KNOWLEDGE AND POWER

Knowledge and Power

A Discourse for Transformation

BRAJ RANJAN MANI

MANOHAR
2014

First published 2014

ISBN 978-93-5098-030-9

Published by
Ajay Kumar Jain *for*
Manohar Publishers & Distributors
4753/23 Ansari Road, Daryaganj,
New Delhi 110 002

Printed at
Salasar Imaging Systems
Delhi 110 035

The history of human knowledge is a cemetery filled with wrong empirical observation, false reasonings, and pseudo intuitions.

PITIRIM A. SOROKIN

What goes by the name of Sacred Books [of Hindus] contains fabrications which are political in their motive, partisan in their composition and fraudulent in their purpose. ... They [who defend such writings] are more selfish than any other set of beings in the world, and are prostituting their intelligence to support the vested interests of their class.

B.R. AMBEDKAR

Knowledge is not a loose-leaf notebook of facts. Above all, it is a responsibility for the integrity of what we are, primarily of what we are as ethical creatures. You cannot possibly maintain that informed integrity if you let other people run the world for you while you yourself continue to live out of a ragbag of morals that come from past beliefs. That is really crucial today.

JACOB BRONOWSKI

No race has a monopoly on beauty, or intelligence, or strength, and there is room for everyone at the convocation of conquest.

AIME CESAIRE

Contents

Acknowledgements

The origins of this book go back a long time. But the actual work began when I was a fellow at the IIAS, Shimla. There I met S.P. Singh and his wife Vandana who had more faith in me (as an engaged writer) than I had in myself. I take this opportunity to tell them that their encouragement and love became the initial inspiration for this work.

My previous book, *Debrahmanising History* (2005), brought me closer to some of India's finest thinker-activists—G. Aloysius, Kancha Ilaiah, Gail Omvedt, Bharat Patankar, Rajendra Yadav, B.L. Mungekar, Sunil Sardar, Vasanthi Raman, Surendra Jondhale, Vivek Kumar, N. Sukumar, Cynthia Stephen, Hari Narke, S. Anand, Raj Kumar, K. Satyanarayana, Jitendra Kumar, to name just a few. I have been enriched and illuminated by their creativity, criticism, and solidarity.

Many friends—Gail Omvedt, Sukrita Paul Kumar, Anjali Deshpande, Cynthia Stephen, Ashish Alexander, Grant McFarland—read at various stages different versions of the typescript and gave their suggestions and comments for improvement. I am grateful.

Family and friends came forward with precious support when this work was in precarious progress. I am indebted to all of them, though it is difficult to acknowledge everyone by name here. Special thanks to my brother, Priya Ranjan. To Sunil Sardar, Dan, and Shiv Kumar. To Madhu Singh. To a dear friend who does not want to be named in the debt department.

I dedicate this book to my elder brother, Prem Kumar Mani, who animated a village cottage in Bihar with his writing and introduced me to the world of Tolstoy and Premchand, Marx and Ambedkar. He had high expectations of his younger brother, but I failed miserably—I can only write a book like this. This is all I can present him in gratitude and love.

BRAJ RANJAN MANI

Introduction

> *Who controls the past, controls the future: who controls the present, controls the past.*
>
> GEORGE ORWELL

> *It is necessary to draw attention violently to the present as it is, if one wants to transform it.*
>
> ANTONIO GRAMSCI

A Socrates dissatisfied (another philosopher thought) is a better prospect for humanity than a fool satisfied. Similarly, Hegel believed that the unhappy consciousness is the source of progress. Indeed, most of the path-breakers who struggled to broaden humanity's horizon—Buddha and Jesus, Phule and Ambedkar, Helen Keller and Simone de Beauvoir—were not angels with a happy consciousness. However, the world is diverse and all people cannot, must not, think alike. There are people in every society who are happy with the world as it is. Those who succeed and profit more than they deserve are spellbound by the progress the world has made since the days of Adam and Eve. Ensconced in their elegant world, they have no need or desire for change: the world has changed enough to ensure their comfort. History, politics and ideology, they say, have come to an end. The 'lesser' people's sweat and blood that have made their material and intellectual luxuries possible does not prick their conscience. In fact, how to keep the latter off their conscience, forms the bedrock of their knowledge. Their number is small but they have domesticated democracy (to their special interests), enchained globalization (to their greed and profit), and a neoliberal theology (tethered to the belief that democracy can't survive without unbridled privatization and plutocrats). For them, God may or may not be in heaven, but all is well with the world.

Injustice in its myriad forms gives strong enough ground to question all the answers of the power and knowledge establishment. Political and philosophical debate on justice will continue to rage as long as the world remains unjust. For obvious reasons, the powerful tend to cast aside—or depoliticize—the issues of injustice and exploitation, as if we have outlived them, or simply because they are no longer directly proclaimed or defended, as now we have in place rituals and a rhetoric of democracy with a subtler means of oppression. Due to this concealment and an effective takeover of democracy despite the formal existence of democratic structures (Chapter 2), it is all the more necessary for people seeking justice to keep alive the debate on fundamental issues. Without such a debate, it is not possible to grasp and change the world. With this understanding, I attempt to probe the formation of a world with a million millionaires and a billion hungry people (The Merrill Lynch-Cap Gemini World Wealth Report, 2010; and *The Economist* 2009), and ask what went wrong. The objective here is not solely oppositional, it is also reconstructive, blended with empathy for the downtrodden. Searching the seedbed of old and new dominance as well as the ideas and movements for social justice, this work recognizes the terrible odds in political, economic, and in the intellectual-ethical realms, but carries the hope that the excluded and the insulted will call into question the nature of existing power and social relationships, and will unite and break their shackles, and by freeing themselves will reinvent humanity.

Towards a Criticism of Everything Existing

My *Debrahmanising History*, in many ways the predecessor to this work, could be read as a people's history of India and a critique of the larger brahmanic paradigms of society, and of Indian historiography and Indological studies. This work covers a larger canvas and attempts an understanding of knowledge and power in their widest possible sense. I offer a sharp review of dominant canons and constructs, both old and new, Indian and Western, to arrive at a diagnosis.

Astonishing material and political changes notwithstanding, a few profitably regulate the circulation of money, power and information, pushing a large number of people into a daily struggle for survival. India's procedural democracy and progress paradigm are fattening a favoured minority and multiplying inequalities with the reproduction of caste and class. The democratic promise of the passage from exclusion to inclusion, from corruption to honesty, from bad principles to good ones remains, by and large, confined to the realm of constitutional provisions and public rhetoric. Life remains oppressive for 77 per cent of Indians who live on less than a dollar a day. Like the legendary emasculation of Ekalavya, Shambuka, and Sita, the life and creativity of their descendants are snuffed out and the authorities refuse to take any notice of such a waste of human resources. An indebted farmer committing suicide in Maharashtra; a dalit child in Madhya Pradesh gasping for life in the absence of basic medical treatment; an adivasi woman in Jharkhand forced to forsake her land to a housing colony, and her daughter leaving her to become a domestic help in Delhi; a bright teenager from Bihar leaving school to become a slave in some farm or factory in Punjab: millions of such stories of dehumanization in everyday life seldom make news.

There is a global consensus that access to food constitutes one of the most basic of human rights. No government disagrees in principle with Norman Borlaug's suggestion that 'food is the moral right of all who are born into this world'. So, what is the news on food situation?

In 1974 Henry Kissinger, then America's secretary of state, told the world food conference in Rome that no child would go to bed hungry within ten years. Just over 35 years later, in the week of another United Nations food summit in Rome, one billion people will go to bed hungry. (*The Economist*, 19 November 2009)

Years ago, writer-activist Frances Moore Lappe (1971) captured the essence of the world food crisis when she argued that starvation was caused not by a scarcity of food but by a global scarcity in democracy. 'Our "modern" farm economy was actively creating scarcity from abundance, in part by feeding a third of the world's grain to livestock' (Lappe 2008). Evidence accumulates that the powerful countries, corporations and individuals have violated human rights of the global poor, aggravating poverty and disease. Roughly one third of all human deaths are due to poverty-related causes that are preventable through better nutrition, safe drinking water, vaccines and medicines (*The Hindu* 2011). The links between inequality, powerlessness, and poor health have been analyzed and confirmed in a remarkable study (Marmot 2004). In less direct ways, deprivation and a low status weaken people's self-esteem and dignity, so that their capacity to perform diminishes too. Being powerless 'constricts and constrains; it chills the livelihood' (ibid.); it really does make people lesser people.

Obviously, there are forces in society that do not allow resources and power to be distributed fairly. The powerful forces, hidden behind the mask of liberal politics and economics, represent an influential body of thought that is deeply suspicious of true democracy. Democracy, they think, works best not because the public are actively involved in decisions, but because different elites compete for power. As the powerful have succeeded in capturing and domesticating democracy in most countries, they claim to have a *vision* and *commitment* to empower the people and redeem the world. Democracy is undermined and devalued through, more than anything else, such misrepresentation, abstraction, and rhetoric:

The characteristic vices of power include not only the familiar sins of oppression, arrogance, deceit and theft, but also subtler vices like

> the use of abstraction. The main currencies of politics are words, images and fictions, the stories and claims which lend legitimacy to power. In democratic politics, perhaps even more than in non-democratic politics, these fictions can become traps. Abstractions override realities; vague rhetoric about values or identities masks failures, and leaders all too easily come to confuse announcements with reality, laws passed with outcomes achieved, believing that so long as they can solve a problem through a turn of phrase the problem will go away. (Mulgan 2006: 320)

Words like injustice and oppression are rendered meaningless, either by juggling statistics (painting a rosy picture of people's empowerment), or by arguing in forked tongues that life prefers the talented few to amass wealth so that they can redeem the poor, with the occasional blunt assertion that life is unfair, and that there will always be winners and losers in the competition that is life.

With formal equality and procedural democracy, it is easier for the privileged to hide behind the logic of biological naturalism or merit mythology that the world gives individuals just what their natural and acquired abilities may entitle them to. The argument is made that the differentials of property, power and education are located not in the structure of society but in individuality (personal achievement or failure). Reflecting this attitude, the media, the school and *sarkari* propaganda give the impression that educational and economic success is a function of personal achievement and worth, not the hierarchies of caste, class, and gender. Earlier, the division between the privileged and the commoners was seen as a divine dispensation—God made them master and slave, brahman and shudra, and ordered their estate. The only difference from this view in today's secular world is that the *educated* people now attribute the extremes of wealth and poverty, power and powerlessness, to individual merit, luck and pluck rather than to the divine providence. Such naturalization—de-politicization—of caste-class inequalities with the new fairy tales of fairness, equality, and individual choice conceals the structural privilege and discrimination.

When caste, class, and gender inequality can be naturalized by individual differences, hegemony is at its strongest.

Such normalization of power and powerlessness leaves aside the overwhelming role of the accident of birth. Interwoven in the fabric of social, economic and cultural institutions, birth-based inequalities persist in all walks of life. If the established order is so natural (as its beneficiaries suggest), what was—is—the need of its institutionalization and intellectual-moral justification that we find all around? The answer is, hierarchy has been socially constructed, and though normalized in all societies in varying degrees and guises, it is not natural or integral to the human condition. One has to get behind appearances to discover reality. The sun appears to revolve around the earth, but the truth is its opposite. All attempts to understand the social world will be superfluous, to paraphrase Marx, if its outward appearances and the underlying reality are one and the same.

The most disturbing aspect about unequal power relationships is that the oppressed, notwithstanding their rebellions and resistances that dot the history of all societies, are compelled to adopt and internalize the repressive views about themselves planted by the oppressor. As the words, images and constructs of the oppressor penetrate the imagination of the oppressed, and take control of their minds, it starts an insidious cycle of violence. It erodes the self-respect of the oppressed in a social situation that reminds them at every turn just how worthless they are. They begin to see things through the eyes of the oppressor. Once they come to perceive themselves as inferior, they accept their subordination. A critical grasp of history tells us the story of how men made women accept their inferior position, and how the working people, peasants, and artisans were degraded in caste hierarchy and forced to accept their dehumanization as shudra or untouchables in India.

Domination then became systemic and hegemonic. Agreeing to play by the rules of the oppressor also kept the oppressed divided from within. United by suffering, they were divided by ignorance. Unable to see their common oppression, they were set to fight each other for scarce resources and social respectability. In modern society, they have become the official foot-soldiers that safeguard the system and the nation. Violence is always delegated to the oppressed to keep other oppressed groups within the system.

The privileged convince themselves—and then others—to see the world as a just place where people ultimately get what they deserve. Through this system justification theory, which has a variety of versions, the ruling class justifies hierarchy and injustice. Thus, those who put out the people's eyes, reproach them for their blindness. But no one ever wants to be a victim on his or her own accord, and victimization, whether social, economic, or sexual, is never impersonal; it always has its enforcers and its victims. As Gramsci (1971) has shown, dominance even with consent of the governed is never automatic but achieved through political action and organization of the powerful.

Domination of the majority by one group brutalizes all. It diminishes everyone's humanity by destroying the possibility of love, understanding, and cooperation. When all are dehumanized to a greater or lesser degree, dehumanization itself does not seem terribly immoral or bad. That is why, in the dominant discourse, the reality of social injustice is obscured or watered down by euphemistic—noble-sounding—names, and justified on *moral, religious* and *scientific* grounds. There has never been shortage of intellectuals who have made a living out of quoting God, scripture or science to give an intellectual-moral gloss to the reality of oppression and dehumanization (Chapters 1 and 4). Unfortunately, it is the same people—the dominant, the elite—who have made laws and set the standards.

With their control over the media, academia, and public discourse—that is, the means of symbolic reproduction in society—the powerful do not allow the powerless to see the things as they are. By not allowing the people to see that the state, the cultural establishment, the education system and institutionalized religion all converge to validate a system that favours entrenched interests, the powerful manufacture social consensus. Sometimes the more obvious a thing is, the more difficult it is to see and understand that. Thus, injustice results from elitist coercion and manipulation as well as from a common acceptance of the unjust system as 'normal' or 'natural'.

Today, the most vital link in maintaining the status quo is *education*—increasingly privatized and commercial—that keeps young people trapped in the power relations by covering up every trace of contradictions in society. By concealing the reality of privilege and exclusion, the structures of school and university carry a hidden curriculum in pedagogical practices, feeding the myths that reinforce the established order (Chapters 1, 4 and 5). The grammar and idiom have changed, but not the normativity of up-classing some and down-classing others. As the procurement of education remains a race against others, it encourages a sense of entitlement in the elites. In India, the pundits remain in eloquent denial of caste and the roots of many contemporary discriminations. They praise 'national' values of tolerance, and the spirituality of the Indian tradition. By encouraging rote-learning and regurgitation, the system discourages people from asking searching questions about the structures of caste, class, gender, ethnicity, language, age, and other categories. Far from generating an intellectual atmosphere conducive to desirable social change, elite-led education reinforces an uncritical assimilation of dominant norms and values in people's minds.

Those who suffer discrimination are thus diverted from locating the cause of their subordination in society. The people are made to invest more faith in the system than the system has in itself. They are deluded by the false promise that anyone can rise in life, provided he or she is industrious and talented enough. The stories of a few individuals from humble origins who succeed spectacularly against great odds are kept in constant circulation to elide the entire systemic discrimination. One superman, one super-success: no need to think about structural stacks against the disadvantaged. The myth of merit and social mobility hide the truth that without equality of conditions and opportunity, right to equality amounts to nothing. Genuine equality of opportunity requires equality of conditions which can only be ensured through social transformation and a shift in mindset. Mass poverty, suffering, and violence flow from an unjust system which cannot be set right by individual effort or compassion.

Understanding the world as it is, not as it is said to be is a transforming exercise, as it involves not only making new things familiar and familiar things new, but also discovering matters hidden from public view, and exposing distortions that obscure or limit the vision of a more humane world. As 'the past is altered by the present as much as the present is directed by the past', it is imperative to understand the past in order to understand the present and vice versa. This will enable us to grasp how the old and obnoxious socio-religious fundamentals have subtly morphed into modern and secular-scientific avatars (Chapters 2, 3 and 4). To take an example, the 'civilizing mission' of the Vedic-brahmanic culture (and its contemporary reproduction in material and ideological forms) has to be deconstructed for what it has been—a process of caste colonization of India. The ancient brahmanic worldview was not a description (the mirror of its times) but a prescriptive, imposed, caste-based model of culture and religion. This has to be analyzed in the context of its historical exploitation and violence. And that includes not just physical violence but also the symbolic one—the violence of words; of stigmatizing women and toiling communities as 'low born' and 'low caste'. We need to grasp that there is an intellectual-moral violence in the way this oppressive tradition has been glorified, modernized, and equated with an 'inclusive' Indian tradition in the contemporary secular and communal discourses of caste elites (Chapters 1 and 4).

As long as the oppressed abandon their own reason and are content to rely upon authority, there will be no end to the reproduction of injustice. Understanding and overcoming oppression requires knowledge of the real world, in particular of how society is actually organized and how power relations work. Privilege and power are better hidden in the high-tech capitalist democracies in which they are more diffuse and indirect than in the pre-modern forms of explicit hierarchies. New mechanisms of power, their techniques and tactics which govern the individual and society function most effectively when they remain concealed, or rather when they are disguised as friendly forces. Decades ago, following Max Weber's study of bureaucracy, sociologist C. Wright Mills had pointed out the exceedingly complex and technology-enabled networks of modern power.

> Rather than the direct power exerted by the factory owner over his employees and the autocratic ruler over his subjects, modern power has become bureaucratized and thus less easy to locate and recognize.... The new face of power in mass society [is] a corporate one, an interlocking hierarchical system.... [The earlier order that rested on the family, the school and the institutionalized religion has been replaced by] the corporation, the state, and the army, each embedded in a technology, a system of interlocking processes. (Mills 1956)

Beneficiaries of existing conditions do not, cannot, and will never challenge existing understandings to bring in emancipatory change. They conflate their own power and achievements with the empowerment of society as a whole. Nothing changes unless a new consciousness replaces the oppressive one, and generates ferment for transformation. Justice becomes a possibility only after the oppressed groups become conscious of their subservience and decide to act autonomously and fight the system. For this, they have to grasp that once a hierarchical order is in place, cultural or educational discrimination gradually replaces brute force, and becomes the main conduit for reproduction of inequalities. Elite-led knowledge-construction, be it theology, philosophy, history, social-political theorization, or any such, normalizes or keeps hidden the designs of domination. Interrogation of the prevailing hegemonic knowledge system requires a critical understanding of that ingrained system. This means that the entire spectrum of social world and knowledge-systems has to be reread, reassessed and redefined alongside reimagining education for an exploitation-free world (Chapter 5). To be genuinely radical, as Marx proposed, is to go to the root of the problem, which can only be done with 'a merciless criticism of everything existing'.

Civilization and its Intellectual Corruption

Contrary to the fairy tales of textbooks, the story of civilization is not a story of glory alone, but also of barbarities and bombs. People discovered fire, invented myths, wrote epics, interpreted the world; people waged wars, killed innocents, turned might into right, and lies into truths. The institutions of social order and power—patriarchy, family, caste, class, state, religion, morality—that marked the arrival of civilization were, on the whole, guided by the thinking of the dominant. As the establishment was created, endowed, and privileged to uplift some and downgrade others, it ran parallel to justice and fairness. Freedom and dignity became the casualty of order and discipline. This blood-soaked duality of civilization, however, has been the choice of the dominant few, not the need of humanity. Walter Benjamin (1969: 256) points out, 'There is no document of civilization which is not at the same time a document of barbarism. And just as such a document is not free of barbarism, barbarism also taints the manner in which it was transmitted from one owner to another.'

Now, if humanity and history are to change for the better, we have to recognize that the road to civilization was paved with fraud and fabrication as with truth and generosity. As Freud pointed out, 'Civilization began when men stopped throwing stones and started cursing.' A more plausible explanation was dug out by Rousseau who argued that civilization came into existence with the origin of inequality when one impostor claimed a plot of land—a part of nature—as his own and got away with it. In the Judeo-Christian creation myth, an act of disobedience—an act of free will by Adam and Eve in eating of the apple from the prohibited tree of knowledge and the resultant Fall of Man from God's grace—is the beginning of world history. In the Vedic-brahmanic myth, the wheel of civilization comes into motion with the creation of a hierarchical body politic when the cosmic *Purusha*, the Divine Man, split himself—and divided humanity—into four unequal castes, in which brahman is the head, kshatriya the arms, vaishya the thighs and shudra the feet.

If anything, such attempts to grasp the origins of society and body politic point to the reality that civilization was not born in innocence and justice, but in hubris and selfishness. Civilizational development was marked by duality of speech and language, religion and morality, tools and technology. Necessity, material conditions and relations of production along with human will and wile, war and plunder have shaped the contours of civilization, bringing us where we are today.

We often hear that education is a great leveller, and that knowledge is the currency of power today, not weapons. We hear catchphrases like *knowledge society* and *knowledge economy* to underline the fairness and justice of the new world. Broadcasting about the arrival of knowledge empires, however, is part of a bigger propaganda that with liberal democracy and market economy we are witnessing a great civilizational movement from darkness to light, from the closed, conservative society (of the past) to the open-ended globalization of today. The truth is, the power of knowledge is not a new phenomenon but the emergence of a new form of an old power—*knowledge power*. At the same time, knowledge, as we will see in Chapters 1 and 4, is not wisdom or certainty, but has in fact a deeply dual character. It is worth noting that that all hierarchies—and especially the inequalities of caste, class, and patriarchy—were built on the claims of knowledge, both of temporal and supernatural religious variety. History is witness that those who own wealth and control the means of production hold the real levers of power and turn knowledge into a privilege and a further, cynical justification of their wealth and power. As such, increasing knowledge does not often lead to a more inclusive world, but to a more cunning, covert, and compelling defence of established power.

It is notable that the world's first professional intellectuals—priests—were hostile to liberty and equality in every society. They fabricated the fiction of divine hierarchy and sanctified ruling feudatories as God's ambassadors on earth. It was the nexus of the priest with the prince that constructed hierarchy and patriarchy across the world. The collusion of intellectual and political elites covered both the secular and religious realms, and together played havoc for the common people. But for some exceptions, the individuals who dealt in intellectual-moral wares such as Plato, Aristotle, Kautilya, Manu, Machiavelli and their modern-day incarnations (Chapters 1 and 4), threw in their lot behind the forces of power and privilege. This hoary tradition appears in the knowledge society and knowledge economy, where intellectual scoundrels far outnumber public-spirited intellectuals.

For the elite, knowledge has for long been a great source of power. As early as the sixteenth century, Francis Bacon had said, 'knowledge itself is power'. Baconian 'knowledge of causes, and secret motions of things' was meant to admit the knowledgeable to 'the enlarging of the bounds of human empire, to the effecting of all things possible' (Bacon [1626] 1974: 239). The English Bacon explored the social and political implications of scientific knowledge in great detail, while his French contemporary Rene Descartes set the epistemology for science and the modernist project that came with it. The goal of new science—science is the Latin for knowledge—was to make mankind 'masters and possessors of nature' (Descartes [1637] 1968: 78) and set up the 'empire of man over things' (Bacon 1623). Thus, the driving force behind the new learning was a hunger for empire. Empire, as we know, is an extensive sphere of social, political, and commercial activity controlled by a person or a group. Obviously, scientific knowledge, to be generated and employed for a new empire, implied the conquest of both the natural and the social world.

Bacon and Descartes pioneered revolutionary methods in science that went on to change the face of the earth, but in terms of recognizing knowledge–power nexus they had many predecessors. Except the catchphrase 'knowledge is power' and its new scientific celebration, this understanding was not unique to them. In ancient India, the non-scientific brahmans not only rapturously chanted the mantra *shabda brahma hai* (word is the supreme power) but also went on to put it into practice. They monopolized *shabda-shakti* (word power) as their *brahma astra* (ultimate weapon) to subjugate society into the mould of caste in which everything was rigged in their favour. They mastered grammar, rhetoric, and logic, and used these to construct a caste-centred worldview and metaphysics. Their quest of knowledge—the Vedas, Upanishads and Dharmashastras—went hand in hand with appropriation of power and privilege at the cost of the many who were made servile—and kept away from learning and knowledge. The *dharma* the brahman envisioned was the cosmic order maintained by the correct performance of sacrifice, which in turn was dependant on maintaining the requisite social hierarchy. The brahman would not establish dharma (which implied righteousness as well as justice) unless he himself presided over it, unless dharma upheld caste hierarchy, unless righteousness was bound to the caste order and polity, unless justice was one with *dandaniti* (the rule of force) and *matsya nyaya* (the law of big fish swallowing smaller ones).

As Ambedkar, Dumont and some other scholars have shown, the primacy of caste in India—revealed as the governing conception of the contemporary caste structure—could be explained as being of religious essence (that is, the hierarchical ideology enshrined in ancient religious texts) that contained the economic and the political. The social law conceived by the brahmans and executed above all by the kshatriyas was grounded in the belief that the real power lies in holding knowledge. *Veda* means knowledge. In the Veda itself, the Vedas are declared equal to *satya* or truth, or to *vac*, 'speech' also in the sense of 'truth'. *Vac* is the 'mother of the Vedas', and the Vedas are equated with the *brahman*, that is the universal principle that is the ground and the end of all knowledge (Smith 2012: 4–5). Put simply, the brahman authors of the canonical Veda—'knowledge' and 'truth'—were also the architects of varna or caste. To ensure the exclusivity of the all-powerful knowledge the brahmans made Sanskrit the language of divine revelation and forbade the other castes from acquaintance with it. They were the only group to enjoy the privilege of knowledge; all others were required to remain unlettered. This was the most enduring triumph of the brahman, and the most lasting damnation of the rest. All this was done on the strength of knowledge power—the knowledge that blurred the boundary between faith and reason, hierarchy and harmony.

In Greece Plato paved the same path to power and propagated the same lesson—*justice is inequality*—on a purple philosophical plane, as we shall see in Chapter 4. He would exclude the possibility of realizing his Republic as long as highborn philosophers like him would not reign over it, as long as justice was not bound to power, as long as justice was not one with force.

What is strikingly common in the Platonic–brahmanic philosophy is a tradition of knowledge-construction in which some people are more equal than others. And this tradition of deceptive education, thanks to the collusive obfuscation of modern pundits, still flourishes all over the world, and in astonishingly ever-renewing grammar and idiom. The corrupting nature of power is well known and well theorized, but the understanding of knowledge–power nexus is rather new, still confined to a small section of academia, and as such it has yet to become a commonsense, a part of people's intellectual equipment. Sorely missing, from the viewpoint of the oppressed, is a debate on the politics of knowledge. Instead, there is a predominant tendency to accept knowledge as wisdom, and embrace any education as desirable. There is a crying need to debate afresh and vigorously the dark side of knowledge, and how the abuse of knowledge has been a constant in history, as we will see throughout the book. Everyone should know how some of the world's leading knowledge-makers invoked the laws of nature, the hand of providence, and the ruse of reason in a variety of ways, and did whatever they could to institutionalize social hierarchies.

The elite knows that power becomes more effective and enduring when it combines with knowledge. Conquering and coercion become easier with cognition that hides the violence involved in the former. When violence (of caste, class and patriarchy) embellishes itself with a seductive ideology, it is able to hide its true nature and acquires the ability to destroy lives without killing.

This is not to argue that good people have not used knowledge for freedom, justice, and human rights but to stress the point that the fabrication of false knowledge has been a major tool of oppression in the hands of the wily and the wealthy. This requires a major overhauling of our social knowledge for which it is imperative to grasp that it is intellectual corruption, more than anything else, which paves the way for the commission of all other crimes. The knowledge society is notable far more for 'the enormous variety of ways of compelling language to lie' than for producing knowledge professionals who bring truth to our lives, let alone speak truth to power and hold it to account.

The Delusions of Development, Market, and Technology

The market and technology do not reach the heart of humanity and the unbalanced development that we see all around us. Too much of everything—glamorous lifestyle, cutting-edge technology, nuclear arsenals, superhighways and space shuttles—may or may not be good for the rich and their children's future but the cruelty of coping without nutrition, sanitation and education are certainly destroying the deprived around the world. Anyone with a conscience can see how the two—gluttony of the few and hunger of the many; 10,000 nuclear weapons and the global lack of schools and hospitals—are intertwined. The establishment remains blind to this link, as it frets at the symptoms, sidestepping or suppressing structural sources of mass misery. The semiotic trickery of 'inclusive growth' and 'people's empowerment' goes hand in hand with buttressing the extractive structure of the economy.

The intellectual engine of this power politics is the theory that the free market, advancing technology, and wealth creation will on their own conquer all social problems, bestowing universal peace, prosperity, and democracy. Known as the 'modernization theory' formulated first by Seymour Martin Lipset (1959), it has several local and global versions, and a huge following both within and outside the academia. The highbrow among them proclaim that what we are witnessing today—in the form of liberalization, privatization, globalization—is a final victory in a war between the forces of light (capitalism) and darkness (socialism) that has brought an end of history, ideology and politics (Fukuyama 1992). The lowbrow among them beat the drum that *The World is Flat* (Friedman 2005) and demystify the flattened new world by suggesting that once a country gets enough McDonald's restaurants, democracy, prosperity and inclusive institutions are bound to follow.

But the biting reality of growing inequality, financial frauds, ecological crises, and disastrous wars mocks such fantasies. Beneath the veneer of neo-liberalism festers the ugliness of *managed* democracy and crony capitalism which perpetuates many old and new crimes against humanity. Extractive economics thrives on a narrow politics, hidden behind the facade of democracy, and this arrangement can only advantage the top at the expense of the rest (Chapter 2). As a major new study shows, 'Capitalism is failing to produce what was promised, but is delivering on what was not promised—inequality, pollution, unemployment, and, most important of all, the degradation of the values to the point where everything is acceptable and no one is accountable' (Stiglitz 2012: xviii).

Thus, neither the market nor democracy is free; and globalization, to borrow Jimmy Carter's phrase, is a policy, not an act of God. The most dangerous aspect of globalization is that it brings about not only a market-based economy but also a market-based society (Gray 1998). This was first underlined by Karl Polanyi (1957) in a groundbreaking work:

> A market economy can exist only in a market society. . . . A market economy must comprise all elements of industry, including labour, land, and money. But labour and land are no more than the human beings themselves of which every society consists and the natural surroundings in which it exists. To include them in the market mechanism means to subordinate the substance of society itself to the laws of the market.

The market thus has not only economic power but also enormous political and cultural clout to influence the way we think, behave, and desire. Overwhelming parliament, educational institutions and the drawing rooms, it has acquired the ability to subjugate citizens into consumers, keeping them glued and gullible to endless publicity and, thus, ignorant about the larger reality (Chapter 3). The market fundamentals are so strong today that even human-rights activists are forced to deal with the 'practices of global commoditization of human and social suffering and tendencies which all too readily convert human rights movements into human rights *markets*' (Baxi 2012).

Contrary to the promise that social problems will disappear in a free market, the dominance of caste and class has reinvented itself with changing times (Chapter 2). The pervasive hold of inequality, which permits the old hierarchies to reinvent themselves and become capable of resisting social change, is a fact—and this precisely is the problem. Market, technology, and digitization of manufacturing—the leading engines of the third wave of industrialization—take on the form and structure of the society where they operate. Of course, they are the great enablers to the well-born and well-connected, but they also multiply the problems of the have-nots who face a host of historically accumulated deprivations and hidden systemic disadvantages. Egalitarian progress is much slower compared to the breakneck speed of the technological march, as the former has not undergone the kind of immense transformation we have witnessed and are still witnessing in the latter. This has led to a situation where some people enjoy private jets, yachts and cutting-edge knowledge, while many are stuck without bicycles, and struggle to educate their children. Previously, religion and tradition could be blamed for keeping the common people subjugated and backward. But now, for all the alleged help people are getting from the government, the market and technology, they seem to have become more vulnerable than earlier.

Lopsided development has led to not just widening income inequality but also unprecedented cultural violence and dislocations. Advancing technologies and tele-media apparatuses may have facilitated some democratic openings here and there, but much more than that, they have enhanced the scope of massive misunderstanding. No change operates in a vacuum but in a milieu managed and manipulated by powerful private interests. In the absence of a significant social change, science and technology tend to empower privileged groups far more than the rest, while hiding the true nature of the interests they serve. Big business, for example, has harnessed the mass media and information technology to enhance their profit and domesticate politics in their favour. People have full freedom of expression to listen and respond to chatter on film, fashion, cricket and other frivolities, but the 'open system' remains firmly closed on issues like the concentration of wealth and huge salaries at the top and people struggling below with multiple deprivations and unemployment.

Like the market, the dangers of instrumental science and technology are that they assume a status and role they don't deserve (Midgley 2011). The power elites have convinced us to idolize science like a new religion with sovereign power to solve all problems. Politicians like Jawaharlal Nehru reposed their faith in science, turning it into a liberation theology:

> It is science alone that can solve the problems of hunger and poverty, of insanitation and illiteracy, of superstitions and deadening custom and tradition, of vast resources running to waste, of a rich country inhabited by starving people. . . . The future belongs to science and to those who make friends with science. (Nehru 1960: 564)

Nehru spoke of the new industrial complexes and nuclear reactors as 'the new temples of India', and saw science as a 'moral signpost that could take the place of religion'. It was beyond the likes of Nehru to think of it

> as something likely to produce industrial pollution, or the invention of refined methods of torture, or opportunities for profiteering, or a concentration of weaponry, or overuse of chemicals on farms, or computer viruses, or irresponsible currency speculation made possible by the latest computers, or the wholesale waste of resources on gadgetry. (Midgley 2011: 23)

While lauding scientific temper, planned economy and people's democracy, Pandit Nehru was blind to the fact that he was presiding over an essentially bourgeois-brahmanic regime. He could not see what Ambedkar and Periyar easily saw, and which could be summed up in the words of Martin Luther King, 'When scientific power overturns moral power, we end up with guided missiles and misguided men.' The misguided men that Nehru led allowed the privileged to appropriate the developmental state, industrialization and public institutions. The public sector was overwhelmed by private interests and big business (Chibber 2006). State-funded universities, technical colleges, and a few centres of excellence like the Indian Institutes of Technology and Indian Institutes of Management worked as new fiefdoms of the privileged. On the whole, these institutions educated the elites on government subsidies, equipping them with the intellectual capital that they were to use in the age of privatization beginning in 1991. Now, the same elements that reaped the most from Nehru's state socialism and elitist scientism are blaming the 'socialist era' for India's backwardness and pushing for the aggressive privatization of everything (from natural resources to education) as a panacea for illiteracy, hunger and other problems afflicting India.

This is not a plea for the rejection of the market, or science, or technology but a refusal to subordinate life to them. Even at their best, they can only be an instrumentality, not a panacea. Excessive faith in them as an inherently liberating force in a class-and-caste-divided society is dangerous, if not mischievous, since they are, in the first place, neither free nor benignly apolitical. No technology or economics can liberate the oppressed unless they are driven by the ethics of inclusiveness as the measure of human progress. This can only be ensured by the political and philosophical task of evolving an inclusive vision—and making them a lived reality through inclusive institutions. As Ambedkar pointed out, 'History shows that where ethics and economics come in conflict, victory is always with economics. Vested interests have never been known to have willingly divested themselves unless there was sufficient force to compel them.' This insight—that real transformation does not come without a decisive struggle between the powerful and the powerless—has been validated by a new global research on power, poverty and prosperity:

> Inclusive economic and political institutions do not emerge by themselves. They are often the outcome of significant conflict between elites resisting economic growth and political change and those wishing to limit the economic and political power of existing elites. Inclusive institutions emerge during critical junctures, . . . when a series of factors weaken the hold of the elites in power, make their opponent stronger, and create incentives for the formation of a pluralistic society. (Acemoglu and Robinson 2012: 332)

Foregrounding the Struggle against Profit-over-People

Against the aristocratic tendency to make the world the fiefdom of the few, mistrust of might and money has a long lineage in all cultures, exemplified best by the indelible signatures of Buddha, Jesus, Muhammad, and Nanak. Buddha shunned the glamour of power, seeing in it a self-inflicted sickness that smothers the best in the self and society. Jesus despised the established order and expelled Mammon-worshippers from the Temple. (Both fought against abuse of power, and rejected legalistic or the sanctimonious claims of brahmans and pharisees.) Muhammad banned usury, built brotherhood and equality among worshippers. Nanak stood with the poor and scorned the rich for exploiting them. The fabled four had different worldviews, coloured by their contemporary milieu and challenges of the times, but they shared a vision of radical inclusiveness. They especially disliked the idea of might over meekness. They reconciled lofty thoughts with earthly pain, arguing that without love and justice, knowledge and power would produce misery and strife, not happiness and harmony. This liberating message was, however, not only subverted by the powers that be, but also distorted by many of their dogmatic disciples. The religions instituted in their names could not make the leap from justice and equality as an ethical ideal to a political and economic one. In spite of elitist appropriation of their legacies, their noble ideals were kept alive by the humble who went on to play a vital role in building social movements towards democracy and equality.

The demand for justice gathered a fresh momentum in modern times, and in increasingly secular terms. As capitalism gained ascendancy in the West, it was not only Marx who stood up against its alienation and inhumanity. Some of his predecessors and contemporaries said the same thing though not in such a compelling manner: 'Capital is dead labour which, vampire-like, lives only by sucking living labour.' Exploitation, earlier veiled by religious and political illusions, was now being substituted by the naked and brutal exploitation of capitalism. But the author of *Das Kapital* was most remarkable for his argument, 'The philosophers have interpreted the world in many ways; the point, however, is to change it.' In this too, he was preceded by others, including the four we mentioned above. As early as 1516, Thomas More raised the idea of collective ownership and social equality in his *Utopia.* In the next century, Gerrard Winstanley grasped the necessity of economic equality for social and political freedom in his *Law of Freedom* (1651). In France, philosophers such as Rousseau in *Discourse on the Origin of Inequality* (1754) and Proudhon in *What is Property?* (1840) laid the intellectual foundations of socialist politics. They were followed by writers such as Balzac who vividly saw 'a crime behind every great fortune.' (Not for nothing had Marx said that Balzac's novels enriched his knowledge of capitalism more than bulky treaties on economy.)

Even the liberal democrat J.S. Mill in a review of Tocqueville's *Democracy in America* saw the emergence of commercial civilization (not democracy as 'tyranny of the majority', as the biased French aristocrat had fretted), as a dangerous development. He warned that when 'petty pursuit of petty advancements in fortune . . . treading upon the heels of one another' becomes the norm, humanity would be in grave danger. 'Let the idea hold that the most serious danger to the future prospects of mankind is in the unbalanced influence of the commercial spirit' (see McMahon 2006: 344–5).

The amassing of profit and power amidst a sea of suffering spawns a pathology that spares no one. A sage-like figure of our time says, 'There is more to life than having everything', implying that conspicuous consumption does not make up for the lack of intimacy or aesthetics. Jotirao Phule asked in the nineteenth century: 'How can a person be called human, if he has no concern, love and service for others?' The have-lots, however, strive to get wealthier, but is not affluence one of the most pathetic goals to strive for, when others' children—anyone's children—go to bed without food?

The wisdom that 'charity is no substitute for justice withheld' dawned on St. Augustine in the fifth century. But this is what the best of billionaires resort to in their finest moments, today. And so do most governments that preside over systems rigged in favour of the wealthy. Charity only reproduces the social patterns of domination. Disguising the root causes of injustice in society, it only reinforces the fundamental dependence of the disprivileged on the privileged. 'Whether public or private, charity indicates a return to societies divided by class. This is ethics denied in favour of moralism; citizens' rights converted into clientalism' (Saul 2004: 60). 'All charity,' August Strindberg saw clearly, 'is humiliation.'

Even while giving a big tax cut to the corporate sector, the people-in-power relate it to some 'common good', or 'public interest'. Mortgaging the earth to the corporations, they speak about 'ecological balance'. Thus, the old authoritarian norms and rules have been outwardly discarded, and replaced with nice-sounding phrases, a rhetoric of inclusiveness and politically-correct hospitality.

The lip service paid to democracy makes the reality of oppression more insidious. 'Political language is designed to make lies sound truthful and murder sound respectable, and to give an appearance of solidity to pure wind' (Orwell [1946] 1981: 171). Democracy, thus, has been reduced to a system that gives priority to power dinners for the overfed over bread for the hungry. What Helen Keller said in 1911 about the US democracy applies, after a century, to all procedural democracies that flourish in the globalized world: 'The country is governed for the richest, for the corporations, the bankers, the land speculators, and for the exploiters of labour'.

The success of a system appears, as Herbert Marcuse once said, when it makes alternatives unthinkable. This is the kind of success the brahmanic-bourgeois forces seem to have cemented in recent years. Relying on the triumphalist arrogance that *there is no alternative*, the contempt of the powerful for the powerless has crossed all limits. It was evident in Joan Robinson's 1962 quip, made in response to underdevelopment in south-east Asia: 'The misery of being exploited by capitalists is nothing compared to the misery of not being exploited at all.'

Ways of Seeing and Forging Alternative Possibilities

As the tyranny of the few persists and the world remains divided between winners and losers, all justice-loving people are forced to ask if the idea of a fair world is an illusion. Will the world be always governed by vested interests? Will humanity give up the hope of a paradigm of humanity with room for everyone? It is human to fail and suffer but we also have the ingenuity to think beyond what *is* to what *might be* and what *should be*. The question we often ask *who I really am* is innately related to *what sort of person I ought to be*. As Marx said, we do not make our life arbitrarily: we build it under conditions structured by the past. Structures condition us, but we have the power to transform them or even recreate new ones. In this lies the hope of new initiative and creativity. Humanity has many holes but one of its hallmarks is that it sees the present as passing and hence changeable. No power is permanent; no empire everlasting. There have been uprisings in the past, and the uprisings to make the world decent and fair—through movements like the World Social Forum, Occupy the Wall Street, Debrahmanize India and the world—will continue in the future.

However, change must not be directed by the templates of existing norms and principles. Essential for change are an uprooting, and the sowing of new seeds of human value and social relationships. There are things in the world that are not for exchange, and these things—inclusiveness, justice, and understanding—are so precious that they will become the basis for exchanging the things that are exchangeable. Thus, there could be new ways of seeing the world and ourselves, leading to a way of producing and distributing goods in society where human needs would come first rather than gambling on everything for the profit of the few. There could be new politics and new economics which place human need at the centre of all activities, and protect the planet's biodiversity. A new kind of democracy with socialism, or socialism with democracy—combining the best of democracy, reformism, Marxism, Phule-Ambedkarism, feminism, liberation theology, engaged religiosity, environmentalism—where individuals cease to view one another in instrumental terms, where education, freedom, progress are available to every child, could be the future of humanity.

The world could be reorganized on the principle that no race, sex, caste or country has a monopoly on intelligence. A world where competition is fair and an incentive for mutual excellence, with a new sensibility that is almost instinctively repulsed by exploitation and violence, is worth dreaming about and striving for. We have the ability to tame our pride, to harness our imagination, and join hands to do much better things. Our shared ways of thinking and acting, far from being a stultifying constraint, open up the possibility of being innovative and creative.

Our ability to tell our stories and struggles is empowering in itself—a foretaste of liberation. All of us have something to say to each other, something valuable to do together. Opening up, sharing our personal stories as well as canonical ones that are greater than ourselves will enhance our empathy and understanding, and sow the seeds of insurgency against iniquities and callousness. Endowed with a capacity for reflection, action and reinvention, every human is born with a gift for the fight.

The possibility of the impossible is an imperishable dream of humanity. No matter how exhausted the social and political situation is, as Raymond Williams put it, we cannot exhaust all the alternatives. Envisioning alternatives, however, demands a level of imagination that is as uncommon as it is necessary. In the absence of imaginative efforts and fresh perspectives to understand the reality of society, we are confined to the collective delusions of convention and custom that severely limit our capacity to see what is apparent, to visualize what is possible. There are, of course, no easy and ready-made answers. The questions that confront all are to be sought and fought by all.

This work is a part of such an effort—to see the world in an enlarged and emancipating perspective that can help in bringing a change in the nature of knowledge, power and relationships. Since such a reconstruction involves not only dismantling the structures of oppression but also challenging and changing encrusted ideas and prejudices, this work stresses the necessity of self-criticism and self-struggle along with a broader emancipatory philosophy and social action. Profound changes—authentic revolutions—are anchored in love and understanding. Reason alone is never going to produce justice for the neighbour and the stranger.

This work draws on many sources, ideas and literatures from across the world that may help us to see the forest, not just the trees. For this, it casts its net deep and wide, and travels back and forth to show how the forces that earlier conspired against justice and humanity have now changed their names, stripes and spots, acquiring a modern wardrobe and a secular vocabulary (Chapters 2 and 3). Since things have merely changed their appearance, giving the illusion of change, this work searches for alternative possibilities, and strives to build an ethical and intellectual foundation for a liberating cultural struggle—a struggle over how history shall be understood and presented; a struggle to identify the progressive and regressive elements of knowledge; a struggle over the appropriation of values, cognitions and symbols (Chapters 4 and 5). To challenge and change the status quo, let us see things with new eyes, and attempt a holistic understanding of knowledge, power and politics that can enable us to ask the right questions and seek answers outside the old, failed frameworks.

In an attempt to establish connections between bodies of knowledge that have hitherto been unconnected, the chapters are open-ended, overarching, and fluid. There is a free-flowing interaction of key ideas and issues that have been raised in the preceding pages and the first chapter. Intended to be accessible and useful for general readers, this book makes certain assertions about history, culture and knowledge with little regard for academic technicalities, euphemism and obfuscation. For the same reason, the book adopts an approach which is discursive. This explains its lack of methodological and structural cohesiveness in academic terms. There is a conscious attempt to eschew as far as possible the academic opaqueness for which professional scholars have rightly earned a dubious notoriety. The idea is to effectively convey what really matters rather than follow the academic conventions of 'objectivity' or 'neutrality'. In fact, the problem of an amoral intelligentsia constitutes a vital part of this book.

Above all, this book sees human liberation as an act of culture, and a critical education as the locomotive of all change. An integral part of the book is an appendix 'Resources for Transformation', which lists and briefly discusses a wide range of radical and emancipatory works to help interested young readers and aspiring intellectuals generate thoughts and perspectives for transformation.

CHAPTER 1

Understanding the Fundamentals

Evils which are patiently endured when they seem inevitable become intolerable when once the idea of escape from them is suggested.

ALEXIS DE TOCQUEVILLE

No type of enslavement can be abolished unless all enslavement is destroyed.

KARL MARX

Critical education is the third eye that can see through slavery, leading to liberation.

JOTIRAO PHULE

To make the revolution, one must first and foremost remould oneself.

HO CHI MINH

Justice is a beautiful idea, so compelling that even its adversaries have created a cobweb of romance around it. Justice, liberty, and equality have become the catchphrases of this age in which the rich make structural and ethical transformations impossible. Despite all democratic change, the powerful are able to keep the world demoralized—in thrall to power, wealth, status—in a way that even the most democratic of persons find it tough to lead a life that respects the demands of equality. To know and say that we are free, fair and equal has a certain emotional—and universal—appeal. But this appeal fades in comparison with the dominant sense that most people have internalized a conviction of social superiority to some and inferiority to others—a sense engendered by all-round inequality and power relationships.

Knowledge of the self vis-à-vis the hierarchy and the obligation of keeping one's place in the established order bolsters the idea and institution of inequality that has been handed down to us through generations.

The rhetoric of justice without practice or reciprocity legitimizes the assumption that a pecking order of some sort is essential for society and civilization. It was on this assumption that inequalities of patriarchy, caste, class, ethnicity, language, etc., had been established by their progenitors who invoked all kinds of natural and supernatural justifications of hierarchy, and did whatever they could to make it a sacred fact of life. It is notable that the word *hierarchy* by its very etymology (in Greek) associates two ideas: ruling and the sacred. True, there has also been a tradition of opposition to the idea and institution of hierarchy in all societies. In fact, the demand to break the spell of hierarchy on moral, natural, or supernatural grounds—all humans are created equal—has enjoyed popular support for centuries. But it has not made a radical difference, even with the backing of modern democratic laws, because the assumption of self-evident equality (because all people are born equal) is non-existent. We see pervasive inequalities from the cradle to the grave. This conflict between the ideal and the ugly continues, though in theory and in public the privileged pretend that the issue has been resolved with the mere declaration of formal equality.

The war against social inequality has been waged all over the world ever since it came into existence. In India, from Buddha to Ambedkar, there has been a glorious tradition of ideological and political resistance against caste and brahmanism (Mani 2005). In the modern West, one of its first and finest proponents was the French philosopher Jean-Jacques Rousseau. His *Social Contract* (1762) opens with the famous claim that 'Man is born free, and yet everywhere he is in chains.' Freedom as we know it is the ability to make unforced choices, and as such, it is not a given, or a gift of nature, but the challenge of life. But the great point Rousseau was making was about the enslavement induced by hierarchy, which can be grasped with the next line in the same paragraph: 'Many a one believes himself the master of others, and yet he is a greater slave than they are. How has this change come about? . . . What can render it legitimate?' (Rousseau [1762] 1998: 5). What he is suggesting here is at the heart of democratic imagination—power, unless mutually agreed upon and shared, is not right. Might does not make right. Might is *not* right because a system based on arbitrary power cannot escape envy and enmity, dissension and counter-violence. Rousseau proposes that the only powers that all people are under obligation to obey are legitimate ones. This he calls the social contract, which serves everyone's interest in a fair and non-partisan way. In other words, he was dreaming of democracy, and demanding the autonomy of all individuals and their full participation in common decisions.

On the other hand, the dominant class with its power and intellectual cunning has taken the fullest advantage of democratic deficit of hundreds of years, giving the established power relationships the appearance of being facts of life, thus, making man-made inequalities seem natural and inevitable. Their facts may be right but facts do not speak for themselves, so their interpretation is free—and flawed. Skin colour, for example, is a fact; no one can deny it; but is racism based simply on this fact? Or, does the fact of two sexes—female and male—warrant or justify sexism and patriarchy? Or, can the mere existence of foreign lands and people give birth to xenophobia? So also are caste and religion-based violence in India merely the reflection of the facts of caste and the facts of religion? In all such cases, the logic of *fact*—the inevitability of hostility—is only a ruse for prejudice, ill-will, and violence against the other. Caste, class, and gender are not pre-given facts about society; they are manufactured facts—conceived and cultivated through the persistent (though not always visible) exercise of power. They exist and matter in society today because their powerful beneficiaries created them on purpose. But none of these facts or categories is permanent or compulsory identity that one cannot transcend. In other words, the way the world operates is a reality, but it is not a reality that cannot be changed; if people come together and fight the status quo, things will change.

How the facts like caste, class and gender have been manufactured as social tools—and put to a deliberate, self-conscious use to subjugate the others—can also be grasped from another angle. In social or cultural debates, we often see how the powerful distort or change facts when they don't fit their self-serving theory. This explains why they are now in denial of the very existence of social hierarchy. When there was no demand or movement for justice, there was no need for such denial. Earlier, brahmans would proudly own the authorship of caste; now, they want to ban any political or public discussion of caste in the name of existing political equality or national unity (as we will see in Chapter 2). For the powerful, facts have to normalize or hide their power and privilege, otherwise they are discarded and discredited.

Mere fact or information, thus, is not knowledge, let alone understanding or wisdom. Our understanding of the social world advances not by parading known or unknown facts, dates, and statistics but by getting rid of false knowledge, false constructs, and false canons. We advance knowledge by learning and unlearning, and developing a perspective.

The decision therefore to oppose inequality does not depend merely on the fact that all people are born equal. Even if people are born unequal, many of us might demand the removal of socially constructed inequality. In fact, the demand for equality and justice is the demand for equality of conditions, which is the fundamental idea behind democracy. (In absence of equality of conditions, and the historically accumulated discriminations that many communities face, a democratic society tries to be fair to the disadvantaged groups by positive discrimination or affirmative action. Such measures are affirmation, not negation, of the egalitarian vision of democracy.)

Dialectics of Formal Equality and Actual Inequality

The demand for equality is grounded in an ethical imagination and a political vision, which now universally enjoys—at least in principle and in law—validation. But this ideal, despite the United Nations' Universal Declaration of Human Rights (1948) and the global ascendancy of democracy, has not become a reality due to the hostility and hypocrisy of the privileged groups everywhere. In fact, formal equality allows elites to throw a veil over the deep social and economic structures of inequality, which also eases their guilt about their complicity in maintaining unequal conditions. This explains why procedural democracy with the show of elections has been unable to resolve deeper economic and social contradictions in society. In other words, real democracy has not and will never come from the top, but from people getting together and fighting for justice. As the battle for democracy is far from over, it matters where we stand and with whom we stand. Such a decision, however, is not just political but deeply personal and ethical as well because the political is never separate from the personal and the ethical.

As suggested earlier, our decisions relate to some facts of social life, but they are not derived from these facts. The same facts of life can give birth to divergent decisions. Similarly, our decisions cannot be derived from other kinds of facts related to what we call human nature. Humans do not have an essential nature as is often assumed. What was the human essential, for example, between Hitler who killed six million innocent Jews and Mother Teresa who gave her entire life to serve the poor and the sick, many of them shunned even by their families, in a country far away from her birth? What we see more commonly is that even within a single individual, there are contradictory strands of good and bad. Few people, if any, are either completely good or completely bad. A bewildering range of human eccentricity, emotional intensity, intellectual non-conformity and so on make a mockery of a fixed notion of human nature. The popular concept of selfishness as the defining human characteristic is fallacious since humans also act altruistically—without any expectation of gain, sometimes at great personal cost and without the desire to advertise it to the world. This means that not all human decisions or actions are selfish, predictable or socially determined. Said Margaret Mead (1951), 'Individuals are born with different combinations of innate potentialities, and it will depend upon how they are reared—to trust and love and experiment and create, or to fear and hate and conform—what kind of human beings they will become.' One thing is clear, though: individuals who are motivated solely by self-interest pose a threat to society—and themselves. Even Adam Smith, the free-market philosopher in whose name much of the logic of greed and selfishness is justified, held the view that 'the wise and the virtuous man is at all times willing that his own private interest should be sacrificed to the public interest' (Smith [1759] 1984: 235).

A defining human trait is our ability to think, reflect, and consider. There is something like a human way of thinking, but all humans do not think the same thing and in the same manner. Our thinking is indeterminate, unpredictable, and not always perfect. Multiplicity of ways of seeing and thinking have produced languages, cultures, ethics, and normative laws all of which have evolved historically. Our civilization, thus, is circumstantial, and culture by its very definition is not nature. Culture, unlike nature, is a human invention. The tension between nature and culture, convention and innovation is central to civilization, and at the heart of the great movement of justice and equality. Our ability to think and consider gives us some ability to shape things rather than simply be shaped. But this is just ability: we may or may not use it, and worse, we may use it for the wrong purpose.

As our mindset and character are formed in the stream of social life, our nurturing or environment influences us even more than nature or genetics. A child psychologist recently made an interesting observation that when a mother picked flowers from the garden, the child processed it as 'flowers are worthy but not the grass!' Indeed, the way we see things is affected by what we are made to know and what we come to believe. As products of time and place, we are formed by circumstances and what we learn from others and on our own. We make our own lives but not under conditions of our choice, as Marx ([1852] 1978: 595) underlined, 'Men make their own history, but they do not make it just as they please; they do not make it under circumstances chosen by themselves, but under circumstances directly encountered, given and transmitted from the past.' The individual, in other words, is small and the context—circumstances—large.

Living in a stratified society, brought up to respect ascriptive views and values, most of us think, feel and behave in a way that aligns with the status quo of possession, power, and vanities. Ideas and outlooks have a special force when they are familiar, easy to grasp and imbued in long-held prejudices. Customary views and institutions appear to be natural and fair because they have survived for so long and their principles and prejudices have come to be internalized even by the victims. There are no conditions of life to which a person cannot get accustomed, especially if she sees them accepted by everyone around her. Exceptions apart, the education we get, the books we read, the films and television programmes that we see moulds our tastes and morals, to opinions and intellect that gel with the established order. Dominant opinion and prejudice pervade every nook and cranny of our lives. Familiarity—of the established power and social relationships—brings comfort. Cultural and political passivity infuses our life, making us sleep along with the others, and for the privileged, as Paulo Freire once put it, it is quite a 'comfortable slumber'.

The establishment rewards its conformists and punishes the 'troublemakers'; a practical, cautious, domesticated mentality reigns supreme. Even the rebels among us, beneath the skin of a radical vocabulary, are not immune from the viruses of caste, race, or gender. The few who disdain privilege and power are considered cantankerous, if not dangerous. Such dissenters seldom become role models or leaders with a mass following. As a result, human relations continue to revolve around a play of power, money and manipulation, and our capacity for human empathy remains stunted.

There is nothing natural or essential, however, about the established order of power, wealth, and status. If hierarchical relationships are widely accepted, even by the underdog, it is because their norms and values have for centuries been reinforced by the dominant culture, acquiring institutional expression in language, in humour, and in music and the media. In other words, the groups with the power to define reality have created values and ideologies that reflect, legitimize and safeguard their interests. To take the glaring example of gender inequality, the reason for male dominance is falsely attributed—as more and more studies in recent years bear out—to a host of reasons such as sex chromosomes, hormones and even brain size. 'The characteristics of the powerful, whatever they may be, are thought to be better than the characteristics of the powerless—and logic has nothing to do with it,' as Gloria Steinem tells us in a famous satire:

> A white minority of the world has spent centuries conning us into thinking that a white skin makes people superior—even though the only thing it really does is make them more subject to ultraviolet rays and to wrinkles. Male human beings have built whole cultures around the idea that penis-envy is 'natural' to women—though having such an unprotected organ might be said to make men more vulnerable, and the power to give birth makes womb-envy at least as logical. (Steinem 1978)

The point is, if things are not changing in an equalitarian way despite the arrival of political democracy, it is because exclusions are glossed over even in the new discourses of morality, religion, and science. As the dominant groups still mould the public mind and manipulate the system in their favour, the mindset of hierarchy persists; only it has learnt to hide itself better behind the veil of politically correct language. In many ways, in different guises, anti-democratic prejudice and practice persist. Indoctrination of privilege and discrimination runs deep—and the history of this brainwashing has not yet been written into history. The masterminds that created the ideologies of caste, class and gender are still glorified, as we shall see shortly, as benign and disinterested philosophers. Progenitors of brahmanism, patriarchy, and race are (still) portrayed, explicitly or subtly, as intellectual role models in academic tomes and school textbooks. So much so that many of their hierarchical ideas—and divisive legacies—are carried forward (with a little bit of spin doctoring) by the elite groups as the basis of social justice and social morality!

Gandhi's much talked about but little understood 'freedom struggle', for example, was grounded in a nostalgic vision of an indigenous tradition that valorised brahmanic power relationships within society in the name of anti-colonialism. His politics and rhetoric of Hindu spirituality, cultural authenticity, and social harmony subsumed the issues of caste violence, exploitation of the peasantry, and subordination of women in a way that validated traditional caste-class inequalities. Contrary to popular perception, Gandhi never opposed the exploitation according to caste by brahmanism; he only opposed the practice of untouchability, considering it as an anomaly with the *Varnashrama Dharma* (classical caste system) which he portrayed as just, fair, and harmonious. The upper-caste elites knew the value of Gandhi's paternalistic politics and they made him a modern-day avatar. They put him on a pedestal so high that his face remained invisible to the masses (Mani 2005, Chapter 7).

In other words, it is the elitist stranglehold over public discourse—and other means of symbolic reproduction in society—that does not allow democratic norms and values to take root. Today's story may be very complex but the reality of continuing cruelty, callousness and cynicism is stark. Hunger, humiliation, and dehumanization are all around us. A large number of people live with feelings of failure and many suffer from a deep sense of insufficiency, lack of security, and sense of degradation, as a contemporary writer painfully stresses (while defining the essential role of literature):

> Yes, the greatest dilemmas facing humanity are still landlessness, homelessness, and hunger. . . . What literature needs most to tell and investigate today are humanity's basic fears: the fear of being left outside, and the fear of counting for nothing, and the feelings of worthlessness that comes with such fears; the collective humiliations, vulnerabilities, slights, grievances, sensitivities, and imagined insults, and the nationalist boasts and inflations that are their next of kin. (Pamuk 2007: 413)

Under the beautiful Constitutional laws, India is producing hundreds of billionaires, the flip side of which is the state's connivance in the perpetuation of mass poverty. The system apologists make the point that democracy can only assume people to be equal and grant them equal citizenship but that does not make them equal in ability, industry and character. This half-truth obfuscates the real issues. True, people are vastly different, unequal in mental and physical abilities; there are innate individual differences like biological sex, intelligence, health and age about which nothing much can be done. But is it fair to misname and misuse such differences, making them the basis of insult or discrimination? In reality, we have as yet very few cultural patterns for relating across our human differences as equals. The tendency to see what is different as inferior and to oppose the differences remains strong.

Even if we leave aside the historical injustices, there are tremendous odds and current ills that cripple the poor. If institutionalized discriminations are eliminated along with a reconstruction of society where each person could have every possible advantage of food, medical care, education, and housing, much of what we call 'natural' or 'inherent' differences would tend to gradually disappear. When the artificial inequalities disappear, so will the domination of one group by another. When 'distinctions of rank are blurred and privileges abolished' (as Tocqueville grasped in the 1830s, even though he was studying the American democracy from an elite perspective), 'when patrimonies are divided up and education and freedom spread, the poor conceive an eager desire to acquire comfort, and the rich think of the danger of losing it' (Tocqueville 1988: 531). He took note that when everyone is put on more or less equal level, even the slightest discrimination is noticed and resented: 'The more equal men are, the more insatiable will be their longing for equality.'

True, society needs some sort of organization and division of labour. But such organization must be based on a consideration of everyone's interests, which alone can engender social cohesion, a sense of community and voluntary cooperation. Respect for individuality can only be ensured through equality—a fact that elitist individualists ignore with impunity because that will mark the end of their privileges. Social progress, in other words, implies abolition of all entitlements and privileges, overt or hidden. Progress in this sense implies a continually growing freedom of the individual, enabling everyone to choose their kind of life and work. With the institution of equality in social relations, individual differences will be seen in an entirely new light. Equality means that the rights of the individual as an equal citizen are primary and universal, and all particularized rights are secondary and situational. Obviously, every person is equal with others in a number of dimensions and also dissimilar in other areas but with distinct individuality, every person is valuable and unique. We have chosen the foundational principle of equality because it is our best bet to build and hold together a diverse society in a framework of human rights and justice, irrespective of the ways individuals are not equal.

Equality in social relations is a moral and ideational concept, grounded in intelligent humility rather than in arrogance. It is an idea and an aspiration, and it is an ongoing struggle. Our individuality, or personal identity, is in perpetual conflict with any arbitrary divisions into caste, class, or gender. But this is what the essentialism of hierarchy does: it makes the individual faceless in a homogenized category—'he is a shudra, she is a brahman'; 'she is black, he is white'. Hierarchical societies represent individuals symbolically, identifying them by their sex, caste, and rank. A person is perceived as bright or dull, desirable or undesirable, according to her ascriptive identity rather than her own personality. To a casteist or sexist person, the individual simply does not exist; he sees only groups, never individuals; he sees bodies (buttocks and breasts) rather than eyes or faces; he sees the colour of the skin rather than character. He may admit the reality of dissimilarities within a caste or sex group, but it is only the alleged unequal qualities—biological or natural inequalities—between castes and sexes that have great meaning for him.

Put otherwise, our individuality—our being different from each other—is not inherited or fixed at birth, but gradually formed in community. Everyone performs some job or work and this is recognized by others. Judging work as lowly or lofty on whatever basis is another matter, and a contentious one. There are so many respects in which one person may be superior or inferior that there is no person who is entirely superior or inferior to another in every respect. It is often seen that those who are not good in one faculty are compensated with some talent in other areas. Such diversities of individuality create community and provide the intellectual and ethical basis of unity and equality of all humankind, a fact that is distorted or trivialized by the privileged in their exclusionary thinking and behaviour.

As the powerful groups have not embraced equality in actual life, they use their power and knowledge to maintain injustices while paying lip service to democracy and freedom. At unguarded moments, they justify inequality by arguing that many people are (or can be) miserable even without being oppressed. But there is a basic difference between personal suffering and external oppression. It is no one's argument that an equal society will cure all our problems, least of all our personal sorrows, but it will certainly alleviate the pathologies caused by the violence of hierarchy, power, and wealth. True, personal suffering has to be dealt at personal level, at the best with loving support from friends and family. There are only individual solutions to individual problems. But most human problems have social origins and social solutions. No one is immune to the social forces that shape us. We are interrelated and interdependent; each one of us is responsible to every other person. Why then should one individual have the huge privileges of wealth, education and technology, while others remain bereft of the bare minimums of life? Such injustice damages not just the victims but the whole of society because it does not allow many to create, contribute, or bring out their best to society.

Potential for evolution and creativity is immense in each child. Herbert Read rightly underlined, 'Great changes in the destiny of mankind begin in the minds of little children.' No child dreams of becoming a failure, a criminal, a burden on society. But millions of children are still denied the opportunity to go to school. Many are even sold into the slavery of child labour and human trafficking. Although it may be facetiously argued that even in the unfair system, a deprived but determined and deserving child may create her own opportunities, there is little doubt that her way will be paved with all kinds of difficulties. Society puts severe limits to such possibility. It is rare for the children who live in deprivation to cultivate intellectual, artistic or creative skills. Those who face hunger also face despair and social devaluation and a tripping-away of self-esteem. They face multiple hurdles and discriminations in getting an education, or making a decent life. They seldom get the chance—the level-playing field—to improve their lives. The poor are mostly illiterate or poorly educated, and without access to health care and sanitation. Such chronic problems ensure that people who are born poor also die poor. Desperate situations engender hopelessness, lethargy, and even self-destructiveness.

On the other hand, those born in privileged families start their lives with multiple advantages. With wealth, education and associated privileges behind them, the rich don't start the race with the same odds as the rest. The veil of political and technological change, however, allows today's gentlemen to feign ignorance that they are (still) mostly born rather than made. In India, the urban upper castes hiding behind the 'middle class' identity remain ignorant about their power, wealth, and social network that enormously privileges them over the rest. They remain in denial that discriminations against the poor run deep and work at multiple levels in every sphere of life—in education, in employment, in getting loans, in allotment of homes, in provisions of public services. They have no clue about endemic and deep-rooted discriminatory norms of caste and class.

The promise of democracy is to break the chain of discrimination and sever every link in it. This ideal is routinely trashed in a democracy like India's. That we all share the same Constitution and its rule of equality does not mean we are really all the same. Without knowing quotidian experiences of the oppressed—how they cope with deprivation; how they pay higher prices than others for the same needs met; how they fight among themselves for scarce resources; how they suffer humiliation due to their dehumanizing stereotypes—it is difficult to see that layers and layers of economic and cultural barriers have been raised against them. It is difficult to see the reality of oppression as it really is. Marilyn Frye, a brilliant feminist theorist, has given us an illuminating meaning of the word 'oppression', and her penetrating words are worth quoting:

> The root of the word 'oppression' is the element 'press'. *The press of the crowd; pressed into military service; to press a pair of pants; printing press; press the button.* Presses are used to mould things or flatten them or reduce them in bulk, sometimes to reduce them by squeezing out the gases or liquids in them. Something pressed is something caught between or among forces and barriers which are so related to each other that jointly they restrain, restrict or

prevent the thing's motion or mobility. *Mould. Immobilize. Reduce.* The mundane experience of the oppressed provides another clue. One of the most characteristic and ubiquitous features of the word as experienced by oppressed people is the double bind—situations in which options are reduced to a very few and all of them expose one to penalty, censure or deprivation. . . . You can't win. You are caught in a bind, caught between systematically related pressures. (Frye 1983)

Our life and experiences are shaped by social structures, but they are advantageous to some groups and oppressive to others. They impact the life of the privileged and the powerless in a fundamentally different way. Frye gives the metaphor of a birdcage to explain the reality of multiple and interconnected structures of inequality. Class, caste, race, and sex, each make up one bar of the birdcage. Myopically inspecting only an individual wire up and down the length of the cage does not reveal the network of wires that imprison the bird. Likewise, studying only the elements of oppression—even sympathetically as some conscientious elite intellectuals do—without seeing the structure of oppression as a whole (including cultural constructs and common sense, the patterns of behaviour and relationships, resource distribution and social control) will leave us without understanding that 'there are people who are caged, whose motion and mobility are restricted, whose lives are shaped and reduced.' Restrictive forces and barriers that the oppressed face are not occasional or accidental 'but are systematically related to each other in such a way as to catch one between and among them and restrict or penalize motion in any direction. In the experience of being caged in: all avenues, in every direction, are blocked or booby trapped' (Frye 1983).

As the patterns of culture remain more or less hierarchical, despite the rise of political democracy, getting out of the ghetto of oppression is not easy for the oppressed. In democracies like India, extreme inequalities which are 'visceral and commonplace' give birth to what a scholar terms the 'culture of avoidance'.

> The experience of inequality is so existentially disturbing that it is often kept at bay for a whole series of interdictions and stratagems. For those at the bottom of a deep well, the mere act of looking up at the heights to be scaled is dispiriting; for those at the top, the act of looking to the depths at which human beings are confined is likely to cause vertigo. The net result is taciturn avoidance played out in Indian homes and streets.... Powerful representation of this reality—like the astonishing literature produced by Dalits—are politely acknowledged, but rarely internalized in our consciousness ... because they represent an assault on the elaborate psychological fortifications we have constructed to cope with a reality we know all too well. (Mehta 2012b)

A fundamental problem for even the kind-hearted among the privileged, who are themselves largely isolated from the lives lived under the conditions of injustice, is to figure out what justice really means. The basis for concern and acting justly towards others is our shared humanity—'kindness'. The quest for justice presupposes first of all, to use Cornel West's words, 'allowing the suffering to speak, allowing the victims to be visible, and allowing social misery to be put on the agenda of those with power'. Distance or estrangement from suffering obscures the structural sources of injustice, and instead represents the oppressed themselves as the problem. Implicit in the language of problems is the notion of solutions and the implication that the right thinking and action from the above can heal people at the bottom of the social pyramid. This diseased mindset leads the privileged to see the oppressed as passive recipients of charity or subsidy, not as people who help create social assets and whose devaluation of labour power makes the rich richer. Stereotypes reduce the oppressed to simple categories and convert assumptions into realities. Ignorance, prejudice, revulsion, denial, fear, and sheer contempt for those who threaten their sense of living in a civilized society delude the privileged to resist any autonomous move of the oppressed for justice. The most positive response that the privileged are able to muster towards the oppressed is pity, reducing the latter to the objects of condescension and charity. Such thinking privileges the role of the saviours from the above, reinforcing patterns of domination and jeopardizing the possibility of genuine change by toying with one superficial solution after another, and harking back to some real or imaginary justice in the past.

Thus, hiding the pervasive injustices in India, the caste elites never tire of narrating the 'great nation-building contributions' of Gandhi and Nehru. But such glorification of the great leaders and their 'sacrifices' for the oppressed serve no purpose other than self-congratulation. Supposed movements against social injustice elicit feel-good notions of battles fought and victories won. Such narratives neither help us understand what actually happened in modern India nor provide clues as how to cope with (let alone overcome) the aggressive castes' appropriation of power in the name of nation-building. In such narratives, the opposition from below led by the likes of Phule, Ambedkar, and Periyar is either kept out of the view or mischievously misrepresented as a sideshow of casteist politics that failed to understand the greatness of Gandhi and Nehru (Mani 2005). Nothing has a more divisive and alienating effect upon society than the elitist promotion of the romance of casteism-reformed-and-bias-defeated since caste and class are not simply mental blinders that can be easily removed or exorcised. In fact, the convenient assumptions which bias the privileged can enmesh with popular prejudice so that the traditional principles of power and patronage seem normal, not fundamentally antithetical to a democratic polity.

Asking some simple questions and imagining possible scenarios can illustrate how a large number of Indians have been marginalized under the mask of democracy. Imagine an India since 1947 in which every prime minister has been either a dalit, adivasi, OBC, Muslim, or Christian (who together constitute 85 per cent of the population). Imagine an India in which almost all top bureaucrats, judges, business leaders, professionals, and public intellectuals are dalit, adivasi, and OBC. (Caste elites almost totally monopolize these areas.) Imagine a history of India in which shudras enslave brahmans, prohibit the latter from learning and education and force them to adopt shudra supremacist language, culture, and religion, abusing the brahman as 'low caste', 'untouchable', 'chandala', 'worse than animals'. The degree to which any or all of these seem unimaginable is the degree to which the caste elites assume a norm—a viciously undemocratic norm—and fit their expectations to it, making a mockery of justice and freedom.

One does not have to be a Phule or Ambedkar to know that justice demands the opposite. Justice demands that caste elites become uneasy with their unjust overrepresentation in different levers of power, admit their bluff, their injustices of the past and present, and come forward to build a democracy in which there is no privilege and no exclusion. Justice demands that the privileged groups contribute to build a society in which equality of conditions is established in such a way that it eradicates their historically accumulated privileges that allow them to marginalize the majority and monopolize power through reproduction of elitist culture, education and politics.

THE LONGSTANDING ABUSE OF KNOWLEDGE

The light of knowledge dispelling the darkness of life is a universal and exquisite dream of humanity. Knowledge, however, (as we briefly saw in the Introduction and shall probe further in Chapter 4) is neither wisdom or certitude, nor its use necessarily noble or disinterested. Centuries ago, Buddha was forced to assail the brahmanic knowledge-system for its fundamental immorality. Rejecting its supremacist language and ideology as 'pernicious to people's well-being', Buddha argued that 'what mattered was not the letter but the spirit, not the detail but the overall picture, not one's memory but one's understanding' (Hamilton 2006: 55). In a different context, classical Greek dramatist Euripides made the same point succinctly: *To know much is not to be wise.*

As knowledge can be both healing and oppressive, as well as a messy mixture of the two, its history has had a rather uneasy, if not adversarial, relationship with freedom and justice. Though the consequences of use and abuse of knowledge is yet to be fully assessed, there is little doubt that it has played a deeply dual role in history. 'Thanks to words, we have been able to rise above the brutes, and thanks to words, we have often sunk to the level of demons' (Aldous Huxley, quoted in Bassham 2002: 119). Thus, knowledge, like other things in life, is what we make of it. Very little depends upon our knowledge, and everything upon our practical and political demands or upon our will for framing principle or policy that we decide to adopt. Two things, however, stand out clearly: removal of false knowledge is necessary for right understanding; and, if our knowledge does not enlarge our empathy, it does nothing morally, and detached from generosity, it acquires the potential to be dangerous.

It is axiomatic that a little knowledge is a dangerous thing. Knowledge becomes dangerous, not just inane and barren, when it insulates itself from justice and social responsibility. The individuals, for example, who made the atom bombs that destroyed Nagasaki and Hiroshima were some of the finest scientists of their time. But they were easily purchased by the US regime to make the technology of mass killing. And they were no exceptions; only exceptional scientists or knowledge-wielders have ever refused to be bought over by the wealthy and the powerful. Many are known to have sold their brilliance and expertise to inhuman ends. Hitler and Mussolini did not have to do much to drag in the entire scientist community of their countries. Countless poets, artists and intellectuals are known to have squandered their best talents on pleasing their patrons. Men like Firdausi, a self-seeking scholar writing the *Shahnama* (the hagiography of a king) for a few gold coins, or maybe a fortune, has never been out of fashion.

Few intellectuals have displayed virtue to withstand the highest bidder. Complicities of the intellect with the power, invoking 'truth', 'reason', or 'morality' to lie, loot and murder are scattered all over history. Consider this: the East India Company (which turned many countries into colonies through its bloodstained business and laid the foundations of the world's biggest empire) did not just manage to buy off the parliamentarians back home but also recruited the country's top intellectuals such as Thomas Macaulay, Edward Strachey, Thomas Love Peacock, and both James and John Stuart Mill. Some intellectuals are known to have sold their souls even for free. Else, how does one explain racialist thought in Carlyle and colonialism in Ruskin? Then there is Rudyard Kipling extolling empire-building as 'white man's burden', and its 'savage wars of peace' as an enlargement of the horizon of intellect and experience. There is no dearth of their Eastern counterparts either; pundits like Ananda K. Coomaraswamy (1909; 1943) and S. Radhakrishnan (1957; 1962) would use their punditry to see unparalleled beauty and pluralism in caste-centred brahmanism.

A lie is an allurement, a fabrication that can be embellished into a fantasy; it is much more interesting and profitable than cold and sober truth. The educated elitists know this, and contribute their mite in finding compelling ways of avoiding, concealing, or distorting reality. One of the greatest 'achievements' of the modern times, in Jules Henry's phrase, is 'the enormous variety of ways of compelling language to lie'.

Perhaps the greatest modern example of knowledge and politics joining hands is Social Darwinism (and its various new and sophisticated variants that have sprung up in recent times) that rationalizes hierarchy and oppression as 'natural' and 'scientific' because the human world, according to its enthusiasts, is subject to inescapable laws of nature (in which big fish devours smaller ones). By insisting that everything happens by biological necessity, the dogma of DNA essentially glorifies the idea of pre-determined fate, leaving no scope for the idea of free will. Its implication is unmistakable: humanity cannot, must not, escape the hierarchies and cruelties in nature. One way or another, directly or subtly, its votaries insist that big man must smash small man because humans, too, are part of the animal kingdom.

The process of applying the laws of the jungle to the affairs of humanity, however, did not begin in the nineteenth century with Darwin's theory of evolution, when reactionaries turned it into a tool for justifying racism, colonialism, and violence (Chapter 4). Its genesis may be seen much earlier when humans were still in some ways a part of the jungle. Its pioneers were those who invented the hierarchy of caste and patriarchy, dividing the human world into different castes like the different species of animal kingdom, thus laying the intellectual-moral foundation of a vicious human civilization. Under various guises and nomenclatures, Social Darwinism—its articulation, justification and promotion in theory and practice—began with the brahmanic propaganda of caste hierarchy in ancient India and the Platonic-Aristotelian philosophy of slavery in ancient Greece. The Indian and Greek philosophers who justified caste and slavery in their quest for 'truth, beauty and the good life' had not only paved the way for a deceptive intellectual discourse (which continues to flourish in various schools of scientific determinism, religious obscurantism, and neocon theories) but also much of the dehumanization and bloodshed in history.

The brahman conceived and institutionalized the caste system and patriarchy, involving physical and psychological violence against the weaker castes and women, on the grounds that hierarchies represent an 'integral part' of the food chain—the big fish does devour the smaller one and this natural order of things, they insisted, has a divine sanctity. Thus, justice became inequality, and was made the basis of the brahmanic religion and culture centred on caste. Caste was basically a religious hierarchy that encompassed the economic and the political, as Dumont has demonstrated in *Homo Hierarchicus*. Likewise, in Greece, Plato argued that the classes of workers, soldiers, and guardians must stick to their natural—inherited—work because that alone would ensure perfect justice in a just Republic. Plato, who came from the patrician class and clandestinely represented its interests in his philosophy, tells this 'lordly lie'—his own phrase; he knew what he was up to—because his intention was to establish a regime in which inequality was justice, and this lie the supreme truth. In *Open Society and its Enemies*, Karl Popper has shown that Plato's *Republic* is actually a caste state and his (much-misunderstood) philosopher-king a ruthless dictator. John Dewey and Bertrand Russell have castigated the *Republic* as a 'totalitarian tract' but sadly the number of intellectuals who are in thrall to Platonic philosophy far outnumber the others.

Plato's equally celebrated disciple, Aristotle, defended slavery and the subjection of women on the grounds that it was 'nature's intention'. How he discovered this 'intention', however, is hardly a mystery. Aristotle, like Plato, was simply giving voice to the vested interests of the wealthy Greek aristocracy of his time.

Apparent differences in articulations apart, both brahmanism in India and racism in the West were founded on the core ideas of what we know today as Social Darwinism. Both flourished on the caste-patriarchal matrix of grinding down women and the working class. It was the brahmanic celebration of the domination of the strong over the weak—expressed in phrases such as *matsya nyaya, dandaniti*, and *vira bhogya vasundhara* (the ethic of the strong exploiting and enjoying the earth)—and the Greek glorification of aristocracy along with slavery of the working class and subjection of women as a necessity for the good life of the chosen few, that firmly laid the intellectual-moral foundation of hierarchy and oppression.

Social Darwinism, combining the concepts of selfish gene, biological determinism and social jungle, presents a scientific version of the theory of predestination. (To quote Aldous Huxley: 'Nature is monstrously unjust. There is no substitute for talent. Industry and all the virtues are of no avail.') It may be a modern scientific phrase but the fundamental idea behind it has a long philosophical as well as socio-religious lineage in civilized societies. It can also be grasped by the fact that much before the rise of science-inspired Social Darwinism, the reductionist idea of humans as selfish and greedy creatures had decisively triumphed in the West (Hirschman 1977). Among others, Adam Smith had famously endorsed the selfish nature of humans in his 1776 classic *The Wealth of Nations*. His much-quoted words about the self-interested butcher, brewer, and baker went on to become the intellectual bedrock of capitalism. The crux of his logic is well known: the pursuit of individual self-interest in the marketplace will lead to the general good by making available more and better and cheaper goods. In his earlier work, *The Theory of Moral Sentiments* (1759), he rhapsodizes that selfish motives are transmuted by interaction to yield the most unexpected of results: social harmony. Above all, he saw an 'invisible hand' directing profit-driven activities that served the common good of humanity. This seems like the language of theological reductionism rather than critical enlightenment.

History has disproved Adam Smith's market fundamentalism that when everyone pursues his self-interest (even without equality of conditions), the outcome will be economic betterment for everyone. As of now, Smith's 'invisible hand' has produced ten million super-rich wallowing in luxuries, and one billion people bereft of basic necessities. For all his greatness, his glorification of *laissez faire, laissez passer* (let it be, leave it alone), he was unable to foresee that rampaging private interest, set free, can wreck social harmony and create extremes of wealth and poverty. In the scramble for wealth, it is the creed of greed that prevails over the values of public spiritedness and cooperation.

The father of capitalism was standing on the shoulders of

many giants who had glorified greed, self-aggrandisement and power in the previous centuries. In a resurgent Europe on the cusp of modernity, humanism was many things to many people, but the common idea was the belief that human nature was many sided, and that individuals were capable of shaping their own lives through means other than the mere pursuit of wealth and status that was the most important thing in a hierarchical society. It was this idea that was appropriated and variously undermined, attacked, and destroyed by a long line of intellectual charlatans in favour of self-interest.

Francesco Barbaro (1390–1454), an Italian humanist, defended acquisition of wealth as a great virtue in a famous leaflet. Lorenzo Valla (1406–1457) wrote *On Pleasure*, cocking a snook at Jesus' self-transcending ethics and lavishing praise on gratification as the highest human value. Niccolo Machiavelli mocked morality, glorified the theory of 'end justifies the means' and made human nature synonymous with selfishness in his iconic book, *The Prince* (1513). The French writer La Rochefoucauld (1613–80) brilliantly reinforced the idea that humans are basically selfish and greedy.

In 1714, Bernard Mandeville published *The Fable of the Bees* whose moral is captured in its subtitle, *Private Vices, Public Benefits*. It is the story of a hive in which the bees come to realize their own selfishness and decide to reform and act with the good of others in mind. But reform proves disastrous; everyone loses his job. The richness and variety of life, however, return with embracing the old, selfish days, when the bees acted out of vanity and greed—a time when

. . . every Part was full of Vice,
Yet the whole Mass a Paradise;
. . . Such were the Blessings of that state;
Their Crimes conspir'd to make them Great.

(see Ball and Dagger 2004: 61)

In short, the theory that man is a selfish animal was propagated with a vengeance by many great and not-so-great minds of the time. This led to the idea that everyone should unleash their animal spirits and pursue their private interests. From the eighteenth century, arguments in support of power and profit flooded the intellectual climate in the West. Though these ideas were still unknown to the ordinary people who could not read or write, the brainwave to create a selfish paradise hit the ambitious lot, especially those who went on to lay the foundations of colonies and empires in many parts of the world. If greed and glory required selling one's soul, prostituting intellect, and killing 'savages' to plunder their lands and resources, how could one help it?

In other words, political arguments for imperialism and capitalism preceded their actual triumph—and the emergence of science-led Social Darwinism. Herbert Spencer was not the only one who had begun to think in evolutionary terms—captured in the phrase 'survival of the fittest' that he coined—before Darwin's *Origin of Species* appeared in 1859. Social Darwinism was born before Darwinism, but the latter gave the former a 'scientific' justification in the age of science, helping it ram home the point that helping the weak impedes individual freedom and retards progress by holding the strong back. The doctrine of evolution provided crucial scientific support for predatory capitalism—and the genocides in the coming decades, as we will see in Chapter 4.

Though Social Darwinism lost its sheen and its champions scampered to cover their hideous nakedness after Hitler put the bloody idea into practice in the Holocaust, the toxic proposal behind it survives in new elitist schools of thought such as socio-biology, evolutionary psychology, neo-conservatism and neo-liberalism. Not long ago *The Economist* carried an article 'Why We Are, As We Are' (2008) which more or less equated Darwinism with Social Darwinism, justifying hierarchy, status, sexual crimes, and gender pay gaps, etc., as products of evolutionary—and unavoidable—forces, exhorting governments and policymakers to profitably use Darwin's insights in the process of policymaking.

The Economist has been propagating this brand of Darwinism since its inception in 1843 with the avowed mission of taking part in 'a severe contest between intelligence, which presses forward, and an unworthy, timid ignorance obstructing our progress.' (It carries this mission statement in every issue.) On the staff of this periodical in his early years, Herbert Spencer said the poor were undeserving of any aid and should be eliminated: 'The whole effort of nature is to get rid of such [the unfit, the poor], to clear the world of them, and make room for better' (see Hofstadter 1944: 5). He explained this and similar theories in his *Principles of Biology* and *Principles of Sociology*, which had a notable impact on the rise of sociology as a discipline. His biological base to the study of society gave the aura of science to the fledgling discipline of sociology. Similarly, Walter Bagehot, the editor of *The Economist* from 1861 till his death in 1877, made a colossal effort to apply the idea of natural selection to the study of society and economics. The sociological justification of imperialism and capitalism after 1850 in Europe came into vogue with Bagehot's brilliant essay, 'Physics and Politics'. The subtitle of this 1872 work was 'Thoughts on the Application of the Principles of "Natural Selection" and "Inheritance" to Political Society.' Justifying the logic of domination and expansion, the essay exhorted the imperialists to fulfil their racial and national mission, arguing that *might is not just right but marvellously moral*:

> In every particular state of the world, those nations which are strongest tend to prevail over the others; and in certain marked peculiarities the strongest tend to be the best. . . . The strongest nation has always been conquering the weaker. . . . The majority of groups which win and conquer are better than the majority of those which fail and perish. (Bagehot [1872] 2007)

The Economist is permanently tethered to the supremacist economics and politics which it keeps replenished to march with the changing times. Corporatist privatization of economy, technological inevitability, and intellectual property rights—its three magic bullets for all the world's ills—are just reworked versions of the Social Darwinists. Beneath the skin of a new vocabulary, it never fails to give fresh perspectives for hierarchy and domination. We know how seriously the governments and policymakers around the world takes *Economist*, which describes itself as the *capitalist cadre*. The point is, big fish—corporate sharks—may fight or be friends but there is no confusion or dispute among them that little fish are to be eaten.

What remains constant between the old and new forms of hierarchy are the mindset of dominance and misrepresentation of reality. Manu and Kautilya, Plato and Aristotle, Spencer and Bagehot were not just individual intellectuals; their power philosophy represented a university which never fails to fascinate the powerful who dominated much of human history and knowledge-construction. They still control economy and polity, culture and education, which they form, formulate, and reform from time to time in order to maintain their power. It is their continued hold on people's minds that enables them to uphold their power in the contemporary world.

In the case of India, the reproduction of knowledge and education—with some exceptions of challenging attempts in recent years—remains biased and brahmanic, despite the dazzling democratic façade and politically correct vocabulary. Contestations to the dominant discourse and meta-narratives by the marginalized majority remains confined to the margins. In place everywhere are refurbished brahmanic canons and constructs blithely flaunted as 'Indian'. The Indian elite's winning trick, from the colonial nineteenth century to the present, is to selectively cull from modern democratic ideas and institutions, and ingeniously align and integrate them with the traditional structures of caste and class. The basic design behind such *change with continuity* is to preserve and innovate upon traditional dominance over the masses. As in the past, so in the present, the over-all objective is to mislead, exploit and exclude the majority.

Elitist Pedagogy and the Pedagogy of Liberation

Our social world and relationships continue to be ascriptive and power-driven, and the established knowledge has no interest in changing the situation. Social sciences, by their mandate, are empirical and produced to understand, explain and thus sustain the existing social formation. They are not driven by the urge to challenge and change the world. The point is, individual interests of intellectuals, the fiction of disinterested academia notwithstanding, have always impacted knowledge-formation. Identity or location of the scholar (in terms of caste, class, gender, age, nationality) influence, if not determine, the orientation or emphasis of their work. History is always told, as Habermas points out, with specific 'interests' in mind, the first of which is communicating. And this *interestedness* is not necessarily impartial, let alone ethical, as philosophers like Paul Ricoeur would like us to believe, simply because (as he says) what we consider communicable and memorable is also valuable. Ricoeur stresses that most worthy of being preserved in memory are those 'values which ruled the individual actions, the life of the institutions, and the social struggles of the past' (see Kearney 2002: 154). However, the choice of memories that are preserved, whether in the form of narratives or abstract treaties, is coloured by the social and political position of the writer, and may be the opposite of ethical and most valuable. For example, the brahman authors, both ancient and current, who are *official* recorders sui generis of the memory of India and things Indians, are not only notorious for killing memories that threaten their supremacy but also for erasing the basic difference between description and prescription, fact and fabrication, as we will see in Chapter 4. Moreover, knowledge-generation and dissemination, on the whole, has a long tradition of patronage by the powerful vested interests—earlier by the monarchs and merchants, and now by the governments and corporations. Scholars and experts may boast of their objectivity and intellectual freedom, but the rampaging corporate and political interests have on occasion reduced knowledge-production to an outright industry—the knowledge industry—for maximizing their profits and tightening their control over society, culture, and economy.

By producing knowledge, the dominant groups manufacture consent for their politics and power. Claiming to represent the national or global interest and carrying the conscience of society, they mask their interests as common interests through weaving a system of knowledge that constitutes power and through which power is exercised. Even when they take recognition of injustice and oppression, they indulge in ahistorical and wilful assertions about the past and present and do not allow the powerless to think and speak for themselves. The ruling groups nurture and promote their own intellectuals and social scientists—from their own social background—to articulate and formulate social problems. The elite recognises only other elite voices as authentic. Even the best among them betray this mindset. Singing praises to the *Argumentative Indian* and the glorious tradition of public reasoning in India, intellectuals like Amartya Sen develop a discourse that reinforces brahmanic half-truths about history and culture. They uncritically glorify Gandhi, Nehru, Tagore as God's gifts to modern India, while keeping the lives and struggles of dalit-bahujan revolutionaries such as Phule, Periyar, and Ambedkar hidden from the public view (see Chapter 4). When they occasionally drop Ambedkar's name in their discourses—tokenism necessitated by the growing democratic clamour of dalit–bahujans—such gestures are lauded as a radical exercise in social reconciliation.

Cultural tokenism is a feel-good device for elitist minds. They keep critical social and political issues outside the people's gaze, but give the impression of conducting an open-ended debate. They speak on behalf of the voiceless but turn hostile when the silenced and the suppressed—dalits, adivasis, subaltern women—start telling their own stories, telling their raw experiences as their truth, as human truth. The elites become angry and afraid because when the people who are kept down think and speak on their own, they break out, they subvert. The subalterns threaten the established order when they think and write. As they do not know how to play with words and make abstract theories in a nice, unthreatening way, their writings are quietly set aside as biased, outrageous, or reckless—improper for serious intellectual discussion! Ambedkar, for example, was not only attacked throughout his life for his struggle against caste and cultural oppression, but was also told by the pundits not to enter the sacred realm of scholarship: 'I have already been warned that while I may have a right to speak on Indian politics, religion and religious history of India are not my field and that I must not enter it' (Ambedkar, *BAWS*, vol. 7: 11). Pointing out 'the intolerance of the Brahman scholar towards any attempt to expose the Brahmanic literature,' he writes,

> If any non-Brahman were to make such an attempt the Brahman scholars would engage in a conspiracy of silence, take no notice of him, condemn him outright on some flimsy grounds or dub his work useless. As a writer engaged in the exposition of the Brahmanic literature I have been a victim of such mean tricks. (ibid.: 241)

When the conspiracy of silence does not work, as in the case of some popular oppositional writers, the latter are accused of politicizing and polluting the sacred realm of knowledge. The kidnapping of a lower-class writer, as George Orwell once observed, happens the moment he puts pen to paper. To the intellectual establishment, elitist constructions of the past and present seem natural and apolitical; only the demand for change and inclusion seem motivated by a political agenda. When Kancha Ilaiah, a dalit–bahujan scholar, wrote *Why I am Not a Hindu* (1996) when the militant Hindutva forces were threatening to make India a Hindu state, he was greeted with derision not only by the upper-caste reactionaries but also by many leftist-liberal academics.

Among them were the likes of Romila Thapar, a progressive historian. In her magisterial manner, she dismissed Ilaiah's book as 'not history or social science'! Pundits like Amartya Sen who have never bothered to reflect about brahmanism, caste, or its consequences, maintained a studied silence. One wonders whether professionals like Thapar and Sen would ever honestly engage with Phule and Ambedkar's critiques of caste and Indian culture, or dare to dismiss the brahmanic obfuscation of history by the likes of Gandhi and Nehru, and point out that the duo had no training in social science, so we should not take their writings on history seriously. On this issue, Ambedkar has made a pertinent point:

> [T]he selfish interest of a person or of the class to which he belongs always acts as an internal limitation which regulates the direction of his intellect. . . . [T]he intellect of a Brahman scholar is severely limited by anxiety to preserve his interest. He suffers from this internal limitation as a result of which he does not allow his intellect full play which honesty and integrity demands. For, he fears that it may affect the interests of his class and therefore his own. (Ambedkar, ibid.: 240–41)

Elitist intellectuals dismiss pro-people writings as political and partisan, while presenting themselves as benign custodians of objectivity and truth. The best among them take recourse to the fact that history is very complicated. They sneer at the suggestion of bottom-up history: 'Who built Thebes of the seven gates? In the books you will find the names of kings. Did the kings haul up the lumps of rock?' (Brecht [1935] 1959: 108). Social sciences are more complex and nuanced than ideological wish fulfilment, they remind us, themselves unconscious of the blindness that prevents them from seeing conflict and contestation in history. Thinking they have a great soul and vast views beyond the comprehension of the commoners, the power pundits blithely equate their knowing with seeing, their knowledge with illumination, and their writing with truth. But as Daniel Wall confesses in a poem:

When / My contentedness / Is in,
I cannot see / Discrimination . . .
I have to allow myself to feel / —uncomfortable
To kick my contentedness out . . .
My words can speak / In all colours
And not allow the power / Of my whiteness
Words can speak / In all shades
And not show the power / Of maleness
Close your eyes / I could be any male.
Open your eyes / I am a white one. (Wall 2001: 108–12)

Howard Zinn's maxim 'you can't be neutral on a moving train' applies to the Sens and the Thapars. One's partiality or politics is related to one's identity, whether inherited or acquired or a complicated mixture of the two. Every idea has an owner, and every idea, if we read closely, reflects the owner's identity and politics. 'In acquiring one's conception of the world one always belongs to a particular grouping which is that of all the social elements which share the same mode of thinking and acting. We are all conformists of some conformism or other, always man-in-the-mass or collective man' (Gramsci 1975: 324). In the Aristotelian sense, any piece of writing is a political act—though the Athenian philosopher would have vehemently contested this description for his own writings, like other elitist writers.

Know yourself—the timeless wisdom of the ancient sages—must apply equally to everyone, especially to those who are in the business of knowledge-production. One must know that knowing others—understanding society—is far less challenging than knowing oneself. To have political views is not a form of guilt; to hide it is guilt. The claim to be neutral or apolitical is actually to be taking a position—a partisan position. Thomas Mann says in his *Culture and Politics* that being apolitical is nothing less than being anti-democratic. Assertion of being apolitical is dangerous because it is often used as a ploy to keep elitist ideas and ideologies beyond questioning.

Much damage has been done to the cause of good social science by those who pretend disinterest to the point at which their research conceals opinions that covertly structure their conclusions. No one is truly objective, certainly not about the nature of society—there are too many personal stakes involved for that. (Hoover and Donovan 1995: 9)

All writing is based on elective affinities, and incorporates, subliminally or consciously, the relationship of writer to subject. All writers approach their subjects with a certain value system which affects the way they interpret situations or facts that they cite. There is nothing like a neutral narrative, since all accounts are presented from an individual's point of view, and every writer has to make a choice whether to support the existing order or oppose it, whether to support injustice or to stand by humaneness. Knowingly or unknowingly, every writer takes a moral or political position on issues facing a society at a given point of time. As Ngugi forcefully argues, 'Every writer is a writer in politics. The only question is what and whose politics.' It is, therefore, important to ask, 'Who writes? For whom is the writing being done? In what circumstances? These . . . are the questions whose answers provide us with the ingredients making a politics of interpretation' (Said 1983: 7).

In other words, a critical understanding—and debunking—of the elitist construction of knowledge and education becomes necessary for dismantling the structure of oppression. By showing their real face, we can deny the elites one of their most effective rhetorical tools. As the politics of knowledge plays a crucial role in the design of dominance, Cherryl Smith is right in insisting that 'colonialism, racism and cultural imperialism do not occur only in society, outside of the gates of universities' (cited in Linda Smith 1999: 37). That there is no such thing as a neutral education process is the major theme of Freire's celebrated work ([1970] 1996). Education either functions as an instrument which is used to facilitate the integration of people into the logic of the established order and bring about conformity to it, or it becomes the 'practice of freedom', the means by which people deal critically with reality and discover how to participate in the transformation of their world. Central to Freiro's emancipatory pedagogy is the idea of the act of reading leading to the ability to read the world and 'learning to perceive social, political, and economic contradictions, and to take action against the oppressive elements of reality.'

Thus, emancipatory pedagogical activity will not be the fiefdom of a few professional intellectuals but a concrete social activity in which all people are engaged. It means that people must think for themselves. And, though all people may not be intellectuals, as Gramsci argued, everyone is capable of independent thinking and developing their own conception of the world. Common people, like the privileged, are capable of producing from within their own ranks their own intellectuals who do not simply describe social life in accordance with the established rules, but articulate the feelings and experiences which the masses could not express for themselves (Gramsci 1996: 5–23; 323–4).

Above all, emancipatory education requires defining things afresh: seeing things not simply as they are, but also how they have come to be that way. Redefining things means looking at situations as contingent (dependent on conditions), not inevitable. It means seeing the existing situation as the result of a series of historical choices made by people, and gaining the insight that the facts of society are not natural or predestined but made by humans, and therefore changeable and reversible. Thus it is not enough to understand what happened in history and how a particular culture formed but also what didn't happen—and why. What happened in history was not a historical inevitability; they could have been different and better. Not looking for another perspective could be a false outlook.

It is important to see the human world interconnected and interwoven against the tendency to see people in fragments and get a distorted picture. A big obstacle in a holistic and critical understanding is the trend of specialization and sequestering of knowledge that dominates social science frameworks. Academic specialization thrives on one-dimensional approach, notwithstanding pretentious claims of its professional practitioners. Professionalizing of disciplines makes the experts acquire a monopoly not only over the production of knowledge, but also over the production of the producers of knowledge. The way in which these knowledge-producers are produced ensures that they remain confined to their own ghettos, unmindful of the big picture. The disciplinary ghettos force professional scholars to think more or less alike and churn out dangerously similar works (Menand 2009).

Today, specialization is especially unfortunate as peoples, countries, cultures and human activities are becoming exceedingly connected and complex. Isolated from the broader cultural and historical setting, specialists spin their yarns with less and less cotton and have hardly any substance or wherewithal to integrate them meaningfully. Academic specialists are like the proverbial blind men who visited an elephant and made futile and fragmented identifications. As the parable goes, each of them touched a part of the beast; each one of them had a portion of the truth which they held fanatically and bitterly contested the claims of others. But the shape of the beast eluded them because they refused to piece their individual parts together. Academic specialization approaches its subject in a similar manner, peddling half-truths as total reality. The jealously guarded business of specialization, moreover, alienates the academic from the public, 'lay people'; the ordinary people in their turn are tempted to dismiss academics as impractical and useless. No wonder, the dominant connotation of the word 'academic' is impractical, someone who is divorced from real life.

The current trend overwhelming academia is to objectively study a subject and stick to the 'impossible premises of stating nothing at all'. But behind the veneer of neutrality, professional scholars are known to hide their conformist prejudices and reactionary politics, as we saw earlier. Edward Said (1994: 305) points out, 'The intellectual community doesn't operate according to principles and doesn't consider itself bound by responsibilities toward the common weal. . . . The large body of American intellectuals is basically provincial, drawn only by virtue of expertise.' This also applies to Indian pundits. The scholars who claim to practice objective or disinterested scholarship seldom serve any purpose other than obscuring the reality of caste and class. They mask social reality because coming from privileged backgrounds they stand to gain from the status quo. The establishment does not even have to persuade them to serve the system; the pundits willingly come to the establishment and corporate houses on the tacit understanding of playing by the rules, which consists mainly in concealing reality. To give but one striking example, the brahmanic academics have churned out more than 5,000 academic tomes on caste (in English and Indian languages) during the last 150 years or so, only to hide the inhuman face of caste.

The reconstruction of knowledge requires transcending the established academic framework and a grasp of how most of the world's festering problems grew out of the old paradigms of caste, class, and gender. Their reproduction in different ways, though not easily recognizable in many cases, continue to dominate the world. Michael Oakeshott's comment can also be read in a radical light: 'The past in history varies with the present, rests upon the present, is the present. . . . There are not two worlds—the world of past happenings and the world of our present knowledge of those past events—there is only one world, and it is a world of present experience' (Oakeshott 1966: 107–8).

'History may be servitude, and history may be freedom', but we must have the astuteness to sift the one from the other. The need is to go to the fundamentals of society and polity, the nature of power, and see what the dominant discourse tells us and what it doesn't. This is possible only when we see the whole and the parts, the past and the present, by meaningfully piecing together diverse human experiences and narrative fragments. Few of us think about our experiences and thoughts that are related to the fundamentals of society and culture. Fewer think deeply about them; even fewer think deeply about everything that matters. The need for a critical education (which 'not only raises consciousness but also develops actions to change oppressive structures') cannot be overstressed.

Reason, Imagination, and the Question of Religion

The question of religion and science, imagination and reason, is old but far from resolved. The dominant tendency to either pit the one against the other or hierarchize them is flawed. Science and religion, like other things in life, should be judged by content and outcome rather than form. This implies that the right way to see the complex and difficult situations that define our life incorporates both the light of reason and the lamp of imagination. A character in Dostoevsky's *Brothers Karamazov* makes the point, 'If everything on earth was rational, nothing would happen.'

The trajectory of traditional religion and those who abide by it are well known, and have become unfashionable in this age of science and scepticism. What is not so well known is the fact that many of the science enthusiasts have turned science into a religion, with its own theology and theory of salvation, the glimpse of which we saw in the Introduction. But science is not conscience or an ethical system. It is a strategy for learning about life and the universe. A motor, a wonderful product of science, provides energy, not direction; a driver has to know where to go. Science may be capable to giving us everything we desire but it cannot tell us what to desire. Its limitations was seen best by Helen Keller, 'Science may have found a cure for most evils, but it has found no remedy for the worst of them all—the apathy of human beings' (Keller 1927: 162). Science could have easily overcome the world's poverty, instead the world is awash in a trillion-dollar weaponry, even as a billion children go to bed hungry. This is not to denounce science but to argue that what really matters is what we do with the power of science.

For the change we want to see in the world, empathy is more important than reason. Justice comes from character, not competence. Schopenhauer (1995: 210) makes an excellent point when he says, 'Whoever is morally noble reveals by his activities the deepest knowledge, the highest wisdom, however much he may be lacking in intellectual excellence.' Belief in the superiority of reason over imagination is not just misplaced, but also damaging to the cause of a humane world. Our heart and mind work better together, each augmenting the other. Our emotion and intellect are not separate, they are intertwined. This is the point the students of the Sorbonne in 1968 were attempting to make when they wrote on the walls of Paris, 'Power to the imagination'. They were proclaiming that science and logic and combinations of the already known are insufficient for a fair and noble world. Einstein had come around such thinking in the preceding decade, 'Logic will take you from A to B. Imagination will take you everywhere.'

At their highest level, emotion and reason unite. Intellect, without compassion, is too feeble, too rudderless to get us to the heart of humanity. Great joy or ecstasy, epiphany or illumination, visions of another world or another level of living have seldom come from professional science and professional philosophy. Severed from empathy, professional intellectuality has often been put to destructive uses. Functioning on the proposition of segregating values from knowledge, science leads to nuclear bombs.

Just as in science, so in the case of religion, we have to evolve a nuanced and critical perspective. Just as we resist the inhuman application of science for making nuclear weapons, we oppose the religious establishment for its dogmatism, sectarian violence, and nexus with right-wing forces. But this opposition should not be extended to rejecting the whole domain of religion (which embodies, whether we agree or not, the 'sacred' for a large number of people in this cruel and unjust world), and handing it over to the reactionary forces. As Gramsci once said, 'I don't go to church. I am not a believer. [However] We must be aware of the fact that those who believe are the majority. If we keep on having cordial relations with atheists alone we shall always be the minority.'

The futility of refusal to engage with religion can also be seen in Marx's famous statement ([1843a] 1978: 54),

> Religious suffering is at [one and] the same time an expression of real suffering and a protest against real suffering. Religion is the sigh of the oppressed creature, the heart of a heartless world, the soul of soulless conditions. It is the opium of the people.

The important point is that Marx is not only unmasking the illusion of religion but, equally, is committed to unmask 'human self-alienation in its secular form now that it has been unmasked in its sacred form' (ibid.).

As Marx saw the looming dangers of secular deceptions overtaking the world, he wanted to transform 'the criticism of religion into the criticism of law, and the criticism of theology into the criticism of politics'—a fact ignored by most atheist-secularists. Marx criticizes religion historically, not metaphysically. We know that his Promethean scheme is based on the idea that people make their own destiny under conditions structured by the past. The question is: has religion, for good or for worse, not been an important player in shaping the past we inherit and deal with? If the answer is yes, can one afford to ignore the legacy and politics of religion? Religion, in this Marxian sense, is not an illusion, but a palpable cultural construct, one of the most enduring institutions of history. Even in its unorganized form, it is a clear and present reality in the lives of many people. Merely rejecting religion by equating it with obscurantism will not do; we ought to historicize it, boldly critique it, strip it of its supposed supernatural aura and authority, and argue that even the sacred texts must be debated, questioned and read in context. A critical, open-ended study of theology and sociology of religions may help to grasp what are noble and worth embracing, and what are ignoble and dross about them.

It is also important to differentiate between broadly egalitarian religions like Buddhism, Christianity, and Islam—which despite their many contradictions and pro-patriarchy nonsense, abide by the basic idea, at least in theology, that *all humans are created equal*—and the brahmanic Hinduism, whose defining characteristic, as we shall see in Chapter 4, is a fundamental inequality of humans. Without caste there is no Hindu—hundreds of castes (ranging from the most sacred to the untouchable) placed one above or below the other in the human hierarchy. Hinduism is innately incompatible with the democratic ethos (see Mani 2005). Even the caste elites concede this point in moments of candour: Hinduism 'constructed a deep, enduring and disfiguring ideological edifice of inequality. This framework, with its fusion of coercive, ideological, economic and religious power, pitilessly condemned large masses to the most insidious forms of subordination mankind has known' (Mehta 2012b). If the worst corruption is a corrupt religion, Hinduism even in its pristine form is an embodiment of such corrupt religion. Rooted in the iron laws of caste, it is incapable of eliminating the hierarchy implicit in it, and must be squarely rejected (as did Phule, Ambedkar, Periyar, Pandita Ramabai, and many other greats in modern India). Faiths or belief-systems like brahmanism that are toxic, pose danger to civility and social amity, must be annihilated.

Fighting brahmanism, however, is not fighting all religions and the religious people whose faith inspire them to fight injustice. It would be an intellectual folly, an ethical bankruptcy, not to recognize that our life will be uglier—bloodier—without the likes of Buddha and Jesus, Muhammad and Nanak. In fact, rediscovering and retrieving their legacies from the clutches of right-wing fundamentalists should form an integral part of the emancipatory struggle. It is due to some liberating luminaries that religion, in one form or another, will always survive as a source of spiritual solace, self-transformation and transcendence—even for the people who are not religious in the conventional sense.

Though non-believers are right in insisting that religion has no bona fides as an explanation of the world and the everyday life, atheism or anti-religiosity is not the necessary basis of revolutionary action, as many of them claim. It is historically false that philosophical materialism and atheism have been intrinsically bound to struggles for justice. All atheists are not revolutionaries like Marx. Aggressive atheism of the likes of Richard Dawkins (1976) is merely a ruse to celebrate greed and aggrandisement of the corporatist society. At the heart of the militant atheists' programme is the 'selfish gene', not social justice. By glorifying basic instincts, the new atheists' godlessness merges with the dominant ideological values of the consumerist culture.

Religion—*religion without religion*—is too important to be left to the brahman or bishop. As the Marxist Marathi poet Narayan Surve says, *Tyanche rajya udyache, Buddhache aani Christache* (Buddha and Christ's—their realm will come tomorrow). In other words, alongside revolutionary political struggles, there are other important and beautiful struggles. We can empathise with the heart-cry of noble souls like St. Francis of Assisi: 'Lord, make me a channel of thy peace. Where there is hatred, let me sow love.'

If we can open our souls we can also see how Marx, too, was 'praying and weeping for an age in which the rich stop feeding off the most defenceless people in our society, off minorities and immigrants, women and children. This is the best side of Marx, the most enduring side, his prophetico-religious side . . . [That is why] . . . certain versions of Marx's atheism play so well in the churches of the poor. That is also why . . . the distinction between theism and atheism is a little more unstable than people think' (Caputo 2001: 17). Those who disdain such reading of Marx should read him closely and sensitively. He never wavered from what he thought was the highest human choice, which he articulated with characteristic brilliance in his youth. Till his end he never gave up the unselfish quest that animated his early invocation of Jesus, as 'the ideal being' who lived and died for other people, as a model of virtuous behaviour:

> History calls those men the greatest who have ennobled themselves by working for the common good; experience acclaims as happiest the man who has made the greatest number of people happy; religion itself teaches us that the ideal being whom all strive to copy sacrificed himself for the sake of mankind, and who would dare to set at nought such judgments? If we have chosen the position in life in which we can most of all work for mankind, no burdens can bow us down, because they are sacrifices for the benefit of all; then we shall experience no petty, limited, selfish joy, but our happiness will belong to millions, our deeds will live on quietly but perpetually at work, and over our ashes will be shed the hot tears of noble people. (Marx [1837] 1975: 8–9)

Marx went on to become a merciless critic of religion (as it existed) and he constructed the philosophy of historical dialecticism. Like all great thinkers, he was right in many areas and wrong in some. But what makes him outstanding was his passion to integrate his philosophizing with the suffering humanity and his struggle to liberate them. His life and struggle should be assessed in this light by all those who want to change the world, whether Marxists or non-Marxists. This should be the approach to assess all movements and people who strove for a better world.

One ideology, one revolution cannot end all kinds of problems and exploitations in society. The fad of the pure and the absolute—either science or religion, either socialism or feminism—is a dangerous myopia. 'It may be a mistake,' as Bertolt Brecht (1944) suggests, 'to mix different wines, but old and new wisdom mix admirably.' In harnessing new and old resources for freedom struggles, we may have to face opposition not only from the fundamentalists who stake their exclusive claims on Buddhism or Christianity, but also from many well-meaning but fossilized Marxists, feminists, or postmodernists. Such obstacles will be tough to overcome unless we have the imagination to combine the emancipatory visions of the likes of Marx, Phule, Hellen Keller, Pandita Ramabai, and Ambedkar into a new subjectivity and a new aesthetics of transformation. A proponent of critical realism seems to capture the essence of such radical syncretism when he sees symmetry between the quintessence of real spirituality and radical social change:

> Now if you take the ideal from Mahayana Buddhism of the Bodhisattva, he may be the most realised human being but he will postpone his enlightenment, his own bliss, his own nirvana until the realisation of every other being in the world. That is very similar to the standpoint of Marx—and Marx was an atheist—when he said that in a communist society the free development of each would be the condition of the free development of all. . . . That is also precisely the standpoint of Buddhism. And if you go into it deeply enough, at some level, this is the standpoint of all great religions and also even political inspirations and aspirations. . . . There is no contradiction between spirituality and radical social change. (Bhaskar 2002: 301)

All sorts of good thoughts and good struggles should come together for a civilized living, as there is a limit to both the arrogance of science and the claims of faith. 'If we are to deal with uncertainty [of knowledge] effectively, a margin of tolerance for alternative forms of understanding is essential. Without it, we are likely to transcend the boundaries set by our human qualities' (Hoover and Donovan 1995: 145).

The blending of the socio-political with the ethical-spiritual will also take care of—and correct—our narrow and flawed understanding of history, freedom and democracy that tend to present them as the gifts of the West. Justice and freedom—as well as rationalism and science—are not unique to the West; they are universal values and assets pursued by humankind over a long arc of history. Democracy is an outcome of the evolution of the global arc of political civilization, and it is the common people everywhere who have been in the forefront of such struggles. Whatever genuine democracy we have today is the result of the long, protracted historical struggles of ordinary and exploited people who aspired to build an inclusive world. Daniel Paul, a Canadian aborigine, has pointed out in a recent work that Thomas Paine, the pioneering philosopher of democracy (who was a leading figure of the American War for Independence as well as the French Revolution) 'used the [native] Indians as models of how [a democratic] society might be organized' (Paul 2000: 333).

The pre-modern East, pretty much like the West of that time, might be simpler and less knowledgeable but it produced some of the most evolved and enlightened minds. The minds that set ethical and intellectual benchmarks for universal justice, laying the foundation of a decent and democratic society. Buddha, Jesus, Muhammad, and Nanak—none of whom came from the West—did perhaps more to engender democratic ethos in human culture than the ancient Athenians (who coined the word 'democracy' and brought it into existence but grounded it in what was essentially a slave society) and the modern capitalist-democratic rulers of the West and elsewhere. Egalitarian ideas and sentiments that went into the making of democracy, freedom and human rights had been strongly present in the native cultures and the various streams of counter-cultures in India, China, West Asia, Africa, and North and South America. To deny this, especially in the context of India's radically inclusive Buddhist, Bhakti, Sufi, and Sikh traditions, amounts to not only accepting the hegemony of the Western canon but also equating the Indian tradition with the exclusionary Vedic-brahmanic tradition, ignoring the humanist-democratic tradition that the struggles of Buddha, Ashoka, Kabir, Nanak, Tuka and many others made possible.

Summarizing, the dogmatism of both the reactionary right (conservative obscurantism) and the doctrinaire left (absolute scientism) have left us debilitated and demoralized. The crisis that religious and secular fanatics have unleashed on humanity will not be overcome unless we rethink on the basic issues and redraw our priorities.

Self and Society: Cultivating the Better Nature

'I found one day in school a boy of medium size ill-treating a smaller boy. I expostulated, but he replied: "The bigs hit me, so I hit the babies; that's fair." In these words he epitomised the history of the human race.' This is what Russell writes in his *Education and the Social Order.* He forgets that children also carry within their little selves an instinctive love for fairness and a revulsion against injustice. Charles Dickens, a better observer of children than Russell, writes in *Great Expectations*: 'In the little world in which children have their existence, whosoever brings them up, there is nothing so finely perceived, and so finely felt, as injustice.' Indeed, all of us can remember disgust or anger at being treated shabbily by siblings and other children, and conversely, our delight at being treated fairly by friends and family. We often hear children yell 'that's not fair'; to which parents reply 'the world is not fair, get over it.' This shows that it is the joint responsibility of family, school, and society to nurture and strengthen the better instincts of children so that they can grow into healthy, thoughtful and compassionate individuals.

Individual is *in-divisible* from society, etymologically as well as in practical sense. No one can become human on her own. We need other people in order to be people. No woman or man is an island but society itself is an interweaving and interworking of its individual components. Individual actions affect other lives and contribute to social effects, which in turn influence the individual life. One cannot be grasped without grasping the other. It was this fundamental point that feminist Carol Hanisch underlined in her acclaimed 1970 essay: 'One of the first things we discover in these groups [of women] is that personal problems are political problems.' A decade earlier, C. Wright Mills had made a similar argument in *The Sociological Imagination* (1959), emphasizing the need to see links between apparently personal problems of the individual and important social issues:

'Know that many personal troubles cannot be solved merely as troubles, but must be understood in terms of public issues.' His point was to create a new paradigm, to convert 'personal troubles into public issues, and public issues into the terms of their human meaning for a variety of individuals.'

Contrary to the current notion of individualism, individual freedom can only be ensured with larger social freedom. People can engender the conditions in which the good of society becomes integrated with the good of each individual and in which they both work in harmony to enrich each other. Only freedom of each and every individual—and a unity based on it—can help build an authentic community of persons, paving the path for everyone to thrive. A good life entails a sense of belonging and indebtedness, not just concentration on one's own self. A maxim in the Talmud expresses this beautifully, 'If I am not for myself, who will be for me? But if I am only for myself, what am I?' In other words, what is at stake for achieving a fulfilling and meaningful life is not making a choice between

> either/or: either you focus on self-realisation or you lose yourself in worldly involvements. Instead, it seems that a well-lived life must somehow combine both these orientations. Self-possession is necessary in the modern world, because it is important to know how you feel about things and to candidly express your views. But . . . such a practice serves its proper social role only when it provides the basis for an open and respectful exchange of views with others about issues that matter to the wider community. (Guignon 2004: 164)

To act and live in such reciprocity is a necessary condition for individual evolution and social progress. Justice, reconciliation, and the abatement of suffering are the moral imperatives to steer our thought, behaviour, and action. Indifference to the suffering of others—hungry children, harassed women, hunted immigrants—is to exile them from our conscience. Such indifference in the face of oppression amounts to complicity in the crime. It was for this reason that Dante reserved the hottest places in Hell for those who remain neutral in times of moral crisis. Similarly, the experience of the Holocaust (when millions of Jews were segregated and slaughtered as a whole nation stood by) gave Elie Wiesel the insight that indifference is the epitome of evil, the greatest enemy of humanity. Because of indifference one dies before one actually dies (Wiesel 1960). And it cuts both ways: turning our backs on social responsibility threatens our right to freedom and justice. When the neighbour's house is in flames, our own safety is at stake.

Human world is as interdependent as the natural world. The celebrated nature-preservationist phrase *Lost there, felt here*—coined by the Conservation International to underline that our natural world is one integrated system and when species, forests and ocean life are depleted in one region, their loss will eventually be felt in another—applies to the social world and interpersonal relationships in equal measure. It is this human bond that singer John Denver evokes in his moving song 'It's About Time':

There is a man who is my brother, I just don't know his name
But I know his home and family because we know we feel the same
And it hurts me when he is hungry and when his children cry
I too am a father, and the little one is mine.

Exclusion of any one part of humanity starts an endless regress of exclusions from which no one is immune. Each of us shares responsibility for injustice anywhere because it threatens peace everywhere. In a democracy, as Camus said, everyone is responsible. Good citizens don't sleep when there is a wailing in the neighbourhood. It is this empathic connection with the larger humanity that impels so many writers and poets to envision a revolutionary role for literature. Here's Ezra Pound in his poem 'Commission':

Go, my songs, to the lonely and the unsatisfied
Go also to the nerve-racked, go to the enslaved-by-convention
Bear to them my contempt for their oppressors.

Speak against unconscious oppression
Speak against the tyranny of the unimaginative
Speak against bonds. (Pound 1952: 97–8)

Such exquisite radicalism must include turning the gaze on ourselves as well. We cannot transform life and ourselves without honest self-reflection and connecting our public reason to our character. Along with eliminating oppressive contents in our culture, we will have to deal with the contents of our character. Personal behaviour is an outward sign of the kind of society we want to create. What we emote, think, say, and what we do to ourselves and others have consequences—and those consequences define and form life. A highly strung figure like Foucault, who was even more terrorising in his tortuous personal life than in his scorching cultural theories, recognized this and remarked a little before his tragic death in 1984, 'At every moment, step by step, one must confront what one is thinking and saying with what one is doing, what one is' (see Miller 1993: 9).

Bereft of self-criticism and ethical moorings, many revolutions fell apart. The holier-than-thou arrogance of their leaders and their refusal to accept the validity of a sensibility other than their own corroded their souls and destroyed the dreams of millions. Octavio Paz, a fellow traveller, put it elegantly in his poem 'San Ildefonso Nocturne':

The good, we sought the good: To straighten out the world.
We did not lack integrity: We lacked humility.
What we wanted we wanted without innocence.

While elitist forces remained united in their opposition to justice, many radicals bickered and betrayed their own cause. Hans Enzensberger expressed it in his famous poem *Karl Heinrich Marx*:

I see you betrayed / by your disciples:
only your enemies / remained what they were.

Self-reflection often yields images that we dislike, but it is important for our inner and attitudinal change and must form an integral part of the new politics of transformation. It is not just oppositional forces or adverse circumstances that frustrate our endeavours for change; we, too, let ourselves down. Russell said sardonically, 'We have two kinds of morality side by side: one which we preach but do not practice and another which we practice but seldom preach.' Indeed, many of us have an alter ego in the aristocratic woman in Tolstoy's 'The Freezing Coachman' who visits the Moscow Arts Theatre and sheds copious tears on witnessing on the stage unwarranted suffering while she has no thought for her coachman who is shivering outside in the biting cold of the Russian winter. All too often in our abstract love for humanity, we forsake our suffering neighbours. But saving the life next door is the first important step towards saving the world.

Even the best of us have our foibles, jealousies, ambitions. But for the deluded few, we are imperfect and far from enlightened. Einstein said tongue-in-cheek: 'Two things are infinite: the universe and human stupidity. And I am not sure about the universe!' Let's first recognize this and the duality of our ideal and actuality. It's a good idea to start from where we are, not where we would like to be. Sensitizing ourselves to prejudices of internalized sexism, casteism and other oppressive categories is healthy and desirable. Freud's overarching theory of sex underpinning every human motive alongside his penis-envy or male chauvinism, now rightly stands discredited, but we can read as a cautionary tale his characteristically muddled essay *Civilization and Its Discontents*, written between the two World Wars, in which he brings forth umpteen examples of brutalities in history and the selfish side of human nature (Freud [1930] 2002).

Examples abound of how victims fall to fashionable views and turn into monsters when power comes their way. The Israeli ruthlessness against the Palestinians is a living example of how the people who survived the Holocaust can be capable of perpetrating such sustained ruthlessness against other people. Not long ago, we discovered a world of prejudices in us—the existence of which we were unaware—with the groundbreaking texts of feminism and anti-colonialism that brought these truths out in the open. In the context of anti-colonial movements, Frantz Fanon (1963; 1967) taught us that even freedom fighters have had to face up to and resolve forms of self-hatred inherent in oppressive structures. Similarly, women's self-devaluation, self-loathing and internalization of patriarchal values have been pointed out by a range of feminists, beginning with Simone de Beauvoir's *Second Sex* (1949).

It is a tragi-comic irony that we know the universe but do not know ourselves. Poverty of our inner life and lack of integrity corrode our personal and social life. Our concern for suffering remains only in our heads. In turn, the neglected, the unloved find it hard to trust and love anyone. When we despise a person, no matter however subtly, he guesses that we despise him and he pays us back in the same coin. Social pathologies abound, but we remain self-obsessed. Many people suffer their whole lives from the failures of others to recognize or respond to them as thinking, feeling, worthwhile humans. Hindi poet Nirala felt: *Swartha ke avagunthanon se hua hai lunthan hamara / Gahan hai yeh andhakara* (Selfishness has made us rot in the hell of self-humiliation / So dark and deep is this darkness).

The point is, our inner life feeds and forms our social behaviour, and to ignore our personal failings is to arrest our political growth. Two battles rage in the heart of a morally alive person. One is internal and intensely personal: for overcoming one's vulnerabilities, a sense of incompleteness, and selfish or negative tendencies lurking within us. The other is external and social: opposing injustices inflicted by the powerful on the powerless. The more we evolve and change, the more society benefits. When we are balanced, just, and wholesome from within, our social struggle does tend to acquire a moral force and momentum, which cannot be easily subdued.

Our greatest resources do not come from lands and forests, tools and machines, but from our minds and hearts. Our skills and knowledge go to waste or remain dormant when we are unable to connect with fellow humans. When our minds and hearts open up and meet with others', they engender trust, civility and fairness, paving the atmosphere for a better and higher creativity. Our honesty and openness create ambience for social conversation without which no authentic individual or collective transformation is possible. But true dialogue is not possible without breaking the habits induced by hierarchy and power. The importance of such exchange to the process of understanding and change has not been fully realized.

> In a true dialogue, both sides are willing to change. We have to appreciate that truth can be received outside of—not only within—our own group. If we do not believe that, entering into dialogue would be a waste of time. If we think we monopolize the truth and we still organize a dialogue, it is not authentic. We have to believe that by entering in dialogue with the other person, we have the possibility of making a change within ourselves, that we can become deeper. Dialogue is not a means for assimilation in the sense that one side expands and incorporates the other into its 'self.' Dialogue must be practised on the basis of 'non-self.' We have to allow what is good, beautiful, and meaningful in the other's tradition to transform us.
>
> (Hanh 1995: 9)

The greatest principle of transformation lies in principled choice, and our ability to put this choice into everyday practice. No revolutionary struggle will be effective without a revolution-from-within. A social revolution requires an individual revolution. The transformed individual carries the message of the transformed life. The seed of radical change is individual moral courage, and such courage is contagious. In her novel *The Dispossessed,* Ursula K. Le Guin makes this point thus, 'You cannot make the Revolution. You can only be the Revolution.' When we change from within, we become the catalyst of change, kindling similar spirit in our friends and neighbours. As we connect with each other, our happiness and our struggle become one.

NOTHING IS NOBLER THAN ENDING EXCLUSION

Those who want to change society must not allow themselves, whatever the cost, to become like the system they oppose. To make the difference, we must take the road less travelled. The politics of change goes beyond the idea of power conceding nothing without a demand. Instead of getting something from the unjust power, it tries to challenge and change the very nature of that power. It tries to dismantle the structure and mindset of discrimination. Revolutionaries do more than respond to their opponents with reciprocal respect or contempt. The Phules and the Ambedkars do creative social criticism for changing life and society. Pambatti Sittar, the medieval Tamil saint-poet, recited poems with the oppressed to kindle a creative subversive spirit:

We'll set fire to divisions of caste,
We'll debate philosophical questions in the market place,
We'll have dealings with despised households,
We'll go around in different paths. (See Kailasapathy 1987: 391)

Many people from humble origins dreamed of people's democracy in the age of feudalism and dared to 'debate philosophical questions in the market place.' Some of them such as Kabir and Ravidas, Basava and Tuka somehow survived brahmanic attempts at marginalization. Yet many of those who fought against injustices rest in unswept, unvisited tombs, undiscovered and unsung. The legacy of their creative struggles, however, needs to be resurrected in a broader context because whatever changes have taken place in history have taken place because of the struggles of rebels like Basava, Akka Mahadevi and Mirabai. St. Francis of Assisi, William Tyndale and Thomas Paine. Heroes like Samuel Gompers, the American labour leader, whose dream of more books and fewer guns, more schoolhouses and less jails remains relevant to this day.

What we need is not fashionable or *inane* academic discourse but a profound engagement with the fundamental issues facing humanity. 'The first problem for all of us, men and women,' we recall with Gloria Steinem, 'is not to learn, but to unlearn.' Unlearning our narrow views and prejudices is necessary alongside the bigger struggle for straightening out structural problems. Contrary to the Vedic verse *ekam sad viprah bahudha vadanti* (the truth is one and the pundits express it in different ways), truth never exists in the singular. Claims to a singular truth are often coded claims to power that rely on intellectual arrogance, and could only lead to oppression of one kind or another, reflected in the dictum *vaidiki hinsa hinsa na bhavati* (the Vedic violence is no violence).

The best possible approach to truth we find in the suggestion of Pierre Bourdieu: 'If there is any truth at all, it is that truth is a stake in struggles.' Greater truths—or better ideas—emerge through a free, fair and fearless exchange in the marketplace of ideas. The best way to have good ideas, as scientist Linus Pauling suggests, is to have lots of ideas, and then to discard the bad ones. This was also the idea of J.S. Mill, who argued about the value of allowing many partial truths to compete so that ultimately a more complete truth would prevail. We see the utility of this approach in everyday life as access to a wide range of views facilitates informed choices.

Seeking truth and justice, however, is never a finished business, which is a good thing because there is more uncertainty than certainty in life, and the construction of absolutes enslaves us to a dangerous pseudo-reality. The ability to embrace uncertainty 'is a sign of human consciousness and intelligence, not fear' (Saul 2004: 211). Intelligent and honest discord is better than false accord. Whether religious or secular, reliance on the absolutes leads to fanaticism and becomes a haven for scoundrels who claim privileged access to the truth and want to rid the world of those who hold a different perspective and do not share their worldview. Threatened by the fanaticism of others, other people start creating their own extremism. One absolutism thrives on—and rears—another absolutism, creating a vicious web of bigotry, intolerance, and violence.

Above all, absolutism leads to the danger of blurring the line between difference and discrimination. There is a world of difference between discrimination and difference. As we cannot have both freedom and uniformity, we cannot wish away difference and diversity. Diversities of cultures, languages and perspectives need to be cherished, not feared or forbidden. Freedom of expression is central to a democratic society. Let a hundred thoughts contend; let a hundred flowers bloom. If we let dissent turn into discussion and differences into diversity, there is a possibility of turning conflict into cooperation. What we should target and fight, therefore, are privileges and discriminations, not differences and diversities. What we should reject is pretension and pomposity, not the marketplace of ideas. Diversity, if shared and celebrated, fosters mutual understanding, cooperation, and the possibility of a free and fair society.

Varieties of cultures, religions, languages, and worldviews are needed not just to tolerate differences but also to ultimately converge them into an emancipatory meaning and celebration of life. Grasping and following this will ensure the triumph of vision over short-sightedness, of imagination over pessimism. Buddha suggested to the Kalamas, the simple village folk, who had asked him for guidance to a good life:

Do not believe in anything simply because you have heard it.
Do not believe in sayings because they have been handed down for generations.
Do not believe in ideas merely because many accept them.
Do not believe in anything simply because it is found in your religious books.
Do not believe in anything merely on the authority of your teachers or elders.

Do not believe in specious reasoning, or a bias to which you have become attached by habit.

Have deliberation and analyse, and when you find a proper reason for accepting anything which is also conducive to the good and benefit of one and all, accept it and live up to it.

(Kalama Sutta in *Anguttara Nikaya* III. 65;
tr. based on Woodward and Hare 1932–6: I. 188–93;
also see Holder 2006: 19–25.)

CHAPTER 2

Understanding the Modernization of Oppressive Tradition

Just because everything is different doesn't mean anything has changed.

IRENE PETER

Capitalism is the extraordinary belief that the nastiest of men, for the nastiest of reasons, will somehow work for the benefit of us all.

J.M. KEYNES

Democracy in India is only top dressing on an Indian soil which is essentially undemocratic.

B.R. AMBEDKAR

If Thomas Hobbes, who wrote of human life as 'nasty, brutish and short' in 1651, were to visit our world, he would be dazzled by the opulence of 10 million millionaires with their $39 trillion worth of wealth (The Merrill Lynch-Cap Gemini World Wealth Report, 2010). But he would also witness a billion people who go to bed hungry (*The Economist* 2009). He would see a sea of humanity still submerged in that wretched condition that he so eloquently described—not in a state of nature (as was the case in his time) but under his highly recommended all-powerful state, *Leviathan*. Beyond the affluent islands of upper and middle classes, he would see the endless slums and shanties still stuck in the wretchedness, especially in a country like India. He would read the United Nations' Human Development Report 2000: 'Global inequalities in income increased in the twentieth century by orders of magnitude out of proportion to anything experienced before.' And he may hear Nelson Mandela (2005) say in London, 'Massive poverty and obscene inequality are such terrible scourges in our times—times in which the world boasts of breathtaking advances in science, technology, industry and wealth accumulation—they have to rank alongside slavery and apartheid as social evils.'

Seeing the worlds of those who chatter and fix the system and those who sweat and suffer, Hobbes would have sensed an effective strangling of global democracy despite the structures of parliaments and elections. Perchance visiting India, his suspicions would have been confirmed by Navin Kumar, a brooding and broken young man from Madhya Pradesh, who surely would confide in him:

> After Independence, every successive government's agenda is India's poor people's agenda (*Bharat ki gharib janata ka agenda*). But they all do the exact opposite of what they tell us. Our democracy has become like an expensive call girl who warms the bed—and begets scions—of the corporate and political mafia, and at the times of elections, visits the streets of common people, strutting her stuff. . . . Democracy in India has become a form of government which stops the exploited from fighting the oppressor. (as said to me in Bhopal in August 2009)

But in the desert of deception and injustice, Hobbes would also see oases of human love and cooperation. Biting realities and vaulted ideals would make him realize that he had missed a crucial point by overemphasizing bloody conflict and competition; others are not just feared competitors and rivals, but also sources of mutual security and support. As creatures whose abilities and life skills are learned from others, humans have great potential to be each other's best source of cooperation—a potential that has been little tapped by advancing civilization. Taking note of many state-sponsored genocides of the twentieth century that snuffed out 200 million lives, Hobbes would have realized that social dialogue and understanding, not a strong state, is the way to resolve outstanding conflicts. He would concede that his theory of human savagery in a state of nature—'war of each against all'—was wide off the mark, as some recent researches on hunting and gathering societies have suggested.

> [O]ur ancestors . . . had other ways of keeping peace. . . . [S]ocial and economic life was based on systems of gift exchange, food sharing, and on a very high degree of equality. These served to minimize animosity and keep relations sweet. Forms of exchange involving direct expressions of self-interest, such as buying and selling or barter, were usually regarded as socially unacceptable and outlawed. These patterns demonstrate the fundamental truth: systems of material or economic relations are systems of social relations. (Wilkinson and Pickett 2009: 198–9)

As the existing tribal cultures in India and elsewhere indicate, societies before the emergence of strong governments were not necessarily brutal; nor did their ancestors live in a vicious state of continuous warfare. It was this point that was tapped in Margaret Mead's 1928 classic *Coming of Age in Samoa*. Its description of an idyllic pre-modern society free of social violence and sexual restraint may have been exaggerated, but its central point that so-called primitives were not savages makes eminent sense. Though their side of the story—and the moral therein—has rarely been recorded by themselves or others, what one Cauca Indian in Columbia spoke in 1976 seems to be a fairly true picture of the egalitarian culture of tribal peoples everywhere:

> We are Indians because we believe that the things of the world are made for everyone. It is like saying that since we are all equal, the means of living should also be equal. . . . Because of this, we believe that the land, just as the air, the water and all the other things which keep us alive should not be only for the few. The land should not be owned, but should be communal. . . . This is why we like the reservations. Because there, the lands must all be shared out between all the members of the community. (Corry 1976: 43)

Contrarily, belying the hopes of the likes of Hobbes, civilizing centuries of strong government—regimes ranging from monarchical and feudal to authoritarian, fascist, and capitalist democratic—have only enabled the wealthy and the wily to seize the lion's share of development, leaving the much bigger part to suffer in subjugation.

Visiting the world today, Hobbes might remember a great contemporary of his, Gerrard Winstanley (1609–76) whose book *The Law of Freedom* came out in the same year (1651) as *Leviathan*. Against the Hobbesian idea of a strong ruler with a very long stick to keep the brutally competitive people in check, Winstanley suggested that only a genuine equality among citizens could guarantee a civilized and decent living. Instead of looking for an authoritarian redeemer, he proposed the creation of a level playing field without great disparity of wealth and power. Winstanley and James Harrington, the author of *The Commonwealth of Oceana* (1656), were among the first moderns who grasped that economic equality was essential for political liberty. Unlike Hobbes, they recognized that whatever the formal claims made by constitutions, the interests of those in power and those whom they served were unlikely to coincide given wide gulfs in wealth and opportunity. They grasped that 'states are likely to care most about legitimization when the underlying facts of power force them to do so—when they need the people's acquiescence or support' (Mulgan 2006: 188).

Turning disturbing thoughts in his mind, Hobbes might be forced to brood over Kant's biting remark that the problem of setting up a state can be solved even by a nation of devils. He may wonder whether the state is the 'organized use of force by one class to bring another into subjection'—the highest form of organization set up to guarantee the property and interests of the privileged. Hobbes might be tempted to read Marx and Engels who made the above point, and argued that at a certain stage of economic development, bound up with the cleavage of society into classes, the state arose out of the need to hold class antagonisms in check:

[B]ut as it arose, at the same time, in the midst of the conflict of these classes, it is, as a rule, the State of the most powerful, economically dominant class which, through the medium of the State, becomes also the dominant class politically, and thus acquires new means of holding down and exploiting the oppressed class. Thus the ancient State was above all the slave-owners' State holding down the slaves, as a feudal State was the organ of the nobles for holding down the peasantry, bondmen and serfs and the modern representative State is the instrument of the exploitation of wage-labour by capital. (Engels [1884] 1978: 753, slightly modified)

Above all, while mulling over how the world has and hasn't changed, Hobbes would be struck by Tocqueville's searing reading of the double-faced modernity in the year 1835 when he visited Manchester, the world's first truly industrial city and an early symbol of the modern age:

> From this foul drain the greatest stream of human industry flows out to fertilize the whole world. From this filthy sewer pure gold flows. Here humanity attains its most complete development and its most brutish; here civilization makes its miracles, and civilized is turned back almost into a savage. (see Harvey 1970: 42)

Since then, the world has become more dichotomous as the class and the mass live worlds apart in a global village as vastly different and alienated neighbours. As the rich luxuriate in opulence, one half of the global population lack basic nutrition, sanitation, and healthcare. More than half of such multifariously deprived people live in India alone. To provide them the necessities of life would cost a fraction of what the world currently spends on arms but the power elites in India and everywhere are least interested in that. India, currently the world's biggest importer of arms, spends far more money on purchasing killing machines and bailing out the corporate mafia than it spends on public health and education. As the prospects of self-employment have dwindled globally with the rise of corporate capitalism, and unemployment threatens even the most industrialized nations, slavery—or the condition that approximates slavery—flourishes in many new forms. Human trafficking agencies point out that there are more slaves in the world today than ever before. All this is poignantly captured in the World Food Programme saying (in the wake of rescue packages for the financial frauds whose plunder caused the global economic meltdown in 2007–8), 'Let's talk about the human rescue plan. Trillions are being spent on financial rescue packages. Just 1 per cent of that could turn hunger into hope for 59 million hungry school children. Think about it.'

Things Changed but Not in a Way that Ended Injustices

Nothing is as perennial and pervasive as change. But change can also be illusionary and treacherous. To use Ellen Glasgow's words, 'All change is not growth, as all movement is not forward.' When we talk of social and economic change, we should ask first who are at the centre of change. For, change does not bring change in a similar way to everyone—many are left behind or hardly affected or even turned into victims of change. One person's development can be, has often been, another person's destruction. This is especially true of the intimate history of the modern world, and the still unfolding story of how the progress of civilization empowers and uplifts, but also maims and kills.

The greatest story of change in recorded history—the astonishing rise of the modern West—is entwined with the greatest genocide in history. The 'civilizing' slaughter of the native South and North Americans, Australians, and Africans along with the erasure of their cultures and acquirement of their lands were intimately enmeshed with the project of colonialism—and the ascendancy of the West.

> Conquest through colonization by industrial nations destroyed millions of indigenous peoples and countless cultural groups. Most surviving indigenous groups lost their political independence and now have only a precarious control over their resources. As of 1997, an estimated 220 million indigenous peoples were scattered over the world, usually in the remote areas that are prime targets for resource development by outside interests. (Bodley 1999: 1)

The Western imperial expansion into places rich in raw materials, whether it is rubber in Southeast Asia or gold in the Congo, or cotton in India and Egypt, is well known. Now we know better the dark histories—the decimation and demoralization of the aborigines—buried behind those splendid stories of progress, thanks to the writings of indigenous truth-tellers and a few conscientious descendants of the colonizers. When Charles Darwin returned from his world voyage on the *Beagle* in the 1830s, he wrote: 'Wherever the European has trod, death seems to pursue the aboriginal' (Darwin 1962: 433–4).

One of the worst imperial crimes in history, the Belgian barbarities in Congo, has been vividly captured by Joseph Conrad in his novel, *Heart of Darkness*,

> They were conquerors, and for that you want only brute force. . . . It was robbery with violence, aggravated murder on a great scale, and men going at it blind. . . . The conquest of the earth, which mostly means the taking it away from those who have a different complexion or slightly flatter noses than ourselves, is not a pretty thing when you look into it too much.

But what Conrad's character adds after this is more significant for our discussion, as it carries a canonical example of oppressive knowledge: 'What redeems it is the idea only. An idea at the back of it; not a sentimental pretence but an idea; and an unselfish belief in the idea—something you can set up, and bow down before, and offer a sacrifice to' (Conrad 1988: 10). With the help of an idea, the stench, brutality and ugliness of conquest can be set aside, and the fiction of the imperial gift of progress to the subjected can be manufactured. The idea, in other words, was crucial not only to cover up the actual facts of invasions and conquests, but to embellish it with a civilizational mission that generates self-delusions and compels the world, including the victims, to believe in the myth-history.

The US celebrates a holiday in the name of Columbus, forgetting that he did not just *discover* America, he also kidnapped, tortured and murdered Indians with impunity. The arrival of Western explorers and traders in South and Central America did not simply open up the place for markets and trade and technology; it also led to the wilful destruction of civilizations and the decimation of local people through the spread of disease and warfare. Later, when the European settlers moved into North America, there were large-scale displacements of the indigenous populations, and some 'civilizing' mass slaughtering (Wright 2005; Galeano 2010). It is notable that South America came to be known as Latin America, and Mexico became New Mexico when the US invaded it and captured almost half of it during the war of 1846–8. (And this superpower is often equated with the whole continent when we say America but only mean the USA.)

The natives whose ancestors were killed or conquered in North America now live on the margins, in certain designated reservations. The destruction of their culture has resulted in their ghettoized existence with alcohol, drugs, unemployment and crime. The condition of the aborigines in Australia and elsewhere is no different. To their credit, the governments of Australia and the US have recently apologized to the aborigines, revising some of their exclusionary policies. When the US formally apologized in 2010 to five tribes of the Native Americans, an old tribal chief remarked, 'It is difficult to issue an apology and sometimes it is difficult to accept one.'

The invasion and occupation of Iraq and Afghanistan affirms that this process is continuing into the present, albeit with claims of democratizing the undemocrat, like the earlier civilizing the savage. As a historian points out,

> Here in the United States, we are brought up to believe that our nation is . . . uniquely moral; that we expand into the other lands in order to bring civilization, liberty, democracy. But if you know some history, . . . you know we massacred Indians in this continent, invaded Mexico, sent armies into Cuba and the Philippines. We killed huge numbers of people, and we did not bring them democracy or liberty. We did not go into Vietnam to bring democracy; we did not invade

Panama to stop the drug trade; we did not invade Afghanistan and Iraq to stop terrorism. Our aims were the aims of all the other empires of world history—more profit for corporations, more power for politicians. (Zinn 2006: 164)

Many of us Indians (with the injustices of colonialism fresh in our minds) have been vocal critics of the old and new imperialisms, especially of the US expansionism. But do the Indian elites have the right to take the high ground and still remain silent on atrocities of the Indian state against our own people, especially the aborigines and other vulnerable communities? Dreaming in their luxurious dwellings of becoming the world's new superpower, the proud descendants of caste culture, the most vicious system of hierarchy and oppression, are hell bent to emulate what their ancestors did in ancient India (by burning forests and destroying life in it as described in the ancient literature).

During the colonial period, the British Raj took all common and forest lands, rendering millions of adivasis (indigenous communities) legally dispossessed from their common property rights and ancestral sources of livelihood. After Independence, a new Constitution was framed whose Fifth Schedule states that all scheduled areas which are forest reserves and inhabited by scheduled tribes are to be administered by governors of the states by appointing tribal advisory councils from among the tribals. Similarly, the Ninth Schedule has the land ceiling provision under which cultivable lands occupied by landlords are to be acquired by the government and redistributed among landless peasantry. But these constitutional provisions were never implemented. Exceptions apart, the land ceiling acts are still lying idle in the statute books, and no tribal councils have ever been constituted.

The colonial practice continued as vested interests began a systematic destruction of adivasi lives, livelihoods, and cultures. In the name of nation-building and development, the common property rights of the adivasis that extended to mineral resources were taken over first by the public sector enterprises, and then handed over for mining to private companies, evicting the residents in these forests. As a result, in region after region, adivasis have been uprooted from their lands, denied their sources of livelihood, dehumanized as bonded labour, and their women exploited to fulfil the sexual hunger of the ruling set.

In retrospect, it seems, India's democracy brought the hapless adivasis only a change in colonizers. And, as the things are unfolding now, perhaps for the worse. As the vast tribal tracts contain not just cultivable lands, timber and forest goods, but also immense mineral wealth like coal, iron ore and bauxite, the state in collusion with private corporations showed a desperate urgency to 'develop' the area in the wake of the economic liberalization that began in the early 1990s. The multinational corporations manoeuvred the government into more than 300 contracts for the Special Economic Zones (SEZs) covering thousands of hectares of prime land in both tribal and non-tribal regions. With bribes and sales totalling billions of dollars, mining rights have been sold to many foreign and Indian corporations.

Pushed to the brink of their existence, some forest dwellers took up arms to defend themselves. Thousands, including women and children, joined the communist insurgents (known as Naxalites or Maoists) to fight state violence. When they refused to vacate their lands, the state-corporate nexus retaliated by doling out massive money and resources to organize militias—Salwa Judums—to eliminate the non-cooperating adivasis, rape their women, and torch their houses. These militias set off a vicious chain of violence and counter-violence. Once a police officer cut off the finger of a two-year old boy, in 2009 in Gompad in the state of Chhattisgarh. *The Hindu* published his photograph on 20 October 2009. 'Not one word or condemnation or remorse' was heard from the government, according to the newspaper (Varadarajan 2010).

There is an uncanny parallel between cutting off the finger of the adivasi toddler and the emasculation of legendary archer Ekalavya, who was compelled to slice his right thumb so that he could not shoot an arrow again. There is an echo of the barbaric past in what is happening in India today. The war of the Aryans against the original inhabitants (Dasas, Nagas, Asuras, and Anaryas) and the burning of forests, and destruction of humans and animals are scattered through the ancient lores, including the brahmanized versions of *Ramayana* and *Mahabharata*. Take this vivid description from the *Mahabharata*: The Aryan lot—led by Arjuna, Janmejaya and Krishna—burn the Khandav forest, laughing as they do so while causing death and destruction to all who live there—purely for possessing what clearly did not belong to them. The epics and myth-histories question neither the mindless burning of the forests nor their possession by the invaders. A clear-eyed scholar writes:

> The Aryans battled the local natives for land across the vast expanses of north India. . . . The marginalization of the local people, the aborigines—Adivasis—of North India is the underlying theme of the spread of Vedic Brahmanism. As the Aryans spread eastwards and southwards from their first settlements in the North-West Frontier Province, they conquered and displaced or absorbed the local communities. (Desai 2010)

Revealingly, the writer adds that he is actually referring to the 'ravaging of the Gondwana tract, which is the locus of the many tribes whom the Naxals are recruiting for their battles.'

Killing, detainment and torture of adivasis on the mere suspicion of being Naxalites is commonplace in many regions. In a high-profile case in 2011, Soni Sori, an activist adivasi woman, widely respected in her community, was arbitrarily arrested and tormented; her third-degree torture included pushing stones into her vagina. More recently, on 29 June 2012, as many as 19 adivasis, 10 of them minors, including two 15-year-old school toppers, were slaughtered in an 'encounter' in Kottaguda in the Bijapur district of Chhattisgarh. A newsmagazine reported matter-of-factly, 'The still photos show the dead as rather young, many of them clad in just vests and shorts, frail and poor—a far cry from dreaded 'enemies of the state' waging war on the nation', adding ominously, '[but] when it involves the lives of some poor or innocent tribals, why bother?' (*Outlook* 2012). Sarita, whose brother was among those killed, said in a broken voice: 'First they kill us, then tell us we are Naxals. Search the entire village and see if you find even a single weapon. Can't they at least say sorry?' The headline of the newspaper that quoted Sarita summed up the reality: 'Top Naxals are two 15-yr-old toppers' (*The Indian Express* 2012).

This is the backdrop of the state's ongoing war against extremism in eastern and central India. The reality of this 'single largest internal security threat' (as the government describes it to whip up public support) is laid bare by a *sarkari* report itself. It pointed out that the biggest internal threat is the incapacity of the state to help the disadvantaged communities. The emergence of extremism need to be contextualized. 'The huge gap between state policy and performance is a feature of these conditions. Though its professed long-term ideology is capturing state power by force, in its day-to-day manifestation, it is to be looked upon as basically a fight for social justice, equality, protection, security and local development' (Report of an Expert Group to Planning Commission, Govt. of India, 2008).

This perspective was held up even by the Supreme Court of India in a judgement of July 2011, when Justice Sudershan Reddy ordered the Chhattisgarh government to disband the notorious Salwa Judum, taking pot shots at the 'new mantra from the mandarins of security and high economic policy of the state—tax breaks for the rich and guns for the youngsters among the poor [to be trained on their own brothers and sisters].' The order created a furore among the ruling set, and had to be subsequently modified. As the high and the mighty were lambasting the order as an intolerable case of judicial overreach, a Bench headed by Justice G.S. Singhvi pointed out that the powerful 'accuse the judiciary of overreach when it entertains public interest litigations espousing the cause of the poor and downtrodden. . . . So far, the courts have been used only for the purpose of vindicating the rights of the wealthy and the affluent.'

The Naxalites and adivasis, who are sometimes clubbed together and sometimes presented as separate groups, are not the only people fighting the state. Millions of destitute dalits, workers, peasants, the homeless and the jobless are also up in arms against brazen denial of justice, equity, and land rights. There have been several popular movements across the country against the state–corporate nexus. But India's upper middle class, which controls the polity (because of its economic power and election campaign donations) and uses that political power in a self-serving manner, are baying for the blood of anyone who comes in the way of corporate investment and 'national development'.

The Nexus of Traditional-Religious with the Modern-Secular

Injustice has been so commonplace in history that many of us have come to accept it as a natural human condition. But this mindset, which afflicts even the victims, is not innate; it has been masterminded by the dominant elite. In pre-modern India, for example, injustices of caste, despite resistance from the lowered castes, became gradually entrenched through brahman precept and kshatriya arm. Centuries of indoctrination backed by political coercion succeeded in overcoming people's protests and counter-movements led by the likes of Buddha, Kabir, and Nanak. Precept and propaganda from above forced the people below to fall in the caste identity and ideology. The immorality and inhumanity of brahmanism became the sacred and stabilizing norms and values of 'Hindu' culture, as scholars claim in different idioms. In modern times, caste elites, including leaders like Gandhi and Nehru, valorized the tradition of caste and brahmanism, and in fact, nationalized it under the fig-leaf of anti-colonial movement (Aloysius 1997; Mani 2005).

The oppressive tentacles of brahmanism (which now hides behind Hinduism) cannot be grasped without an understanding of the dual nature of institutionalized religion. Religion has a political dimension, and has been bent to both worthwhile and base purposes. But in its organized form it has often served the ruling forces as a tool of social control. The idea of a divine will controlling worldly affairs, and the need therefore of personal submission to the supreme will becomes a deadly weapon in the hands of the entrenched interests to foster ignorance, obedience and mass subservience. In this sense, all organized religions, in the well-reasoned argument of Thomas Paine, are 'no other than human inventions, set up to terrify and enslave mankind, and monopolize power and profit' (Paine [1794] 2004). Brahmanism, for example, developed the theory of dharma and karma that justified the slavery of shudra and women in this life as a result of their sins in past lives. Religious indoctrination makes people passive by making them accept their current misery with a promise of heavenly rewards. Religious leaderships encourage people, especially women and the working class, to submit to the established power and their subservient role therein. It helps the well-off man to become the agent of God in relation to his wife, who in her turn is encouraged to thank God for being tied to the kitchen sink—and eating very well while others go hungry.

The historical misuse of religion to keep commoners weak and ignorant for easy exploitation has been well established. The point is, when vested interests could so cynically abuse the sacred realm and appropriate the legacies of Buddha, Jesus, or Muhammad—which ideally should have played a sparkling role in the transformation of human values for an oppression-free world—have they allowed secular forces such as modernity, nationalism, and democracy to challenge and change the extractive nature of power? Have not all these forces been trivialized and harnessed by the privileged to safeguard their power and privilege in the changed circumstances?

The fact is, the entrenched interests, which had a stranglehold over religion when it was a force to reckon with, have now similarly domesticated the secular forces that rule the world today. They have cracked the code of manoeuvring and manipulating the forces that stimulate and shape dominant social and political questions of our time, glimpses of which we saw earlier. They have tamed democracy, nationalism, and globalization in their favour by continued control of education and knowledge. The nexus of manipulation runs deep, enabling the wealthy to turn knowledge into a privilege through which they justify their power and privilege. No surprise, then, that the dynamics of modern secular forces, too, have played a deeply dual role. Each one of them has brought, in different countries and different ways, happiness for the few and miseries for the many.

Take the case of nationalism. Invented on romantic notions that people with common characteristics such as ethnicity, language, religion, and cultural heritage constitute a distinct political community (Anderson 1983), nationalism came into existence in eighteenth century Europe, and then reached to the rest of the world on the back of colonialism. It is notable that the foremost democracy in the West was also the world's leading imperial power. The positive political merits of nationalism are well known, and so are its parochialism and extremism (Calhoun 1997). The Nazis, it may be recalled, had called themselves 'national socialists'. However, its role in maintaining an internal oppression in countries like India has not been adequately addressed and understood. Generally the production and politics of imagined universalism (within the nation) play into the hands of powerful groups who employ the attraction of patriotism to hide the internal slavery of caste and class. In the searing vocabulary of Tolstoy ([1894] 1987: 103), 'Patriotism is nothing but a means of obtaining for the rulers their ambitions and covetous desires, and for the ruled the abdication of human dignity, reason and conscience, and a slavish enthralment to those in power.' Nationalist slogans herd people into a net that restricts and exploits them. Seen from the eyes of the oppressed, Leon Rosselson's sardonic lines say it all:

The state of the nation is all my concern
When I'm gnawing a crust for my dinner
I can't afford meat on the money I earn
And I'm growing steadily thinner
But it's all for the good of the nation.
The nation, the nation, the nation . . . (Rosselson 1981: 13)

To maintain the order of power and privilege, the ruling classes in every country ruthlessly exploit patriotic sentiments. They thus stop the flow of free and rational political debate and validate the atrocities of caste, class, and race. An outstanding public intellectual of modern India, Laxmi Narasu, saw to his horror in the heyday of Indian nationalism that Mohandas Gandhi was defending caste in the name of indigenous culture and Hinduism, to the thundering cheers of caste elites. This gave Narasu the insight, strikingly similar to Phule and Ambedkar's, that

> the spirit of nationality is no better than the spirit of caste. Nationality has sentiment, pride, and fanaticism for its basis, and is found on analysis to be no more than imaginary justification of the will to power and possession. Nationalism is the camouflage by which hooliganism masks its true nature. (Narasu [1922] 2003: 174)

Indeed, the vested interests, hidden behind the mask of anti-colonial nationalism, denounced all those (Phule, Ambedkar, Periyar) who raised the banner of revolt against caste and brahmanism as traitors to the nation (Aloysius 1997; Mani 2005).

More recently, an American historian conveys the same impression, pointing out the nefarious role that narrow-minded nationalism plays in keeping people down:

> We have carved up what we claim is one world into two hundred artificially created entities we call 'nations' and are ready to kill anyone who crosses a boundary. Is not nationalism—that devotion to a flag, an anthem, a boundary so fierce it leads to murder—one of the great evils of our time, along with racism, along with religious

hatred? These ways of thinking, cultivated, nurtured, indoctrinated from childhood on, have been useful to those in power, deadly for those outside power. (Zinn 2006: 164)

Democracy, arguably the most radical force of inclusiveness, has been tamed and made redundant in most countries by the vested interests. Procedural democracy has become shamelessly power-friendly, forsaking its primary role of constructing a fair and just society. Many scholars now admit that the transition to democracy did not disrupt the established social order. Democracy has turned out to be extremely conservative, slow to combat inequality.

> Almost no democracy has seriously expropriated the rich—and there is a case to be made that elites enthusiastically embraced democracy precisely because they recognized that the big fear it once induced, of the poor voting out the rich, proved to be largely groundless. (Mehta 2012b)

In the case of India,

> Democracy proved the surest way of keeping more radical and revolutionary forces at bay. The powerful quickly realized that far from dispossessing them, democracy would allow them to exercise power in new ways. . . . It is fair to say that democracy served the interests of power more than it went against it. (ibid.)

Nothing can be worse than an undemocratic democracy. Hitler and Mussolini were elected to power. We can argue that global democracy was not in commanding heights when the Holocaust happened, but what about the US invasion of Vietnam, and more recent massacres of Rwanda and the slaughter and famine in Darfur? Recently in Gujarat democracy re-elected with a thumping majority Narendra Modi, a man widely seen as responsible for the butchery of 2,000 people in 2002.

There is also the deepening danger of corporate money funding elections. If we add to this the acute absence of inner-party democracy and the rise of the family in political parties, the picture becomes dismal.

Recognizing these things will lead us to face the unpleasant reality that the oppressive forces everywhere took control of new political economy, along with the whole modernist project, and have since then shaped and tamed them in such a way that these forces have been unable to dismantle the structure of oppression. The agencies that rule high-tech capitalist democracies have in fact been providing new and more lethal ammunition, both material as well as ideological, to reinforce the tyranny of the few.

Schooling in Paralysing Chains of Conformity and Conservatism

Behind the veneer of modernity and technological innovations in teaching, market forces are orienting education and pedagogic practices to follow the larger commercial culture. But far from being a new phenomenon, the current commercialization of education has a strong historical foundation. The established education has for long been luring young people with promises of money, power, and higher status. At its core, elite-led education has always revolved around power, wealth and status. The difference is that earlier it was kept invisible under the fig leaf of *dharma* or morality. Take this ancient verse that children are force-fed to recite as the morning prayer in school:

Vidya dadati vinayam vinayaat yatti paatrataam
Paatratvad dhanam-apnoti dhanaat dharma tatah sukham.

This says that *vidya*—education—makes you humble and affable, which in turn enables you to receive as it makes you into a *paatra*, a receptacle, to be filled with wealth, which will bring to you dharma and happiness. This *vidya*—of wealth-driven dharma—has been interpreted as the height of spirituality and handed down from generation to generation under the *guru-shishya parampara*. Such education fanned the fantasy of power and wealth but varnished it with a religious gloss under the notion of dharma. Above all, this tradition worked on the principle of rote-learning, hardly leaving any space for inquiry, interrogation, and creativity. Here, the guru knew everything, and he had absolute authority over pupils as subordinates to direct their learning and life. The *shishya* for his part devoted himself completely to the guru, memorizing everything that the all-knowing guru preached. An ideal teacher was one who filled the students with his *vidya*; the ideal student was one who humbly received and retained everything handed down to him by his guru.

This is a classic example of what Freire has described as the 'banking' concept of education. When education becomes an act of depositing, in which students are depositories, and the teacher the depositor, it not only kills the spirit of inquiry and creativity but also what makes us human:

> Instead of communicating, the teacher issues communiqués and makes deposits which the students patiently receive, memorise, and repeat. . . . They do, it is true, have the opportunity to become collectors or cataloguers of the things they store. But in the last analysis, it is the people themselves who are filed away through the lack of creativity, transformation, and knowledge in this (at best) misguided system. For apart from inquiry, apart from praxis, individuals cannot be truly human. Knowledge emerges only through invention and reinvention, through the restless, impatient, continuing, hopeful inquiry human beings pursue in the world, with the world, and with each other. (Freire 1996: 53)

An education in which the teacher is the subject of the learning process (as he teaches, thinks, chooses, acts) and the students mere objects, mirrors the hierarchical and oppressive society as a whole. By minimizing student creativity, the banking education serves the interests of the privileged. The privileged use their 'morality', or 'humanitarianism' to preserve a profitable situation. The classical brahmanic education is exactly such a system which encourages people to be docile, adaptable, and manageable so that they do not think and question the world created by the powerful groups. It indoctrinates people to patriarchy, caste, and class.

In such and sundry other ways, the past has handed down to the present the fundamentals of commercialization and sterility of education that we witness today everywhere. This is not an imported Western phenomenon in India (as many would have us believe); it is only that the new market mentality has aggravated the materialist perversions of education. With profit-seekers playing a major role—its quality defined by the dominant idea of hierarchy, competition, and selfishness—education has become expensive and exclusive. Though education is now available to everyone, there are various categories of schools catering to students from different income groups. As poor children are forced to study in third-class schools, the marketers for whom education is just another business, argue that privatization and business interests greatly improve educational standards by encouraging competitiveness. Competition between whom? Do not quality private institutions smother all competition when they ask for huge fees that effectively keep the poor out of their premises? Such exclusion is made more vicious by a subtle caste discrimination that still obtains at different levels in India. Adivasis, dalits, other lowered castes are perceived in a negative way for good education and culture.

With the rise of political democracy, it seems, the entrenched interests are now focusing on using college and other knowledge hubs as instruments of power and control. With the gradual withdrawal of state support for education, the personal cost of education is rising sharply. As a result, caste, class, and regional inequalities in education are widening. Elite schools that teach children about things like climate change, the possibility of life on other planets, and how technological innovations have changed the world, keep them in the dark about why a country like India has double the number of mobile phones than the number of toilets. As a commentator put it,

> When urban children beat down lofty essays on paper concerning greenhouse gases and global warming and wax eloquent about environment without batting as much as an eyelid in the glare of rampant segregation and inequitable distribution of educational knowledge, we know the system has succeeded in subverting uncomfortable truths while passing them on to Gen Next. (Gupte 2009)

With the growing privatization of education, there is a renewed schooling in the morality of power and status hiding behind new deceptive terms. For a certain number of hours everyday and for so many years, every child is force-fed a large quantity of mental nutrition that buttresses the dominant ideology of wealth, status, and sex. There is a steady diet of norms and values, ideas and images that validate the established power. But even more damaging is the arrogant claim that such education is true education:

> The great harm done by our system of education is not so much that it teaches nothing worth knowing, that it helps to perpetuate privileged classes, that it assists them in the criminal procedure of robbing and exploiting the masses; the harm of the system lies in its boastful proclamation that it stands for true education, thereby enslaving the masses a great deal more than could an absolute ruler. (Emma Goldman [1917] 1996)

The religious order also ends up teaching the same dominant value system, the glimpses of which we saw earlier. Thus, as in the old system, all these streams—economic, educational, religious—ultimately converge and merge into a new cycle of hierarchy and oppression. When the suffering people protest, the rulers bring in palliative reform but without changing the extractive nature of power. Interdependent and interwoven, various aspects of power protect and buttress each other and together form a cultural common sense which has explanation for everything from the most intimate to the most common. Its prejudices, norms, and values continue to prevail because they are variously disseminated at home, school, places of religious congregation and in the market place. Behind the dazzling façade of spectacular change, the old religious dogmas and the new market fundamentalism meet halfway and breed a fertile ground for new hierarchies and objectifications. People are depersonalized so that the powerful can exploit them at will. Objectification is a process of dehumanization—and this oppressive reality is alive and kicking in the capitalist democracies.

CAPITALISM, MARKET FUNDAMENTALISM, AND THE TAKEOVER OF DEMOCRACY

'The American Beauty rose can be produced in the splendour and fragrance which bring cheer to its beholder only by sacrificing the early buds which grow up around it. And so it is with economic life. It is merely the working out of a law of nature and a law of God' (John D. Rockefeller, quoted by Galbraith 1999: 377). Coming from an iconic capitalist, this is the mentality at the core of the capitalist worldview. Contemporary billionaires and their economists have morally elevated themselves by using such phrases as 'democratic' or 'compassionate capitalism', implying that the production of plutocrats is inevitable for the survival of the have-nots. This has been crystallized into a banal theory known as *trickle down* which assumes that crumbs falling from the high table of the overstuffed into hungry mouths below will liberate the latter. As J.K. Galbraith once described it, if and when the trickle down occurs, it is akin to feeding horses with oats so that something passes down to the road for the sparrows.

Thus, capitalism mocks the argument put by the squirrel to the mountain in a poem of Emerson: 'Talents differ; all is well and wisely put; If I cannot carry forests on my back, Neither can you crack a nut.' It discriminates arbitrarily between different kinds of labour and skills—1,000 million rupees for an Ambani, a corporate fixer; 1,000 rupees for Sunita, a domestic help; 2,000 rupees honorarium to a writer for an essay in a national magazine. The fate of a rebel poet, especially if he comes from an impoverished background, is hunger and humiliation. It compels Pavithran Theekkuni, a poet with ten published books in Malayalam, to become a fish seller and construction worker because his poetry against dehumanization has no market value. His suffering forces him to write:

One day, all of a sudden, right from your midst,
With the fire in his chest and the wing-broken dream in his heart,
He will walk away and vanish
Into his own loneliness,
Into his own home in the invisible valley. (Theekkuni 2012)

When the greatest goal for everyone is no more than becoming richer than one's neighbour, who cares for a moneyless poet and his cry? People and products have to be profitable otherwise they will be dumped. Unprofitable things like affordable housing for the poor, community libraries and health-care centres, quality schools and colleges for everyone will not be produced. Profitable things such as high-rise luxury apartments, banks, insurance companies, skyscrapers, and above all, nuclear weapons, aircraft carriers and submarines will be produced. Where will such desire to prosper at the expense of someone else—less out of real need than in order to put oneself above others—lead us to? This was not lost even on Adam Smith: 'Whenever there is great property, there is great inequality. For one very rich man, there must be at least five hundred poor. The affluence of the few supposes the indigence of the many' (Smith [1776] 2005).

It is true, however, that inequality of wealth is not a capitalist invention; it is a survivor from pre-modern times, a consequence of caste, class, race and other factors. Yet there is little doubt that the resistible rise of capitalism not only aggravated it but also made it sacrosanct. Today's extreme disparity of wealth is largely due to capitalist exploitation. The rich can only be rich because they exploit the poor. 'Since money is essentially nothing but a token of power over the labour of others, great inequality is not only caused by but *essentially consists* in the oppression of the poor by the rich.'

This is not a Marxian discovery; many conscientious thinkers and religious figures—Buddha and Jesus, Nanak and Kabir, to name the prominent few—had for long been saying this in different idioms. Marx's contribution lay in the fact that he was the first to dissect the mechanism by which this dehumanization takes place under capitalism.

Marx analyzed the state of alienation in the class society, and showed that the foundation of this alienation is private property as it becomes the locus of individual rights and takes on the character of human life. As acquisitions acquire a life of their own, they turn into a fetish. The fetishism develops as property evolves from use-value to exchange-value. As it passes from merchandise into money and then capital, the transformation of acquisitions into fetishes is complete. Under such a system, it is not only products, but also people, who are bought and sold. In this buying and selling, the people who have nothing to dispose of but their labour are reduced into a means to serve the end of the propertied class. The propertied class dehumanizes the working class for its wealth and power, but in the brutal process also loses its own humanity. When humans turn into objects for each other, whatever social or individual life is left in them revolves around the world of money.

> Money abases all the gods of mankind and changes them into commodities. Money is the universal, self-constituted value of all things. Hence it has robbed the whole world, the human world as well as nature, of its proper value. Money is the alienated essence of man's labour and life, and this alien essence dominates him as he worships him. (Marx [1843b] 1978: 50)

Against the tendency of classical economists to see capitalism as failure-free and a permanent necessity because of its supposed flexibility and self-righting mechanism, Marx could see that it was not only inherently unstable but grossly exploitative and alienating. Whereas professional economists described the interest gained by capital-owners as 'the reward for abstinence', Marx treated interest, profit, and rent as unpaid labour. He developed the theory of surplus value on empirical evidence, showing how the achievements of colossal productive forces of capitalism and the methods of modern industry had been achieved on the brutalization of the worker.

> Political economy conceals the alienation inherent in labour by avoiding any mention of the evil effects of work on those who work. Thus, whereas labour produces miracles for the rich, for the worker it produces destitution. Labour produces palaces, but for the worker, hovels. It produces beauty, but it cripples the worker. It replaces labour by machines, but how does it treat the worker? By throwing some workers back into barbarous kind of work, and by turning the rest into machines. It produces intelligence, but for the worker, stupidity and cretinism. (Marx [1844] 1978: 73)

These ideas impacted not only Marxists but also economists like John Maynard Keynes who gave a new lease of life to the sick capitalism in the 1930s by introducing state intervention and welfare measures, thus rejecting the dogma that the market had a natural tendency to self-equilibrium. But Keynes did not accept his debt to the Marxian economics for political as well as personal reasons: 'The class war will find me on the side of the educated bourgeoisie' (see Wheen 2008: 114). In a moment of candour, though, he bluntly admitted, 'Capitalism is the extraordinary belief that the nastiest of men, for the nastiest of reasons, will somehow work for the benefit of us all' (see Mooney 2002: 322). Seeing close affinities between Marx and Keynes, the Keynesian Joan Robinson said in 1948,

> In both, unemployment plays an essential part. In both, capitalism is seen as carrying within itself the seeds of its own decay. . . .[A]s against the orthodox equilibrium theory, the systems of Keynes and Marx stand together, and there is now, for the first time, enough common ground between Marxists and academic economists to make discussion possible. (see Wheen 2008: 114)

However, Western pundits caricatured Marx as a violent conflict theorist, disentangled Keynes from Marx, and turned Keynesianism into a new orthodoxy. Refusal to see any systemic defects in capitalism reached a crescendo with the collapse of communism in the Soviet Union. US-style corporate capitalism with democracy in tow could now reign unchallenged globally. Since the world is now one market, they announced, history has come to an end, ideological divides and national boundaries have become irrelevant, and future developments can only be within the model of Western democracy and capitalism. Francis Fukuyama became the theoriser of this powerful illusion spawned in the wake of the 'demise' of socialism: 'What we are witnessing is not just the end of the Cold War, or a passing of a particular period of post-war history, but the end of history as such: that is the end point of mankind's ideological evolution' (Fukuyama 1992).

Such euphoric appraisal elided the difference between the Sovietism and Marxism and equated the former's demise with the end of all ideological divides, as pointed out by Derrida who presented a powerful defence of Marx in the wake of collapse of communism: 'Whether they wish it or know it or not, all men and women, all over the earth, are today, to a certain extent, the heirs of Marx and Marxism' (Derrida 2004: 113). In fact, equating state capitalism, bureaucratic collectivism, and the suppression of liberty that characterized the Soviet regime with the ideology of socialism and Marx was something like equating the tortures of the Inquisition with the teachings of Jesus, but that was exactly what the neoliberal forces propagated with a vengeance. The supposed final victory of capitalism over socialism spawned the delusion of a redeeming globalization under which economics, not politics or arms, would determine the course of history. It was assumed that international growth in trade and commerce would foster global markets that would, in turn, abolish mass poverty and change dictatorships into democracies. In his *Disordered World* (2011), Amin Maalouf sums up the dangerous euphoria that gripped not only such globalizers but also many well-meaning folk before the reality hit them:

'We believed that democracy would now gradually spread until it encompassed the whole planet; the barriers between countries would fall; the movement of people, goods, images and ideas would develop unimpeded, ushering in an era of progress and prosperity.'

Within a decade of those glorious predictions, reality returned. Global poverty and inequality intensified. The market trembled with economic meltdown in Russia, currency collapses in Asia, debt crisis in Africa and elsewhere. The twenty-first century started with 11 September, and the US embarked on a trillion-dollar war in Iraq and Afghanistan. Today, with rising unemployment and about to enter a deadly recession after recovering a little from the meltdown of 2007–8, the US, the centre of the unipolar world, is in serious crisis. Europe is struggling to keep afloat above the problems of joblessness, immigration, racism, terrorism and renewed nationalism. Mocking the logic of globalization, many of these issues are born out of regional experiences and needs, crying out for local and contextual solutions. Contrary to the claims of global harmony and prosperity, the world is grappling with fundamentalism and terrorism, debt crisis, deepening ecological crisis, and a widening rich–poor divide.

Even some free-market devotees began to question its viability. Among them was the billionaire speculator George Soros whose 1998 work *The Crisis of Global Capitalism* showed that the promotion of self-interest to a moral principle under capitalism corrupts democratic politics, and the failure of politics becomes the strongest argument in favour of giving markets an ever-freer reign. Noting that 'market fundamentalism seeks to abolish collective decision making and to impose the supremacy of market values over all political and social values', he argued that a totalizing faith in capitalism blinds its supporters to its crucial instabilities, leading to a crisis that cannot be resolved without democratic intervention:

> Market fundamentalism is today a greater threat to open society than any totalitarian ideology. [It] has become so powerful that any political forces that dare to resist it are branded as sentimental, illogical and naïve. Yet the truth is that market fundamentalism is itself naïve and illogical. The capitalist system by itself shows no tendency toward equilibrium. . . . The owners of capital seek to maximize their profits. Left to their own devices, they would continue to accumulate capital until the situation became unbalanced. Marx and Engels gave a very good analysis of the capitalist system 150 years ago, better in some ways, I must say, than the equilibrium theory of classical economics. . . . But the main reason why their dire predictions did not come true was because of countervailing political interventions in democratic countries. Unfortunately we are once again in danger of drawing the wrong conclusions from the lessons of history. This time the danger comes not from communism but from market fundamentalism. (Soros 1998: xxii–xxvii)

In 1997, a British investment banker working in New York told John Cassidy, the economics correspondent of the *New Yorker*, 'The longer I spend on Wall Street, the more convinced I am that Marx was right. . . . Marx's approach is the best way to look at capitalism.' This prompted Cassidy to read Marx for the first time, and he found 'riveting passages' about globalization, political corruption, monopolies, and the 'enervating nature of modern existence—issues that economists are now confronting anew, sometimes without realizing that they are walking in Marx's footsteps.' He concludes, 'Marx's books will be worth reading as long as capitalism endures' (see Wheen 2008: 118–21).

In 2005, John Perkins wrote a shocking memoir in which he recounted his first-hand experiences as an economic 'hit man' for an international consulting fund, exposing corporate crimes.

> Economic hit men are highly paid professionals who cheat countries around the globe out of trillions of dollars. They funnel money from the World Bank, the US Agency for International Development (USAID), and other foreign 'aid' organizations into the coffers of huge corporations. . . . Their tools include fraudulent financial

reports, rigged elections, payoffs, extortion, sex, and murder. They play a game as old as empire, but one that has taken on new and terrifying dimensions. . . . I should know; I was an economic hit man. (Perkins 2006: ix)

Recent studies in the US have found that many large companies pay little or no taxes. Warren Buffett, the conscientious investor-billionaire, made it public in 2011 that the rich often pay taxes at rates which are lower than those paid by middle-class households. Please tax us (the super-rich), he petitioned the US government. The consequences of the blatantly pro-rich policies are reflected in new statistics that not only show that in the existing democracy, those born wealthy or poor usually stay so, but also that the gap between the two is getting wider. '[C]urrent disparities in wealth and income haven't been seen in over a hundred years. Today, the richest one per cent own more wealth than the bottom 95 per cent, and the CEOs of large corporations earn more than five hundred times what their average employers make' (Bernie Sanders, quoted in Zinn 2006: 89–90).

The US is the role model of capitalist democracy. What is happening there—the flow of enormous wealth to the top, while people are battling for a decent living at the bottom—is happening everywhere. The world's leading tycoons and power politicians have illegally stashed away $11.5 trillion in tax havens like Switzerland, Luxembourg, and the Cayman Islands, according to the Tax Justice Network, an independent London-based group (*Time* 6 April 2009). Global India has now many dollar millionaires, and the number of millionaires growing into billionaires is on the rise. Many of them have huge undisclosed wealth stashed away abroad in tax havens whose banking systems hide the sources of clandestine riches. 'According to the Swiss Banking Association report of 2006, Indians have more undeclared booty hidden away in secret accounts than all the rest of the world combined' (*The Times of India* 2011). If the estimated $1,456 billion of Indian money secreted in offshore banks were to be brought back to the country, most of financial problems in the areas of basic nutrition, health care and education—that destroy the lives of millions of children—can be taken care of. But India does not do enough to pressure the tax havens into disclosing details of Indian accounts in those banks.

Who are responsible for these shady financial centres to shelter the tax dodgers? One does not have to be a Marx to see that billionaires bribe and buy the guys in government. They cheat the tax system. They steal the workers' wages and overpay—and corrupt—the top corporate brass. They pollute environment and endanger the entire ecological system. And then they give a fraction of their wealth to philanthropy, trumpeting their commitment to justice and human rights. In the case of India, see the following account by Malvika Singh as to how the corporate mafia with a colluding media in tow fixes the democratic system:

> Corporate honchos, operating through lobbyists who have access to those who influence our top leadership, are advising the government, and those who hold our natural and human resources in trust, to break existing laws in the name of 'development' that they claim will alleviate poverty. Most such decisions, particularly in the realm where business interests clash with statutory environment protection laws, do huge irreparable damage and only help to line the pockets of a few. The Narmada hydel project near Maheshwar is one where high-powered interventions have reversed, in part, the decision noted in good faith and within the laws by the ministry of environment. . . . These interventions . . . carry huge monies that are doled out in sheer gratitude for a deviation well done. Lobbyists seem to have found their way into the prime minister's office from where top secret decisions filter out. . . . In the recent exposure of a lobbyist hired by two of India's largest conglomerates, information about cabinet formation was given out well in advance of the announcement of portfolio allocation. . . . Those who lobby with government departments and ministries have been kept out of the media glare so far. (Singh 2010)

The alliance between the elected rulers and corporate racketeers who line the former's pockets and finance their campaigns carries with it a mutually advantageous business that necessitates exclusionary and corrupt practices. Commenting on the pattern of state-business nexus in the context of India, even a conservative critic is compelled to admit:

> The problem with India's present form of capitalism is not that it has produced inequality, it is that it has eroded the legitimacy of politics: when the economic dominance of a small number of players threatens to destroy the credibility of the entire political process, a society is in deep trouble. Second, it is now becoming clearer that much of what we call liberalization was directed towards the interest of big business, which got preference in everything from cheap credit to captive power. Access to credit is one key component of building a more egalitarian business environment, but state complicity ensured that big business mopped up most of that credit, often at the cost of small enterprise. A development model that inhibits the creation of small-and-medium sized firms is a recipe for exacerbating inequality; the same is true for a model of capitalism that delivers excessive rewards to those who can manipulate the state rather than those who can productively compete. (Mehta 2012b)

Democracy and capitalism, contrary to the reigning myth, are not interlinked: actually, democracy is made possible by greater equality, and in turn promotes fairness and justice, forcing the state to focus on the needs of the citizens rather than the greed of a few. Capitalism on the other hand requires decline in the effectiveness of the collective decision-making, which is at the heart of a democratic society. Margaret Thatcher and Ronald Reagan, who together laid the ground of an aggressive neo-liberalism in the 1980s, openly disdained community and collective endeavour. Thatcher said, 'There is no such thing as society. There are individual men and women and there are families.' Reagan said, 'Government is not the solution to our problem; government is the problem.' Both agreed that what was needed the most was privatization of everything.

CAPITALISM, CASTE AND DEMOCRACY IN INDIA

In post-liberalization India, privately motivated activities are promoted and perceived as essential not just for the pursuit of private profit, but as the only reliable means to secure public goods. The failure of the state to provide even basic necessities to a large number of people is leading to the very inversion of the democratic topography: public authority represented by the political class—bought off and corrupted by the corporate money—is now increasingly seen as the instrument of private profit and gain, while private entities are seen as the true custodians of the common good. It is not that the people behind such assumptions do not know that it is impossible for private initiatives to fix the democratic deficit. They know that private business cannot provide health, education, and employment to the three-fourths of India's population mired in historically accumulated disadvantages. Their hidden agenda is no longer hidden: render democracy bankrupt, tolerate Parliament and public authority as necessary evils, and promote an aggressive privatization of everything to plunder the country's natural resources and cheap labour.

Today, India (after China and the US) has the world's third largest middle class (250-300 million); 49 enlisted dollar billionaires (black-market economy and overseas banks allow many crooks to remain unlisted); and the single largest concentration of the world's poor (800 million), mostly illiterate or semi-literate. A political analyst, representing the views of Indian elite, calls this 'a new triad of India's political economy', adding, 'The poor were always with us, but billionaire businessmen and a huge middle class were not. They constitute a historical novelty for India' (Varshney 2012). A more empathetic view with compelling stories and statistics, delineating depredations by the elite and the suffering of the people, is brought home in a new book which demonstrates that the economy 'may be in good statistical health', but 'by no means in good social or ecological health.'

Unravelling the social consequences of the growth story, the authors point out that the footprint of the wealthiest Indians is 330 times that of the poorest 40 per cent; and that with each new Special Economic Zone, India lose the capacity to feed 50,000 to 1,00,000 people each year (Shrivastava and Kothari 2012).

Before liberalization (1991), India was a socialist state which actually worked to empower and educate the privileged castes; since then, the same groups, hiding behind a middle-class identity, are reaping the benefits of free-market bonanza while the poor are fully exposed to the relentless inequalities of capitalism. As India is producing thousands of millionaires, it has one-half of the world's malnourished children and one-third of the world's absolute poor. India produces 100,000 students a year in global top 10 per cent and also churns out millions with zero skills. Millions of children, despite the recently introduced Right to Education legislation, are unable to go to school. And those who do continue to be trapped in underfunded, brutal, and ineffective state schools which are among the worst in the world.

The story of the making of brand India—the subject of hundreds of academic as well as popular tomes mostly written by, or on behalf of the corporate houses—conveniently leaves aside the vital question of *who has collared the benefits and in what proportion.* That India is a wonderful democracy witnessing momentous change is the story of a fortunate few. For those who remain bereft of bare minimum in life, India is a very limited, if not a sham, democracy. It is also obvious that by keeping millions in subhuman conditions, India is performing way below its potential. What is the socio-political imperative of such lopsided development? Is violence only by killing, maiming, imprisoning (though even on this score Indian state is guilty of large-scale crimes against the less fortunate), or does it also include displacing, dispossessing, and sentencing people to a lifetime of starvation, deprivation and humiliation? A 2012 United Nations report on India's human rights record says, 'The country's economic policies, driven by the neo-liberal economic paradigm, continue to perpetuate exclusion and violate Fundamental Rights and Directive Principles of the Constitution' (see *The Times of India* 2012).

Under aggressive privatization, with an exploding population and capital-intensive, technology-driven development, the number of the jobless or semi-employed is rising. Private and public enterprises, known as the formal sector, are able to absorb only 10 per cent of the employable people; the rest (the 90 per cent) still work in informal sector. The worst sufferers are the traditionally oppressed groups—the people with combined and cumulative disadvantages of low social status, low education, and little access to bureaucracy and political power. On the other hand, traditionally privileged castes, with generations of education, wealth, and power behind them, are making use of their social capital and systematic networking, cornering all opportunities of development, and preaching the virtues of economic trickle down. It is no gainsaying that the state is not a neutral observer of things even in the era of free market: its policies and actions affect the distribution of income, wealth and power in a major way. Contrary to its professed goal, the state is not keen to help the poor but those who are already capable of helping themselves.

Contrary to the claims of great changes sweeping India, its upper and middle classes are still composed of former brahman, bania, and kshatriya groups. This caste cluster—the heavy preponderance of upper castes in key domains and modern professions—holds true for the social composition of capitalist class and the intelligentsia. According to a recent survey, not even one of the 315 editors and senior leaders of the print and electronic media was dalit or adivasi (Dreze and Sen 2011). Perhaps there were two or three OBCs, who generally hide their humiliating shudra identity for sheer survival. The situation is no different in academia. During 2010–11, nearly half the teaching positions reserved for dalits and adivasis in 24 Central universities remain unfilled. The situation of the OBCs is much worse. As on the 31 March 2011 of the 5876 faculty members in the 24 Central Universities, the faculty representation of dalit-bahujan categories is as follows: dalits 513 (8.73 per cent), adivasis 203 (3.45 per cent) and OBCs 195 (3.31 per cent). The proportion of representation of these groups diminishes drastically as one moves up the faculty hierarchy (Oommen 2013). According to a newspaper editorial, 'The situation is unlikely to be very different in other educational institutions.' The editorial makes the point that 'a loosely defined concept of merit is conveniently used to keep out eligible candidates. Laws and rules are often undermined by systemic bias' (*The Hindu* 6 July 2012).

Though rendered invisible by the elite-controlled media and academia, low caste status still spells disadvantage and disaster. People working as agricultural labourers, scavengers, leather workers, fishermen and the like are almost wholly culled from the toiling castes. Almost all labour-intensive, low-paid work continues to be 'almost wholly shudra-manned. The class position of the shudra communities is thus obvious. It is possible to come across a rich shudra but the reality is that much more frequently it is the poor shudra that we come by' (Chatterjee 2010). The vast majority of those in menial and despised occupations—in the farm, factory and households—belong to the lowered castes, while the overwhelming majority of those in the highest or most coveted professions—industry, business, medicine, engineering, the media, and academia—are from the upper castes (Panini 1996: 32–6). In a sociological study of contemporary India, Satish Deshpande (2004: 120) demonstrates, in every field that offers a promising career,

> the upper castes dominate and the middle and lower castes are more or less severely under-represented. . . . It is no longer possible to evade these realities as being the by-product of historical inequities. We have to face up to the uncomfortable truth that caste inequality has been and is being reproduced in independent India.

Contrary to the refrain that economic growth and expansion of middle class alongside new opportunities of individual mobility have made caste irrelevant (as 'its hierarchy is replaced by competing equalities'), the ground surveys and statistics show the reality of huge reproduction of inequalities in caste terms. Two outstanding studies of existing data on caste and occupation and standard of living confirm this reality (Thorat and Newman 2010; Deshpande 2011). As the author of *The Grammar of Caste* puts it,

> [D]ata point more towards continuation of traditional hierarchies rather than towards their dissolution, with upper castes at the top, Scheduled Castes-Scheduled Tribes at the bottom, and Other Backward Classes (OBCs) somewhere in between. . . . What is very revealing is that lip-service to merit notwithstanding, contemporary, formal, urban sector labour markets show a deep awareness of caste, religious, gender, and class cleavages, and that discrimination is very much a modern sector phenomenon, perpetuated in the present. So it is neither a thing of the past nor confined to the rural areas. (Ashwini Deshpande 2011: xiv-xv)

Another scholar who has studied caste over the years makes a point which helps us better grasp why things are as they are: 'There can be no denying that for centuries [dalits and other lowered castes] have been at the receiving end of all communication—information (nay, disinformation), sermons, commands and the like, and compelled into a position of powerlessness. Not surprisingly, the legacy persists' (Chatterjee 2010: 285). Yet another social analyst more than affirms this, arguing with compelling examples how caste is the main culprit that makes India undemocratic, notwithstanding constitutional laws to the contrary:

> Democracy in India is reduced to that of a few privileged castes who manage individuals to control all institutions. Therefore, it has become in practice only an oligarchy of castes, and not a truly representative form of government. As a result, the spirit of democracy to ensure social justice is lost. (Chalam 2007)

Ambedkar, a prophetic figure for the caste-oppressed and framer of the Constitution, was prescient in grasping that 'democracy in India is only top dressing on an Indian soil which is essentially undemocratic.' He tried hard to integrate elements of social justice into the Constitution, but also underlined that rights are protected not by law but by the social and moral conscience of society. At the euphoric dawn of democracy, his was the lone voice that warned against the life of contradictions that India was going to enter with formal political equality and huge actual inequality in social and economic realms (Ambedkar, *BAWS*, vol. 13: 1212–18). He strove to make the national leadership recognize that caste and brahmanism were structural and ideological obstructions to the idea of democracy.

But the national pundits colluded to ignore caste—and the caste-oppressed—as far as was possible. Only the question of untouchability was debated as its presence was glaring and Ambedkar too insistent to leave it to the mercy of caste elites. Even this charity, led by none other than Gandhi, was cynically exploited to reduce the whole question of caste to the question of untouchability (see Mani 2005: 343–93). Thus, at the height of hypocrisy today, the Parliament debates caste-based reservations and atrocities based on caste (and all political parties play the caste card and distribute electoral tickets mostly on caste basis) but thanks to the brahmanic predominance in the body politic, has never ever debated caste as institutionalized discrimination, let alone doing something about making India caste-free.

Pointing out 'the official and social-moral ban on public discussion of caste in the decades after Independence', a sociologist has explained how the ruling castes moulded the state apparatus and body politic in such a way that caste was reinvented as a modern institution (Deshpande 2004). The transition from the colonial to the independent economy and the introduction of development plans had generated new economic and educational opportunities, but confirming Phule-Ambedkar's worst fears, these were usurped by the dominant social groups (Chibber 2006). The investment priorities of the successive Five Years Plans under Nehru and his successors were enormously biased in favour of upper caste-class sections of society (Sarkar 1978: 25). A nexus of brahmanic-feudal-bureaucratic influence reinforced the hold of the traditional power structure through manipulations of the newly introduced participatory democracy. Hidden behind the innocuous labels of traditional Hinduism or modern secularism, the new brahmanism was equated with nationalism and the shaper of Indian unity, with the corollary to pigeonhole the majority—dalits, adivasis, OBCs, Muslims, Sikhs, and other ethnic-religious communities—into different categories of minorities. It is notable that the upper castes, barely 15 per cent of the population, have never presented themselves as a minority (Mani 2008b). Also, this group—which controls different levers of power and holds the bulk of country's wealth—remains 'the most elusive social group in modern India in statistical terms' (Deshpande 2004: 110).

The many faces of the new dominance developed the communal, secular and liberal discourse in such a manner as to subsume all national space, eliding or evading all issues concerning empowerment and education of the vast majority. All these forces colluded to subvert democracy and reinforced a new hierarchy of caste and class. The dominant castes utilised their money, muscle, and intellectual knavery to debase the new politics as a matter of perception which blurs reality and elections as the publicity to project credibility, thus reinforcing a new hierarchical power structure. The role of caste in democratic politics has changed, yet 'what would not change [is] its structural significance as the ultimate secret of Indian democracy' (Anderson 2012a: 112). Contrary to the popular notion of the 'democratic upsurge' of the marginalized majority, a sociologist rightly points out that the fundamental objective of dismantling the caste system (that earlier animated dalit-bahujan movements)—was

> given up in the wake of the crumbs dropped to them in the form of material benefits. While this certainly did facilitate limited upward mobility in the secular context, the status system anchored in the iron law of the ritual hierarchy remains intact even now. Unless this is interrogated and smashed the ultimate emancipation of dalit-bahujans will remain aborted. (Oommen 2013)

Reservations, subsidies, grants, cultural tokenism, and the rhetoric of democracy, justice and 'unity in diversity' notwithstanding, the basic economics—and politics—of caste remained intact, which moulded the nature of the new classes that have emerged. Though the castes are increasingly getting separated from their former assigned tasks, the link between privilege and high caste status remains strong. And so is low caste status and assignment of most laborious and non-intellectual tasks. Politics is the only arena where traditionally subjugated groups are far better represented (and this gets reflected in the mounting anger of the privileged towards parliamentary politics and politicians). Yet the arithmetic of elections and the dependence of all political parties on corporate houses for fighting elections turn even the best of politicians into worst kind of power brokers. Thus, most dalit-adivasi-OBC-Muslim power politicians have become, directly or indirectly, pliable tools in the hands of corporate billionaires. The locus of power shifted from Parliament to the corporate towers—a fundamental debasement of democracy. The poor casting their votes on empty stomachs, in tattered clothes, is a spectacle, and points to the shenanigans of procedural democracy. Over the years, the accountability of elected representatives has weakened, not increased. Now, even some of the procedural processes, especially in working of the legislatures, are falling apart.

Making things worse are the absence of inner-party democracy (which afflicts all national or regional, big and small parties) and the rise of dynastic politics. A single family, a *democratic dynasty*, has ruled India for most of its democratic existence. The lead (of hereditary politics) given by the Nehru-Gandhi family has now spread to all parties and regions like an epidemic. According to one estimate, two-thirds of democratic space in India have been held hostage to a few families. The analysis of the current Lok Sabha showed that over 65 per cent of Members of Parliament under 40 had a prior family connection in politics (French 2010; Sanghvi 2009; Chisti 2009). At least 200 MPs in the 15th Lok Sabha (out of the total of 543) owe their positions to their lineage.

To place the blame on hereditary politics alone is to miss the point. Politics in India, like elsewhere, has become subservient to business, and only those political families are prospering and winning elections that have struck mutually lucrative deals with corporate houses. It is notable that most of the big businesses in India are hereditary, too. Hereditary politics is dependent on hereditary business and crony capitalism. 'Firms with a past history, rather than new entrepreneurs, have remained the main actors' in the period after liberalization. And the predominant sources of the wealth of Indian billionaires, contrary to popular perception, is not software but rent-thick sectors (real estate, construction, infrastructure or port sectors, media, cement and mining) controlled by the government. Taking these into account, a new research shows that dynastic parties thrive because of the pervasiveness of crony capitalism.

> It is far more convenient for business groups dealing in rent-thick sectors that depend on government largess to deal with a dynastic party in which one individual or family exercises control. There is, therefore, a growing relationship between crony capitalists and India's dynastic parties. A large amount of money earned through rent-thick sectors finds a way into politics during elections. . . . The control exercised by the [dynastic] leaders also means less trouble from individual politicians for a crony capitalist. (Chhibber and Verma 2013b)

The profit-based links between elected representatives, business, and bureaucracy have grown so strong that they have effectively taken over the entire democratic system. If democracy in India does not seem to be failing the people, it is because the situation is more or less the same in the rest of the world. In every country democracy has become the handmaiden of corporate houses, techno-managerial elites, and a globalized intelligentsia, who are connected with their counterparts in other countries for private profit. Thus the powerful in India are not connected with the suffering Indians but with the powerful from other parts of the world. This finds manifestation in the disdain for the deprived and the psychological and even geographical separation from the larger part of the country.

> Modern democracies have been around for long enough for neo-liberal capitalists to learn how to subvert them. They have mastered the technique of infiltrating the instruments of democracy—the 'independent' judiciary, the 'free' press, the parliament—and moulding them to their purpose. The project of corporate globalization has cracked the code. Free elections, a free press, and an independent judiciary mean little when the free market has reduced them to commodities available on sale to the highest bidder. (Roy 2004: 3)

True, but it is not just corporate globalization that has made democracy hollow in India. Such perspective tends to overlook the deep complicity of a brahmanic intelligentsia and civil society in undermining democracy. The basis of democratic stability after Independence was a rigid social hierarchy which worked in favour of upper castes which dominated the state, the civil society, the media, and the intelligentsia. As a recent research shows, the much-lauded civil society in India is constituted of associations that are networks, which rely on 'who one knows', and it tends to support existing social inequalities. Civil society in India is limited as 'a platform of the connected, by the connected, and for the connected.'

> Instead of levelling the playing field, civil associations in India amplify inequalities in access to power by providing channel through which social elites can exercise political influence. . . . The share of the upper castes is around 80 per cent among NGO and trade union leaders, close to 90 per cent in the executive committee of the bar association, and a full 100 per cent among

office-bearers of the press club. . . . Civil society far from bridging gaps between social segments has become a domain that fosters social inequality . . . and undermines democratic governance. (Chhibber and Verma 2013a)

In other words, the capitalist subversion of democracy in India cannot be grasped, let alone resisted, in isolation from its wider social context. Capitalism is corrupt and far more dangerous in India than in Europe-America because of the economics and politics of caste.

Reproduction of Hierarchies and Exclusions

Contemporary India's story is the story of unprecedented success for the few and extraordinary failure of the many. 'The progress of living standards for common people, as opposed to a favoured minority, has been dreadfully slow—so slow that India's social indicators are still abysmal' (Dreze and Sen 2011). India continues to be one of the worst laggards in the Human Development Index, a measure used by the United Nations, which has three components—life expectancy, average income per person, and level of education. A recent report by the Organisation for Economic Cooperation and Development reveals that India's income inequality has doubled in the last 20 years. A survey by the National Council of Applied Economic Research (NCAER) shows that in 2009–10 the top 20 per cent had a share of 50 per cent of the national income—against 37 per cent in 1993–4. In the same period, according to another study by NCAER, the share of the bottom 60 per cent of India's people declined from 39 to 28 per cent.

United Nations figures, World Bank data, and Government of India surveys all indicate that even at a time when India is growing at nine per cent, its social indicators are embarrassingly low when compared to even low-income countries like Bangladesh and Nepal. *World Development Indicators 2011* (online) show that India has been a laggard in eradicating poverty, achieving universal primary education, promoting gender equality, reducing child mortality, and combating common diseases. Only five countries outside Africa have a lower youth female literacy rate than India. Only four countries do worse than India in child mortality. Only three have lower levels of access to improved sanitation. None anywhere has a higher proportion of underweight and stunted children. The statistics are damning, and point to a deeper disease that afflicts India. 'There is probably no other example in the history of world development of an economy growing so fast for so long with such limited results in terms of broad-based social progress. . . . An exaggerated concentration on the lives of the minority of the better-off, fed strongly by media interest, gives an unreal picture of the rosiness of what is happening to Indians in general, and stifles public dialogue of other issues' (Dreze and Sen 2011).

High growth is now generating resources that can overcome mass deprivation, ill health, and illiteracy, but the casteist-exclusionary mindset in its not-easy-to-recognize modernized incarnations is proving too powerful to allow the establishment to engage with key problem areas. Egregious discrimination threatens India's stability far more than any other external or internal factor. As we saw earlier, the spread of the Maoist and other kinds of extremisms in many parts of India against the state—resorted to by the marginalized as the last option—is a direct result of institutionalized discrimination.

The Sachar Committee report on the conditions of Muslims brought out the truth of the terrible conditions in which most of them live. Taken as a group, the Muslims are no better off than dalits, the most oppressed community. In proportion to their population, their representation in the administration, judiciary, legislative bodies, and the army, is very small. They are severely underrepresented in the media, academia, banking, industry and other professions. The only place, the report points out, where Muslims excel and have numbers disproportionately high in comparison to their population is jails. The system is loaded against them.

The appalling living conditions of common Indians were also brought forth by the report of the National Commission for Enterprises in the Unorganised Sector headed by Arjun Sengupta. According to the Sengupta report, a total of 836 million—77 per cent of the population—had an income of less than Rs. 20 per day in 2004–5. The report reveals that 88 per cent of dalit-adivasis, 80 per cent of the OBCs, and 85 per cent of Muslims belong to this 'poor and vulnerable' category of people living on less than Rs. 20 a day (less than half a dollar). As a result, India's rank in the United Nations' Human Development Index has been steadily falling all these years.

Another part of India which constitutes the middle class and upper middle class, and which reaps the most from of the government subsidy on higher education, is not only alienated from the suffering majority but also suffer from the entitlement syndrome. This is what a disillusioned engineer who founded an effective organization that provides solar lighting in rural areas of Karnataka, says about his colleagues:

> I've got through an IIT education through huge subsidies which most of the poor have actually paid for and then I go to Silicon valley or I go to Bangalore with millions and I say that I have made money and I am an IITian. This is exactly the brand for which IIT was not started. . . . Six hundred and fifty million people are there without electricity in our country. . . . Most of them do not have clean water or toilets. . . . IITs have been there for 50 years. How many IITians have done research for a good cooking stove? . . . Where is the contribution of the IITs to the real India? (Hande 2011)

A major cause for the callousness of India's affluent and educated class is the fact that the former are among the world's most status-and-pedigree conscious people. Even among themselves, they practice terrible status-check and obsessively assess each other on the basis of pedigree and power:

> In every new social interaction, you can see the antennae quivering, alert for status signals. We sort people by class, last name,

neighbourhood, accent, and whatever other subtle codes govern our little social groupings. . . . Most Indians are hyper-conscious of the many fine lines that separate us from them. And while preps and toffs are at least mildly comic elsewhere, in India privilege seems wholly admirable. Ascribed status is still valued as much as, if not more than, achieved status. (Gopalakrishnan 2011)

Thus, it is not accidental that the policy of reservation for the suppressed castes is India's most badly implemented policy. It has never been implemented with any sincerity. Even before engaging with the caste question and structural sources of inequalities, the elite prescribe solutions to the problem—'create educational and other infrastructures for the poor but do away with the divisive anti-merit reservations!'. Such caste-blindness has given birth to what a scholar calls the 'culture of avoidance', which only exacerbates the problems:

It is a small wonder that schools are now the site of battles over integration of poor children, colleges are sites of caste conflict, and workplaces are repositories of subtle discrimination. Instead of being sites of new mixing and the evolution of a new consciousness of equality, these have become zones of deep conflict and contestation. ...All the evidence suggests that we are going to have a very hard time, because the culture of avoidance has become so ingrained. (Mehta 2012b)

This culture, Mehta indicates, emanates from a long-standing intellectual hypocrisy about caste and its consequences. 'There are very few writings in Indian intellectual history that treat equality directly as a subject. . . . India has not produced many systematic tracts on equality—a revealing fact in its own light.'

Modern political discourse in India carried this devious trend. From the days of the national movement, its predominantly upper-caste leadership has been playing the game of caste-blindness in public and caste networking in private. The entrenched interests never allowed national heroes like Gandhi and Nehru to seriously acknowledge the caste question, let alone honestly deal with it (Mani 2005). Likewise, the academia has systematically avoided any macro study of caste and inequality. Among over 5,000 scholarly tomes on caste, there is hardly any that analyzes caste as an inhuman system and institutionalized discrimination against the toiling majority. Similarly, school textbooks generally do not teach students about caste as discrimination; many of them fancifully narrate the merits of the caste system!

The caste elites oppose caste as antithetical to democracy, arguing that any caste-based reservation violates the principles of merit and equality of opportunity, and thus is nothing short of a national treason. Such measures, they allege, break the 'national consensus' and corrupt our civic virtue and politics. The self-deception of business and professional elites has reached such a level that they assert that their mere entry in politics will purify it of its casteist corruption and dirt. Print and electronic media often feature these charlatans as the great hopes—'visionaries'—of a new India, and prominently advertise their clichés on inefficiency and corruption in public life. In other words, instead of engaging with the issues of glaring discrimination, the casteist media and academia allow the upper castes to believe that they are victims rather than oppressors. As one of them wrote in a candid moment, 'The upper caste, creamy layer of our society is the most prejudiced, and yet the most dominant minority in any democracy in the world' (S. Gupta 2011).

CHAPTER 3

Understanding the Media, Publicity and Pop Culture

The challenge of modernity is to live without illusions and without being disillusioned.

ANTONIO GRAMSCI

For all their lofty pretences, today's mainstream media are essentially just another branch of show biz.

BILL SLOAN

Publicity helps to mask and compensate for all that is undemocratic within society. And it also masks what is happening in the rest of the world.

JOHN BERGER

The triumph of democracy is becoming the triumph of consumerism.

JEAN KILBOURNE

Worldly appearance and reality mock each other with a vengeance as lip service to moral goods abounds amidst nuclear proliferation, organized violence, and climate change. In this magic realism of illusion, elision and hyperbole, sound bite replaces sound thought and show business gets many times more coverage in the media—from TV to Twitter—than the issues of hunger, unemployment, and the growing rich-poor divide. A great deal of all this is rendered invisible by the consumer culture where for the first time in history, as Carl Bernstein put it, 'the weird and the stupid and the vulgar are becoming our cultural norm, even our cultural ideal.' When we live in such a world, the locus of power shifts from parliament to corporate towers and few of us notice this.

In recent years, ideas like democracy and inclusive development have been emptied of any serious meaning, converted into slogans and pressed into service by the ruling set as a club with which to bludgeon the struggling people and those who struggle with them. In India, this tendency is strengthened by a self-congratulatory smugness in the elite circle that the good life has already been achieved in our system of democracy and market economy. There is nothing new and noble to think and do but just to maintain the established order by making occasional adjustments or corrections in the political-bureaucratic set-up. To the rich perched atop the growth pyramid in which the many are miserable at the bottom, Brand India's esteem abroad matters more than do domestic woes.

With incredible increase in technical apparatus of image making, it is easier than ever for the powerful to mislead people to believe in their lies and appearances. People are subjected constantly to the image-burnishing and opinion-manipulating realms of television, journalism and publishing which become a conduit to elide and perpetuate injustices.

> A society based on image manipulation becomes arrogant and increasingly produces cascading hypocrisies that undermine moral life and, thus, the prospects for common justice. In these conditions, 'justice for all' becomes an empty theme used mendaciously to pit one group against another. Justice becomes confused with trophies and spoils. (Hope 2001: xvi)

The Media Behind the Façade

The media have the power to force the people-in-power to seriously think about removing corruption in governance, providing education and health care to every child, and cleaning up the environment and public life. Through objective reporting and analysis, the media can play a vital role in ensuring real democracy and equality of conditions. Instead, they are being used to promote publicity, sex, and sensationalism and to line the pockets of wealthy media moguls. India's privileged groups, hiding behind the mask of middle class, have monopolized the mainstream media, like other realms of power, to crowd out inconvenient truths. Contemptuous of social democracy, they call themselves 'we the people', make their vested interest 'national interest', and name their interactive television shows 'The People's Court' or 'Face the Nation'. The glib set who mislead people with their sound bites on television also double up as newspaper columnists. Some journalists are known to ghost-write speeches for their corporate bosses or friendly politicians—and then to write a newspaper column praising the speeches. In the words of Arundhati Roy,

> Mainstream media has been captured by a small clique of columnists, editors and TV anchors, an incestuous little coterie with shows on each others' channels and interviews in each others' newspapers. . . . Day in and day out, they chatter away, saying things that comfort each other even when they appear to be shouting at one another. It's . . . like watching an interminable cocktail party. (Roy 2010)

Recently, a national newspaper carried all three by-line articles on its edit page written by members of one family, father, daughter and the son-in-law. Their booming voices are now available all the time on a major news channel which they own. Multiply such examples and you get the picture of how such 'rich diversity' of opinions within the incestuous circle are displayed as examples of India's amazing respect for ideological plurality. Such things help us grasp why the news and views we get from the media are so uniform and repetitive. In a resurgent, connected, buzzing-with-scams India, the media endlessly gloat about the baring and daring of glamour dolls and dozens of Indians making it to the world's wealthiest 500, exemplified by Mukesh Ambani's \$1 billion palace and the £60 million wedding extravaganza of Lakshmi Mittal's daughter. When the *Forbes* announced in 2010 that two of the world's ten top billionaires are from India, the media pundits got into a tizzy to show how 'global greatness is our destiny', and asked rhetorically: 'Isn't the rise of the country as one of economic titans of the world a reason to celebrate for every Indian?'

What is happening in the mainstream media in India is part of a larger global phenomenon. India is just following the corporate lead of a handful of media conglomerates spanning the entire spectrum, which generate the kind of public debate and public opinion that suit their special interests. The title of Michael Wolff's biography of Rupert Murdoch is *The Man Who Owns the News*.

> The communication media are monopolized by the few that can reach everyone. Never have so many been held incommunicado by so few. More and more have the right to hear and see, but fewer and fewer have the privilege of informing, giving their opinion and creating. The dictatorship of the single word and the single image, much more devastating than that of the single party, is imposing a life whose exemplary citizen is a docile consumer and passive spectator built on the assembly line following the North American model of commercial television. (Eduardo Galeano, quoted in Herman and McChesney 1998: vi.)

The most noticeable development in the print media in recent years is the erasure of difference between broadsheet and tabloid journalism—between Page One (which would earlier concentrate on serious political and social issues, at least perceived as serious considering most of it was given to only the deeds and misdeeds of the governing classes and hardly any space given to common people and their concerns) and Page Three (set aside for screen and sports and pictures of half-clad starlets). The production of news and views, like other business ventures, has to bring in more revenue. Such developments are directly related to a widespread malaise mirrored in the rise of a corporate-led commercial culture in which racketeers of all shades have come to dominate politics, business, sports and entertainment:

> The impulse for moneymaking induced by free market economics has been a great leveller. Politicians suddenly find themselves

> in the same compartment with film and sports persons, industry tycoons, liquor barons, stockbrokers, public relations smarties, and similar other species, each with an eye on the main chance: how to make money and even more money. This has meant a widening of the horizon of opportunities for racketeers of all varieties. A common goal unites politicians, film stars, real estate speculators, contractors, cricket bosses and commission agents. Franchises are up for sale . . . the whole system is up for sale, including a vote on a cut motion in Parliament, a seat in a medical college, an allotment for the second generation spectrum; even the judiciary, rumour goes, wants to be a part of the fun and games. The snooty ones may describe this lurid set-up as a snakepit; those single-minded in their devotion to make money will shrug off the invectives. For them, it is a world of choices. (Mitra 2010)

With corporatization of the media, the logic of their existence is little more than making money through publicity, plus serving the interests of the corporations in general and the owners in particular. For big business, the media business is especially attractive as an elevator to the corridors of power. It is a business that promises low investments and high returns. The owners use it to win friends in influential places who can help them make more money. The fabled freedom of the press has become the freedom of the people who own them. Philosopher Onora O'Neill underlined this in her 2002 Reith Lectures, arguing that the classical doctrine of press freedom has become a thing of the past. In neoliberal democracies, press freedom is being used as a clock to shield media conglomerate domination of public discussion 'in which misinformation may be peddled uncorrected and in which reputations may be selectively shredded or magnified'. A free press, she warned, is not an unconditional good because when the media mislead and readers cannot assess their reporting, 'the wells of public discourse and public life are poisoned' (O'Neill 2002).

This does not bother the media houses. By introducing the idea of 'paid news', several media houses in India have even replaced editorials with advertorials—commissioned write-ups for advertisers or sponsors presented in the form of editorial views and comments. This is not unexpected given the fact that editorials had already been sold to the rhetoric of business and political power. One example: some years ago, the editors of various newspapers published in New Delhi sat together in a corporate setting and decided to black out all public protests or rallies (of people from outside the city) because 'such events inconvenience the public.' Only the news of traffic jams caused by protests, not the issues and concerns behind the public protest, the newspapers decided, will be published.

Behind the façades such as 'let the truth prevail', or 'because the truth involves us all', the mainstream media today are structurally committed to conceal the bigger social, political and economic reality. Even a little space earlier available to social sector beats has now disappeared. P. Sainath says, 'Today, newspapers have no labour correspondent, housing or primary education correspondent. We are explicitly telling 70 per cent people of this country that they don't matter to us.' The media, he explains, have a 'structural compulsion to lie' as most media companies have interests in various arms of the economy.

In fact, the media's main concern is to obscure the systemic corruption in high places, especially how corporate business is conducted without transparency and public accountability, and behind the protection of fierce libel laws. This is apparent from its failures to spot the rot in Enron, WorldCom, Satyam, and hundreds of similar but largely unknown corporate scandals. From time to time, some newspapers or television channels bring to light cases of political corruption, with an implicit or explicit attack on the democratic system as the main culprit, but none of them turn their gaze on the corporate towers as the media work within the corporate ethos and setting. The owners hire journalists who fit the bill, and those who are especially inclined to be duped into following the hidden agenda of power go on to become journalistic leaders. As editorial has become advertorial, the delivery of truth rests on the shoulders of the masters of deception. Sooner than later, top journalists and editors are transformed into power-broker businesspeople: they spend more time on business matters and power politics than journalism. Conducting friendly or 'paid' interviews with businesspeople, power politicians, and sleazy entertainers, many journalists in India have morphed into media proprietors overnight, and the media are in the vice-like grip of these mercenary elements. Some time ago, a few journalists who woke up rather late to the phenomenon of 'paid news' and 'the triumph of the trivial' wondered aloud whether paid news could mark the death of journalism. One of them pointed out that there is a conspiracy of silence in the media because everyone is a potential beneficiary—'someone who hadn't considered it yesterday may want to do so today' (*The Indian Express* 2010). Ironically, many of the concerned journalists voicing those noble concerns are themselves known as agents of corporate interests.

The Indian media are as disgusting and corrupt as their Western counterparts, yet no Indian has bothered to write books like John Pilger's *Hidden Agendas*, James Fallows' *Breaking the News: How the Media Undermine American Democracy*, Knowlton Nash' *Trivial Pursuit: How Showbiz Values are Corrupting the News*, or Arthur Rowse's *Drive-by Journalism: The Assault on Your Need to Know*. No Indian has bothered to make films like *Shattered Glass* (2003) which showed journalistic integrity playing second fiddle to entertainment and glamour, or *The Insider* (1999) which exposed television journalism corrupted by corporate self-interests, or *To Die For* (2000) in which Nicole Kidman portrays a young woman willing to murder her husband and corrupt her children in order to get a break on television news.

Summarizing, the media malady is part of a larger and structural problem. As Pilger (1998) has shown in a challenging work, people working in the media are pursuing hidden agendas which they themselves don't know or understand. They have become agents of the power elite, deliberately in some cases and unwittingly in others. Bourdieu's study of television and journalism (1998) too found a system, sustained on 'collaboration' between the intellectuals and the media, where 'all production is oriented toward preserving established values' and where competition 'rather than generating originality and diversity, tends to favour uniformity.' Earlier, in a groundbreaking study, Herman and Chomsky's *Manufacturing Consent* (1988) revealed the same pattern: how an underlying elite consensus largely structures all facets of the news, and how issues are framed and topics chosen in a way that safeguards the interests of the business and political elite.

The Grammar of Entertainment and Publicity

The market economy has created a global climate of consumerism and a commercially packaged youth culture. It has also fashioned a show business centred on basic instincts. Marketers know that a half-naked girl whistling and dancing the shimmy gets a drooling and captive audience. That is why there is no industry as big as the entertainment industry in the market society. Based on the logic that 'if lust and hate is the candy, if blood and love taste so sweet, then we [the marketers] give them [the consumers] what they want', there is a global fun factory, a multi-billion amusement industry which produces and provides non-stop entertainment to everyone—from the cradle to the grave—according to the size of our pockets.

The promise of entertainment is an escape into happiness. Film historian Eric Rhode (1976) defines entertainment as 'our over-fabricated sense of illusion which serves the purpose of asserting escapism defiantly.' Recreation, representation, stories and games egg on the young and not-so young, to crave and consume fun all the time and forget everyday reality. *Ye dil maange more*, so go further in search of more fun, more narcissism, more sex or drugs, or whatever takes your fancy: explore new areas of the forbidden; learn to break or bend the rules but all within the boundary of self-obsession and conformity. 'Never put off till tomorrow the fun you can have today', Huxley said in *The Brave New World.*

In sync with the consumerist ethos, the market-driven media makes the young believe that what matters the most in life are fashion, looks, and the ability to seduce. The message being drilled in the impressionable minds is: *appearance is destiny*. While there is a glut of choices, yet a banal uniformity lurks behind all the choices. The standard response of the media apologists—'use the remote to not look at what offends you'—does not mean much. You may change the channel, but the message remains. A critic and concerned parent bemoans that the little ones are forced to follow the trend, and even if parents interfere, they realize with 'a sense of rage that the whole issue has almost been wrested away from their hands.'

An average teenager sees hundreds of advertisements each day and enters into adulthood with a heavy dose of media-induced fascination for fun, frivolity, and fashion. They are encouraged to take pride in their fashion victimhood and imitate this or that celebrity that keeps them away from the trouble of being or becoming their authentic selves. The popular culture leads them to accept the notion that there is nothing more challenging and rewarding than a career in show business. Not surprisingly, many youngsters say their top choice of a profession is to be a fashion model. Shalini, a 15-year schoolgirl from New Delhi, says: 'I want to be a model. Who does not want to be one? If you are a model or a glamour girl, you have lots of fun and have the chance to get to know the rich guys, and if you marry them, you could end up with a lot of money.' She thinks she is a free spirit. The world surrounding her shields her from any sliver of doubt that all that glitters is not gold, that some of the glittering stuff may be even poison. What else explains her fascination for the pathetic story of Xiaoqing, a young Chinese woman who seeks the (US actress) Jessica Alba makeover to win back her estranged lover who is 'obsessed with Alba, adorning his apartment with her photographs and talking about her constantly.' What takes the cake—and overwhelms Shalini—in this case is the 'large-hearted generosity' of an expensive private hospital that has offered to do for free a series of difficult plastic surgeries to turn the Chinese girl into the American beauty.

Why would a cosmetic hospital be so keen to give a young girl free head-to-foot plastic surgery? Apart from representing the age-old slavery to the ideal of romantic love whereby young people are encouraged to do anything for love, is there a deeper context to her tragicomic story? Isn't she the victim of a toxic culture that compels her to go to such ludicrous depths to woo back her moronic estranged lover?

Allure, an American beauty magazine, some time ago carried an ad, featuring a Chinese woman in a military uniform wearing red lipstick: 'Why six million women who used to carry a little red book now carry a little red lipstick. When nail polish becomes political, and fashion becomes philosophy, *Allure* magazine will be there.' 'The triumph of democracy is becoming the triumph of consumerism, as the global village is reduced to a "trillion dollar market",' concludes a researcher after grasping how a few powerful corporations—Time Warner, Sony, Viacom, Disney, Bertelsmann, and News Corporation—together control most publishing, music, television, film, theme-park entertainment across the world. 'Almost everywhere we look these days, anywhere in the world, there is a message from one of these conglomerates. An ad in *Advertising Age* shows a huge picture of the earth and the headline, "Do You See the Trillion Dollar Market?" ' (Kilbourne 1999: 54).

To capture the world, the trillion-dollar market, however, requires turning citizens into consumers, and this is what the corporations are up to. The public is encouraged to know everything—from Britney Spears' latest one-night stand to Bipasha Basu's latest wink—except what is worth knowing. The difference between people and product is blurred through a never-ending circle of publicity—until the newspaper is thrown away, the commercials on video, Internet and television take over, or the new poster is pasted over in the vicinity.

Publicity is explained and justified as a competitive medium which ultimately benefits the public and the best manufacturers—and thus the national or international economy. Publicity paints a rosy picture of 'the free world' celebrating the spirit of freedom—freedom of choice for the purchaser and freedom of enterprise for the manufacturer. It gives us free choice to choose from a variety of products where one firm or brand of manufacture competes with another but publicity image, as John Berger points out, also confirms and enhances every other—whether this cream or that cream, some cream is essential to make you attractive, and a little more money will fetch you a better cream which will make you more attractive. 'Publicity is not merely an assembly of competing messages: it is a language in itself which is always being used to make the same general proposition.'

Berger gives us an illuminating insight into how publicity and its manufacture of glamour lead to alienation and dehumanization:

> It proposes to all of us that we transform ourselves, or our lives, by buying something more. . . . Publicity persuades us of such a transformation by showing us people who have apparently been transformed and are, as a result, enviable. The state of being envied is what constitutes glamour. And publicity is the process of manufacturing glamour. . . . The happiness of being envied is glamour. Being envied is a form of solitary reassurance. It depends precisely upon not sharing your experience with those who envy you. . . . In this respect the envied are like bureaucrats; the more impersonal they are, the greater the illusion (for themselves and others) of their power. . . . It is this which explains the absent, unfocussed look of so many glamour images. . . . The spectator-buyer is meant to envy herself as she will become if she buys the product. She is meant to imagine herself transformed by the product into an object of envy for others, an envy which will then justify her loving herself. One could put this another way: the publicity image steals

> her love for herself as she is, and offers it back to her for the price of the product. (Berger 1981: 131–4)

Democracy and the free market give everyone the right to enjoy a dream life—the pursuit of individual happiness is their most tantalizing promise. What does it mean to the poor and the unemployed? The existing conditions and culture of publicity make the people who are left behind in the rat race experience total powerlessness. As one falls victim to envy, compounded with a sense of isolation, impotence or old age, one constantly lives in the contradiction between what one is and what one would like to be. The failure shatters him, cuts him off from fellow beings because the popular culture—with its escapist movies, television programmes, pulp fiction, and other entertainment glut—forces everyone to fill in the gap between dream and reality by daydreaming and fantasy (by watching), rather than by participating and becoming conscious of the contradictions and its causes, and joining hands with other people for a struggle for a genuine democracy which ensures a life of dignity to everyone. People are trapped into the wheel of capitalism that knows no destination other than the market.

> The choice of what one eats (or wears or drives) takes the place of significant political choice. Publicity helps to mask and compensate for all that is undemocratic within society. And it also masks what is happening in the rest of the world. Publicity adds up to a kind of philosophical system. It explains everything in its own terms. It interprets the world. . . . The contrast between publicity's interpretation of the world and the world's actual condition is a very stark one, and this sometimes becomes evident in the colour magazines which deal with news stories. (Berger, ibid.: 149–53)

The corporations know that the more people watch glitz, glamour and porn, the less they will know about the social and economic issues that affect them. It is for this reason that corporate media turns film, fashion, and porn stars into brands, presenting them like a cross between the old deities and the medieval royalty. The marketers encourage people to shut out the world and feast on the glitter of what the glitterati are eating, drinking, and making merry with. Exhibitionism, raunchy revelry, and one-night stands of pampered superstars are glorified and promoted to overtake people's real freedom and to pull a veil over the dehumanization of consumer culture.

In an important work on the decline of public discourse in the age of entertainment, Neil Postman compares the dystopias of George Orwell (*1984*) and Aldous Huxley (*The Brave New World*), and makes the point that it is not the Orwellian nightmare—an externally imposed oppression—but Huxley's horror of the mechanized age that has come to haunt the world. The real threat to the free world, Postman contends, is not from a dictatorship as portrayed by Orwell but from a culture satiated by amusement and diversion. No Big Brother is required to deprive people of their autonomy, maturity, or history. People will embrace subjugation on their own accord, adoring the technologies that undo their capacity to feel and think. There would be no reason to ban a book, for there would be few who would want to read the book. There would be no need to withhold information because the truth would be drowned in an avalanche of statistics. The culture would not become captive but trivial. Huxley remarked in *The Brave New World Revisited* that rationalists and activists up in arms against injustice 'failed to take into account man's almost infinite appetite for distractions.' There would be no need to control people through inflicting pain; people would choke themselves with fun and frivolity (Postman 1985).

Indeed, the parallel between *soma*, the pleasure drug easily available to citizens of *The Brave New World*, and today's mass entertainment is unmistakable. Both keep the people happy and hallucinated. Both foster mindless uniformity in thinking and behaviour; both devalue the meaning of life by privileging instant gratification over all else. Ceaseless entertainment and a stream of fragmented truths keep the people away from any challenging reflection and action. Unlike the victims in an Orwellian nightmare, who resent being controlled by the Big Brother but are powerless to resist, the human robots of the mechanized society are willing participants in their own manipulation—they grab *soma* with alacrity. The pursuit of pleasure becomes its own end—the people are enraptured in the merry-go-round of entertainment, free sex and perfect mood management.

A relentless focus on glitz and glamour is to keep people, especially the youth, tethered to consumerist templates. Young people have a natural affinity for idealism and nonconformism. Many of them dream to be a part of some noble cause. It is important for the marketers to get them early, bombard them with the images of addictive products, get them hooked to narcissism, and alienate them from real human connection. For this, the market culture creates a climate of self-centred, self-righteous individualism that disdains social engagement. It creates a climate of thoughtlessness and acquiescence in the system that closes the eyes to the possibility of alternatives. Through its mass deception and a cynical distortion of everyday politics, it will not allow the public to see things as they are. It gives no space and scope to perceive alternatives, to look at things if they could be otherwise. It keeps people atomised, aloof, and distant from the power and politics of change.

The market and the media tell us in words and images that entertainment should be valued above all else. That entertainers are the real culture heroes: that they are burning with the desire not only to entertain us but also to make the world a better place. News like Jimena Navarrette, the Miss Universe 2010, wanting to 'inspire peace and unity by looking hot', and 'Poonam Pandey going nude to motivate the Indian cricketers' are regularly and prominently splashed. It is not accidental that most of the contemporary symbols of alleged accomplishment and achievements come from the world of entertainment. With their banal quips, super earnings and glamorous lives, it is the entertainers—film actors, television presenters, rock stars, beauty queens, porn stars, ramp scorchers, flashy footballers and cricketers—who stop people from a serious engagement with life and themselves.

The market logic goes something like this: since the entertainers do so much to add colour and excitement to our drab lives, they must be at the centre of our life. Their entertaining examples have to be followed and multiplied by leaders in other domains. After all, everything in life is a show and the world is a stage, so politics, too, has to be a sort of spectacle, a part of the entertainment business. Politicians have to be well-turned-out clowns who can entertain us with their colourful personality and funny speech. Some politicians may well be decent people seriously thinking about social and economic conditions and trying to improve the situation but they all have become characters in the media's representation.

The culture of entertainment ensures that clothes and cosmetics, not ideology and commitment, should dominate politics, with the logic that only those who make us laugh or lose our mind are our real heroes—and worthy of our attention, allegiance and emulation. No wonder, the term 'sexy' has come to mean anything that is worthwhile or noteworthy. As sexiness becomes central to the way people mark what is good and valuable, 'sexing up' of not just politicians (and their dossiers) but any 'achiever' worth his or her salt in any field has become mandatory. Noticing this trend, in which achievement does not bring the limelight but limelight is the achievement, a columnist remarks, 'What else can explain the inordinately diminishing ways in which respected figures of our establishment, from judges to generals, are converting their professions into a kind of publicity contest, seeking validation not in professional norms, but some inchoate idea of public esteem?' (Mehta 2012a). The centrality of the idea of publicity in which no achievement is achievement unless it is exhibited, 'proclaims the spirit of a culture in which all public discourse increasingly takes the form of entertainment. Our politics, religion, news, athletics, education and commerce have been transformed into congenial adjuncts of show business, largely without protest or even much popular notice' (Postman 1985).

The Roman emperors used bread and circuses to enslave citizens and make them slog for the glory of the empire. Today's corporations have their celebrities, entertainers and advertisers to perform the same role. People are encouraged to escape from their own humdrum existence by riding on the coat-tails of those celebrities whose exotic lives are the stuff gossip columns are made of. The manufacturing of escapist entertainment is meant to dumb down and depoliticize the people.

Supersexualised Market and the New Body Politic

In the market culture, relationships, like other things in life, are the function of wealth and possession. Money forms the ties of affection and love. This is reflected in the promotional ads which seldom depict a man's economic success without his possessing a playgirl or a trophy wife, the more (women) the merrier. This fits in with the concept of possession—possessing property leads to possessing fetching females. The neatness of the fit between economic and sexual success reflects the same old ideology and value system. The modern capitalist commodification of woman is just an updated version of the patriarchal objectification of woman as a *maal* (property). The commercial culture only packages the old heterosexual stereotypes in a new feisty vocabulary of female empowerment and an exuberant celebration of the body.

Since nothing defuses the arbitrariness of capitalism like sex, the three-letter word, especially female sexuality and its pornographic commercial celebration has taken centre stage. To lure customers and sell things (from car and sofa to food and drinks), the presence of a half-clad model with bedroom eyes has become mandatory. The female flesh does not merely sell, it is sold, as the clear-eyed Margaret Atwood (1992) sees it,

> Money flows into this country or that country, flies in, practically crawls in, suitcase after suitcase, lured by all those hairless pre-teen legs. Listen, you want to reduce the national debt, don't you? Aren't you patriotic? That's the spirit. That's my girl. She's a natural resource, a renewable one luckily, because those things wear out so quickly.

The market appeals to naturalness and ubiquity of sex to sell products, but sexuality thus unleashed and celebrated is never free in itself. It is a symbol, as John Berger says, of the good life in which you can buy whatever you want. 'To be able to buy is the same thing as being sexually desirable . . . the implicit message [is:] if you are able to buy this product you will be lovable. If you cannot buy it, you will be less lovable' (Berger 1981: 144).

The market commercializes sex by stereotyping sex roles. Inculcation and normalization of masculine and feminine stereotypes is necessary for boosting sales and turning sex itself into a thriving industry. The market-induced standards of hot body (that rarely match what most women and men actually look like) immensely enhance the scope to give hopes—sell things—to *the less feminine, the less masculine*. The bottom line is: solution to your sexual problem is something you have to pay for. Buying the product will make you supersexy. In advertisements, the tag line goes something like, *Hey guys! Want to become an alpha male, a seductive female! Want to heighten your sex appeal and overall confidence! Then, buy the magic grooming products and colognes!* 'Instinct' from Axe, 'Swagger' by Old Spice, 'Magnetic Attraction Enhancing Body Wash' by Dial. Body wash. Face wash. Exfoliating wash. Deodorant. And, of course, shampoo, conditioner and hair gel. According to a 2010 report in *The New York Times*, worldwide retail sales of such products for boys ages 8 to 19 would be around $2 billion. And sales of beauty products for young women, of course, would be many times higher. Sex sells!

For profit-maximization, the market exerts pressures on people, especially youngsters, to embrace and engage in casual sex. The market is saturated with sexual imagery and content whose effect is to enforce the idea that sexual activities are central to our life. Teenagers are bombarded with publicity that shows premature sexual activity as a benchmark of being cool, trendy, and advanced. The latest gimmick is to present children in sexually provocative clothing and poses to sell products—a marketing method that has come to be known as 'corporate paedophilia'. Even the most reputable companies indulge in such crime to up their sales. Clive Hamilton (2009) contends that corporate paedophilia is so 'widespread and unremarked that it stands as testimony to the Freudian denial on a mass scale.' Citing the phenomenon of young cheerleaders as sex symbols, he says that the delusion of the mothers who insist that their daughters' routine are in no way sexual—despite the short skirts, clingy tops and bottom-thrusting—would be shattered if they 'spent five minutes with their ears open, listening to the lechers on the terraces as their daughters performed'. Such consent has been 'extracted by subtle coercion—not by the other party but by social groups and the wider culture'.

Since the market is already saturated with sex and porn, there is a mad race among the marketers to produce even more stimulating words and images to get public attention. The love of lucre blinds them to the fact that seeing sex as panacea is as reductive and dangerous as seeing sex as sin. The market and sex radicals, however, have succeeded in brainwashing people to see 'free sex' as liberation. Earlier, sin used to be 'to give in to one's sexual desires'; now, it is not to have full sexual satisfaction. Indiscriminate sex being hailed as a substitute for the anxiety of aloneness and emotional poverty compounded by a dwindling community life was noticed by philosopher Rollo May (1966) at the very dawn of the sexual revolution:

What goes into building a relationship—the sharing of tastes, fantasies, dreams, hopes for the future and fears from the past—seem to make people more shy and vulnerable than going to bed with each other. They are more wary of the tenderness that goes with psychological and spiritual nakedness than they are of the physical nakedness in sexual intimacy.

Earlier, she wanted more intimacy and he wanted more penetration; now she has caught up, well . . . overtaken him in divorcing sex from intimacy, if we are to believe libertarians like Catherine Millet whose sensational memoir *The Sexual Life of Catherine M.* is advertised by the publisher as 'a manifesto of our times—when the sexual equality of women is a reality and where love and sex have gone their own separate ways' (Millet 2002). Her thesis statement is: 'F . . . is an antidote to boredom. I find it easier to give my body than my heart.' She gives explicit accounts of hundreds of sexual encounters, especially orgies in which she is penetrated in every orifice. She boasts of having had sex with a hundred men in a single night. She admits she cannot remember most of them and did not even see many. But she is so sure that only through such sexual abandon can we find full freedom and that any criticism of her remorseless sexual orgies is not just neurotic but oppressive as well.

This form of free and depersonalised sex is being hailed by the society set as a major triumph of female power, rather than actualization of primordial male or female fantasy in which all finer feelings drown in a sea of testosterone.

Such biological model of sexuality is a dangerous nonsense because sex is not simply a natural bodily function. Of course, sex is a drive or instinct, but like all human drives and instincts, sex, too, is developed and cultivated in society. Though natural, sex involves a decision, a judgement. Even for the believers in free sex, it is neither involuntary nor indiscriminate. A definition of sex as purely biological can be questioned from many anti-essentialist perspectives. Foucault demolished the sexuality-as-biology thesis in his *History of Sexuality*, along with the assumption that such a natural, biological sexuality could be 'liberated' outside society and culture. Sexual identities are not merely the expression of natural instincts, but are social and political constructs as well. 'Sexuality has always been the site where the future of our species, and at the same time our truth as human subjects, are formed.' Foucault rightly sees sexuality as a historically and culturally constructed domain of experience that is shaped by social relations of power.

The assumption—and theorization—of the Freudian Marxists and feminist radicals of the 1960s and 1970s such as Herbert Marcuse (1956), Wilhelm Reich (1969), and Shere Hite (1976) that took a categorically biological view of sexuality, along with the optimism that sexual liberation will overcome capitalism and transform the social order, was naïve. In fancifully yoking Marx and Freud together—by proposing that workers and women couldn't be free until they were liberated from sexual repression and the tyranny of traditional family structures—Reich and Marcuse overlooked the social and material conditions under the capitalist order. Their fascination with the body and the pleasures of consumption (mass market kitsch, shopping malls, television soap-operas) displaced the traditional Marxist focus on conditions of material production. They forgot that Marx himself had dismissed free love as a 'bestial' prospect, tantamount to 'general prostitution'. He wrote in the *Communist Manifesto* ([1848] 1978: 488), 'Our bourgeois, not content with having wives and daughters of their proletarians at their disposal, not to speak of common prostitutes, take the greatest pleasure in seducing each other's wives.' He followed this up by asserting that only the abolition of the capitalist system of production would lead to the abolition of prostitution 'both public and private.'

The New Left's fond hopes that the unfettered libido will not only liberate sexuality but also oppressive structures of power and patriarchy did more harm than good to the cause of a social revolution. Their tendency to see sexuality as biological was essentialist, one-dimensional, not very different from the dogma of evolutionary psychology. No wonder then that sex-centred radicalism ended up with women simply internalizing male ideas of sex and power. The concept of free sex was easily co-opted by the capitalist forces which went on to build a massive industry of pornography and prostitution in the wake of the sexual revolution. Now it is clear that far from unalloyed pleasure, 'free sex' is also the site of extreme selfishness, promiscuity, relationship risks, commercial exploitation, male violence, rape, pornography, and prostitution. Sex is no exception to the truth that the extreme of anything leads to absurdity and sickness. Sex has its place in life but when it is employed as a therapy to fill up social insecurity and emotional vacuum, and taken as a substitute to social action and transformation, it becomes dark and dangerous—and a tool in the hands of oppressive forces.

Exclusion of labouring bodies and concealment of less than perfect figures in the corporate media tell the story of sex, lies and advertising. The gap between an iconic perfect body and the natural body produces shame in the less endowed. When shame permeates the core of both the emotional and personal self, the market steps in with magical slimming pills and surgery so that her body can be an object of pride and measure up to the ideal of beauty. In advertisements, women's bodies are often fragmented in parts—the lips, the breasts, the legs—each requiring a product-solution to enhance their value. The market-induced fetish of a perfect body and obsession with weight and shape has led to the mushrooming of the cosmetic surgery centres.

In its pursuit of profit maximization the market has even appropriated or domesticated feminist ideas against an unbalanced and sick society. A feminist sociologist explains this nefarious trend:

> Cultural images of women's beauty—and implicit ratings of their bodies—are replete throughout the culture. . . . Advertisements admonish women to be afraid—afraid of aging, afraid of food, afraid of being alone, afraid of having too small a bust. They promise that with the right products, a woman can be beguiling and seductive,

> as long as you change how you look.... And, if the ads don't work, the articles tell you month after month how to please men ... so not only do advertisements tell women exactly what they have to buy to have the right look, they have also appropriated the women's movement by claiming that new freedoms allow you to buy the right products. (Anderson 2003: 56)

While being commodified, women are made to believe in their new subjectivity and empowerment through a discourse of playfulness, freedom and choice. Women are encouraged to cultivate erotic appeal and capitalize upon every aspect of it because sexual attractiveness is a personal asset that offers money and mobility. A post-feminist scholar gleefully argues that women can—and should—use 'erotic capital' to enhance their power 'in the bedroom and the boardroom' (Hakim 2011). 'Midriff advertising', Rosalind Gill points out, 'adds a further layer of oppression. Not only are women objectified now as they were before, but through sexual subjectification they must also now understand their own objectification as pleasurable and self-chosen' (Gill 2009: 107). She argues that this is a ploy to re-sexualize women's bodies within a rigid heterosexual economy, in which power, pleasure, and subjectivity are all presented in relation to traditional relations. It promotes a uniform standard of female beauty and sex appeal that excludes a large number of women who cannot meet these standards.

The more women are ensnared in this kind of body politic—accepting looks as the key to their self-image—the worse they think about themselves and others. In a US survey some time ago, over half of young women said they would prefer to be hit by a truck than be fat (Rhode 2011). Consumer culture targets both women and men with standardization of femininity and masculinity, but women become more vulnerable to such an ideal because the female body is displayed as an object of power, and that power is based on beauty (not strength). Though images of men in popular culture are also stereotyped, they are generally shown in dominating, self-assured postures—as masculinity still means 'natural' power and control—while the new femininity is like consuming and celebrating a kind of emancipatory nakedness. In other words, if man and woman are defined and judged by just their anatomies, he is still the mover and she is the shaker. As the popular culture pushes women to 'channel energy into being seen rather than into being strong, attracting becomes a substitute for acting.'

The pursuit of erotic perfection does not lead to personal or social bliss; it leads to a sex industry that lures women and men with promises of sexually-oriented shortcuts to success. *Want to buy a Rolex, a Merc, clothes from Gucci . . . Don't worry if you don't have money . . . You have a pretty face, a wonderful body that you can use and get those dream items.* All kinds of prostitutions are flourishing today—in addition to the traditional body trafficking induced by abject poverty and force which continue to blight millions of lives. (According to the UNICEF estimate in 2010, 1.8 million children are forced into the sex trade each year.)

Perhaps for the first time in history, thanks to the rise of the consumerist culture of raunch, classy prostitutes and painted, perfumed gigolos have gained a global respectability. With the consumerist fever sweeping the world, the item girls, the porn actors have become the role models—and envy—of many middle-class youngsters. Now, call girls, playboys and their patrons are penetrating the public sphere and even parliaments. This phenomenon, represented by the likes of Silvio Berlusconi, the former billionaire playboy prime minister of Italy, is currently more visible in Euro-America, but the trend is gaining ground globally.

There is no dearth of defence lawyers of prostitution such as Camille Paglia (1994) and Catherine Millet (2002), who are outraged by any criticism of prostitution. The decision to become a prostitute, the argument goes, is a free choice no different from becoming a schoolteacher, a waiter or a truck driver. In this view, sexual morality or coercion is a myth, and negative stereotyping of prostitutes is solely due to crass ignorance and outdated moralism. This constitutes a discourse that sex—impersonal, paid, or anything—is more enjoyable when it is free of any expectations, obligations or intimacy. Decades ago in India, Durga Bhagwat, a Marathi author of repute, made a similar point, arguing that prostitutes render a valuable service to society, and that the flesh trade is a noble profession, to which Raja Dhale, a dalit writer, retorted, 'Then, why don't you join the noble profession?' The debate ended there and Dhale overnight became famous for that wisecrack.

The condemnation of prostitution is not based on a puritan bigotry but on an obvious reality that our body and we are not two entities but one, and by selling the body we sell our dignity and integrity that anchors our humanity. When we put a price on our body, we debase not only ourselves but also all those who value us as individuals. Our sexuality is not a commodity that can be prised free from our beings, and sold in the market like other products. The marketing of human sexuality is not a tribute to either physical beauty or human freedom but a perversion of both. Prostitution and pornography are human trafficking.

> The case against pornography is the case against the interest that it serves—the interest in seeing people reduced to their bodies, objectified as animals, made thing-like and obscene. This is an interest that many people have; but it is an interest at war with our humanity. (Scruton 2011: 138)

The pornification of market society, however, is part of a bigger phenomenon in which the power and wealth of those who prostitute their bodies are nothing in comparison to the corporate honchos and power pimps who prostitute their minds to the highest bidder. Prostitution, physical or intellectual, never fails to debase relationships and values. But the prostitution of mind is perhaps more odious, because it prepares the ground for perversion and corruption of an entire culture. (Intellectual prostitution, though seldom recognized, has for long afflicted humanity, and has in fact been far more prevalent than the business of selling one's body.

However, the business of selling one's mind and body has never been as flourishing as it is today, thanks to the ruling market forces which give the powerful prostitutes several other glamorous identities to hide their primary profession. Today, the most successful prostitutes, of both physical and intellectual variety, are those who remain invisible as prostitutes.)

On the surface, sex roles appear to have changed in a radical way, but has it brought more satisfaction to women and men? Has it really liberated women? If yes, how many and from which caste-and-class background? As Meena Kandasamy, a young Indian woman who writes on the politics of the body, observes,

> If one realizes that we belong to a caste society that once demanded that untouchable women bare their breasts and not wear blouses, we'll move closer to understanding the male gaze that predominates advertising today. . . . The stereotype of a sexually liberated woman desperately yearning for the zipless you-know-what is another corporate creation that only manifests male supremacy and female subjugation. . . . The promotion of this licentiousness serves the material interests of the ruling classes. Those who advocate such a de-moralizing of society have no tolerance to declass and decaste it. [It] . . . is an absolutely apolitical project. The nude woman in a corporate advertisement . . . cannot speak at all, not even to save herself. . . . *Sex and the City* and its many clones may be about lusty and liberated women but they do not have a single care about the rest of the world. (Kandasamy 2011)

The consumerist culture celebrates hypersexuality and peddles the idea that the young and the sexy means new brains and new bodies that bring in new approaches and new ideas. But behind the facade of celebrating youth power and sexual freedom, it indulges in a new kind of reactionary politics. The supersexualised market and its validation encourage the assumption that feminist and all equalitarian struggles have ended, that equality for all women and men has been achieved, and the deserving lot can now have anything they want. Its sexy-selfish template trivializes all social commitment and mocks any serious engagement with arts, literature, politics, or spirituality.

Debasement of Inner Resources, Emotions and Relationships

In the market culture, those who excel in the art of selling their bodies and minds to the highest bidders have become the cultural icons, and advertising such 'talents' has become one of the predominant art forms of our time. It has become so popular that its messages are the only ones being heard. Messages such as *bad is the new good; greed is glorious; diamond is a girl's best friend; selfishness is the axis of excellence; winning is everything; winner takes all.* In this all-or-nothing world, if you are not a winner, you are nothing. Those who advertise in this manner also create a culture in which every girl or boy is expected to look like the models in Pepsi-Coca Cola ad. And the softdrink ad look-alike must be dedicated to the motto of *having fun* and *anything goes*. They must consume the right brands and revel in latest jokes, gags and thrills. Spew obscenities, shed clothes, do anything to get attention and above all, refuse to grow up—always remain young!

The name of the game is dumbing down through a pernicious kind of censorship, not allowing people to think and reflect beyond the sleaze of sex, glamour, money, and status. Consumerist culture teaches a new ethic in which the offence is not selling one's body or soul, but the inability to lead a dream life—a life of indulgence and unlimited pleasure. The market is no longer a mechanism to satisfy our various needs, but primarily a means of generating superfluous needs and then satisfying them. 'Areas of personal and social life that…were well beyond the purview of the market have become infused with the market's value, transforming how we think about them. Choosing a mate, education, and entertainment, for example, have become increasingly commodified and are thus considered in terms of their capacity to deliver pleasure' (Hamilton 2009: 14).

The consumerist spirit thus pushes people to goals such as wealth acquisition and sexual conquest, instead of wasting life on intrinsic aspirations such as intimacy, self-actualization and contributing to the community. What were once the deadly sins—lust, gluttony, greed, sloth, wrath, envy, and pride—have now miraculously morphed into the prized virtues.

Consumer culture bombards people with messages that mock all notions of social ethics and individual sensitivity. It encourages the cynicism that all people are tricks and all relationships acting, and so it is better to gravitate our life to the pleasures of acquisitiveness. Placing products above people, it teaches the art of emotional numbing—feeling nothing for neighbours and others. Your possession and power should talk, not your conscience and inner voice. It is very good to sleep around, only you should not get intimate, or emotionally involved.

Generation Now doesn't want to be nice, gushes the media as if it is a great achievement. 'Being nice is no longer nice; the worse the better, that is the mantra. . . . It's hip and happening to be reckless, profane and unapologetic about it.' The reporter who writes this brings in a film actress who talks about her new film, 'My character is bad through and through. No apologies. No justification. She just enjoys being bad.' Then the reporter meets a hair stylist to get this pearl of wisdom, 'Nice is boring. . . . Today, it is politically correct to be obnoxious. The mean ones get the maximum attention' (*The Week* 2009). Read closely, these statements show that the movers and shakers of pop culture reinforce rather than merely reflect the trend of being rude, crude and lewd.

The *I-me-myself* culture teaches the young that becoming outwardly sexy and exciting, and inwardly cold and calculating is essential for survival in the marketplace of relationships. Since there is no difference in the templates of personal relationships and marketplace transaction, the call girl-call boy ethic reigns supreme—don't sell yourself cheap, hold out for the highest bidder! Commercial culture gives the impression that lots of money and products can take care of our emotional needs and relationships as well. Advertising promises us that acquisition of this or that thing will deliver what in fact they never can. As addictions to products and profits take root and flourish, as Jean Kilbourne says, relationships with family and friends flounder. The corrupting power of advertising—which makes lovers things and things lovers—pervades our whole culture and has made inroads in our inner lives and emotions:

> We are surrounded by hundreds, thousands, of messages every day that link our deepest emotions to products, that objectify people and trivialize our most heartfelt moments and relationships. Every emotion is used to sell us something. . . . Everything in the world—nature, animals, people—is just so much stuff to be consumed or to be used to sell us something. . . . It may be that there is no other way to depict relationships when the ultimate goal is to sell products. But this apparently bottomless consumerism not only depletes the world's resources, it also depletes our inner resources. It leads inevitably to narcissism and solipsism. It becomes difficult even to imagine a way of relating—to ourselves, our children, our partners, our environment—that isn't objectifying and exploitative. (Kilbourne 1999: 77–8)

The custodians of commercial culture, however, have an arsenal of arguments to justify its necessity. They have developed compelling ways of selling their half-truths with semi-empirical statistics. Their voices—relayed in many versions to target men, women and children from different segments of society—are the only ones to be heard today. As a propaganda branch of the market, the mass media club together with the corporate interests to stifle alternative views and perspectives. Being path-breaking in sensitivity, art, or aesthetics is no longer of any value. All that matters is a race to the top—being first, earning more than others, and defeating them all.

Ideas are judged on the basis of the monetary values of their expected commercial exploitation. Forget the excitement of a new insight, a pioneering thought. Being first is not a matter of discovery, but of gaining the highest number, the top position; box office figures, not cinematic quality, bestseller lists rather than literary value. The competition may involve a contest of physical and mental prowess, or artistic skills, but the judgement is qualitative. Who is first, and who is not. Winners and losers. (Gyan Prakash 2010)

There is a role for commerce in life but when we apply commercial logic to everything, life itself becomes a business. Competition for wealth, success, glory may have virtues, but how is a fair contest possible in an unfair world filled with fear, suspicion and mass poverty? Isn't the idea that one's success and happiness, possession and consumption, must come at the cost of the lesser mortals emotionally damaging (even for the triumphant) and socially destructive? Doesn't this kind of Darwinian competition make individuals alienated and community atomised?

That what we long to attain tells more about us than what we win. 'Our greatest fear should not be failure, but succeeding at something that doesn't really matter.' Shakespeare makes the same point, 'A peace is of the nature of a conquest; for then both parties are nobly subdued and neither party loser.'

The absence of a moral compass, flirting with the dark side, and obsession with self-interest at any cost will lead everyone to a dark alley, to a psychiatric ward where the healers will be as neurotic as the patients. Psychotherapy cannot be a substitute for human connection and warmth, the lack of which drives us into the arms of the former. Connecting to neighbours and nurturing relationships are more important than connecting to the dot-com bubble. Communication technology can enormously extend our reach but only connecting with real people in real life teaches us the great fundamentals of life. What really redeems us and gives us joy are honest relationships, good work and a humbling sense of belonging to a vast community and the cosmos. We are social creatures who live in a wider and interconnected world. We are vulnerable, disease-prone and finite, and we need friends, warmth, and mutual support. We need each other to be alive and effective. But anyone who tries to say these things in the market society is looked down upon. Any dissenting voice against commercialization of culture and relationships, any view that is at variance with market values, is dismissed either as cheap moralizing, utopian daydreaming, or the ideological posturing or paranoia of anti-capitalist conspiracy theorists. Voices of dissent, of human values and public ethics, have never been so marginalized and muted by the vested interests in which the successful, the safe, the profitable drive out all uncomfortable truths from our view. As everything is about selling to the world, the market and those who control it have emerged as the supreme arbiters of values.

Powerful tools of mass communication—television, films, the Internet, newspapers—have become the means of mass mobilization in favour of the standards, values and tastes set up by the market. From news and views to the so-called public opinions and public surveys, almost all things in the media are sponsored by corporate interests—and fixed. The world is as the corporate elites say it is.

Do the best lack all conviction, to paraphrase W.B. Yeats, while the worst are full of passionate intensity? No, this is not true, or just partly true. The best do not lack conviction; they are kept down—mocked and rendered invisible by the commercial forces. People with passion for justice and truth are kept on the margins. No journalist interviews them; no talk show features them. To be in the limelight, the alleged do-gooder has to be a talk shop, or some sort of power-friendly harmless drudge—there is ample scope for them to amplify their cause. But the individuals who question the system with the oppressed are not allowed to emerge as role models because there is no cash value in them. Worst of all, they may become a threat to the established power.

As life has become television and television life, the biggest pedagogues today are not parents, teachers, and schools, but television and its siblings like the movies and the Internet. Today, commercial publicity and infotainments exert far more influence on impressionable minds than schools and teachers. An average urban student spends more time in front of television and the Internet than at school. And when they read, they read the American or British-style pulp fictin that is available all over the world. Earlier, stories and myths that influenced people the most were specific to a particular community and culture. However good or bad, they did not have a universal reach. But modern stories and myths are more and more mass-produced in singular corporate clichés for the trillion-dollar global marketplace. 'For the first time in human history, most of the stories about people, life, and values are told not by parents, schools, churches, or others in the community who have something to tell, but by a group of distant conglomerates that have something to sell' (George Gerbner, quoted in Kilbourne 1999: 56). This is true, but we miss the point that the corporate stories too carry a great deal of the old prejudices of power and wealth. In newer forms, most of the films, television shows, and items on the Internet teach people the same old values, norms and attitudes of dominant culture though in a murderously uniform and far more damaging and dehumanized manner.

CHAPTER 4

Understanding the Politics of Knowledge

All knowledge that is divorced from justice must be called cunning.

SOCRATES

The arrow shot by the archer may or may not kill a single person. But stratagems devised by a wise man can kill even babes in the womb.

KAUTILYA

Bad men increase in knowledge as fast as good men, and science, arts, taste, sense and letters are employed for the purpose of injustice as well as for virtue.

JOHN ADAMS

As long as there are entrenched social and political distinctions between sexes, races or classes, there will be forms of science whose main function is to rationalize and legitimize these distinctions.

ELIZABETH FEE

In the pre-modern world, the predominant asset to production was land; capital became paramount with the Industrial Revolution; today it is increasingly knowledge and technology. That is, privilege and power that were earlier based on birth or wealth have now been replaced by knowledge and expertise. We often hear that knowledge, not weapons, is the currency of power today; that ours is a knowledge society and knowledge economy. This is very close to what the empire-loving Winston Churchill had fondly predicted in the last century (as the colonial imperialism was coming to an end), 'The empires of the future are going to be the empires of the mind.' More recently, social scientist Ernest Gellner made the same point but with a different emphasis and a darker undertone, 'At the base of modern social order stands not the executioner but the professor.' He made it clear by adding that the 'monopoly of legitimate education', that is the 'monopoly of legitimate violence' is now central to the process of the integration and reproduction of social order (Gellner 1983: 34).

In the acquisitive society teeming with ambitious individuals, knowledge, more than ever before, is an instrument of wealth and power. People think that knowledge always pays off . . . or ought to, and the test of genuine knowledge is just such pays-offs. The powerful and the wealthy must be the men of most knowledge, otherwise how could they be where they are? Such assumptions are tantamount to saying that power is knowledge and wealth is knowledge, but this is exactly what has happened to the kind of experience that knowledge has come to be. 'Knowledge is no longer widely felt as an ideal; it is seen as an instrument.' Sociologist C. Wright Mills wrote this in 1956. Knowledge has become more dismal and devastating since then. In the era of global finance capitalism, knowledge society and knowledge economy are merely euphemisms for an economic information society. This means that more and more of social and economic life have now come under the controls of saleable knowledge. Such knowledge has been developed into an industry—knowledge industry—in which experts of business and politics interpret and orient oceans of new information in their favour.

It is notable that in the catchphrases *knowledge capital*, *knowledge economy*, *knowledge industry*, knowledge is a mere adjective; the noun that anchors or captures it is either capital or its ally. Similarly, in the buzzwords *human capital* (what you know), *social capital* (who you know), *economic capital* (what you have), *cultural capital* (what makes you click), it is *capital* that occupies the driving seat. This is also being extended to the new *powerful* categories such as *relationship capital* and *erotic capital* (Hakim 2011). And, of course, there is perennial *time capital*—time is money!

We see now an infiltration of capital into areas of life, with knowledge in tow, that was earlier unimaginable. Knowledge as capital finds its most blatant expression in the idea and institution of *intellectual property rights*. Legitimizing knowledge as the property of individuals and corporations is a new and wonderful way of colonizing culture and community. What it means in actual terms can be grasped through the example of life-saving drugs in which 'the human right of a corporation to protect its intellectual property trumps the need of a sick man.' As a public intellectual puts it, 'For a civilization to attempt to live off licensed knowledge is the intellectual re-creation of the old absentee landlord problem. Abruptly it is to be believed that owning knowledge—that is, controlling rather than spreading the use of our imaginations—will make societies and their citizens rich' (Saul 2004: 282).

In the market society, knowledge is being marketed as a form of expedient—and often misleading—information to maximize profit and power. We are swamped by statistics and information that confuse or conceal rather than reveal the real world and the larger reality. The more information we have, the harder it is to distinguish the useful sort from the trash. The information glut does not slack the tightening of elitist control of knowledge that has become the master key to the empire of capital, not just one of the fundamentals of power. But the elitist appropriation and abuse of knowledge has a long historical background, as we saw in the Introduction and Chapter 1. Let us now probe the production and politics of knowledge to grasp its duality and complicity in the design of dominance. A subversive understanding of knowledge is necessary for developing a suspicious relationship with the 'ruling ideas of the ruling class.' Reconstruction of knowledge and life will not be possible without such a deconstruction.

The Dark Side of Knowledge: Duality, Falsity, Fabrication

The *knowing* few who assume the role of telling fellow people the reality of the world and how things really work acquire the power to both reveal (lead) and mystify (mislead). As biologist Humberto Maturana points out, 'When one human being tells another human what is "real", what they are actually doing is making a demand of obedience. They are asserting that they have a privileged view of reality' (cited by Senge 2004: xi). It is in this sense that knowledge is power. Like power, knowledge (especially social and political knowledge) can be, and has been, used in many different ways—for both good and bad purposes. It is important, therefore, to grasp social aspects of production and dissemination of knowledge, especially its historical role in engendering or justifying inequalities of caste, class, gender and other oppressive categories within a country or of the races or peoples around the world. This dark side of knowledge has been erased or ignored by the ruling minority, which, for obvious reasons, glorifies constituted knowledge or the intellectual tradition that legitimizes their power and wealth.

Let us begin with two philosophers, John Locke and David Hume. In *An Essay Concerning Human Understanding* (1690), Locke explores the operations of the mind in order to know what knowledge is and how it is constituted and acquired. Denying the existence of innate logical or moral principles, he famously pictures the mind at birth as a white paper—a blank tablet—on which experience and reflection write the script. He is categorical that reason or knowledge springs from the fountain of experience. Born of our experience, our knowledge is relative. (To take his own case, Locke could believe in equality and Christianity, yet was comfortable with slavery.) Following Locke, Hume, in his *Treatise of Human Nature* (1740), argues that since all the data of reason stem from experience (which is always subjective), there is little possibility of certainty in knowledge. In a famous phrase, he asserts that reason 'is, and ought only to be, the slave of our passions; and can never pretend to any other office than to serve and obey them'. He clarifies that reason is a most useful slave as it helps us grasp and guide our competing passions, but alone it can never be a motive to any action since desire arises not from reason, although it can and ought to be directed by it. Being thus suspicious of the powers of reason, Hume was alive to the dangers of intellectual charlatanry: 'No man need despair of gaining converts to the most extravagant hypothesis who has art enough to represent it in favourable colours.'

Elements or sources that constitute knowledge give weight to Hume's suspicion about absolutist claims of 'clear, certain and perfect knowledge'. As we know, experience, reason, testimony, and memory are four major sources of knowledge. All these are finite and fallible: our senses can deceive us; our reasoning can be unsound; testimony of others can knowingly or unknowingly mislead us; and our memories can be partial, selective or distorted. Now we know that our memory of even objective facts is coloured—distorted—by our present feelings and motivations, and this applies more to our experience, reasoning and testimony. As our individual perceptions about the world are limited, we depend on a collective and accumulated knowledge created by experience, observation and articulation of other people, written or recorded either by themselves or others. To be persuasive, however, knowledge has to be well organized, well reasoned, and well articulated. Knowledge thus produced with a collective and well-documented memory—in the form of tracts, books, journals, or new electronic databases—becomes a prized human possession. But still there is no guarantee that our current knowledge cannot be wrong. Even standard or commonly accepted knowledge is not always flawless, disinterested, or true for all time. Moreover, false knowledge is not solely a product of human failure (as in the realm of pure science); individuals or groups for quite selfish reasons can knowingly—perversely—fabricate knowledge, as we can see in many instances of social and political issues.

Knowledge, thus, is a treacherous terrain, and defining it is difficult, but a functional definition is feasible, like the one provided by *Oxford Dictionary of English*: 'facts, information, and skills acquired through experience or education; the theoretical and practical understanding of a subject'. Proven facts or information are not disputable but what is a justified belief or true understanding as opposed to opinion can—and does—vary within a community and among countries and cultures, creating controversy, dissent and worse. In this sense, all human knowledge takes the form of interpretation. Even though the generation of knowledge is a cumulative and collective process, it involves assimilation or interpretation and comes from interaction between individuals and the world. All of us continually organize what we know, structuring and restructuring our knowledge. In other words, knowledge is not readymade ('out there' to be discovered), but something that is constructed, communicated, trusted, or contested.

That knowledge is a *social construction of reality* is the crux of a well-known treatise by Berger and Luckmann (1966) who reinvented the earlier 'sociology of knowledge' that was pioneered by the likes of Karl Marx, Max Scheler and Karl Mannheim. They, despite mutual differences, shared the perspective that knowledges, including belief systems and ideas, are products of existing social order. Berger and Luckmann move from the social determination of ideas to the social construction of reality itself. Theirs is an idea of knowledge that guides and is produced by everyday life. Not merely an offshoot of society or culture, knowledge and reality 'existed in dialectical and reciprocal relationship of mutual construction'. All knowledges are generated by social interactions, and it is in this sense that knowledge and reality are socially constructed. Thus, what we call knowledge in everyday language is not very different from the parable of the blind men and the elephant. What everybody knows about society is an 'assemblage of maxims, morals, proverbial nuggets of wisdom, values and beliefs, myths, and so forth'. As people, not some infallible power, produce knowledge, it is not a loose-leaf notebook of proven facts that cannot be questioned. Any knowledge, especially social and political knowledge, is open to further inquiry because the questions we ask and the answers we get are shaped by context and location.

In other words, many of our knowledges can be—and are—false. And false knowledge, or fabrication, is more dangerous than ignorance. As early as the sixth century BCE, the great Buddha sounded a profoundly sceptical note regarding claims of truth and knowledge, and suggested in his famous *Kalama Sutta* some universal criteria to avoid the pitfalls of false knowledge. Many centuries down the line, empiricist Roger Bacon (*c*. 1214–94), almost in the same vein, pointed out four major obstacles to grasping truth, which hinder even the wisest of people to win a clear title to knowledge. The obstacles he enlisted are: submission to faulty and unworthy authority; influence of custom; popular prejudice; and concealment of our own ignorance accompanied by the ostentatious display of our knowledge (Bacon [1267] 1928: 4). No wonder, philosopher Pitirim A. Sorokin came to the sad conclusion that 'the history of human knowledge is a cemetery filled with wrong empirical observation, false reasonings, and pseudo intuitions' (Sorokin 1957: 181).

It is not surprising, then, that knowledges (a lot of which are questionable and false) have been used far more to defend the power and privilege of the few than for securing justice and dignity of the multitude. Elite groups everywhere want to hire and harness knowledge to perpetuate their domination, and have so far wonderfully succeeded in turning knowledge into their privilege. From the dim and distant past, knowledge has a sordid history, playing second fiddle to power and perverting itself to yoke together liberty and property, morality and power.

In his *Discourse On the Origin of Inequality* (1754), Rousseau discovered this unusual truth when he argued that the idea and institution of inequality originated from advances in knowledge, and gradually got established through the civil society. 'Inequality', he said, 'derives its force and growth from the development of our faculties and the progress of the human mind, and eventually becomes stable and legitimate through the establishment of property and law.' In his famous words, the first person who having fenced off a plot of land, took it into his head to claim it as his and found people simple enough to believe him, was as much a founder of civil society as the institution of inequality. 'What crimes, wars, murders, what miseries and horrors', he adds, 'would the human race have been spared, had someone pulled up the stakes or filled in the ditch and cried out to his fellow men: "Do not listen to this imposter. You are lost if you forget that the fruits of the earth belong to all and the earth to no one!"' (Rousseau [1754] 1987: 60).

Rousseau pointed out that the idea of property was part of a larger phenomenon, which had already been in play for a long time. It was not formed all at once in the human mind but had a long background of events and advances in knowledge—all ultimately leading to the notion of private property and hierarchy of human relations. This insight was at the heart of his worldview that made him deeply suspicious of the progress of civilization and prompted him to denounce arts and sciences as the handmaiden of a scheming elite who used their intelligence to keep the commonality in servitude. Noting that 'it is contrary to the law of nature for a handful of people to gorge themselves on superfluities while the starving multitudes lack the necessities of life', Rousseau, a man of humble origin, mounted a fierce attack on the faith in reason at a time when science and reason were emerging as new gods and advances in knowledge seen as Enlightenment that would liberate humanity. Instead, he demanded that increased knowledge ought to serve a moral purpose; as he did not see that happening, he 'rejected the elegant, cosmopolitan culture of his day as immoral, and declared it the source of man's evilness rather than the crown of his achievement'. He argued that our increased knowledge might increase our pride and multiply our errors (Bronowski and Mazlish 1963: 326–8).

Placing ethics above knowledge, Rousseau suggested that the regeneration would come about not by scientific and technological improvements but by humanity's rediscovery and renewal of itself. Implied in his critique was a demand for recognition of human emotions combined with a political and ethical remaking of the world (Cassirer 1954). His writings, especially *Social Contract*, carry an impassioned argument for the autonomy of each individual and his or her full participation in common decisions, and this perspective, as we know now, is at the heart of a democratic ideal.

In retrospect, it seems that Rousseau could peer into the abyss of the modern trinity of wealth, power, and knowledge that gradually replaced the traditional socio-religious forms of inequality and injustice. He was the only major thinker in the age of reason who could see the dark side of culture and knowledge. Perhaps it was this Rousseauesque insight that was developed in the twentieth century by Horkheimer and Adorno in a landmark work of modern philosophy (1947), in which they set themselves the task of 'nothing less than finding out why humankind, instead of entering into a truly human condition, is sinking into a new kind of barbarism'. Whatever their faults or inability to give some viable solution, the question posed by them (and enlarged by their intellectual movement known as the Frankfurt School) was so important that it went on to become the central issue of modern philosophy and social theory. This question—why the incredible brilliance, wealth, and technology of the modern world are used for preventing rather than constructing a more decent and humane society—was sought by intellectuals like Walter Benjamin, who thought, Rousseau-like, that culture and barbarism go hand in hand, and that the most modern scientific-technological advances can actually be a manifestation of old savagery. In 'Theses on the Philosophy of History', he bemoans, 'there is no document of civilization which is not at the same time a document of barbarism. And just as such a document is not free of barbarism, barbarism also taints the manner in which it was transmitted from one owner to another' (Benjamin 1969: 256).

The 'tainted transmission' of historical and social reality brings us to the dual nature and function of knowledge. Eugene Meehan makes the illuminating point that knowledge, at the most fundamental level, is organized experience, and, thus, the search for knowledge is a 'search for patterns of organization. The organization is always created and not discovered' (see Hoover and Donovan 1995: 47). Thus, the questions such as how is knowledge generated, and who transmits it and for what purpose become crucial. On this understanding (that there is no text without context), the new sociology of knowledge argues that all knowledge—especially commonsensical, everyday, and cultural, including what we call truth or morality—is derived from and maintained by social interactions in a historical context, and, thus, is partial and questionable, not universal and absolute. This gives us the insight that knowledge construction is coloured, if not determined, by the specific individual attributes and background of the knowledge-maker, including factors such as class, caste, race, gender, cultural conditioning, and age. This viewpoint finds devastating articulations in the fashionable intellectual current of postmodernism which rejects all claims of rationality, objectivity, and the very possibility of absolute or universal truth (Anderson 1996). A leading figure of this school argues that knowledge and power are actually synonymous terms—the effectiveness of power is knowledge, and the effectiveness of knowledge is power (Foucault 1980).

Postmodernism rejects not just modernist—positivist—dogmatism (of perfect knowledge) but the very ideal of absolute intellectual purity in favour of 'partial epistemologies that recognize the historical and socially constructed nature of their own knowledge claims and methodologies'. Ironically, postmodernists themselves end up making absolutist claims of impossibility—even undesirability—of not just pure reason or objectivity but of any coherent worldview or meaning of life (Jameson 1992). We can reject relativist nihilism, but cannot easily dismiss the notion that truth is a matter of perspective and that every view is only one among many possible interpretations.

In other words, from the rational Buddha to medieval mystics and to postmodernist naysayers, the acceptance of the impossibility of absolute knowledge has a long lineage in history. Indeed, absolutism of whatever kind is not the hallmark of an evolved mind. A thinker is satisfied with telling a little more of the truth than other people did. By dint of hard work and cultivated intelligence, this is what the best of minds are able to accomplish. If we combine the structuralist theory of language with the paradoxical nature of our conscience and identity, it is difficult to avoid the inference that language is inadequate to explain total reality. Stressing the impossibility of saying it all, Lacan makes an excellent point. 'I always tell the truth: not the whole truth, because the whole truth is something one never comes to the end of. To tell the whole truth is impossible, materially: the words are lacking' (see Clement 1983: 22).

All grandiose attempts to discover the final truth flop because there is no super language that can separate reality from falsehood. Since appearance and reality are cleaved together and language is lacking in fully extricating them and conveying the whole truth, knowledge is neither absolute nor holds the same meaning for everyone. Relative to the knower, the same knowledge can have different meanings for different individuals or groups. Marcel Proust refers to this when he observes, 'Each reader brings to each work of literature only what is within himself.' What really matters is not our knowledge, but what meaning we give to it. Knowledge, in other words, cannot be grasped in isolation from our understanding and feelings.

Construction of reality and the representation of that reality has the power to tweak the reality. People with knowledge gain the ability not just to know or understand and make others so, but also to manipulate the natural and social world. Thus, knowledge is a double-edged weapon as its function can be twofold: one for the personal and social ideal of understanding the world and making us better, setting us free; and the other, as an instrument of power and manipulation. It is true that as an ideal, knowledge only strives for understanding and illumination, but in reality it can be—and has often been—reduced to an instrument of masking reality and manipulating people, and thus coercing and misleading society for selfish or sectarian purposes. History is witness to countless instances in which religio-cultural formulations or scientific-technological applications have been used for power, wealth, or the urge to dominate others.

The noble Socrates had naively equated knowledge with virtue, believing that 'to know the good is to do the good'. (He was wise enough, though, to clarify elsewhere: 'All knowledge that is divorced from justice must be called cunning.') But Francis Bacon (1561–1626) was wiser to the ways of the world and closer to reality when he associated knowledge with power. Power is inherently a social and political question, and generally a bad host to justice and wisdom. The corrupting nature of power has never been in serious dispute. The Actonian thesis—'power corrupts and absolute power corrupts absolutely'—is well known, but there is also a longstanding intellectual school that thinks that power is sacred. The Kautilyas and the Machiavellis have for ages been singing paeans to power: a ruler (they argued) can lie, cheat and kill if he has to retain power. They rejected conflict-resolution through dialogue and justice because virtuous acts would lead to the loss of power. Machiavelli preached that the end justifies the means and Kautilya, the greater rogue, prescribed that 'those who seek to achieve success should show no mercy' (Scharffstein 1995). 'One should not be straightforward. Go and see the forest. The straight trees are cut down, the crooked ones are left standing' (Kautilya, see Greene 2004: 211).

The aim of Kautilya and Machiavelli was to assist the powerful, not to liberate the weak and the defenceless. The elites portray them as great political philosophers because (though it is never made explicit) their writings give legitimacy to 'Machiavellism'—the disregard of moral scruples and use of deception and force for political ends—and its relentless employment to keep the common people in awe of the ruling class. No wonder the title of a major study of political theory in India, China and the West is *Amoral Politics: The Persistent Truth of Machiavellism* (Scharffstein 1995).

In short, knowledge does not have to be right to be influential. Pervasive but false ideologies of caste, race, and patriarchy are its classic examples. Their widespread acceptance are not the proof of their validity. The greatest defence of such categories—that also works as a very effective psychological weapon—is simply their ubiquity and longevity, besides the earlier lack of enduring success of any demonstrable alternatives. Though the dominant ideas and institutions did not go unchallenged, their tenacious hold continued through the ages as the accepted order. History reveals that there were individuals and groups in every society who resisted the oppressive forces, but they were in one way or other overcome by the ruling class.

Thus, knowledge is power that can trap and oppress as well as heal and liberate. Ultimately, it is what we make of it. But when knowledge combines with power, corruption festers. When the pursuit of knowledge combines with prejudice, ill will or evil, the former is reduced to a destructive quest for power. Above all, when the intellect detaches itself from any ability to sympathize with the oppressed, it generates ideas and attitudes of cruelty and crime. History is replete with examples of how unfettered knowledge containing the seeds of bigotry and hatred became the handmaiden of oppression, serving immoral ends and leading to gratuitous violence.

The abuse of knowledge for power and wealth has dominated the human civilization so far, and this oppressive reality shows no signs of abatement in our time. In fact, the knowledge–power nexus has acquired a more lethal edge in the technological–financial capitalism of today. Drawn by the power of knowledge, the power elite gathers all kinds of knowledge-producers to shore up the worldview that legitimizes existing structures of power. The power elite needs the knowledge elite, but the former brings in the latter not as peers but as hirelings whose task is to somehow explain away the current ills of society. If the system is a procedural democracy, as is the case today, the power intellectuals have to work harder to weave novel narratives and theories to hide how the system is rigged in favour of the powerful. Prostituting their intellect is incumbent on the knowledge elite associated with power.

Oppressive Language: the Theory, Violence: the Practice

We celebrate the classic rivalry between the letters and the arms assuming that they are worlds apart, representing two different worldviews. We assume that the word represents the virtuous through which we can take on the sword of evil and oppression. But history gives us countless examples of how they can also work in tandem and play havoc together. One can hold a holy book in one hand and a weapon in the other. People have been killed in the name of God. Also, our identity or ideological disposition can change the meaning of a word in a dramatic way—one man's terrorist is another man's freedom fighter. In his novel *1984*, Orwell showed us a deadly vision of a bureaucracy devoted to doublespeak and reconstructing language concepts to enhance the power of an authoritarian regime. In more recent times, one may recall Reagan's press secretary who would defend the lies of his boss by claiming that the President had misspoken. 'Tinkering with the meanings of concepts, one can play with the foundations of human understanding and social control' (Hoover and Donovan 1995: 20).

It is words through which we forge all relationships, friendly or adversarial. As Durkheim says, 'The word is a way of entering into relations with persons.' Thus, language does not just represent reality, it also has the power to create situations. If people define situations as real, in W.I. Thomas's celebrated maxim, they are real in their consequences. Whatever people believe to be real will produce real consequences, regardless of whether the believed thing is real or not. Language is symbolic and the agency of such bewitchment. Threatening, humiliating, four-letter words do hurt; words mask and manipulate, deceive and sting. The author of the *Manusmriti* (the brahmanic manifesto of caste) used words to commit crimes against humanity.

The oppressor denies and disproves the experiences and feelings of others by using 'words that make the wound, the split between subject and object, exposing and exploiting the object but disguising and defending the subject' (Le Guin 1992: 400). Ignoring, excluding, or distorting the interpretations of others not only makes them invisible or unimportant, but also lowers them in their own eyes by damaging their self-image. A confining, demeaning or contemptible portrayal can inflict harm, can be a form of oppression.

An oppressor objectifies the other in many ways. It is to ease his guilty conscience that the oppressor gets into the habit of seeing the oppressed as subhuman; for this he invents a web of words, images and theories. Accustoming oneself to treating the other as less than human requires some intellectual and moral justification. The principle—the method in madness—is old and well known: 'Call a dog bad. Call a dog mad. Then shoot him.'

When the oppressor's mindset acquires social currency and ascendancy—and starts affecting and infecting people's minds—a pattern in culture is established that devalues the oppressed (as the embodiment of ugliness and stupidity, evil and depravity) and supervaluates the oppressor (as the personification of beauty and purity, excellence and virtue). The makers of dominant culture and language encourage such stereotypes based on the binary opposition of 'deserving us' and 'undeserving they' which first pervade the *high culture* and then infiltrate down to every sphere of social life, including the domain and mindscape of the very people who are humiliated by such constructs. With relentless propaganda from above, such prejudices and stereotypes gradually insinuate themselves into people's psyche. Some examples:

The rich are fit—biologically, intellectually and morally—and the poor unfit. (Science, the theory of evolution, explains it; or God has made them so.)

Women are weaker and inferior to men. As the second sex, they are—have to be—subservient to the first one. (This is again either the law of nature or God; mere mortals should not mess with it.)

There are superior and inferior castes or races. (Again, the cause is natural or supernatural. It is enshrined in our Dharmashastras, and proved by the latest science! What can we do about it?)

We are the torchbearer of civilization—the original source of knowledge, the first philosophers, the first scientists. Our forefathers wrote everything that really matters, and you will find them in the Vedas. Our caste, religion and language are obviously the best in the world. (It's written in the Vedas! Western scholars acknowledge it! Dalits and shudras should understand this.)

We are the modern world's greatest country. We are a chosen people, one nation under God. (We have 10,000 nuclear weapons and our mandate is to spread democracy and free market around the world. We have the right to bombard the countries that do not accept our command and superiority.)

Big fish swallow up small fish. There is a logic or justice in injustices, cruelties and perversities that we see in life as everything is willed either by God or the law of nature. (I have a divine and biological right to keep you down!)

Hundreds of similar clichés enslave the gullible:

Women are emotional, men are rational.

One can identify a person's status, worth and level of education by looking at her dress and appearance.

Greed and self-interest are wired in our genes, a part of our evolutionary psychology—and they are glorious, in everyone's interest.

Privatization of resources—corporatization of economy—uplifts everyone, especially the poor.

Such stereotypes—first conceived and promoted by vested interests—slowly acquire currency and a mass following. Some of these and similar stereotypes are too blunt to be missed but some others are so seductive that they go on to acquire the aura of benevolence. Most languages, for example, devalue women in two ways—either by denigrating conventional feminine attributes or by glorifying them as a model of virtue. A woman is either a whore or a goddess. In either case, she ends up bearing a disproportionate burden of coercion and exploitation. Such sexism is so encrusted in public parlance that men—and women—are often not aware of the sexist nature of their reactions. So too for various false assumptions about caste, class, and race. All of them come together to form a general theory of society and human nature that explains and justifies differences in the character and culture and the roles therein of the dominant and the dominated.

Oppressive language is any language that fosters oppressive behaviour and practice. Every language has a vocabulary of words that wound and oppress. Implicitly or explicitly, such words disparage, diminish, and demonize the other, and give credence to oppressive practices in personal and social relationships. The symbolic violence that oppressive language represents is ultimately sucked into real violence. Oppressive language, as Toni Morrison said, does more than just represent violence; it is violence. Sexist, casteist, racist language continues to be one of the root causes of oppression of women and lowered castes or races. Attitudes of ridicule and contempt towards 'inferior' people have spawned a rich vocabulary of insults and abuses, only a fraction of which appears in standard dictionary and formal language. Though there is a progression of lesser insults for dalits (from chandala and untouchable to depressed class and dalit) and African-Americans (from nigger and negro to black and African-American), the hate or dehumanization that infuses these words survives, perpetuating psychological and social discrimination against them. Offensive and wounding words still pervade our cultural milieu, and they are used in everyday speech. Being poor, black, dalit, or adivasi still evokes a negative image because the dominant forces in control of the language and culture have over the centuries denigrated these categories in various ways. Such humiliation has become rather better hidden in a new vocabulary but it has not yet become history.

The relationship between power and naming is obvious enough. The act of naming confers power over the people or thing named. 'Names set up a field of power' (Trouillot 1995: 115). Those with the power to name and define things establish themselves as standard-bearers of society. Their interests become common interests and their worldview the measure of all things. In India, one section monopolized knowledge and in the process committed all kinds of intellectual frauds in order to acquire dominion over the rest of society. They called themselves brahman, pure and superior, and branded the working class shudra (and atishudra), impure and inferior. This history is yet to be fully understood and written, but one thing is clear. The brahman male literati in India and the white male elite in the West—and their counterparts everywhere—established their supremacy through a process of cultural and linguistic manipulation. They glorified themselves in various ways and fabricated degrading images and narratives against women and supposedly inferior castes and races. Over the centuries, they invented thousands of wounding words and phrases—*neech* (a person of lowly origins who deserves to be hated), *shudra* (worthless), *kameena* (the toiling bastard), *achhuta* (the untouchables), bitch, broad, fag, dyke, nigger, *rakhel* (a woman who is kept for sex and domestic service), to name just a few—through which lowered races, castes, and women were reduced to subhuman creatures, fit only for slavery and drudgery.

Germaine Greer, in her *Female Eunuch* (1970), fills four pages with anatomical terms and words for animals and pets, implements and receptacles, fruits and vegetables, all of which are used to humiliate the female person. The prevalence of the male principle in family and culture reigned supreme till the rise of feminism in the twentieth century. Writing on the phallic-centric world, Lacan says,

> The origins of our culture are too closely bound up with what we can only call the vagaries of the paternalistic family . . . to impose the male principle in the various psychological guises fostered by the family; the partiality of this principle is reflected in the moral dimension accorded to the term virility. (See Clement 1983: 82)

It is notable that the other side of the male principle inscribed in the word virility is virginity, the dissimulation of the feminine principle beneath the masculine ideal. In a culture of patriarchy, virginity is valued only in women, and through this and similar double standards a woman's sexual freedom is denied or curtailed.

All societies have traditionally been stratified, suffering from pathologies of hierarchy and exclusion. But no society or country can beat the caste culture of India in terms of verbal violence, or *vakparushyam,* as the pre-modern brahman would call it. Sublimation of violence in language is the defining feature of some of the most ancient and sacred Sanskrit texts. Historian Ranajit Guha points out that the ideology of caste hierarchy moulded the very grammar of Sanskrit in its own image. A ground rule of Panini's grammar, he says, can be interpreted in such a way as to make the caste hierarchy itself a compound of the *dvndvasamaas* class and put these together in their ascriptive order descending from brahman to shudra (Guha [1983] 1999: 41–2). Vocabulary of Sanskrit could serve for caste markers. The standard expression for superiority or excellence in Sanskrit is *utkrishtata*, etymologically derived from *utkrishta*, or high born; while the opposite is *nikrishtata*, from *nikrishta*, or low born. The word shudra—the last varna or caste in the brahmanic social order—is derived from *kshudra*, which literally means contemptible, without any worth or value. But shudra, as a scholar of Dharmashastras informs us, was also the code word for anyone, especially the Buddhists, Jains, and foreigners who would not accept superiority of the brahman. The word identified the enemy and it encompassed a wide cross-section of society. 'The reason why foreign ruling classes, such as the Greeks, Shakas, Persians, and Chinese, have fallen to the level of Shudras ... is their lack of devotion to Brahmins' (Olivelle 2005: 39). Likewise, in the Sanskritic parlance, women are commonly referred to as *dhana*, property of the male. If someone works on the glossary of abusive words for *stree* (women) and *shudra* in the brahmanic literature and orature (where they are assumed to be born in sin and slavery—*paapyoni*, to use the phrase in the *Bhagavad Gita*)—it will run into several hundred pages!

Brahmans manufactured a vast body of literature to create and enforce a vicious system of discrimination and dehumanization. Words became their most effective weaponry to demoralize and divide the lowered castes. Knowing that those who control words—and their definitions—control the world, the brahman positioned himself to be in the exclusive custody of the words and their meanings. The *Manusmriti* (11. 33) says, 'Speech is the brahman's weapon, and with that he should slay his enemies' (Olivelle 2005: 216). Brahmanic texts vie with one another to stress the 'sacred injunction' that toiling castes (shudras) and women ought to be completely excluded from the world of knowledge. The punishment to a shudra for reading or hearing the Vedas, Smritis, and other 'sacred' literature was brutal and barbaric:

> If a shudra listens to a recitation of the Vedas his ears shall be filled with molten tin or lac. If he recites Vedic texts his tongue shall be cut out.... He who tells [religious] law to a shudra and he who teaches

him religious observances, he indeed together with that shudra sinks into the darkness of hell called Asamvritta. [Such invocations are common in many brahmanic texts, for example in Shankar's *Brahma Sutra*, *Gautamdharma Sutra* (12: 4), and *Manusmriti* (8: 270).]

Hundreds of such violent utterances against shudras are scattered through the brahmanic texts. Then there are instances in the scriptures like *Gita* where hatred and antagonism against the commonality are better hidden, in literary excellence. But *Gita*, too, glorifies caste in the name of karma and killing in the name of dharma (see Mani 2005: 59–68). Though correspondence between language and social control is not unique to brahmanism, the extent of its pervasiveness remains unparalleled. As Ranajit Guha has pointed out, what was sought to be controlled was not the spoken word alone, but also the zero sign of utterance—silence used formally and yet eloquently enough as 'a significant absence' of speech. The ban on various kinds of conversation could announce the subordination of junior kin to senior, of wife to husband, of low caste to high caste and generally of the underclass to the elite. Guha cites several sociological studies that show the linguistic imposition of domination and subordination in everyday life.

> In Gujarat a Patidar youth was not to initiate conversation in the company of his elders, and . . . in an Andhra village a young man would be sharply rebuked if he tried to put in a word edgeways 'when big people are talking.' In the same village nuptial songs would insist that to 'keep silent in your husband's house' was part of a young bride's novitiate. And silence was a sign of subordination to authority in other spheres too. In Orissa, a Bauri untouchable was not to speak to a high caste person unless spoken to, while in a UP village 'one frequently finds a lower-caste individual sitting or standing at a slight distance from a higher group engaged in discussion, listening to what is said, but not participating. In parts of southern India a servant would cover his mouth while receiving his master's command in a sort of metalinguistic acknowledgement of the latter's power over himself. In Bengal a landlord would feel it

an affront if a peasant were to speak up to him. (Guha [1983] 1999: 46–7)

Such invasive hierarchies were directly related to the long-standing intellectual politics of brahmanism. Thanks to increasing resistance from below, the use of casteist-sexist words are on the decline but their resonance still pervades the social world and has become the basis of acute discrimination. Ascriptive identity still matters more than any other, despite the Constitutional laws to the contrary. In a recent judgement of the Supreme Court of India related to live-in relationships, two presiding judges used the word 'keep' for a woman, and in their wisdom noted, 'If a man has a "keep" whom he maintains financially and uses mainly for sexual purpose and/or as a servant, it would not be a relationship in the nature of marriage. Merely spending weekends together or a one-night stand would not make it a "domestic relationship."' (M. Katju and T.S. Thakur delivered the judgement on 21 October 2010.) The epistemic-semantic mechanism that keeps people in their place is still strong. Our marketplace, schools, and cultural institutions tend to teach us to listen to—and follow—the privileged people-in-power. Directly or suggestively, we are taught not to listen to common men, women, and children, at least not to hear their talk as a valid language or discourse. Miller and Swift (2001), who have extensively studied pervasive sexism in language, point out that learning through language and other symbols begins in the home, and is reinforced by institutionalized religion, the educational system, the media and the market.

Language and symbols are used not only to interpret one another and the reality of the world but also to misread others and create a false reality, or to hide some aspects of reality. For example, when children learn from their school books about Indian society, caste and patriarchy appear to them as symbols of a harmonious division of labour because they are not informed about their dehumanizing effects on the lowered castes and women. The social brutalities that lurk behind the stories of Sita, Shambuka, Ekalavya, and Karna are kept hidden in the sanitized versions of the stories that children are told. Above all, history as taught to children remains 'his' and not 'her' story. It remains centred around powerful male characters, primarily brahmans and kings, not about the bulk of the people and their dreams, struggles, creativity, or achievements against all odds.

Thus, language has so far been used more as a tool in the creation and maintenance of an oppressive power than an instrument to challenge and change that power. It is so because not all writers or intellectuals seek a public role or stand on the side of justice and truth. Many wordsmiths are indifferent to suffering. Some even take up the cudgels on behalf of oppressive forces. Exceptions apart, the intellectual class seldom engages in a radical critique of power, let alone siding with the weak and challenging the unjust system. We also see that when intellectuals or academics come to the point of contact with the circles of the powerful, they come not as peers but as hired or willing-to-fall-in-line experts who have no compunction in misusing their talents to devise theories and ideologies to prop up the established power.

The voices of those who dare to use knowledge ethically and humanely continue to be muzzled and muted. If knowledge is not wisdom, it is not simply because the former is just cognition but also because most knowledges about our social and political world are prejudiced and partisan. No wonder then that the objectivity of knowledge has in recent times been a subject of huge debate among conscientious intellectuals. It is good that the reality of the power–knowledge nexus is now out in the open. While some of the world's top intellectuals are known to have openly opposed or problematized the ideas of equality and justice, others have invoked truth, beauty, justice, as we shall see later in this chapter, only to justify injustice, slavery, and patriarchy! Such actions have been variously performed in the name of good sense, divinity, or the laws of nature or science. This tradition of oppressive language and knowledge has only been replenished in recent times. 'Passion and prejudice govern the world only under the name of reason,' John Wesley said.

INTELLECTUAL MYTHS, DECEPTION AND THE VIOLENCE OF BRAHMANISM

Today, the pundits in India make an expedient use of the fashionable relativist theory according to which human knowledge, truth, and morality exist only in relation to specific culture and context, and as such are neither absolute nor universal. Stretching this logic to propound that no set of social or cultural values is better or more useful than any other, caste elites normalize their caste-centric religion and culture by arguing that they are a uniquely Indian way of managing human differences. They ignore the truth, which is that the cultural values of any society are seldom random or innocent. They are not the same for rich and poor, brahman and shudra. In fact, many features of a culture are directly—causally—connected to the degree of social stratification and stage of economic development. In his suggestive study, *Hierarchy, History and Human Nature* (1988), anthropologist Donald E. Brown has debunked some of the misgivings of cultural relativism by exploring the relationship between the quality of historical writing and the degree of closure or openness in a wide range of societies. Why has, he asks, the study of history flourished in some cultures and not in others? Why did historical-mindedness develop in ancient Greece and China but not in India?

Brown points out that all societies experience stratification, but the degree of hierarchy is not the same in every society. Less hierarchical societies are more open and inclusive, with more avenues and scope for social mobility, whereas rigidly hierarchical societies are closed and conservative, where only those from the privileged families or castes are able to get ahead. In more open societies, success depends in a large measure on an individual's skills and initiatives, giving rise to an interest in history as a repository of facts and interpretations about why certain individuals succeeded and others did not. Open societies have a propensity to be interested in the accurate recording of chronology, biography, and realistic portraiture as well as a common educational philosophy, social and political science, the pace and direction of change, the shape of things to come, and, above all, belief in the idea of the universality of human nature. By contrast, closed societies—of which pre-modern and caste-dominated India is a prototype—tend to represent individuals symbolically, identifying persons through the symbols of their caste or rank rather than depicting their individual characteristics. In producing images, art and literature that are highly stylized, symbolic, and non-representational, the objective of the ruling castes in closed societies is to perpetuate illusions and mystification about society and culture, thus keeping people away from the reality of historical truth. For this reason, closed societies like India have traditionally elevated myths and legends over historical facts, hagiography over biography, iconography and symbolism over realism, superstition over rationality or science, education of the few over education of the many, and above all, casteism and sexism over humanism and egalitarianism, etc.

This explains why the brahman in India wrote only *Itihasa-Purana* (myth-history and legends), which, unlike historical narratives, are a make-believe account that conceals the reality far more than it reveals. The point is not that mythology is undesirable or inferior to history—it may not be an inferior mode of thought either, as many critical traditionalists argue—but it cannot be a substitute for history. By mixing the natural with the supernatural and fact with fiction, myths allow us to read whatever we like to read. But if a society is left only with myths, it will be well nigh impossible to understand the past—anyone could read anything into those myths. This was however the precise purpose of the brahman literati—to hide actual history and destroy as far as possible the evidence of real events and their nefarious role therein so that the truth could not be reconstructed.

In pre-modern India, the iron laws of caste gave little or no opportunity to dalits and other lowered castes to advance according to their merits. The social closure of caste was even stricter in principle than it was in actual practice. The brahman perched precariously atop the social pyramid in which the many were oppressed at the bottom had strong incentives to develop canons and constructs to justify their privileges and the others' miseries as natural or divinely designed. The surest way to do this was to propagate the idea that the perquisites of knowledge, power, and wealth were a birthright, a matter of social status rather than individual merit. This was what the pundits proclaimed and propagated. Denying the universality of human nature, they developed the notion of biological and psychological differentiation along caste and gender lines, and asserted that since people did not share the same nature, they did not deserve the same rights. The criterion of caste divisions is not 'hereditarily appointed work'; it is 'unequally divided rights' (Bougle 1991: 64). The *Manusmriti* (8. 267–8) has different punishments (dependent on caste identity of the wrong-doer) for the same crime: 'For assailing a brahman, a kshatriya ought to be fined 100 [panaas], and a vaisya 150 or 200; but a shudra ought to suffer corporal punishment. A brahman should be fined 50 for abusing a kshatriya, 25 for abusing a vaishya, and 12 for abusing a shudra' (Olivelle 2005: 181).

Classical brahmanism is also a viciously patriarchal system where the women of all castes are treated either like chattel or eternal minors to be constantly guarded by their male relatives. Malicious, misogynist expressions such as *na stri swaatantryamarhati* (women should never be given independence) and *striyo hi mool doshaanaam* (woman is the root cause of all evil) abound in the canon.

> Even in their own homes, a female—whether she is a child, a young woman, or an old lady—should never carry out any task

independently. As a child, she must remain under her father's control; as a young woman, under her husband's; and when her husband is dead, under her sons'. She must never seek to live independently. . . . Day and night men should keep their women from acting independently; for, attached as they are to sensual pleasures, men should keep them under their control. . . . A woman is not qualified to act independently. (*Manusmriti* 5.147–9, 9. 2–3, tr. Olivelle 2005: 146, 190).

There are frequent co-references to women and shudras in the literature—both are life-long slaves from birth to death. Manu and Yajnavalkya, the premier law-givers, hold that even when released from slavery they are not emancipated because slavery is inherent in them (Sharma 1983: 45–8). The anti-woman, anti-shudra epistemology is enshrined in the brahmanical sacred texts. Even truth telling is not an unconditional imperative in the brahman's book. Manu is categorical: for the sake of a brahman, falsehood is even better than truth. Thus, justice and jurisprudence were reduced to a farce. In the words of Kosambi ([1965] 1992), 'Crime and sin stand hopelessly confused, while juristic principles are drowned in an amazing mass of religious fable which offers ridiculous justification for any stupid observance'.

Above all, the privileged castes safeguarded their entitlements to the good things in life by making them hereditary: they prohibited intermarriage between individuals of different social strata. By doing so, they made a good genealogy the most prized of all assets. The self-styled highest caste traced his lineage to many mythical gods and deities. Wonderful royal (kshatriya) genealogies for the ruling feudatories and aspiring kings were concocted for a price and the promise to defend—and put in force—the caste system. The status of kshatriyahood was made mandatory for according legitimacy on kings and aspiring rulers. It was done through a ceremony *hiranya garbha* (the golden womb), representing symbolic birth into caste society, by which tribal chiefs and other casteless entities acquired kshatriya status and agreed to maintain the caste order and convert the rest of the tribe or ethnic community into a subject (shudra) peasantry (Kosambi [1965] 1992: 171). Through such guiles and frauds the caste system was institutionalized and forced on the Indian people.

This understanding gives a plausible explanation to why did the brahmans fictionalize and do not historicize their—and India's—history. It gives us the reason why they wrote all kinds of myths and legends, but no history or narrative of what had actually happened. The very origin of caste was explained through a myth in the *Purusha-sukta* of the *Rig-Veda.* The tendency to base the origin of caste on a supernatural agency, fictitious claims of descent from mythic figures and similar mythifications were essential and integral to the bigger ploy of keeping the people in the dark about how they were enslaved in the caste system. Opting for myth over history (where accurate names, facts, and chronicles are needed and understanding of the past is animated by an objective concern about what exactly happened) became necessary to hide the hideous historical truth. The literati who wrote misleading accounts kept their own identities hidden from the public eye. It is striking that most brahmanic works remain either anonymous or attributed to fictitious or false authors. Manu, for example, is not the real name of the man who wrote the *Manusmriti* (Mani 2005: 125–6).

By filling the public space with misleading stories and legends, by blurring the difference between myth and reality, the brahman destroyed the very possibility of any meaningful discussion about society and its actual functioning. In the Puranas statements about events were made in the future tense, although they were written much after the events had happened. Similar falsification–mystification are evident in the Dharmashastras, the Sanskritized epics of the *Ramayana* and the *Mahabharata,* and other sacerdotal texts in which the general design is to confuse brahmanic prescription with societal description. So fraudulently was fiction interwoven with selective facts that the anti-caste and non-brahmanic traditions, especially the Buddhist-shramanic movements, were erased, suppressed, or at the best, grossly misrepresented in some fleeting references. For example, a Puranic text depicts Ashoka, one of the most benevolent kings in history, as a hated Buddhist and a despised shudra. In brahmanic eyes, the Mauryas, the dynasty to which Ashoka belonged, was *shudra-prayastv-adharmikah*—mainly shudras and unrighteous (Thapar [1961] 1999: 12). The brahmanic records completely ignore Ashoka until the time when, ten or twelve centuries afterwards, all danger from his influence had passed away. Expunged from the Indian history, Ashoka had to be discovered on the basis of his rock edicts and the Ceylon chronicles.

Ashoka's icon, Gautam Buddha, the greatest Indian who ever walked on this earth, fared no better as the brahmanic forces tried to destroy the Buddhist ideology and movement through a criminal conspiracy and large-scale violence that stretched over centuries, as a new work has brilliantly demonstrated, showing the complicity of modern elitist historiography to hide the real history of India (Verardi 2011). When Buddhism was a strong force and Buddha a household name, the brahman tried to subsume him as one of the avatars (incarnations) of Vishnu. Buddha was an avatar but no temple or memorial was built in his honour. The objective, clearly, was to ahistorise him, and then to give a quiet burial to his memory. After a long and vicious campaign, brahmanism succeeded in banishing Buddhism from India before the marauding Turks snuffed out its flickering existence in the twelfth and thirteenth centuries. So much so that there was a raging debate among historians in the first half of the nineteenth century about the historicity of Buddha and whether he was an Indian! Buddha had to be rediscovered after centuries of forced oblivion in a country whose pundits take great pride in advertising their brilliant intellectual legacy.

Not only did the brahmans not keep any specific chronologies or sequences of events, they also destroyed the records and literature of their supposed adversaries. A group of fanatics led by Pushyamitra Shunga, a disciple of the famed grammarian Patanjali, hatched a plot and beheaded the last Mauryan king Brihadratha in 185 BCE. The period following this regicide saw the rise of militant brahmanism which indulged in a large-scale vandalism of Buddhist shrines and violence against Buddhists. It was also the period in which the pundits indulged in massive forgeries to recast Indian culture in the brahmanic mould. They suppressed facts, changed names, confused places and periods, proffered false data, created fictitious dynastic pedigrees, frequently revaluated and tampered with their Vedas and Puranas, Sanskritized the *Mahabharata* and *Ramayana*, and above all, brutally censured all oppositional voices and events.

The use of Sanskrit as the language of the rituals, and royal genealogies concocted for the ruling chiefs and aspiring kings helped create a pan-India brahman elite. These pundits, however, never showed any interest in the study and analysis of various guilds and city records that existed through the ages. Instead they created a socio-religious canon to valorize caste and sabotaged all alternative attempts of developing ethics of justice or equality:

> Indian culture lost the contributions that these numerous groups (tribal, clan, jati caste, guild, and perhaps civic) could have made. The civilizing and socializing work of the Buddha and of Asoka was never continued. The tightening of caste bonds and of caste exclusiveness threw away the possibility of finding some common denominator of justice and equity for all men regardless of class, profession, caste, and creed. As a concomitant, almost all Indian history is also obliterated. (Kosambi [1965] 1992: 173)

The genesis of Sanskrit literature is traceable to the period of brahmanic resurgence. Up to then, there had been no literary work in Sanskrit. The brahman revered Sanskrit as *devabhasha*, the sacred language of the gods, in which there was no place for profane worldly literature. Sanskrit was made a highly contrived and inflexible language, and then jealously guarded, used mainly as a vehicle of sacerdotal gobbledygook. The widely spoken and written languages in the north were Pali (in which Buddha taught) and Prakrit (the natural tongue that common people used), with their many regional varieties, while Dravidian languages were the means of communication in the south of the Vindhyas. The *Mahabharata* and *Ramayana* were long current in the Prakrits before they were rendered into Sanskrit. The epics were re-written in Sanskrit, involving translations and elaborations of Prakrit originals, in the early years before and after the beginning of the common era (Keith 1948). The portrayal of society in the Sanskritized epics is on the line of prescriptions in the Dharmashastras, for which both the reworked texts show tremendous zeal. But this is only a part of a bigger story of the Sanskritization of Indian thought and the brahmanization of Indian culture. 'There is hardly any Sanskrit composition which has not been tampered with, altered or added to by them. There is no famous *rishi* or teacher in whose name they have not concocted scriptures. There is no sacred book into which fiction and legend and imaginary history have not been interpolated' (Dharma Theertha [1941] 1992).

Tampering and tinkering with the original *Mahabharata* are evident from linguistic scrutiny. The conversion of the original heroic adventures into a sort of bible was not always cleverly done, for in the Sanskrit redactions the priestly interest overshadows the heroic, and the legends related are often distorted to suit the brahmanic viewpoint. Sidhanta, in his *Heroic Age of India* (1929), has comprehensively shown that everything is viewed from the brahman's angle, and instead of a straightforward narrative, there are many didactic digressions on the sanctity of the brahman.

Similarly, the Sanskritized *Ramayana* carries the indelible imprint of brahmanic tampering. Walker says, 'The pronounced brahmanical tone did not characterize the original work, but was given to it at the time of the revival, when much additional material was also introduced.' In the brahmanized text, to cite one example, Rama is represented as saying that those who accept the teachings of Buddha must be punished. The author has even made Rama use the word *chora* (thief) for Buddha in the *Ayodhyakanda* (Varma

1974: 297). The reference to Buddha clearly indicates that the *Ramayana* was recast in the post-Buddha period and represents a brahmanic reassertion against Buddha's anti-Vedic teachings.

Besides the epics, a great deal of secular literature in Sanskrit—poetry, the fables and the fairy tales—are translations and elaborations from Prakrit originals. The *Katha-saritasagar,* the best-known Sanskrit collection of stories, is said to have been based on an earlier work composed in Prakrit (Walker 1983, vol. 1: 364; Kosambi [1965] 1992: 203–4).

Contending that the story of forged texts in Sanskrit has yet to be written, Walker argues that the period of the brahmanical revival was the age that fixed the criterion for every subsequent interpretation of Hindu life and culture. It was at this time when the ancient Indian traditions as they existed in the regional languages were taken over, adapted to the brahmanic bias, and hammered into the new mould of Sanskrit. The earlier tomes were rendered into Sanskrit for the deification of the brahman and the damnation of all others, especially shudras and ati-shudras. The oral literature and Prakrit writings were first Sanskritized and then the whole of Sanskrit literature was brahmanized. Local and original names were altered to fit the Sanskrit alphabet; native sentiments were put through the mill of Sanskrit syntax, and a great deal of indigenous material irretrievably lost. This whole-sale change and substitution was nothing short of calamity:

> Interpretations of pre-Sanskrit and what might be called 'un-Sanskrit' life were further distorted by wilful tendentiousness that shaped into orthodox from the mythology, history and even the geography of ancient India. Its corruptions crept into the regional languages by its insistence on its own sanctity and stilted rules. And in most instances it debased what it influenced. The noble early poetry of Tamil, characterized by simplicity and realism, never recovered its freshness after contact with Sanskrit, and Tamil literature was thereafter subjected to the artificialities of the northern tongue. Practically every vernacular literature has

suffered in like manner as long as it lay under the shadow of Sanskrit influence. (Walker 1983, vol. 1: 364)

That Sanskrit monopolized the intellectual and cultural space after this period is also attested by an analysis of inscriptions. The brahmanical revival climaxed during the Gupta period (fourth to sixth centuries), after which Sanskrit elbowed out Prakrit. Prior to the Gupta age, more than 95 per cent of inscriptions were written in Prakrit and concerned non-brahmanical groups, mainly Buddhist and Jain, and only five per cent in Sanskrit concerned brahmanism.

> The position is almost entirely reversed in favour of Sanskrit and brahmanism in the post-Gupta period. The power of the priesthood must have been tremendous, almost tyrannical, to have achieved the phenomenal reversal. The number and nature of spurious inscriptions after the seventh century AD confirm the continuance of this tendency. (Walker, ibid.)

By obliterating historical facts, records and events when Buddhism opposed brahmanism, and the memories of the people—considered 'enemies' and hence lowered and ensnared in the caste hierarchy—the brahmans destroyed the possibility of a realistic understanding of what really happened. Instead, they (mis)represented India through the rigmarole of myths and legends which served the purpose of hiding the real history. Besides, Shastras and Puranas were frequently altered and rewritten over the centuries to incorporate elements (that were felt necessary for the brahmanic supremacy) that in historical terms were simply lies.

Power politics, in other words, was at the heart of the brahmanic knowledge-production. For all this, it was essential that the people lived in ignorance and remained uninformed of historical truth, even the truth of their own lives. In order to establish caste order and a religion based on it, brahmanism had to promote mass ignorance and prohibit any learning for the lowered castes and women.

It was this fear of facing the ugly reality that made many brahmanic minds profoundly distrustful of history. 'I believe',

Mohandas Gandhi wrote in his trademark didactic style, 'that a nation is happy that has no history' (Gandhi 1967: 128). He turned selectively to brahmanic narratives, stories and legends instead—but without ever encountering characters like Shambuka, Sita, Ekalavya, or Karna whose stories bring out the horrible injustices of caste and patriarchy. Instead, the upper-caste conservative that he was, he contrived to incorporate into the caste culture many beautiful elements of the folk and dalit-subaltern Bhakti traditions as well as Christian morality. To defend his right to take liberties with historical facts and events, Gandhi would quote Emerson, that consistency was the hobgoblin of foolish minds, and uphold the brahmanic mythification of India's past by asserting, 'I look upon Gibbon and Motley as inferior editions of the Mahabharata' (ibid.).

It is this supremacist arrogance that is carried forth by the neo-Gandhians like Ashis Nandy when they fulminate against Western modernity, history, and rationality (ironically with formulas, phrases, and jargons borrowed from the postmodernist scholarship in the West), presenting the brahmanic mythography as vastly superior to the Western historiography. Taking the cue from their godly Gandhi, they argue that historicizing India and Hinduism is unIndian and unHindu. They fear—and not wrongly—that 'historicizing us will destroy our India and Hinduism', as U.R. Ananthamurthy, the Kannada writer, put it in the context of the Babri mosque-Ram temple debate. Another elitist writer shows the same anxiety, arguing that eclipsing the social question is necessary for a quality intellectual discourse about the past. To assess and appreciate 'a great tradition' and create 'space for larger questions of meaning, ethics and ontology', he fatuously suggests, demand that we remain tethered to reverence—*shraddha*—for the past and self-satisfaction—*swantaha sukhay* (Mehta 2011).

The discerning reader can see that the real motive that inspires such pious thoughts in the heart of the modern pundit is to keep the socio-historical fraud of caste and brahmanism hidden from public view. They have come up with several fanciful theories to falsify the nature and agency of caste. Suffice here to say that while some more imaginative scholars see caste as a colonial construct (Dirks 2002); others accept its pre-modern existence but argue that caste was not a preconceived grand plan thought by brahman and put in practice by political power (represented by kshatriya), but a pre-brahman development in which common people were willingly and actively involved. The point is, caste may or may not have pre-brahmanic origin, but there is little doubt that caste as an archetype of social stratification was not the handiwork of those who were not its beneficiaries, namely the shudras, atishudras, and adivasis. Irrespective of its origin, caste as a system of graded hierarchy—with 'an ascending order of reverence and a descending order of contempt', to quote Ambedkar—was a brahmanic construction.

In other words, our understanding of caste will remain forever incomplete without understanding the politics of knowledge that nurtured and normalized it from the dim and distant past to the present time. In all societies, the structure of inequality is anchored in an ideology that justifies hierarchy. In India, it is brahmanism that provides the socio-religious and cultural logic of caste. Symbiotic and twinborn, one cannot grasp caste without grasping brahmanism. Caste is a system of discrimination, not mere difference, as its apologists would have us believe. Race, class, and sex—the fundamental axes of oppression in any society—are interlocked in the caste-brahmanic system which makes it a permanently organized force of domination. The salient feature of Indian culture, as they say, is 'continuity', and the main vehicle of this (discriminatory) continuity is caste. For those who have been on the receiving end of the caste order—the dalit-bahujans and their visionary leaders such as Phule, Periyar, and Ambedkar—caste is nothing but a socio-religious system that keeps the toiling majority divided, demoralized, and dehumanized for exploitation. Caste, as Ambedkar famously said, is not a division of labour but a division of labourers—into hundreds of hierarchically arranged and mutually antagonistic castes and sub-castes.

The system of caste was basically a religious hierarchy that encompassed the economic and the political. Caste was first and foremost an intellectual—and 'moral'—construction, beginning with its naturalization–sacralization in the Rig-vedic *Purusha-sukta*. The oppressor has always wielded knowledge as a psychological weapon to colonize the minds and bodies of the oppressed. Kautilya refers to this when he boasts of brahman's epistemic power to destroy his adversaries generation after generation, 'The arrow shot by the archer may or may not kill a single person. But stratagems devised by a wise man [a brahman] can kill even babes in the womb' (cited in Greene 2004: xix). Kautilya, as he emerges from the pages of myth-history, was a slimy and scheming character who never doubted the wisdom of his cruel precepts and prescriptions. But he was more than an individual; he represented the mindset of caste and brahmanism. He had a whole battalion of soulmates and supporters to assist in his epistemic conspiracy. (Some brahmanic scholars still adore him for his 'nasty but necessary' pragmatism—*we produced our own Machiavelli, a more lethal one, so long ago!*)

Discrimination was justified by the *varna dharma* (the religion of caste) with its key assertion that various castes and genders have different essences and so deserved differential treatment. The Dharmashastras are actually a manifesto of a caste-based hierarchy and exclusion (Omvedt 2003: 133). The priest-prince combine of brahman and kshatriya—the nexus of intellectual and political elites—strove over the centuries to build a patriarchal–hierarchical society, a caste–feudal political economy and an exclusionary religio-cultural establishment. It was the 'brahman precepts and kshatriya arm', to use Kosambi's phrase, that succeeded in establishing the caste system in India.

Relentless socio-religious propaganda indoctrinated the people with the values of caste, class, race, and gender, forcing them—often with political and psychological manipulation—to internalize self-oppressive norms and values. 'Slavery is inborn in shudras and women' is a common refrain in the brahmanic religious texts. To validate and normalize such slavery, the brahman literati employed everything, from divine discourse to profane arguments, often resorting to abusive expressions to demonize shudras and women. Sylvain Levi, one of the first modern scholars of the Vedic-brahmanic texts, came to this startling conclusion: 'It is difficult to imagine anything more brutal and more material than the theology of the brahmanas. Notions which usage afterwards gradually refined and clothed with a garb of morality, take us aback by their savage realism' (see Rhys Davids [1902] 1981: 240).

But Levi was rather an exception. Scholars and Sanskritists, both Indian and Western, have grossly misrepresented classical Sanskrit literature. A.K. Coomaraswamy and S. Radhakrishnan not only conceal the ascription and violence of brahmanism, they even discover unparalleled ethical and spiritual beauty in those texts. Elitist scholarship seems to be singularly dedicated to shielding the oppressive tenets and contents of brahmanic literature. When they describe or define the brahmanic—or Hindu, as they say now—socio-religious worldview, real history evaporates, actual meanings in the Sanskrit texts are marginalized or muted and what one gets is a distilled, idealized version of brahmanic religion and social order. With amazing verbal jugglery and sophistication, the brahmanic works of ancient India are hoisted as the height of ancient Indian intellectualism, even spiritualism!

The Vedic-brahmanic celebration of power and violence is usually drowned in fantastic elaboration on some stray ethical verse, didactic phrase or abstract philosophical proposition. Even the greatest of modern pundits (Gandhi,

Nehru, Radhakrishnan) and many progressive intellectuals (Amartya Sen) remain enthralled by the philosophical grandeur of brahmanic Hinduism (as we will see later in this chapter). The Upanishadic metaphysical unity of *Atman* (the self) with *Brahman* (the divine) is celebrated as the glorious Hindu spirituality without bothering to grasp how such ideals were interpreted in the real world where corruption and cruelties festered beneath the veneer. The fact that in order to identify *Atman* or *Brahman*, *Atman* has to be separated from the empirical self betrays the utter irrelevance of such ideals in actual life.

As late as the last quarter of the nineteenth century, William Logan came across the tradition of using language as a register of caste status in Malabar, Kerala. The imprint of hierarchical divisions within the society was so pervasive that it was impossible to say anything without indicating the caste relationship between the speaker and the listener. A man's deference towards those higher than himself in caste status was demonstrated in explicit verbal acknowledgements of his own inferiority: in any talk he had to degrade himself by stigmatizing whatever he possessed; convention required him to refer to his own food not simply as rice, but as 'stony or gritty rice', his money as nothing more than 'copper cash', his house as a 'dungheap'. Logan has recorded a list of words for houses that mirrors a terrible hierarchy in the society:

> The house itself is called by different names according to the occupant's caste. The house of a pariah is a *cheri*, while the agrestic slave—the Cheraman—lives in a *chala*. The blacksmith, the goldsmith, the carpenter, the weaver, etc., and the toddy-drawer (Tiyan) inhabit houses styled *pura* or *kudi*; the temple servant resides in a *variyam* or *pisharam* or *pumatham*, the ordinary Nayar in a *vidu* or *bhavanam*, while the man in authority of this caste dwells in an *idam*; the Raja lives in a *kovilakam* or *kottaram*, the indigenous Brahman (Nambudiri) in an *illam*, while his fellow of higher rank calls his house a *mana* or *manakkal*. (see Guha [1983] 1999: 42–3)

Elitist minds, however, only see the beauty of brahmanic philosophy and the 'harmony' in varnashrama dharma: which supposedly provided a peaceful principle of absorbing numerous groups within the Hindu society (see Gandhi [1934] 1993; Nehru [1946] 1996; Radhakrishnan 1962). They celebrate Hinduism for its plurality of texts, beliefs, rituals and practices (thus pointing out its superiority over the monotheistic rigidity of Islam and Christianity) without grasping that the gulf between the high and low—the 'great' and 'little'—traditions is much wider in Hinduism than in any other religion. 'Greater heterogeneity does not necessarily mean lesser toxicality. Shorter in scriptural authority, it [Hinduism] is larger in hierarchical cruelty' (Anderson 2012b). The caste elites seldom bother to unravel the *dharma*, the 'masterly moral code', and 'open the trap doors of the great monuments of ancient Hindu intellectuals' (to borrow Pandita Ramabai's phrase) and 'enter into the dark cellars' of differentiated hierarchies and social cruelties. Hindi poet Raghuvir Sahay has given expression to this blood-soaked history in his poem 'Sanskrit':

Armies kill men
then dig themselves in
and set up camp
somehow the mango tree survives.
The two armies come to an agreement
to go fight somewhere else.
The departure ceremony
takes place under that mango tree.
It was under the same tree
that they had tied up and shot
those eighteen-year old boys
from the Hindi-speaking village
who had refused to give in.
And now these wise old Sanskrit scholars have come
to sing the shastric praises of the mango tree
under that tree.

(tr. Vinay Dharvadker, see Vajpeyi 2000: 87)

Intellects Revolt Against the World's First Democracy (in Greece)

In the glory days of ancient Greece, some brilliant minds took up the challenge of systematizing the organization of knowledge—and society—in a logical way. The man who started a public debate on this—though it had a long build-up with significant contributions from earlier philosophers and poets such as Heraclitus, Xenophanes, Pythagoras, and Solon—was Socrates (*c*. 468–399 BCE). A legend in his own time, Socrates was an archetypal philosopher whose image as a relentless seeker of truth who chose hemlock poison over intellectual compromise has lingered down the ages. He brought philosophy down from the skies and asked fundamental questions of human existence. What is good? What is virtue? How should we live our lives? Through his fabled questioning and cross-questioning, he ridiculed the received ideas and attitudes and insisted on digging deeper into reality, heralding in the process a new a way of investigating the nature of things and the meaning of life. A little gruff and very ugly, this son of a stonemason charmed a city that prided itself on its cult of physical beauty—a good-looking person was thought to possess an inner nobility of spirit as well—by making the point that the noblest reason for living life was to love each other. 'What is the point of walls and warships and glittering statues if the men who build them are not happy?' He was a people's philosopher who pestered fellow citizens, forcing them to think and to account for the principles of their action.

Noble as he was, Socrates believed that 'knowledge is virtue' and 'nobody errs willingly'. Somewhat dismissive he was of the duality of knowledge and human nature. In his nobility and naivety, he allowed himself to be surrounded by a brilliant bunch of aristocratic scoundrels. Around the halo of Socratic intellectualism developed a circle of reactionary oligarchy that was out to destroy the fledgling democracy in Athens. Though the vested interests have suppressed the real story of what actually happened, Karl Popper ([1945] 2010) gives us a realistic picture of what seemed likely to have happened. Following the defeat of Athens in the Peloponnesian War (432–404 BCE), a council of thirty oligarchs assumed power at the behest of the victorious military state of Sparta. Under the leadership of Critias and Charmides, the oligarchs threw out the democratic constitution of Pericles, and unleashed a reign of terror. They hobnobbed with the Spartan rulers against their own people in order to destroy democracy. The Thirty Tyrants, as they came to be known, executed the democrats and former members of Pericles' Council. But they were overpowered in 403 BCE by the Athenian people under the leadership of Thrasybulus who reinstated the democratic constitution. It was under this regime that Socrates perished, held guilty of the curious crime of denying the state gods, introducing new divinities and corrupting youth, as reported in many accounts, including the one by Diogenes Laertius (Popper, ibid.; Stone 1988).

The real reason for Socrates' condemnation was political. The actual meaning behind 'denying the state gods' and 'poisoning the minds of youth' was the accusation of undermining the Athenian democracy by educating some of the most pernicious enemies of the state. Although not personally involved with the excesses of the Thirty, his circle indeed included Critias and Charmides, both uncles of Plato and frontline leaders of the anti-democratic gang, as well as Alcibiades, a close ally of Critias, who even defected to Sparta to give logistic information and advice against Athens, and some other figures of strong anti-democratic tendencies. Among Socrates' followers was Xenophon, the ace conservative writer-warrior, who had eventually settled in Sparta. The aim of the Athenian democrats was to disengage Socrates from this gang—and at the most to exile him—but this plan was defeated by the philosopher who refused to compromise. 'He had never intended to undermine democracy. . . . Had he seized it, and become an exile, everybody would have thought him an opponent of democracy. . . . Socrates' death is the ultimate proof of his sincerity' (Popper [1945] 2010: 207). Orator Aeschines, speaking in 345 BCE, informs us that Socrates was punished because of his association with Critias, a poet and intellectual but the archenemy of democracy.

The man who became famous as Plato was Critias' sister's son and a disciple of Socrates. Full of filial fervour, Plato imbibed visceral hatred for democracy from his uncle Critias. But before we come to Plato's politics and philosophy—centred around an iron state under philosopher-kings who will banish poets, purge dissenters and dominate the life of the citizen from the mating of his parents to his grave—and his betrayal of Socrates, it would be in order to understand the intellectual and political climate of the time.

For several reasons, Athens in the fifth century BCE had emerged as a unique centre of arts, culture and politics. The literary greats of the period (which witnessed the transition from an oligarchic to a democratic government) included the serious writer Euripides and the comic dramatist Aristophanes. To this Great Age belonged the classic conservatives such as playwright Sophocles and historian Thucydides. The outsider historian Herodotus was welcomed in Pericles' city as the author of a work that hailed its democratic politics and principles. The sophist Protagoras and the scientist Democritus, both natives of Abdera, became influential in Athens during this time for their doctrine that language, customs, and laws were human institutions, not natural or magical (as people created them and were responsible for them). Then there was the school of Gorgias led by Alcidamas, Lycophron and Antisthenes who developed the tenets of anti-slavery and a universal unity of humanity. Misrepresented and maligned, the Gorgias became an eyesore to the aristocratic class for their insistence that the greatest criminals were always 'men who come from the class which possesses power.' And, then came Socrates who celebrated human reason but cautioned against dogmatism, insisting that the true spirit of knowledge was rationalism and fair criticism.

Towering above them was Pericles, the statesman of the Athenian democracy, who formulated the principle of equality before the law. But the democratic movement had begun well before Pericles with an imaginative leader called Solon (*c.* 630–560 BCE), who was brought into power at a critical juncture when the class-divided Athenian society was facing an acute crisis. The farming class, the bulk of the population, was neck-deep in debt to an aristocratic and oppressive business class. With one bold stroke, Solon, who was also a poet of rare imagination and sensitivity, cancelled the debts, thus reactivating the citizenry.

> It was a revolution because it clearly demonstrated the precedence of citizen rights over contractual rights. At the same time it was a prudent revolution. Solon *broke the chains*—those were his words and he was Athens's leading poet—but he did so in a way which did not bankrupt the business class. (Saul 2004: 31–2)

Solon accorded respect to individual choices but pressed the point that greed and self-interest had to be restrained in the wider public interest. He said that ethics is a public matter, and when it is given a go by, 'public evil enters the house of each man' (ibid.: 65). Despite this wisdom, and the setting free of some slaves by Solon, Athenian democracy did not ban slavery. The assemblies were banned to slaves, but they did include free poor, commoners and peasants who used the democracy to limit the power of the ruling class (Ste Croix 1997). The presence of commoners and their concerns in the assemblies was significant. Hence the debates between aristocrats and commoners; hence the fear of the multitude evinced by the aristocracy (as we will see shortly). Hence Solon's claims of the fair deal for everyone.

This legacy was carried forward by Democritus and Pericles, two major figures of the Athenian democracy after Solon. Democritus, a leading materialist thinker of his time, is renowned for the statement 'I would rather find a single causal law than be the king of Persia.' Besides the structure of nature, he was concerned with the problem of knowledge and of human conduct and social organization. A scientist and an early champion of democracy, he put forward paradigmatic ideas of equality and universalism against the closed walls of monarchy and aristocracy:

> Not out of fear but out of a feeling of what is right should we abstain from doing wrong.
>
> Virtue is based, most of all, upon respecting the other man.
>
> Every man is a little world of his own.
>
> We ought to do our utmost to help those who have suffered injustice.
>
> It is good deeds, not words, that count.
>
> The poverty of a democracy is better than the prosperity which allegedly goes with aristocracy or monarchy, just as liberty is better than slavery.
>
> The wise man belongs to all countries, for the home of a good soul is the whole world. (see Popper [1945] 2010: 198)

The superior qualities of democracy and equality were best articulated by Pericles, who held that liberty and order, excellence and equality, individualism and public responsibility are compatible and ought to be blended in the common interest of all citizens. Contrasting the democratic vision with the closed mentality of oligarchic Sparta, he told the Athenians that debate and discussion, even doubt and dissent, would make them better and bolder. His Funeral Oration—delivered in honour of the Athenians who fell fighting Sparta during the first year of the Peloponnesian War—remains unsurpassed as an exposition of democratic ideal. In one of the most important speeches in history, he asserts that if all citizens cannot legislate or cannot provide creative leadership, all of them are able and expected to debate the public policy:

> Our constitution does not copy the laws of our neighbouring states, rather we try to be an example to others. Our government favours the many instead of the few: this is why it is called a democracy. Here, everyone is equal before the law; everyone is entitled to

justice. Positions in the government are a reward of merit, not a matter of privilege; we choose persons for public responsibility by their ability and excellence, not by their class background. No one who possesses merit is kept in political obscurity because of poverty. And, just as our political life is free and open, so is our day-to-day life in our relations to each other. . . . We are free and tolerant in our private lives; but we obey the laws, especially those which are for the protection of the oppressed; and we also obey those unwritten laws whose sanction lies only in the universal feeling of what is right. . . . Our city is thrown open to the world; we never expel a foreigner. . . . We love beauty without indulging in the fancies, and although we try to improve our intellect, this does not weaken our will. . . . To admit one's poverty is no disgrace with us; but we consider it disgraceful not to make an effort to avoid it. An Athenian citizen does not neglect public affairs when attending to his private business. . . . We consider a man who takes no interest in the state not as harmless, but as useless; and although only a few may originate a policy, we are all able to judge it. We do not look upon discussion as a stumbling block in the way of political action, but as an indispensable preliminary to acting wisely. (Thucydides [431 BCE] 1954, book 2, Chapters 37 and 38)

This speech leaves little doubt that democracy was at the heart of the Greek debate of the time, and that all Athenians did not support it. (Pericles' statement also explains, why those who shunned public life and public affairs were labelled *idiotes* in Athens—from which we have got the word idiot.) Whereas Pericles claimed the Athenian democracy was an example for all of Greece, its opponents dismissed it as a rule by the mob and instead craved the Sparta-type oligarchic dictatorship. This is borne by a famous pamphlet *On the Constitution of the Athens*, whose unknown author is now commonly known as the 'Old Oligarch'. Of an uncertain date, what is certain about this pamphlet—a bitter, sarcastic, but brilliant diatribe against democracy—is that it was written in the early years of the Peloponnesian War in response to Pericles' Funeral Oration. The gist of its tirade is that democracy gives the 'advantage to rascals, the poor, and the worst elements' rather than 'the rich and good citizens', which is why 'in every land the best element is opposed to democracy' and 'the worst element in every state favours democracy—on the principle that like favours like.' One of its keynotes is to establish somehow the connection between the Athenian democracy and its naval imperialism, and attacking it for the same. Its main target, however, is to demoralize and wean away those non-commons who were on the side of democracy:

> I pardon the commons itself its democracy, for it is pardonable that everyone should seek his own interest. But the man who is not of the commons yet chose to live in a democratic rather than in an oligarchic state sought opportunity for wrongdoing, and realized that it was more possible for his wickedness to go unnoticed in a democratic state than in an oligarchic. (see Bailkey 1987: 174–8; Carroll 1969: 83–5)

The Old Oligarch reflects the viewpoint of those Athenians who wanted to establish an oligarchic government in Athens with the help of Sparta. 'The extreme pettiness of this representative of the oligarchical faction is, perhaps, a minor piece of evidence as to why the Athenian oligarchies established in 411 and 404 were both short-lived and why the Athenians even after the Peloponnesian War preferred to maintain their democratic way of life' (Carroll 1969: 83).

The Old Oligarch, as Popper suggests, was no other than Critias, but more notably he makes the point that the pamphleteer was not an individual but an anti-democracy elitist mindset that has prevailed since then to our own time.

> This ingenious pamphlet, the oldest extant treatise on political theory, is, at the same time, perhaps the oldest monument of the desertion of mankind by its intellectual leaders. . . . Its central idea . . . is the close connection between naval imperialism and democracy. . . . The remarkable pamphlet was to become the first of a practically infinite sequence of works on political philosophy which were to repeat more or less, openly or covertly, the same theme down to our own day. (Popper [1945] 2010: 200)

Philosophy's Perversion: Platonic-Aristotelian Betrayal of Humanity

Plato (429–347 BCE) and his disciple Aristotle (384–322 BCE) came from patrician backgrounds—Plato's favourite uncle Critias (as we saw) was the most notorious enemy of the Athenian democracy—and their philosophy carried the anti-plebeian prejudice of their class. They broke with the popular practice of Socrates who taught in the streets for free, and set up their exclusive schools. Plato founded the Academy and Aristotle his Lyceum for the chosen few, to groom them into a new class of educated elite, the best of whom would be what Plato called the philosopher-kings. The first in the Western world to institutionalize education in the elitist mould, they came up with a new conception of politics in which power was to be combined with knowledge and vice versa, thus pioneering the school that aimed at turning knowledge into a privilege and a tool of social control. Like Socrates, they, too, championed philosophy against the sophistry of rhetoric and mere opinion but their power politics led them to formulate what was essentially a philosophical justification of hierarchy and slavery.

Among the first to use the words *Philosophy*, *Academy*, and *Symposium*, Plato and Aristotle discovered the truth that intellectual contemplation—reflection on the meaning of existence and the nature of things—was in itself superior to action. By creating this gratuitous hierarchy as if our thought is inaction or our action has nothing to do with our thought, they discounted the reality that one acquires knowledge by intelligent action, and that the knowledge thus acquired enables one to act more intelligently. What Plato overlooked, as John Dewey points out, is that 'there is no such thing as genuine knowledge and fruitful understanding except as the offspring of *doing*' and that 'knowledge furnishes the means of understanding . . . what is to be done' (see Cahn 1970: 201). However, 'discovering' the superiority of knowledge over action helped them to reach a set of foregone conclusions. No sooner did they discover this truth than they turned it into a self-serving lie, arguing that since those who possess knowledge represent the best of the human race, the rest should assist and follow the former. Plato (with his construction of authoritarian philosopher-kings) and Aristotle (with his assertion that 'man is by nature a political animal') insisted that the precious life of the chosen few required a particular kind of politics—one that supplied them with a number of enslaved men and women to do the menial and domestic chores so that they could pursue the life of excellence. Thus, the superhuman life of aristocrats required the subhuman life of slaves and the working class. Slaves and subjected women were made to labour for aristocrats but labouring was in Aristotle's view, 'the meanest, because the body is the most deteriorated'. In this way, the superiority of the intellectual life was bound to a contempt for labour and to the evil of slavery and women's subjection. Morality, justice and truth were to be defined and based on this oppressive ideology.

Plato gave the philosophical lead for this power politics. Far from being apolitical or disinterested, as Karl Popper says, 'the philosopher-king is Plato himself, and the Republic is Plato's own claim for kingly power'. Derrida has explained it brilliantly:

> Plato excludes the possibility of realizing an ideal state as long as philosophers do not reign over it, as long as the kings and sovereigns, the 'dynasts' who dispose of power are not philosophers—that is as long as *philosophia* is not bound to political power: in other words as long as justice (which must be distinguished from law) is not bound to power, as long as justice is not one with force. (See Glendinning 2011: 88)

That is why Plato and Aristotle wax philosophical on virtue and justice, and yet glorify a chosen and self-perpetuating elite entitled to subjugate workers and commoners. Behind the veneer of their philosophical sorcery that to this day mesmerizes many as a unique model of a society of individuals unified by a shared purpose, they indulged in an elitist essentialism—a hierarchical foundationalism—as they theorized knowledge to give an intellectual-moral legitimacy to the idea of social exclusion. For them, people's rights were not only nonsense but also a dangerous recipe for anarchy and violence. With a cold-blooded apathy to common people, their fundamental vision was anti-democratic and their metaphysics and epistemology reflect and encourage hierarchy and oppression.

In their ideal state—represented in Plato's *Republic* ([c. 380 BCE] 1957) and Aristotle's *Politics* ([c. 350 BCE] 1992)—everyone would perform what was appropriate to their 'essential' nature. The gist of their logic goes like this: by nature some beings command (as they are superior—and qualified to be governors) and others obey (as they are inferior—and prone to slavery), so if people of all classes and sexes adhere—of their own accord or by force—to their work according to their inherent nature, society will be healthy and harmonious. With everyone excelling in his or her natural or fixed function, there would be social equilibrium and justice where the interest of master and slave would be identical. On the other hand, equality among people would lead to contention, dissension, and bloody democracy. Thus social hierarchy alone would engender permanent civil order and harmony. According to this logic, education and excellence are a class prerogative, and to quote Popper, *justice is inequality*.

Plato's extraordinary literary gifts helped him write in a captivating style. With the poetry, the eloquence, the metaphysics of which he was a master, Plato's real agenda was to establish that justice is hierarchy and he sought to institutionalize it. The dialogic style of *Republic* betrays the truth that first Plato persuaded himself against democracy and freedom, so that it became easy for him to persuade others. Plato's is a classic case of self-deception turned into mass deception with the help of intellectual power.

He charmed all intellectuals with his brilliance, flattering and thrilling them by his demand that the learned should rule. Although arguing against justice he convinced all righteous men that he was its advocate. . . . Plato thus became, unconsciously, the pioneer of many propagandists who, often in good faith, developed the technique of appealing to moral, humanitarian sentiments, for anti-humanitarian, immoral purposes. (Popper [1945] 2010: 212–13)

To discredit democracy, Plato uses Socrates as his mouthpiece for the *Republic* even after departing so widely from his teaching. He misrepresented the meaning of Socrates' death. Socrates, we are made to believe, criticized the multitude as well as the leaders of democracy for their lack of wisdom; he wanted the enlightened, the wise to rule; and so he was killed by democracy. Plato knew that he was betraying Socrates.

Plato's continuous efforts to make Socrates reinterpret himself are at the same time Plato's efforts to quiet his own bad conscience. By trying again and again to prove that his teaching was only the logical development of the true Socratic doctrine, he tried to persuade himself that he was not a traitor. (Popper [1945] 2010: 208–10)

The poor Socrates is made to propound the caste theory by arguing that human groups were of varying worth and could be categorized like different metals. The ideal state would have three classes: guardians, led by philosopher-kings; soldiers; and workers, peasants, and other commoners (virtual slaves). Although Plato facetiously maintains that membership in the royal and military classes should be based solely upon the possession of appropriate skills, he presumes that future rulers would typically be the offspring of those who presently hold power. If the people express any resentment against their servile roles, he suggests that the servile class be told the *useful falsehood*, the *noble lie* that God fashioned human beings like diverse metals, allotting them different natures that fit each of them to a particular function within the operation of the society as a whole. The god who fashioned all people 'mixed gold in the composition' of those people who were to rule and 'put silver in the guardians, and iron and brass in the farmers and craftsmen' (Plato [380 BCE]

1957; Popper [1945] 2010: 149). These metals—the metaphors for racial characteristics—are hereditary, implying that by nature some would be rulers and others servile and that this would provide the basis for a just society.

Plato's philosopher-kings are brilliantly educated and enlightened. They would provide people with an education of sorts but much of this schooling will be lies and falsehood to keep them in their proper place. In a hideous travesty of his proposition (put of course in the mouth of Socrates) that philosophers are those who love truth, Plato declares that it is one of the royal privileges of the sovereign to make use of deceit: 'It is the business of the rulers of the city, if it is anybody's, to tell lies, deceiving both its enemies and its own citizens for the benefit of the city; and no one else must touch this privilege' (Plato [380 BCE] 1957: 86–7; Popper [1945] 2010: 146). The banal justification is a collective utility—'the benefit of the city'.

In other words, Plato's principle of predestined specialization becomes the justification for a chosen and self-perpetuating elite whose business will be to 'administer a great many lies and deception' to maintain the republic. (The English 'Republic' for Plato's Greek word which only means a State or a City State is itself a fabrication of translators.) The metaphor of the four metals (gold, silver, iron and copper) comes tantalizingly close to the four-fold caste division in ancient India. Like the propagandists of caste, 'Plato saw each quality as belonging to a different political class: reason for the guardians, the elite; courage for the soldiers; sensual appetite for the farmers and artisans' (Saul 2004: 11).

Similarly, Plato's philosopher-king bears a close resemblance to the brahmanic concept of *rajarshi*, the Sanskrit for the king-philosopher. Like the brahmanic paranoia about admixtures of castes leading to social chaos and loss of power for the elite (visualized in the dreaded *kali yuga*), Plato, too, is paranoid about miscegenation. He warns against possibility of admixtures between metals and corresponding changes in status in the story of the Fall of Man: 'Iron will be mixed with silver and bronze with gold, and inequality and inharmonious discrepancy will arise, results which always produce war and strife whenever they occur' (Plato [380 BCE] 1957: 299; Popper [1945] 2010: 149–50). Plato makes the prophecy that 'the city must perish when guarded by iron [shudra] and copper [vaishya].'Therefore, he suggests that every effort should be made towards widening the gulf between the governors and governed. The stronger the feeling that the ruled are a different and altogether inferior race, the deeper will be the sense of unity among the rulers.

Also striking is Plato's cynical exploitation of religion to persuade the common people into submission. As with the brahman, for him too, religion is nothing but a fabrication of the ruling class to subjugate the masses. He wants the guardians to use lies and myths for brainwashing the people so that they can never dream of thinking independently. They will propagate the fiction that the gods have made men of different metals (castes) and that each should know and keep his place. Make-believe tales, Plato suggests, should also be created to induce women to have sex with the guardians. This is in the context of his proposal that the guardians should not marry. The latter should also secretly fix the ballots that allot mating partners in order to bring forth the best children. Like dictators of all ages, he wanted to determine the whole life of all citizens, not only during war but also in peace, and from the earliest childhood on:

> The greatest principle of all is that nobody, whether male or female, should ever be without a leader. Nor should the mind of anybody be habituated to letting him do anything at all on his own initiative; neither out of zeal, nor even playfully. But in war and in the midst of peace—to his leader he shall direct his eye and follow him faithfully. And even in the smallest matter he should stand under leadership. For example, he should get up, or move, or wash, or take his meals . . . only if he has been told to do so. In a word, he should teach his soul, by long habit, never to dream of acting independently, and to become utterly incapable of it. There is no law, nor will there ever be one, which is superior to this. (Plato, tr. Popper [1945] 2010: 109)

Can any idea be more opposed to J.S. Mill's classic defence of individual freedom: 'Over himself, over his own body and mind, the individual is sovereign.' Not only commoners but writers and poets, too, will be strictly monitored and censored in his ideal state. The rulers' duty would be to keep a close eye on all authors and force them to fall in the officially approved line of right and wrong, aesthetic and unaesthetic.

> Our first duty . . . is to set a watch over the makers of stories . . . [and] we shall have to throw away most of the stories they tell now. . . . The fights of the giants and the other many and varied strifes of gods and heroes with kinsfolk and friends must not be told . . . the poets must be compelled to make [agreeable and approved] stories.
>
> (Plato [380 BCE] 1957: 71–4)

In the last part of the *Republic*, Plato declares, 'we shall expel poetry from the city' (p. 387).

Plato's description of democracy, like the Old Oligarch's, is vivid but an intensely hostile parody of the political life of Athens, which we find in Pericles' funeral speech. Of the five forms of government—aristocracy, timocracy, plutocracy, democracy and despotism—Plato dislikes democracy the most. To him, when the poor wage war on the propertied classes and win, the result is democracy. Though there is a difference, democracy, he says, inevitably leads to despotism. He considers the transition from aristocracy to democracy and despotism a step-by-step decline in the quality of the state, corresponding to a gradual deterioration of the moral character of the rulers and the ruled. Democracy is most odious for its principle of equality and freedom for everyone—even the dogs in a democracy, he mocks, exhibit equality and freedom by refusing to move out of the way in streets. A democratic ruler is a tyrant because he is 'full of promises to the individual and to the public; he grants release from debts, distributes lands to the public and to his party, and pretends to be gracious and good-natured to all' (Plato [380 BCE] 1957: 329). Liberty and free speech are rife everywhere; anyone is allowed to do what he likes. All such equality and freedom, he says, stem from a soul whose order has been shattered.

Identifying liberty with lawlessness, freedom with license, and equality before law with disorder, Plato succeeded in turning many brilliant minds against democracy, and 'we may wonder how much damage his poisonous writing has done when presented, unopposed, to lesser minds' (Popper [1945] 2010: 42).

The popular image, however, is of Plato as a benevolent philosopher and a Christian before Christ. Take this typical textbook glorification of Plato and his philosophy:

> Plato went beyond his master [Socrates], asserting the existence of universal truths (the Platonic Ideas), and upon them constructed a philosophical system. Known as idealism, this system has exerted an incalculable influence on the history of Western philosophy and religion. . . . Platonists are born and not made, and Plato himself tells us . . . that it will be understood and accepted only by 'some few who are able with a little teaching to find it out for themselves.' [It] . . . is founded upon the belief that the things that are seen are temporal, whereas the things that are not seen are eternal. . . . The senses inform us about what is unreal and imperfect, while only the reason, identified by Plato with the soul, can grasp what is perfect and eternal. Confronted by these two worlds, the task of man is to follow the dictates of his reason—or soul—and concern himself as far as possible with the higher and real world, the world of thought or spirit. . . . [His idealism notwithstanding] Plato was essentially a practical philosopher whose theories were intended both to serve as goal posts along the road whose goal is the good life for man, and to inspire men to create a state in which that life could be lived.
>
> (Bailkey 1987: 204-5)

Aristotle followed his master, as closely as his temperament permitted, and if we leave aside superficial differences between them, his political and philosophical outlook was entirely dominated by Plato's. Much is made of Plato's idealism and Aristotle's empiricism, but that does not obstruct them from coming together to uphold a racist-casteist view of society. Aristotle systematized Plato's theory of hierarchy by arguing that nature follows orderly, discoverable laws, and humans, though special, are part of the natural order and behave according to nature's laws. Asserting that everything was defined according to its inherent powers and effects, he applied this understanding to uphold slavery and patriarchy. As he observed an acorn becoming an oak, a slave doing manual work, a woman giving birth to and raising a child, he jumped to the conclusion that slaves were made by nature for slavery and girls become women in order to procreate and take care of domestic chores. Since slaves were toiling in the field, and women working in the kitchen, that was all they were meant to be. Women's inferiority was evident to Aristotle because he believed that men had more teeth than women! He believed this because with horses the stallion has more teeth than the mare. (He was married twice but presumably never asked his wives to open their mouths to have their teeth counted.)

Aristotle discounts the idea that individuals are free to be whatever they choose to be, stressing instead that some men are born to rule whereas most men and all women are slaves by nature. Slaves and women, unfit by nature for any intellectual or governing work, are not citizens in the Aristotelian world. As he writes in *Politics*, 'Someone who, being a man, belongs by nature not to himself but to someone else is a slave by nature. He belongs to someone else if, being a man, he is an article of property—and an article of property is an instrument which aids the actions of and is separable from its owner.' On such arguments, he upholds slavery, patriarchy and unequal social relations. Starting with the structure of the household, Aristotle puts property-owning man (husband and master) in charge of his wife (production and reproduction), children (potentialities), and slaves (animate objects used as instruments). The household provides the model by which the larger social structures and the state are to be organized and developed (Aristotle [350 BCE] 1992).

Plato and Aristotle were different kinds of idealists who justified, in contrasting idioms, social stratification as the prime requisite for a civil order. Plato was a sort of aristocratic communitarian who wanted to separate power from property since he feared that material possession and wealth would lead to conflict and dissension among the ruling class. In his ideal state, the guardians would have great power but common property, and there would be common ownership of women and children as well to avoid disunity. But only babies born from approved mating would be allowed to survive! No parent would know his own child, nor any child his parent. Children would be raised, not by individual parents, but by the state. All the elite men and women will live together, sharing their property and their bodies (Plato [380 BCE] 1957: 181–2). On the contrary, Aristotle was a hardcore individualist and an ardent advocate of private property. He thought that the property-owning class should enjoy their wealth and rule with an iron hand. But both feared and hated people's democracy as the worst of all political systems, agreeing on an authoritarian state under the control of the chosen few.

To be fair to Plato and Aristotle, it must be said that they read like philosophers while the brahman authors like Manu and Kautilya read like propagandists. The brahman would fatuously insist that mere humans cannot mess with their inherent superiority as it was divinely designed. A well-known verse of Manu reads, 'Whether he is learned or not, a brahman is a great deity . . . Even if they engage in every undesirable act, brahmans should be honoured in every way; for they are the highest deity' (*Manusmriti* 9: 317–19, tr. Olivelle 2005: 206). Compared to India's vulgar pundits, the Greek philosophers developed their theories of social stratification on a purple philosophical plane—and in much mellowed terms. Unlike the brahman literati, they did not use abusive terms like *rakshasa, chandala, shudra*, or *achhuta* for the commoner. Unlike the former, they gave an air of philosophical detachment. Despite these differences and superior quality of their works, Plato and Aristotle shared with the brahman a hierarchical view of life, which went on to become the dominant paradigm of the Western civilization for two millennia. Like the brahman, both Plato and Aristotle concealed the nexus between power, property and knowledge, and the fact that they were man-made. In their philosophies, power justified itself by pointing to powerlessness in the subjugated, as proof of an innate inferiority. Both ignored the social forces and cultural power that moulded people into one role or another, and provided a justification of that power in nature. No wonder, in subsequent centuries, their philosophies provided a standard to the entrenched interests to justify hierarchy and exclusion. Their lasting legacy, like the legacy of brahmanism in India, is the reification of human hierarchy.

> For Aristotle, the great philosopher of the classical period, reared to accept slavery and pursue self-centredness, the Greek was human. The European barbarians were not human, because they were unskilled; nor were Asians human, because they lacked strength and character; women were not human either; women were halfway human and children were only potentially human. The human being par excellence is the free man of the polis of Hellas. (Enrique Dussel, quoted by Soccio 2001: 186)

Aristotle trained the Macedonian king's son, later known as Alexander the Great, to be a philosopher-king in the manner of Plato's dream. Alexander is reputed to have enjoyed the company—and advice—of philosophers even in midst of his military campaigns. And he shed more blood than any of his contemporary rulers. And what kind of political leaders—philosopher-kings—did Plato nurture at his Academy? Apart from the fact that Plato travelled to Italy at least three times to teach Dionysius the Elder, tyrant of Syracuse in Sicily, many of his students turned out to be murderers, some of whom even killed their fellow philosopher-kings! (Popper [1945] 2010: 144–5). Yet the moral philosophy and the scientific tradition of Western civilization are essentially the achievements of Plato's thought (Stumpf 1993: 47). Platonists, John Saul (2004: 161) says, are 'the eternal governing party of Western civilization.'

Reductionism of Science, Social Darwinism and Enlightenment

Emperors go, but empires remain. If we leave aside the superficialities, there is little difference between the old Platonic-brahmanic ideology of hierarchy and the new pseudo-science of Social Darwinism that links evolutionary ideas to social inequality. In their essence, both are based on the assumption that different castes or races differ genetically—fundamentally—in their abilities and inclinations. Such innate differences create the conditions of inequality in the human world, which is not just natural but desirable too, according to their logic. Several of the world's top minds have over the centuries produced and promoted diverse forms of supremacist ideologies such as brahmanism, Platonism or Social Darwinism by cunningly intermixing nature, knowledge, and politics. In India, Manu, Kautilya, Kumarila Bhatta, Shankar, Dayananda Saraswati, Bal Gangadhar Tilak, Vinayak Damodar Savarkar, and in the West, Plato, Aristotle, Machiavelli, David Ricardo, Herbert Spencer, Thomas Huxley, Arthur de Gobineau and Friedrich Nietzsche, despite apparent intellectual differences among them. Hundreds of other intellectuals—some of them better hidden under their better-formulated ideas—came one way or the other to support different brands of Social Darwinism. The essentials in their ideations are unmistakable—in intellectual-biological development of humanity, hierarchy is inevitable. The weaknesses of the weak, the poverty of the poor, the oddity of the alien are either their own fault, or a law of nature, or a curse of God.

Herbert Spencer, an early cheerleader of ethnic cleansing, wrote that suppression of the inferior is simply the nature's way of ensuring 'the survival of the fittest'. He coined this phrase ten years before the publication of Darwin's *Origin of the Species* in 1859 (Dickens 2002: 19). Arguing that the poor were undeserving of life, he wrote, 'The whole effort of nature is to get rid of such [the unfit, the poor], to clear the world of them, and make room for better' (see Hofstadter 1944: 5, 41). The doctrine that the weak has to suffer or die so that the strong can thrive came to be known as Social Darwinism after Darwin's evolutionary theory. Though Darwin's work highlighted not only the cruelty in nature but also the common ancestry of humankind and the fact that 'only those species survived which collaborated and improvised', many of his supporters such as Spencer, Huxley and Bagehot brazenly applied the evolutionary theory to justify natural inequality: to ideas of race superiority, military warfare, and national mission.

Social Darwinism was based on two key assumptions. The first was that there are underlying and unstoppable forces acting in the human world which are like the natural forces that operate in natural or plant communities. The second assumption was that our social and economic laws are, or ought to be, like natural laws to produce evolutionary progress. Its gist is best represented in the words of a Russian sociologist who became, ironically, a peace activist in his later life:

> Since societies are organisms, one can deduce a priori that they will conform to all the laws of biology. . . . Nature is a vast field of carnage. Between living creatures conflict takes place every second, every minute, without truce and without respite. It takes place first between separate individuals, then between collective organisms, tribe against tribe, state against state, nationality against nationality. No cessation is possible. Living means fighting. . . . This subordination of the less fit individual and collective organisms to the more fit, this is justice in nature: an incorruptible but implacable justice which knows no pity, but which gives to each with absolute impartiality the place due to its merits. It is the struggle for existence which determines this place. If one animal is less perfect than another, he must serve as prey. If one society is less perfect than another, the first must work for the second. (J. Novicow, quoted in Langer 1992: 554)

The Darwinists saw themselves as high priests of an omnipotent science, and tried to convince the losers in the evolutionary race that there was no perversity in their oppression or destruction since their life was worthless—and it was all part of the natural law. Likewise, their message to the kind-hearted: don't mess with the evolutionary process; allow the deserving—the superior—to make mincemeat of the inferior to ensure human progress. 'If we do not like the survival of the fittest', argued a leading Social Darwinist in the US, 'we have only one possible alternative, and that is survival of the unfittest. The former is the law of civilization; the latter is the law of anti-civilization' (William Graham Summer, cited in North 1976: 61). Some of them openly applied the evolutionary theory to justify violence and war. The discovery of humanity's common ancestry with animals provided such psychopaths a wonderful means of justifying their murderous intentions and actions. Though Spencer and Bagehot, while glorifying the achievements of war in the past, hoped that in the future the struggle for existence might be restricted to intellectual and economic spheres, there was no dearth of Darwinists who went on to popularize the idea that physical combat and battlefields were evolutionary necessities to decide the best in human civilization.

Ernest Renan, the French historian and philosopher, who discarded the supernatural element in the life of Jesus in his eponymous 1863 work, found solace in this way: 'War is in a way one of the conditions of progress, the cut of the whip which prevents a country from going to sleep, forcing satisfied mediocrity itself to leave its apathy' (see Langer 1992: 556). The argument was made that as political and economic struggle raises the best to leadership in the domestic domain, in the global arena, war and bloodbath separate the degenerate races or nationalities from the strong, thus benefiting the human species. Lester Ward wrote in a 1905 discussion of war, 'When races stop struggling, progress ceases' (see North 1976: 64).

Debate continues because the difference between Darwinism and Social Darwinism is not as dramatic as is commonly assumed. Evidence accumulates to show that Darwin himself tended to blur the difference, and as Fernandez-Armesto contends, Darwin was not 'the embodiment of disinterested science'. Neither was his discovery strikingly his own—the theory of evolution was in the air of his day. Other naturalists were on the track of natural selection or had reached the idea on their own. Alfred Russel Wallace put forward the theory of evolution independently at about the same time in the 1850s when Darwin was published (Bronowski 1973: 291–308). The important thing, however, is not that Wallace was as much the discoverer of the evolution theory as Darwin, but the fact that the doctrine of natural selection was never meant to be an all-encompassing explanation of how evolution works. Thomas Huxley, who took pride in describing himself as Darwin's bulldog, never believed in natural selection. 'Darwin himself was barely faithful to it, at times preferring "sexual selection"—the elimination of unfavoured types in the joust for mates—as the "main agent" of evolutionary change' (Fernandez-Armesto 1995: 456). In his later writings, especially in *The Descent of Man* (1871), Darwin laid extra emphasis on sexual selection: intelligence and muscular power was developed particularly among males. Sexual selection, for Darwin, accounted for the physical differences of races (Dickens 2002: 18). Darwin spoke with approval of the savage custom of eliminating the weak, so that only the strong would survive: 'we civilized men do our utmost to check the process of elimination':

> With savages the weak in body or mind are soon eliminated, and those that survive commonly exhibit a vigorous state of health. We civilized men, on the other hand, do our utmost to check the process of elimination; we build asylums for the imbecile, the maimed, and the sick; we institute poor laws; and our medical men exert their utmost skill to save the life of every one to the last moment. There is reason to believe that vaccination has preserved thousands who from a weak constitution would formerly have succumbed to smallpox. Thus the weak members of civilized society propagate their kind. . . . The aid which we feel impelled to give to the helpless is mainly an incidental result of the instinct of sympathy, which was

originally acquired as part of the social instincts, but subsequently rendered, in the manner previously indicated, more tender and more widely diffused. . . . We must therefore bear the undoubtedly bad effects of the weak serving and propagating their kind. (Darwin [1871], quoted in Tierney 1992: 560)

Though his admirers hotly contest it, Darwin himself, as the paragraph above shows, was prone to blurring the divide between 'scientific' and 'social' Darwinism. A product of the time when the empire's sun was shining bright, Darwin's science served the interests of a particular race and class by giving credence to the theory of the White Man's Burden.

Various forms of oppressive practice appeared on the stage of history prior to the modern period, but none of them had had such crushing support from science. Darwin's science proved to be the nub around which the new supremacist theories were woven, aided and abetted by the matching ideas emanating from the fields of biology, and the newly founded disciplines of sociology and anthropology. Spencer theorized his brand of Darwinism in *The Study of Sociology*, which had a notable impact on the rise of this new discipline. Likewise, the French aristocrat Gobineau saw the key to history and civilization in race and 'worked out a ranking of human races in which Aryans come out on top and Blacks at the bottom'. In his four-volume work on the inequality of human races, published in Paris between 1853 and 1855, Gobineau laid the foundation of anthropology. There was also Darwin's cousin Francis Galton, who exploited Gregor Mendel's discovery of genetics in the 1860s to champion eugenics and build a movement based on it. All these 'scientific' theories came together to create an intellectual monstrosity which has no parallel in human history.

Genetics provided an explanation of how one man could be inherently and necessarily inferior to another by virtue of race alone. The anthropology of scholars in the tradition of Gobineau supplied what passed for evidence. Darwin helped provide a justification for the subjection of naturally inferior races to those better adopted. . . . Early modern empires had been erected with much less comprehensive theories—of the rights of tutelage of developed cultures, or the limits of the protection of natural law; the appropriation of untenanted territory, or the fiction of purchase from unsophisticated occupants; the imperfection of the sovereignty of pagans, or Aristotle's doctrine of the 'natural slavery' of the conquered men. Now, just when White power was at its most penetrative and most pervasive, scientific theory helped to ram it home. Imperialists from the White west could confront the rest of the world in confidence. (Fernandez-Armesto 1995: 458–9)

In its most brutal form, Social Darwinism provided the intellectual underpinning to the genocides of Nazism. Adolf Hitler used it and a quasi-science of genetics to justify his racist and eugenic agenda. His regime murdered six million Jews and other 'inferior' people before and during the Second World War. Blaming Hitler alone, however, for the Holocaust is tantamount to absolving a large number of scientists, intellectuals, and celebrities who were in thrall to Darwinism and eugenics. We know about the sinister role of many German scientists with regard to the Nazi race policy, but racism and eugenics were neither their invention nor were these pseudo-sciences confined to them.

The eugenics movement was based on an overtly racist fear that the best humans were not breeding as fast as the inferior ones, and that this was leading to the deterioration of the human race. The eugenists thought Jews were largely feeble-minded, and so were blacks and many foreigners. It has been established lately that their movement was actually a social programme masquerading as a scientific one. What is not as well known is that it commanded the support of many scientists, writers and politicians around the world. Its supporters included statesmen like Theodore Roosevelt, Woodrow Wilson, Winston Churchill, writers like H.G. Wells and Bernard Shaw, scientists like Alexander Graham Bell and women's rights activists like Margaret Sanger. Research was funded by distinguished philanthropists, and carried out by prestigious universities in Europe and the USA (Hofstadter 1944; Hawkins 1997). Many honourable people lent their powerful voice to stop the feeble-minded and feeble-bodied from breeding by sterilization or isolationist arrangement. Many took recourse even to religion and Jesus—If Jesus were alive, they fancied, he would have supported their effort! The not so religious joined the chorus from the other side. Margaret Sanger, the heroine of sexual freedom and the birth-control movement, angrily invoked Spenser's words, 'Fostering the good-for-nothing at the expense of the good is an extreme cruelty . . . there is no greater crime to posterity than that of bequeathing them an increasing population of imbeciles.' Socialist Bernard Shaw opined that only eugenics could save mankind. H.G. Wells fulminated against 'ill-trained swarms of inferior citizens.' President Roosevelt thundered, 'Society has no business to permit the degenerated to reproduce their kind' (Hofstadter 1944; Hawkins 1997).

Underpinning the importance of remembering the eugenics story as a cautionary tale, a science fiction writer bemoans, 'Biographers of the celebrated and the powerful did not dwell on the attractions of this philosophy to their subjects, and sometimes did not mention it at all. Eugenics ceased to be a subject for college classrooms, although some argue that its ideas continue to have currency in disguised form' (Crichton 2006: 575–8).

Darwinism, scientific and social, cast a spell on many great minds, which in their turn spellbound millions of lesser minds. Take the case of Friedrich Nietzsche (1844–1900), one of the most influential of modern thinkers. The key strand in his much talked about but little understood philosophy accords neatly with the Darwinian theory of evolution. Nietzsche's main idea was that all of history was a metaphorical struggle between two groups, those who express the 'will of power', the vital life force that creates civilizational values, and those who do not, primarily a debased class of commoners produced by Christianity and democracy. As he put it, the poor and the weak impoverish culture whereas the strong and the powerful enrich and embellish it. All civilization owes its existence to 'men of prey', Aryans. They were the 'noble caste' which was the 'barbarian' caste. 'Spontaneously creating values' for itself, it creates its own definitions of right and wrong, truth and falsity. On the other hand, Nietzsche bemoans, 'Morality is the creation of the underclass. . . . Morality negates life' (Nietzsche 1968a; 1968b).

Nietzsche pours scorn on Christianity, calling it the religion of the underclass and the progenitor of democracy, and rhapsodises Aryanism, which is best embodied, he says, in the brahman. He praises Manu and his 'noble and spiritual' laws, for so thoroughly crushing the common people and turning them into worthless chandala. For the same reason, nothing can be filthier and more perverse than the Christian religion of love because there is no such thing as a right to live, a right to work, a right to be happy for ordinary people (Nietzsche 1968b). His contempt for women was equally vicious: 'In revenge and in love, woman is more barbarous than man.'

Nietzsche wrote most of his books when he was seriously sick, suffering from syphilis, and wildly deluded. But this did not stop his influence among morally blind intellectuals in thrall to 'scientific objectivity' and one or another kind of Darwinism. Nietzsche's announcement of 'God is dead' and his replacement of the dead God with the magnificent blonde brute lording over the underclass 'certainly sound like evolution, the law of the jungle, with natural selection in operation' (Watson 2000: 40). It is not surprising thus that Nietzschean thoughts fired the imagination of Hitler and animated the Nazi worldview. Mussolini regarded Nietzsche, along with Machiavelli and Mazzini, one of his ideological mentors. However, scholars such as Walter Kaufmann disingenuously defend Nietzsche as a supremely disinterested philosopher, and not in any way responsible for his appropriation by the Third Reich and the Nazi monstrosity (Kaufmann 1974). As a brilliant new study shows, instead of providing a serious reckoning with one of the greatest philosophers of power, Kaufmann built a massive Nietzsche industry for the Anglo-American world, neutralizing his frontal attacks on democratic equality and Christian morality and erasing the darker elements of his philosophizing, and presenting him as a charming and inoffensive existentialist—a 'King-Kong-in-chains . . . under heavy sedition' (Ratner-Rosenhagen 2012). William Shirer, the scrupulous chronicler of Nazi Germany, pointed out the connection between the Nietzschean philosophy of power and Hitler's megalomania. Though there were many Europeans who provided the intellectuals roots of the Third Reich, Hitler was particularly fascinated with Nietzsche and his prophecy of an elite who would replace the 'dead God' and rule the world, and from whom the superman would spring. 'That in the end Hitler considered himself the superman of Nietzsche's philosophy cannot be doubted' (Shirer 1991: 97–113).

Ambedkar, one of the first Indians to study Nietzsche, had come to a similar conclusion. Seeing the fascist thought in the German philosopher, he argued that Zarathustra is a new name for Manu and *Thus Spoke Zarathustra* is but a new edition of the *Manusmriti* (Ambedkar, *BAWS*, vol. 3: 74–6).

Another intellectual stalwart in thrall to Darwinism was Sigmund Freud (1856–1939), the trailblazer of psychoanalysis, discoverer of the unconscious mind and one of the greatest influences on the making of the sexual revolution. If Nietzsche was a cultural Darwinist, Freud was a psycho(logical) Darwinist. A positivist in the mould of a die-hard Darwinist, Freud was an aggressive, not revolutionary, atheist who drew up a sharp distinction between religious faith, which he termed illusionary and uncorrectable, and scientific inquiry which would enlighten and emancipate humanity. His one-dimensional thinking and psychoanalytical discourse were greatly influenced by the reductionist propositions of the evolutionary theory. The fad of biological naturalism led him to the theory that 'man, and for that matter woman, is sex, and beyond nothing' and a sexist worldview in which 'there is nothing in the world so wonderful, powerful, important and worth having as a penis' (Miles 1988: 260–3).

> Whenever a comparison was made which seemed to be unfavourable to their sex, the ladies were able to express a suspicion that we, as male analysts, had never overcome certain deep-rooted prejudices against the feminine . . . We had only to say, 'This does not apply to you. You are an exception, in this respect you are more masculine than feminine.' (Freud, quoted in Miles 1988: 244)

Alongside seeing sex in everything, Freud essentialized aggression and destructive instincts in humans—the dark side of human nature—with his characteristic colour and force:

> . . . [T]heir [humans'] neighbour is not only a potential helper or sexual object, but also someone who tempts them to take out their aggression on him, to exploit his labour without recompense, to use him sexually without his consent, to take possession of his goods, to humiliate him and cause him pain, to torture and kill him. . . . Who, after all that he has learnt from life and history, would be so bold as to dispute this proposition? . . . [I]t manifests itself spontaneously and reveals man as a savage beast that has no thought of sparing its own kind. (Freud [1930] 2002: 48)

Freud's key idea (that all humans are burdened with an unconscious in which lust, rage, and repression constantly battle for supremacy) led him to theorize in his best known essay, *Civilization and Its Discontents*, that the human animal, with his potent sexual and aggressive drives, must always remain an enemy to organized society, which exists largely to trample on animal desires.

Though his reputation remains high as one of the great liberators of human mind, Freud's mind, as a perceptive author has put it, 'dealt more strikingly with problems of neurotics than with matters of aesthetics'. He was 'powerfully reductive' (Davies 1977). Critics have argued that Freud was wrong in thinking of the unconscious, like his sweeping reading of human nature, as an unmitigated evil. Abraham Maslow points out that the unconscious 'also carries in it the roots of creativeness, of joy, of happiness, of its own ethics and values. There is a healthy unconscious as well as an unhealthy one.' Mocking Freud's formula, he says

Explain it away. If I am a kind man, this is a reaction formation against my rage to kill. Somehow, the killing is more basic than the kindness. And the kindness is a way of trying to cover up, repress, and defend myself against realizing the fact that I am truly a murderer. If I am generous, it is a reaction formation against stinginess. I am really stingy inside.

This is a strange—utterly unscientific—way to see human life. Why did Freud not say that killing people was perhaps a reaction to loving them? It is just as legitimate a conclusion and, as a matter of fact, more true for many people (Maslow 1970).

This is not to suggest that all intellectuals supported Social Darwinism; there were many compelling voices against it. Thinkers such as Thorstein Veblen and Peter Kropotkin saw through the science of biological naturalism and challenged the supremacist politics that underpinned it. They objected to elitist attempts to yoke together the logic of unfettered capitalism with Darwinism. They rejected the argument that social excellence and economic success could be equated with the biologically fittest. Veblen's *Theory of the Leisure Class* (1899) turned such logic on its head, arguing that the type of characters 'selected for dominance' in the business world were little more than barbarians, a throw-back to a more primitive form of society. Similarly, Kropotkin argued in his 1902 work *Mutual Aid*, like fellow Russian Michael Bakunin, that although competition and conflict were a fact of life, so too were collaboration and co-operation, and that liberty for everyone was assured only when people lived together in free associations of equals. Like Veblen, he presented an alternative to Social Darwinism in which violence and domination were condemned as abnormal.

Yet it is really sad that the Darwinian absolutism enthralled even some socialists. It is a tragic irony that Engels did not see any conflict between Marxism and Darwinism. In his speech at Marx's graveside, he said, 'Just as Darwin discovered the law of development of organic nature, so Marx discovered the law of development of human history' (Engels [1883]

1978: 681). Darwinism as a political sociology buttresses the idea that there can be life which is worthless, injury to which or destruction of which does not matter. Socialism, on the other hand, is a philosophy of hope even for the most desolate and defeated, and looks forward to a time when a new culture of harmony is established. To make them synonymous was a blunder.

The menace of direct Darwinism and eugenics has subsided in recent times. Reference to them—under popular democratic pressure—has acquired a negative and condemnatory tone. But this change in outlook is skin-deep. Softer forms like evolutionary biology, evolutionary psychology, and the neo-conservative economic and social theories rule the roost today. An influential periodical like *The Economist*, with whom the leading drumbeaters of Darwinism such as Herbert Spencer and Walter Bagehot were associated, still sells the idea of hierarchy, status, sexual crimes, gender pay gap, as products of evolutionary—and hence unavoidable—forces. It exhorts governments and policymakers to profitably use Darwin's insights in the process of policymaking: '[T]he moment has come to ask how Darwin's insights can be used profitably by policymakers' (*The Economist* 2008).

This amounts to reiterating the basic racist argument that humans owe their existence to nature which has blessed some with superior genes and condemned the rest with inferior ones. Since the fundamental thing about a human, as *The Economist* seems to suggest, is his genetic structure, his mental and moral qualities depend upon the genes, and are, in fact, expressions of it. Theories like this become more vicious when their proponents convince themselves and society at large to believe that their social prejudices are scientific facts after all. In Elizabeth Fee's words, 'As long as there are entrenched social and political distinctions between sexes, races or classes, there will be forms of science whose main function is to rationalize and legitimize these distinctions'(see Steinem 1992: 139).

LEFT, RIGHT AND THE GANDHIAN CENTRE OF NEO-BRAHMANISM

The tyranny of the few has deep and global intellectual roots. Manu and Kautilya, Plato and Aristotle were less individuals than a climate of opinion. They have intellectual heirs who (still) dominate the world of knowledge. More than a century ago, Jotirao Phule had denounced the brahmanic intellectuals who would justify the oppressions of caste and patriarchy in the name of patriotism, as *kalam-kasai*, the pen-wielding butchers (Phule [1873] 2002: 77–8). Later, other stalwarts of the anti-caste movements, especially Ambedkar and Periyar, faced and fought the terrible intellectual abuse of caste elites. The situation has not changed much since their day, as reproduction of culture and knowledge still remains the fiefdom of caste elites, despite some challenging attempts in recent years. The brahmanic stranglehold over the media, academia, and the public sphere allow the dominant castes to claim to be custodians of Indian society and culture. Multiplicity of voices, communal-secular quibbling and competing visions of India notwithstanding, there is an astonishing unanimity among the Indian elites about issues such as Hinduism, cultural nationalism, secularism, and Indianness, which are used interchangeably, making them almost synonymous. There is a division of labour between the secular-liberals who use politically correct vocabulary to hide the hideousness of caste and brahmanism, and the Hindutva gladiators who sing about 'Hindu India' and hurl abuses at the 'internal enemies' (Muslims, Christians, etc.). Both ignore the festering issues of caste and its consequences. Brahmanism, which forms the axis of communalism and casteism in India, is not even a phenomenon to them. Some even pretend to be innocent of their caste background though they wear their caste in their surnames—Sharma, Jha, Tripathi, Iyer, Chatterjee, and so on.

Like other democracies, India has spawned a rich crop of public figures and public intellectuals, but hardly any dalit-bahujan qualifies for this slot. At the most, intellectual leaders of 'little traditions' are recognized as voices from the margins, representing their particular caste or community. Celebrated at home and abroad, public intellectuals are caste elites who write tomes, make speeches, and suggest philanthropic palliatives for the masses. They get their books released by people-in-power; befriend and win laurels from business and political leaders; and hog whatever space there is for people's issues in the media. They are hailed as the nation's conscience-keepers. Their self-constructed and media-hyped images are those of public intellectuals, not power intellectuals.

Take the case of one of the finest and foremost among public intellectuals, Amartya Sen. A Nobel laureate in economics and an authority on Indian philosophy and culture, Sen has over the years donned the role of a radical public thinker. He has written many tomes on injustice and exclusion in India, yet caste, brahmanism and their consequences fail to qualify as a worthy subject of his scholarly engagement. When he names caste in the categories of inequalities, he shows a strange inclination to minimize its negative impact by invoking the all-powerful and crushing asymmetry of class. This is surprising since Sen is no impassioned believer in class radicalism. He is (contrary to his popular image as a Marxist) a career academic and a sophisticated neoliberal. Sen cultivated the self-image of some sort of a Marxist in the days when socialism not only held popular appeal but was also in academic vogue in India and abroad. His favourite philosophers, as he openly affirms now, have all along been the iconic liberals Adam Smith and J.S. Mill, not Marx who comes a poor third in his list of thinkers who have profoundly influenced him.

Like other brahmanic progressives, Sen plays up class in a banal way that elides caste as an institutionalized inequality. In his essay, 'Class in India', in *The Argumentative Indian*, he keeps repeating the point that 'no other source of inequality is independent of class'. This enables him to assert that caste is not that important in itself; 'caste-related conflicts tend to involve a great deal more than just caste':

> . . . [E]ven though being lower caste is undoubtedly a separate cause of disparity; its impact is all the greater when the lower-caste families also happen to be very poor. The blighting of the lives of Dalits or people from other disadvantaged castes, or of members of the Scheduled Tribes, is particularly severe when the caste or tribal adversities are further magnified by abject penury. Even the violence associated with caste-related conflicts tends to involve a great deal more than just caste. . . . [T]he victims of brutality may typically be low-caste Dalits, yet the predicament of the potential victims cannot be adequately grasped if we do not take note of the poverty and landlessness of Dalits. (Sen 2005a: 207–8)

What is the point of proving a self-evident truth that poverty added to caste is a much greater menace than just caste? Or, that the nexus of class and caste constructs a more vicious hierarchy? Sadly for Sen, it reveals more than it conceals. In obscuring the role of caste in the scheme of domination, Sen is playing the game of not rocking the brahmanic boat. We detect in many of his writings a concerted attempt to suppress any recognition of brahmanic interest in constructing caste. No sooner does the subject crop up than he starts citing most obscure, dubious—and at best exceptional—examples of anti-caste tendencies even in the brahmanic orthodoxy and its ancient literature.

> For example, when in the Mahabharata, Bhrigu tells Bharadvaja that caste divisions relate to differences in physical attributes of different human beings, reflected in skin colour, Bharadvaja responds not only by pointing to the considerable variations in skin colour within every caste, but also by the more profound question: 'We all seem to be affected by desire, anger, fear, sorrow, worry, hunger, and labour; how do we have caste differences then?' (Sen 2005a: 10–11)

Just after this gem, Sen culls another example of castelessness from a most dubious source, the *Bhavishya Purana*, which he calls an 'ancient document' but which was actually written or massively redacted during the colonial period as it contains many references to the reign of Queen Victoria: 'Since members of all the four castes are children of God, they all belong to the same caste. All human beings have the same father, and children of the same father cannot have different castes' (ibid.: 11). It is surprising that Sen does not cite anti-hierarchical views from the anti-caste movements and their spearheads but only from Bhrigu, Bharadvaja and the *Bhavishya Purana*, i.e. from within the orthodox brahmanic tradition. He finds these passages worth repeating several times in the same book (on page 37 again, for example). Knowing that he could rarely find anti-ascriptive views in the brahmanic corpus, he makes the maximum use of the exceptions—the exceptional as the normal.

We find the same citations (of Bhrigu, Bharadvaja and *Bhavishya Purana*) with much fanfare in Sen's 'Foreword' to *Hinduism* (2005b) authored by his grandfather K.M. Sen. A close reading of this Foreword (pp. vii-xxiii) makes it clear that the odd quotes cited above as well as his entire reading of Hinduism, caste system, Indian culture and identity (represented in his *Argumentative Indian* and other works) are actually not the product of his objective intellectual engagement but almost wholly and uncritically derived from the work of the senior Sen. Contrary to the grandson's claims, K.M. Sen's views are not that original, but a typical representation of *bhadralok* 'progressivism' (which saw the key elements of inclusiveness, democracy, and secularism in the old brahmanic tradition) which began with Rammohun Roy's expedient interpretation of the tradition against the more orthodox school which remained loyal to the rather more real (hierarchical) nature of caste and brahmanism (see Mani 2005, Chapter 4).

As he emerges from the pages of *The Argumentative Indian* (especially pp. 3–33) and his other essays referring to Hinduism, culture, and caste, Sen is a proud and faithful adherent of this dubious progressivism. He proclaims that pluralism has a pedigree in the oldest texts of Hinduism, and even traces the lineage of modern Indian democracy to the ancient tradition of 'public reasoning and argumentative heterodoxy'. He does all this marvellously well by deftly deflecting the attention from the construction and institutionalization of the world's most ruthless and enduring system of hierarchy that survives to this day. Like the earlier 'radical' caste elites who saw inclusiveness and enlightenment in the Vedic–Upanishadic tradition, Sen too is averse to recognize the violence of caste and brahmanism. His narrative is wonderfully innocent of the 'brahman precept and kshatriya arm' that cultivated mass conformity and compliance in favour of caste hierarchy. By citing a few stray instances of scepticism, rationalism, and liberalism in the domain of the privileged, he tries to cover up the entire story of brahmanic promotion of mass illiteracy, superstition, and irrationality in India. He reformulates—and embellishes—his grandfather's sanitized and very selective reading of caste and Hinduism, in which we find not a trace of Shambuka, Ekalavya, Karna (that is, the murderous politics of caste), let alone the acknowledgement of the massive intellectual–moral fraud committed by the authors of Dharmashastras and *Itihasa-Purana* (as we saw earlier in this chapter).

Making a brilliant use of his eclectic scholarship, what Sen essentially does accomplish, like other pundits, is to erect a sophisticated defence of brahmanism under the guise of presenting a more balanced and 'open-ended' reading of Indian culture and society. Beneath the surface of attractive phraseology, Sen's perspective, too, is centred around the normalization of caste and exaltation of Hinduism. He is in agreement with the obfuscating brahmanic formulations of his grandfather that

> (1) there were considerable variations in the actual practice of the caste system, even in pre-modern—indeed ancient—periods, (2) 'when an orthodox Hindu suggests that the caste system, as we know it, is an integral part of Hinduism, he is ignoring a substantial part of India's religious literature.' (Sen 2005b: xvi)

At this point, Sen underlines the great vision of his grandfather in 'rejecting the philosophy of homo hierarchicus [human hierarchy] as a quintessentially Hindu view of life . . . to be no more than an abstract reconstruction' (p. xvi). What his epistemic entrepreneurship—addressed mainly to foreign readers and caste elites within and outside India—is up to, thus, becomes clear: first, he tries as far as possible to hide the prevalence and hideousness of caste system, and then, along with his grandfather, strongly refutes any suggestion of symbiosis between caste and Hinduism. All along he remains blissfully blind to the agency that produced and nurtured Hinduism; the term brahmanism simply does not exist in his otherwise wonderful vocabulary.

K.M. Sen was a key associate of Rabindranath Tagore at his Shantiniketan, the grandson informs us, and stresses how great was Tagore in appreciating his grandfather's 'unusual combination of consummate scholarship and undogmatic open-mindedness' (p. xvi)—and in his critical understanding (of the Indian tradition and Hinduism) 'an accurate vision that India badly needed' (p. xviii). And the devoted grandson that he is, he too rediscovers and reaffirms his faith in the unparalleled liberality, flexibility, and criticality in the Hindu tradition. He proclaims that his grandfather's 'focus on liberality of thought and constructive receptivity yields a much more capacious understanding of the diversity and intellectual reach of Hinduism than the narrowness that is increasingly cultivated by the priorities of sectarian politics or by the fanning of religious orthodoxy' (p. xiv).

The Sens were perhaps oblivious that it was Rammohun Roy who used the term 'Hinduism' for the first time in 1816-17 for a faith ('practised by our ancestors', 'well known at the present day to many learned Brahmins') that was traditionally called Varnashrama Dharma, Sanatana Dhrama or simply Brahmanism (Killingley 1993: 62–3). Though the word Hindu (from the river Sindhu) had been in use in the premodern India, more as a cultural and geographical marker than as a religious category, Hinduism, as we know it today, is a modern construction of the brahman literati, aided and abetted by colonial rule and Oriental scholarship (Frykenberg 2001; Thapar 2001). But Amartya Sen sees Hinduism as a millennia-old, conflict-free, all-encompassing, rational and almost national religion. His eloquence on 'liberality of thought, constructive receptivity . . . the diversity and intellectual reach of Hinduism' goes hand in hand with eliding the oppressions of caste and the frauds of brahmanism—facts that an intellectual like him cannot be unaware of.

Through such glorification of an oppressive past, Sen wants to take on the coarse and communal elements of Hindutva—and he is quite eloquent about it in the *Argumentative Indian* and his 'Foreward' to *Hinduism*. But, as with many champions of the Hindu Left and Gandhism and their lovely talk of Hindu–Muslim unity, Sen's tragedy and hypocrisy is that his caste-blindness and competitive exaltation of Hinduism and Indian culture puts him in a close and dangerous kinship to the very sectarian and violent forces he is ranged against. His fundamentally flawed reading of Hinduism, especially his unwillingness to understand communalism as a by-product of the unresolved and festering question of caste, makes him a proponent of a vacuous secularism which only hides the real nature of communal violence. Communalism in India, as Menon (2006) rightly shows, is a deflation of the violence and graded inequality within Hindu society, as the deployment of aggression against an internal Other, the dalit-subaltern, come to be transformed into violence against an external Other, the Muslim or Christian. The disingenuous discourse of secularism and communalism in which people like Sen take the high moral ground creates two polar opposites, comprised of two streams of neo-brahmanism. These subsume all issues related to caste exploitation and historically accumulated discriminations that effectively reduce India to a very limited democracy in which only the façade of secularism can be maintained.

In fact, K.M. and Amartya Sen's reading of Hinduism is as obscurantist as the wild fantasies of some right-wing

Hindu nationalists. The blurb of *Hinduism* reads: 'A product of many cultures and traditions, Hinduism has generated and assimilated the religious movements of India over 5,000 years.' When Hinduism becomes five millennia old and the alpha and omega of indigenous religions, it reinforces the elitist mischief that equates brahmanism with Hinduism and Hinduism with Indianness. This myth is the mainstay of modern brahmanic chauvinism. It is also notable that it was S. Radhakrishnan who asked Penguin to request K.M. Sen, as the latter's grandson informs us, to do that book on Hinduism. Radhakrishnan, as we know, was the high priest who had a penchant for Hinduising India in the brahmanic mould, the kind of pundit who could prove that Buddha was 'born, grew up, and died a Hindu' (Radhakrishnan [1956] 1997: ix).

The Sens thus fully share and celebrate the fraudulent claims of brahmanic chauvinists who make their caste-centred religion co-terminus with India's 'national' religion and culture. Amartya Sen berates 'the combative exponents of religious politics' for 'more aggressive and less tolerant interpretations of Hinduism', and takes recourse to the elitist fictions of 'openness, tolerance and constructivism' of Hinduism and the 'old tradition of cogent interreligious discussions'. There may be some truth in his claims but to present such half-truths as the reality of India is a dangerous and blatantly brahmanic proposition. This power-friendly expediency takes him to a point from where he glibly philosophizes as if there were no problems in religious and social realms in the ancient and medieval India. Such glorification of an oppressive tradition—by concealing the corruption and crimes of brahmanism and mixing them up with the broad-minded ideologies of Buddha, Ashoka, Kabir, and so on to show the liberality and openness of the past—is an even more dishonest representation of the past than the visible red tooth and claws of Hindutva (which the oppressed castes and communities can—and will—see, fight, and ultimately crush). It is not that an intellectual like Sen does not understand these things. He does but he does not want to deal with the internalized falsehood of brahmanism which in its turn helps him block out the pain, the anguish, and the worth of the struggles of the caste oppressed. He uncritically glorifies Tagore, Gandhi, and Nehru and their majestic contribution in the making of modern India, and keeps his eyes shut to the freedom struggles of Phule, Periyar and Ambedkar. What can be a more glaring example of intellectual corruption than totally excluding the oppressed and their movements and struggles from the discourse and view of modern India? Isn't this kind of scholarship an attempt at the very annihilation of author of *Annihilation of Caste* (Ambedkar)?

In his determination to avoid any reference to the troubled and contested past, Sen is oblivious to the fact that India, like many other societies, has a deeply dual tradition. He often discusses the difference between *niti* (principle) and *nyaya* (justice), and bemoans that despite its long and brilliant tradition of *niti* India has lacked *nyaya* (Sen 2009: 20–2, 212–13). He thus remains blind to the viciousness of the *niti*, the 'lawless laws' of Dharmashastras that sanctioned the most inhuman and racist discriminations against dalits, shudras (lowered castes) and women. Sen would talk about the 'argumentative Indian' without revealing the fact that in pre-modern India, toiling castes and women were systematically denied access to education under the brahmanic injunctions. 'Do not give education to the common people and women' is a common refrain in the sacred brahmanic texts. He does not see that education under the *guru-shishya parampara* did everything to stifle debate and dialogue and instead promoted a closed and conservative pedagogy. And, of course, he does not see that if there has been a tradition of critical discourse in India, it is largely thanks to the anti-brahmanic philosophies of Buddha, Kabir, Phule, and Ambedkar.

The erudite Sen's scholarship does not extend to the existence and struggles of Phule, IyotheeThass, Pandita Ramabai, Narayana Guru, and Periyar. These social revolutionaries do not figure at all in his list of 'argumentative Indians', or for that matter in any of his writings. And while Ambedkar somehow figures in two books, it is only accidently, as the chairperson of the Drafting Committee of the Constitution, with no reference at all to the huge historical work of emancipation he started in people groups that had been oppressed for centuries. In fact, Sen keeps a very safe distance from the authentic Ambedkar, the anti-caste system-builder whose dalit-subaltern vision of Indian society and culture clash with the brahmanic visions of Gandhi and Nehru and his own. His writings, save the ritualistic name-dropping of Buddha, Kabir, and Ambedkar, reveal no knowledge or acknowledgement of India's long-standing tradition of resistance against caste and brahmanism.

Thus, like other practitioners of academic brahmanism, Sen too does not see in the dalit-subaltern dream of 'annihilation of caste' a vision towards which a new India can move. Nor does he see the point that Gandhi, Tagore and Nehru—and for that matter modern India itself—cannot be understood without understanding Phule, Ambedkar, and Periyar, the other side of the national movement. When he is done with praising Gandhi, Tagore, and Nehru, emperors like Akbar take Sen's fancy because he allegedly paved the 'path of reason' by befriending some pundits of other faiths and making them talk with the courtly kazis about a composite religion and culture which Sen fancifully tries to sell to the world as a remarkable harbinger of secular democracy (Sen 2009: 36–9). He does not see that Akbar's tolerance was not magnanimity but born of political necessity of securing the consent of caste elites to stabilize his rule, a ploy that every wise ruler employs for sheer survival. The British colonisers, for instance, did it even better than the Mughals by employing and accommodating a large number of indigenous elites in the colonial power structure. To see Akbar as a harbinger of democracy and secularism, as Sen does, is a fabrication that hides the fact that he had a harem with 5,000 women and his court was sealed off from public view.

Though Sen does not see in the arrival of Islam into India as 'a dagger thrust in the heart of Indian civilization', his tendency to see the tactical alliance of Hindu and Muslim elites as the foundation of a free and fair India is obnoxious for social democracy. It is this propensity to see the movement toward justice and democracy in brahmans, monarchs, and other merchants of dreams that makes Sen blind to the people's movements and their contribution to whatever democracy and secularism India has. It is not accidental that in his pedantic book on justice, Sen neglects the cultural roots of injustices with the clever but well-worn argument that harking back to the past in search for justice would not do. This does not prevent Sen from voyaging himself to the past and bring back the 'argumentative Indian' and the majesty of the great Sanskritic tradition. He invokes the greatness of the old and medieval monarchs in his discourse but does not want the struggling people to visit the oppressive past to understand their oppressive present. He makes noble noises about justice, but undercuts the fundamentals of power and oppression by saying that we have to accept the reality that 'we're where we are today'. Instead of chasing after the chimera of perfect justice, he suggests, we would be better off concentrating on eliminating remediable injustices around us. This is right but how can one remove the glaring injustices without dealing with structural hierarchy and discriminations? How many people can be caste-free and democratic in a brahmanic social order?

Sen, however, rightly points out that human abilities 'to understand, to sympathise, to argue' can save us from leading isolated lives (Sen 2009: 415). But intellectuals like Sen, whom the elites portray as god's gift to the world's poor and as 'an accessible and exceptional humanitarian' for making such statements never meet the struggling people—the sons and daughters of Ekalavya, Birsa Munda, Phule, Tarabai Shinde, and Ambedkar. They meet only fellow pundits, the people-in-power, and corporate heads, and lobby for years for awards and rewards from the establishment. The point is:

can the oppressed trust elite intellectuals to be their articulate and insightful champions or should they endeavour to grasp the world for themselves? It may be in the elites' interest to overlook the roots of crisis and push occasional charity, welfarism or some nice-sounding abstract idea as a way forward for a decent and democratic society, but would this brahmanic–Gandhian approach enthuse the oppressed and supporters of social democracy?

The powerful groups have always pedalled their selfish propaganda as the noble truth. But the embedded intelligentsia remain in denial about this as well as the fact that many heroes of history and humanity have been an integral part of such truth-selling rackets. To take a great example, the authorized—hagiographical—version of Mohandas Gandhi is very different from the real one. Gandhi found enlightenment in *Varnashrama Dharma* while he was leading the anti-colonial struggle. He reiterated brahmanic myths about caste, Hinduism, and Indian society in the garb of great Indian truths. The upper casteist abstraction and fondness with which he saw the culture of caste made him not only elide its exploitation and violence but also sing its praises—a fact that the intellectual establishment in India has totally suppressed. Writing in *Navjivan*, in 1921–2, for example, Gandhi saw the seeds of Swaraj in caste and argued that the Hindu society had been able to survive precisely because it was founded on the caste system:

> The seeds of Swaraj are to be found in the caste system. . . . A community which can create the caste system must be said to possess unique power of organisation. . . . The caste system is a natural order of society. In India it has been given a religious coating. Other countries not having understood the utility of the caste system . . . have not derived . . . the same degree of advantage as India has derived. (Gandhi, quoted in Ambedkar, *BAWS*, vol. 9, pp. 275–6)

Rebuffing those who advocated social democracy and wanted to do away with the principle of hereditary occupation inherent in caste, Gandhi asserted:

> To destroy the caste system and adopt the western European social system means that Hindus must give up the principle of hereditary occupation which is the soul of the caste system. Hereditary principle is an eternal principle. To change it is to create disorder. I have no use for a Brahman if I cannot call him a Brahman for my life. It will be a chaos if everyday a Brahman is to be changed into a Shudra and a Shudra is to be changed into a Brahman. (ibid.: 276)

Varna, he insists in his 1934 essay '*Varna Vyavastha*', is not a human invention but an immutable law of nature which 'reveals the law of one's being and thus the duty one has to perform, it confers no right, and the idea of inferiority or superiority is wholly repugnant to it' (Gandhi [1934] 1993: 218). After this specious argument, he gives this call: 'What is essential is that one must seek one's livelihood, and no more, from following the vocation to which one is born' (ibid.: 221). This pontification is from the person who himself quit—and so did his forefathers—*tarajoo,* the scale, of the grocery shop, the duty of his ancestral calling in favour of the brahmanic profession of law.

Caste elites portray Gandhi as an anti-caste campaigner, pointing out that he made the removal of untouchability a part of the struggle for independence but that does not mean that he was opposed to caste system per se. In fact, he saw untouchability as a perversity, which had nothing to do with caste system. This explains why he never attempted to convert his anti-untouchability programme into an anti-caste programme as Ambedkar and Periyar, the leaders of the caste-oppressed, were demanding. On the contrary, he wanted to reinforce the caste order in accordance with the brahmanic scriptural injunctions because he saw no inequality or exploitation in the former. The shudra who serves the higher castes as a matter of religious duty and who will never own property, indeed has not even the ambition to own anything, Gandhi wrote, is 'worthy of the world's homage. . . . The gods will shower their choicest blessings on him. One may not say this of the proletariat of the present day. They certainly own nothing, but I expect they covet ownership' (ibid.: 220). It was this regressive mindset which occasionally made him oppose the education of the masses which, he feared, might ignite their minds about the wretched conditions in which they lived:

> What do you want to gain by giving literacy to the children of the peasants? What comfort are you going to add to their life by educating them? Do you want to ignite discontent in his mind for his thatched hut and pathetic condition? ...We are going to do excess when some preach for imparting education for all, without considering its pros and cons. (Gandhi, quoted in Biswas 1998: 267)

Such ideas came naturally to Gandhi since he considered the caste system a natural order of society, perfected religiously and 'scientifically'. 'The caste system', he claimed, 'has a scientific basis. Reason does not revolt against it. . . . I can find no reason for its abolition. To abolish caste is to demolish Hinduism.' Since Gandhi did not want to harm Hinduism in any way, and he saw caste and brahmanism as symbiotic with Hinduism, he refused to accept that they were the matrix of structural discriminations and cultural oppression in Indian society. He could not see that caste benefited upper castes, and debilitated women, shudra, and above all, untouchables. Caste, he argued with Ambedkar, did not discriminate against scavengers or anyone. It was a system that allowed everyone to earn their livelihood and no more. Similarly, responding to the anti-caste radicals of Tamil Nadu, he declared in 1927, 'Varnashrama Dharma is not an unmitigated evil but it is one of the foundations on which Hinduism is built [and it] defines man's mission on earth . . . Brahmins [are] the finest flowers of Hinduism and humanity', adding that he would 'do nothing to wither it' (see Pandian 2007: 191).

In league with the brahmanic forces throughout his life, Gandhi only wanted to remove untouchability so that millions of dehumanized people—whom he patronizingly renamed Harijan (literally, children of god)—could remain forever within the fold of Hinduism as servile creatures, serving the upper castes and swelling the numbers of Hindus. His Harijan politics was driven by the calculation that numbers of Hindus must not dwindle so that the dominant castes could hide their real exploitative identity under the beguiling banner of Hinduism. His real objective, like a typical upper-caste charlatan, was to stop any conversions of untouchables, adivasis, and lowered castes to more egalitarian religions like Christianity, Islam, and Buddhism—all in the name of Indian culture and nationalism. He linked conversion with 'denationalisation', calling the former 'blasphemy' and proselytization 'deadliest poison'. 'If I had the power and could legislate, I should certainly stop all proselytizing' (Gandhi 1935; Vora 1999: v, 44). Speaking in the language of an ace fundamentalist, he would say, 'What of substance is contained in any other religion is always to be found in Hinduism. And what is not contained in it is insubstantial or unnecessary' (Gandhi 1925).

As a perceptive biographer has pointed out, despite his friendships and alliances with Muslims, Gandhi was

> a Hindu politician, incessantly invoking Rama and publicly embracing the ascetic practices associated with Hindu holiness. . . . He never dissociated himself sufficiently from the Hindu communalist wing of Congress. He demurred at being treated as an *avatar* by the masses, but left no doubt that his spiritual aspirations might as well be understood by the ignorant. (Tidrick 2006)

It must be noted however that the celebration of Hinduism and caste culture in the name of nationalism did not begin with Gandhi. Gandhi merely carried the conservative Hindu perspective that was variously expounded in the earlier decades by the brahmanic intelligentsia of different stripes, ranging from Bankimchandra Chatterjee and Dayananda Saraswati to Vivekananda and Bal Gangadhar Tilak. (For a comprehensive understanding of the Gandhian myth and the brahmanical orientation of the cultural nationalism, see Aloysius 1997 and Mani 2005.) Thus Gandhi's understanding of Hinduism and caste differed sharply from those of Phule,

Ambedkar, and Periyar. Phule preceded Gandhi by a few decades, but Ambedkar and Periyar were left with no option but to take on the most powerful defender of caste and brahmanism in modern India. Under their powerful criticism, Gandhi sometimes had to conceal his open support for caste. Citing some of these ambiguous and misleading statements of Gandhi, some pundits claim that Gandhi supported caste in his earlier life, but gradually came out of it, and ended up as a crusader against caste. But to the end Gandhi supported the morality of *varna-dharma*, presenting it as an organic, unifying and inclusive system. In his most revealing essay on caste, written in 1934, Gandhi argued that varna-dharma stressed the community rather than the individual, co-operation as against conflict, and duties rather than rights. As he put it, a stricter 'fulfilment of the [varna] law would make life liveable, would spread peace and content, end all clashes and conflicts, put an end to starvation and pauperization, solve the problem of population and even end disease and suffering' (Gandhi [1934] 1993: 218).

Gandhi found the varna model of society worthy of export: 'Though the law of varna is a special discovery of some Hindu seer, it has universal application. The world may ignore it today but it will have to accept it in the time to come' (ibid.: 219). Warning against the dangers of 'class wars and civil strife' unleashed by Western modernity and materialism, he gave the call to return to the birth-based varna purity to end conflicting inequalities:

> These wars and strife could not be ended except by the observance of the law of varna. For it ordains that everyone shall fulfil the law of one's being by doing it in a spirit of duty and service that to which one is born. Its due observance by a large part of mankind will end the conflicting inequalities and give place to an equality in diversity. (ibid.: 218)

Even the Gandhi-lovers concede that his conception of caste was 'remote from reality, as it did not take into account considerations of superior and inferior rank' (Beteille 1997:

160). This, of course, is a huge understatement. Gandhi's remoteness from caste reality was part of his bigger brahmanic politics (as we saw in his own words), which Ambedkar, Periyar, and other dalit-bahujan leaders clearly grasped and lambasted in the strongest words (Mani 2005). Gandhi's reconstruction of the Indian tradition was not only dismissive of its conflict-ridden past but also derisive of its rich plurality and the popular anti-caste resistances that dot its history. His faith in the wonderful Hindu tolerance continued till Nathuram Godse, a brahman fanatic, pumped three bullets to end his life for his appeal for peace during the partition riots that claimed half a million lives. Intellectuals like Ashis Nandy (1980) naïvely see Gandhi's killing as unique proof of his anti-brahmanic politics, but Periyar was nearer to the truth by pointing out that 'Godse was not an isolated bigot or madman but rather an expression of the very forms of Hindu nationalism that Gandhi had himself done so much to cultivate, and that had become pervasive in India at large' (cited in Dirks 2002: 263). Gandhi, as Periyar saw it, was struck down by a cancer within that was aggravated by his own complicity in the cloying connection of brahman privilege to Hindu ideology. Ambedkar's critique of Gandhi and Gandhism was even stronger and well-known. Incorporating the critical dalit-bahujan perspective, a scholar of modern India comes to this conclusion,

> Gandhi's construction of the ideal–typical tradition is composed of the worst elements of the sub-continental history, elements that kept the masses under social and cultural tyranny. An integral component of such a reconstruction of tradition is the view of egalitarianism, and any other form of aspiration to socio-cultural equality, as foreign imported and Western, and hence to be repudiated ruthlessly. (Aloysius 1997: 207)

However, the caste elites, including honourable intellectuals like Amartya Sen, have to date deftly kept Gandhi's cultural deception hidden from the public eye. What Paul Williams pointed out in another context, fits more in the case of Gandhi's deification: 'The process by which a historical individual is deified is one of exaggeration and exaggerated reverence. It is essentially a process of falsification, the creation of a massive delusion' (Williams 1989: 169). The brahmanic guile in Gandhi's glorification and the global gullibility to accept this mythification remains largely unknown even in the academia, thanks to the elitist stranglehold over production and dissemination of knowledge. Till today, what is known and accepted about India and things Indian—in the academic and popular discourse—is by and large a construction of the brahmanic mind. Without deconstructing this mindset, it is not possible to grasp the Gandhian phenomenon, the structure of power in Indian society, or the reasons behind the pervasiveness of caste.

Beneath the appearance of a humane and all-embracing anti-colonial politics, the Gandhian synthesis of varna dharma, culture and patriotism—though highly successful—was upper casteist and ahistorical. Even a cursory look at the historical record shows that he was wrong about caste and culture. Rooted in nostalgia for an imaginary past, his stress on the moral superiority of ancient Hindu spirituality was an elitist assertion to naturalise inequality and injustice by effectively subsuming the glaring injustices of caste and class. Colonialism provided Gandhi and his upper-caste trumpeters to project brahmanism as the basis of Indian nationalism. More than a stratagem for the anti-colonial struggle, the Gandhian non-violence entailed acceptance of the apparent and indirect forms of coercion implicit in the caste system. All caste elites knew the real Gandhi and revered him for his holy deception. Nehru, for example, would write in a moment of candid honesty of Gandhi's 'muddled humanitarianism' and worse, and then bend over backwards to glorify him as a godly figure.

For years I have puzzled over this problem: why with all his love and solicitude for the underdog he yet supports a system which inevitably produces it and crushes it; why with all his passion for non-violence he is in favour of a political and social structure which is wholly based on violence and coercion? Perhaps it is not correct to say that he is in favour of such a system but . . . he accepts the present order. (Nehru [1936] 1999: 515)

Straddling the worlds of politics and religion, Gandhi donned the double role of a people's saint and a duplicitous politician working at the behest of the caste elites. On the one hand, his concealment of caste-class conflict galvanized the upper castes to build a national politics that reinforced existing inequalities, and on the other he mesmerized the masses with his 'delightfully vague' invocation of the coming swaraj. In other words, he gave the people the consolation of religion, and handed over the reigns of power politics to the privileged. Varnashrama, Ram Rajya and Trusteeship—the three unmistakable status quoist concepts embedded in the traditional structure of power and hierarchy—represented his social, political and economic philosophies. Gandhi would appeal to the poor to suffer poverty and not just spare but trust the rich: 'There are numerous examples extant of the rich and the poor living in perfect friendliness. We have to multiply such instances' (Gandhi 1970: 19).

Far from a call for an inclusive and democratic society, political Gandhism was based on an appeal for a reversal to the status quo ante (of caste and brahmanism) that he would call Hinduism. Knowing the value of Gandhi, the wily upper castes were quick to hand over to him the supreme leadership, equating him with an avatar of god and putting him on a pedestal so high that his real face remained invisible to the people who mistook him for a Mahatma.

True, Gandhi was pious and self-sacrificing. One can say that he was a victim of naïve self-delusion, who personified austerity but on whom wealthy caste fellows showered comforts. Minus his 'half-naked' holiness and demonstrative religiosity (something he and his caste elite constituency knew well), he would be much easier to dismiss. The best defence one can present for Gandhi, as his sophisticated apologists do, is that in his philosophy

> equality has been seen not in terms of political or social relations, but as related to the perfecting of the self. . . . On this view, the primary challenge of equality is not about our relationship with others, it is primarily about crafting the right relationship with one's own self. The root of inequality, in some form or the other, always lies in an exaltation of materialism, which compels us to seek domination over others. (Mehta 2012b)

But even this apologist accepts that 'as a means of achieving equality, it proved counter-productive, for it immediately tied the politics of equality to an idiom [and politics] of renunciation . . . ' (ibid.). Argument like this is basically obfuscatory and indulgent since Gandhi had actively supported caste, brahmanism, and trusteeship, dismissing in most devious ways anti-caste revolutionaries like Ambedkar and Periyar. The Gandhian doctrine of self-denial and moralizing mysticism breeds docile conformists rather than revolutionaries. In the actual socio-political context, the discourses of the finest neo-Gandhians such as Bhikhu Parekh (1989; 2001) and Ashis Nandy (1980; 1983) are nothing but seductive abuse of intelligence to defend and glorify the indefensible. Their caste-class interest makes the elites blind to the fact that Gandhi was 'gripped by a set of regressive personal fixations and phobias, had a very limited intellectual formation, was impervious to rational argument, and entirely unaware of the damage he was doing to the national movement by suffusing it with Hindu pietism as he reconceived it' (Anderson 2012b).

Gandhi's defence of caste and brahmanism was, and is, the basic reason for his popularity among the caste elites. Hagiographic accounts of the 'saintly-godly' Gandhi and his 'ism'—with his own tacit consent and complicity—have been cunningly used by oppressive forces as an apparel to cover their hideous nakedness. As Gandhism and neo-brahmanism are interwoven, Gandhi and Gandhism have become an attractive refuge of vested interests. With the government's propaganda machine at its command since Independence, the neo-brahmanic forces have succeeded in spreading a hagiographic image of Gandhi in all corners in the world.

Billions of rupees—all public money—have been squandered on creating and disseminating the image of Gandhi as 'father of the nation' and the 'Christ of the East'.

It is a measure of the crushing power of neo-brahmanism that even the finest of our public thinkers, including people like Amartya Sen and Ashis Nandy, are not immune from the brahmanic-Gandhian humbug. Intellectuals of lesser ability and integrity, and the caste-blind *savarna* middle classes, are of course totally sold out on the brahmanic myths about India's past and present. Ambedkar's famous poser to the 'progressives' among the caste elites as to why have the brahmans, after monopolizing intellectual work for centuries, failed to produce a Voltaire—that is, a single revolutionary dissenter—remains unanswered and relevant. The era of caste and brahmanism may be formally over, but the subject needs to be open, debated, discussed. Not just because they are responsible for so many of continuing inequalities, divisions, and brutalities, or to remind the dominant castes or groups of their guilt, but mainly to unite and emancipate the oppressed because that past is not yet past. The struggling people will have to produce their new Phules and Ambedkars, their own revolutionary thinker-activists who can build and lead the new emancipatory movement in the twenty-first century.

CHAPTER 5

Emancipating the Mind

Arise, awake and educate—smash traditions, liberate!
SAVITRIBAI PHULE

In a pithy Hindi poem, Uday Prakash says, 'The dead do not think and do not speak: when people do not think and speak, they are dead.' Indeed, silence, born of ignorance, is the root and stem of lifelessness since it submits to whatever is dictated to it. Where ignorance and silence prevail, justice will not. Rousseau described rightless people as those 'whose first gifts are fetters and whose first treatment is torture, yet whose voice alone is free.' When the voice is free, why do the oppressed not raise it in resistance? Because their mind is submerged in the oppressor's language and education. It is in this sense that revolution first takes place in one's mind. Freedom comes from a mental fight, an intense personal struggle as well as a collective one for transformational change. An ignited consciousness—and a freedom struggle based on it—is known by many names. Emancipatory education is one of them. Epictetus, the Roman slave-turned-philosopher, said two millennia ago, 'Only the educated are free.' He was speaking from his own experience—even in his chains, he was perhaps more free than his masters.

That education is the most important differentiator and the most effective multiplier is commonly accepted. J.K. Galbraith had said that there is no educated person who is servile and poor, and no uneducated person who not servile and poor. But a larger social change with genuine inclusiveness and equality of conditions demands change in the very nature of education, which we have discussed variously in the preceding chapters. A revolution in values requires the replacement of the traditional education with an emancipatory one. 'Education', in this sense, in the poetic words of W.B. Yeats, 'is not the filling of a bucket but the lighting of the fire.' In a more prosaic vocabulary, it is not merely the art of reading, writing, gathering information, but the antidote to ignorance and exploitation in all their manifestations. Such education opens our eyes, enables us to understand the world as it is and dream about the one we want to live and work in. It enables us with voice and choice, and paves the way for freedom and reconstruction. A movement from darkness to light, the promise of education is nothing less than remaking the world where justice rolls down like waters and righteousness like an overflowing stream.

The new world is a new eye, not a new landscape. Observing—and interpreting—the world is the first important step towards transforming it. Education ignites change within us, to meet the change outside. It helps cultivate a new mind and new imagination to remake life and ourselves. The ability to think for oneself, to take one's own decisions, to recognize the face of friends and mere pretenders, to assert oneself intellectually and ethically, are inseparable from one's physical way of being in the world. In this sense, education is a life-long affair, not something that begins and ends in one's early years with school and college.

India has a long and glorious tradition of struggle for emancipatory education. Buddha, Kabir, Phule, Ambedkar and many others saw ignorance as slavery and education as liberation. An education that liberates was the focal point of their thinking, and at the heart of their struggles. Their worldviews and approaches to knowledge were multifarious, but they shared a vision that rebelled against the ideas and institutions of dominance. It was for this reason that they rejected the closed pedagogy of brahmanism.

Buddha set a new benchmark of truth-seeking: 'Work with diligence. Be your own lamp. Be your own refuge. Think, endeavour, and experiment if you want to seek the truth.' Stressing on these fundamentals and the need to test and revaluate received ideas and attitudes, he insisted that people must actively work for their liberation. This does not mean turning away from others. Instead he suggested that most of us benefit from the support and guidance of other people working towards a common goal. Through his personal example, he showed how to blend the personal and the social, the spiritual and the temporal, the intellect and the emotions. In word and deed, he suggested that enlightenment was always accompanied by a desire to help and embrace people in need. In this humble and humbling way, he laid the foundation of an ethics and aesthetics that combined knowledge with compassion.

In subsequent centuries, the people's poets and philosophers carried forward Buddha's emancipatory message in their own idioms. Kabir declared war on all forms of injustice and asked the oppressed to acquire true knowledge and join the liberation movement—*Saddho, uthi gyan ki aandhi*! Tuka proclaimed, *Satya asatya ke man ke ne vahi, mane le nahin bahumati* (I have made my own mind with the truth and untruth; I do not accept the opinion of the gullible majority).

In the nineteenth century, Jotirao Phule carried this torch of truth-seeking to new heights and named the radical organization he and his friends founded in 1873, Satyashodhak Samaj—the Society of Truth-Seekers. Perhaps no one has described the inhumanity of caste with as much power and passion as did Phule. In his view, the greatest injustice of caste culture was the relegation of all the lowered castes and women to illiteracy. It was also the brahmans' most emphatic and enduring victory over the people whom they had enslaved. Not only the brahmans were the only acknowledged producers and disseminators of knowledge, the lowered castes were not ever permitted to imbibe this knowledge, let alone develop an alternate knowledge system. It was the lack of knowledge, Phule bemoaned in a legendary poem popularly identified as 'Vidya Bina Mati Geli', that turned India's toiling communities into virtual slaves:

Without knowledge, intelligence was lost;
Without intelligence, morality was lost;
Without morality, dynamism was lost;
Without dynamism, wealth was lost;
All this led to ruination of the lowered castes;
All the tragedy resulted from lack of knowledge.

Phule presented a blistering critique of brahmanic suppression of mass education, which he held as the worst form of treason, and he made democratization of education the locus of his freedom movement. He believed that education—not merely alphabetical competence but an eye-opening education that he metaphorically termed *Tritya Ratna*, the Third Eye, in his eponymous play (1855)—would unleash forces that would break the spell of caste and patriarchy, paving the way for a social revolution in India. He gave the call of *bahujanvad*—solidarity of the oppressed majority—for a casteless society, which could not be achieved (and he was emphatic about it) without a cultural and educational revolution.

Then came Ambedkar, standing on the shoulders of Buddha, Kabir and Phule whom he acknowledged as his three great gurus. A public intellectual unlike any other, he put to use his extraordinary erudition for evolving an emancipatory politics and pedagogy. With a call of *Educate, Organize, Agitate*, he galvanized millions of dehumanized people—known now as dalits—for a liberation struggle which has had no parallel in history. For him, education was the means to annihilate caste, destroy slavery, and awaken the downtrodden to a new life of liberty, equality and fraternity.

Other dalit-bahujan and feminist leaders such as Savitribai Phule, Iyothee Thass, Narayan Guru, Periyar, Pandita Ramabai, and Acchutanand expressed similar views on knowledge, education and freedom. 'Get educated to get freedom' was their common refrain. Savitribai Phule, modern India's first woman teacher and a pioneer of female education with her revolutionary husband Jotirao Phule, wrote in a poem as early as 1854: *Arise, awake and educate—smash traditions, liberate!* (Mani 2008a).

However, as we saw in previous chapters, forces representing caste and brahmanism could never be decisively defeated in India. These forces kept common people in ignorance, uninformed of social reality, even the truth of their own lives. Relentless socio-religious propaganda indoctrinated the people with the values of caste and patriarchy, forcing them—often with political coercion and psychological manipulation—to internalize self-oppressive norms and values. Though challenged from the days of Buddha, the brahmanical social order was normalized by a politics of power and knowledge, glimpses of which we saw in previous chapters.

The brahmans realized that real power lies in holding knowledge. That is why the social laws conceived by them were based on the claim of knowledge—'absolute' and 'sacred' knowledge that their Vedas supposedly embodied. The correlation between Veda and varna—canon and caste, knowledge and power—runs deep, and it is not possible to grasp the one without grasping the other (Smith 2012). Panini and Patanjali, Vyasa and Valmiki, Badrayana and Jaimini, Kautilya and Manu, Shankar and Kumarila Bhatta, and hundreds of authors and theoreticians wrapped in anonymity created an impressive body of knowledge in Sanskrit that took brahmanism to the commanding heights of language and literature. 'With Buddhism and Jainism, the Prakrit languages met with short-lived successes. Until Sanskrit left the devalued circle of the celebrants of ritual sacrifices and became the language of the bureaucracy, literature, and all types of knowledge from the legendary to the erotic.' Sanskrit was however forbidden to non-brahmans, who revolted in pre-modern India by engendering people's poets and philosophers. When Namdev and Tuka, Kabir and Ravidas revolted, and when gods started to speak in Marathi, Bengali, and Tamil, the power of the brahmans was shaken (Deleury 2005: 211). However, during Mughal and colonial rule, the brahmans became entrenched in official and political administration, and successfully staked the intellectual-moral claim of representing Hindu religion and society.

Despite their passionate protests, the anti-caste forces failed to produce an effective line of scholars and writers who could take on the brahmanic knowledge-producers. The early intellectual lead that brahmanism established with the Vedic conundrum over its challengers continued in the medieval and colonial period, despite some setbacks here and there. To give a revealing example, Akbar's court was graced with many pundits; and even an *Allopanishad* was concocted in the Mughal period! And when the British conquered India, the caste elites became their main interlocutors. Colonialism in India, in fact, was more or less the story of how the British in India brahmanized and how the brahmans Westernized for mutual self-interest (Frykenberg 2001; Mani 2005). With the foundation of Asiatic Society of Calcutta in 1784, the British had in a way brought Sanskrit back into fashion. The first books they translated for the modern world were the *Manusmriti* and the *Bhagavad Gita*. The curricula of the Hindu College of Calcutta in 1817 included Sanskrit courses taught in English. Almost all the students of this institution, from 1817 to 1854, belonged to the high castes (Deleury 2005: 265). With the establishment of three universities and the expansion of secondary education in the 1850s, the caste elites studied English, surged ahead and reclaimed from the colonial power their rights as 'natural leaders' of Indian society. Before the birth of Ambedkar (1891), the first matriculate from the dalit community, there were 20,000 matriculates in India, mainly from the upper-caste groups. The near total absence of dalit-bahujans from the realms of higher education and knowledge-production was underlined by Ambedkar when he said that he was the only non-brahman scholar of his time in India. The systemic exclusion of dalit-bahujans from production and dissemination of knowledge explains why the movements led by the likes of Phule, Ambedkar, and Periyar failed to stop the upper castes from appropriating nationalism, taming it to their interest, and emerging as the new ruling class in the post-colonial period.

The new age produced no Rousseau, Thomas Paine and Karl Marx in India. Mohandas Gandhi, the alleged father of the nation, as we saw in Chapter 4, was a conservative par excellence on caste and brahmanism. And Jawarharlal Nehru, the most progressive of the elite lot, contrary to popular perception, 'discovered' India through a brahmanical eye, endowing her with the 'mysterious ability to conquer her conquerors, achieve synthesis and unity in diversity,' thus effectively covering up all flaws, frauds, and failures of the caste system (Nehru [1946] 1996; Mani 2005: 29–36). Not for nothing does he confess in his *Autobiography*: 'A Brahmin I was born, and a Brahmin I seem to remain whatever I might say or do in regard to religion or social custom. To the Indian world I am 'Pandit' so and so, in spite of my desire not to have this or any other honorific title attached to my name' (Nehru [1936] 1999: 118). Obviously, a beneficiary of the ideology and practice of caste could only become the most interested party for its reproduction, and the upper-caste nationalists were no exception to this. Grasping this reality, Louis Dumont (1998: 414) has commented, 'It would be an illusion to suppose that the castes could be abolished without bringing any affliction on the Brahmins.' Seen in this light, it is not surprising why those who could have been India's liberators—such as Phule and Ambedkar—were mocked and marginalized as special interest leaders of 'lower castes' and 'untouchables'. Built on the edifice of selective Westernization and neo-brahmanism, the modernity, the nation-state and democracy that came to India failed to establish the hegemony of egalitarianism. The brahmanical, in the sharp assessment of G. Aloysius (2010), was inscribed in the new India's body politic.

This is truer in the domain of academia and knowledge-construction, where the caste or caste-like fragmentation of Indian society is taken as a given, and even celebrated as a multicultural wonder in which there is a beautiful tolerance of difference, with an implicit assertion that there is no winner and no loser in India. Discrimination is camouflaged either as 'natural' or celebration of difference or a uniquely 'Hindu' combination of both. Caste thus can be seen as canonical, from the ancient to our own days, as a scholar has incisively pointed out:

> The authority of caste derives from the authority of Veda, but more than that caste is made to appear as a social transformation or reduplication of canon. The legitimacy, or even indisputability, of the distinctive social scheme of historical and contemporary India rides piggyback on the unquestionable truth of the Veda, and both are part of the eternal cosmic order of things. Any challenge to either the sociological or the scriptural structure can be debunked as obviously 'unnatural' or false. (Smith 2012: 24)

In short, the new and modernized Manus and Kautilyas overwhelm the academia and they fear the emancipatory potential of real education that Phule evocatively described as the Third Eye. Today, the caste elites cannot openly withhold education from the common people, but they see to it that the education imparted to the people does not encourage critical thinking about themselves and their social surroundings. They ensure that people remain in the dark about how social attitudes, norms, values, and truths have been culturally constructed to empower some and disenfranchise others. In a word, the vested interests have not allowed India to become democratic in education and culture, despite the arrival of formal equality.

Beyond the Ruling Ideas of the Ruling Class

Marx and Phule were among the first moderns to clearly see the interconnection between ideological domination and actual subjugation of the oppressed. While Marx articulated it in the context of the exploited industrial workers of the West, Phule at about the same time in India saw the link between mental slavery of the toiling castes and women and their oppression. In his groundbreaking 1873 work *Gulamgiri* (Slavery), Phule shows that brahmanism enslaved the people in the caste system through an elaborate web of socio-religious ideology. 'Brahmans' main object in fabricating these [temporal and spiritual] falsehoods was to dupe the minds of the ignorant and to rivet firmly on them the chains of perpetual bondage and slavery which their selfishness and cunning had forged' (Phule [1973] 2002). Following Phule, Iyothee Thass, Periyar, Ambedkar, and several other thinker-campaigners brought out the vicious role of brahmanic ideology and religion in the design of dominance (Mani 2005).

Marx's enunciation of how economic power gives the dominant class political power which also entails intellectual power—the power over the minds of the oppressed—is well-known.

> The class which has the means of material production at its disposal, has control at the same time over the means of mental production, so that thereby, generally speaking, the ideas of those who lack the means of mental production are subject to it. (Marx [1845] 1970: 64)

But Marx somewhat underestimated the independent role of ideology by making economics the determiner of everything. 'The mode of production of material life', he argued, 'determines the social, political and intellectual life process in general.' In the Marxist phraseology, it is the infrastructure that forms the cultural-ideological superstructure. Marx's extra emphasis on material conditions made sense when idealism and religious fundamentalism reigned supreme as an autonomous worldview. In fact, superstructure—religious and ethnic identities, ideological factors, and role of elites, etc.—is symbiotic, not superfluous to the economic and social 'base' in his construct. But this was lost on many of his followers who simply reduced Marxism into an inane discourse of economic forces determining the course of human history and politics. This was further perverted by the Marxists in India from upper-caste background who elided the whole question of caste and brahmanism in the name of class struggle. Such Marxist mimics overlooked the role played by strongly motivated elites and the devastating effects that their ideologies and actions have caused.

The relatively autonomous role of ideology and intellectual elites is provided by Gramsci in his theory of hegemony, which may be broadly understood as 'dominance by consent.' Hegemony arises from the power of the dominant class to convince other classes that its interests are the interests of all. The most viable method of social control is to induce subordinates to regulate themselves through a seductive ideology. Hegemony is established not through force, but by largely peaceful means through elite-controlled agencies and apparatuses such as religious institutions, intellectual pursuits, the media, art and literature which present the dominant class interest as the common interest and thus come to be taken for granted (Gramsci 1996). Such ideological indoctrination produces conformist, docile subjects and also helps the dominant class to mystify and mask its repressive machinery (police, law courts, and the military).

At about the same time when Gramsci was theorizing hegemony in an Italian jail, the American academic Harold Lasswell published a remarkable work, *Politics: Who Gets What, When, How*, which shows how easy it is for the elites to manufacture consent and maintain the status quo through a well-entrenched ideology.

> A well-established ideology perpetuates itself with a little propaganda by those whom it benefits most. . . . Systems of life which confer special benefits on the other fellow need no plots or conspiracies when the masses are moved by faith and the elites are inspired by self-confidence. (Lasswell 1936)

Later, combining the insights of Marx and Gramsci, Louis Althusser developed his thesis of ideological state apparatuses. This stresses that ideology is the fulcrum of the state machinery through which the dominant class reproduces its class domination, moulding people into subjects who conform to the norms and values of existing class relations (Althusser 1971). By concealing the whole situation of economic, social, and political domination, the dominant ideology perpetuates ignorance, disunity and lethargy among the oppressed. As Paulo Freire argues, elitist reproduction of culture and knowledge keeps pace with changing times, ensuring that the oppressed do not see through the design of dominance, lest they unite and engage in a struggle for emancipation (Freire [1970] 1996).

Of the different capitals—economic, cultural and social—cultural capital is a 'misrecognisable, transfigured and legitimized form' of the most basic form of capital, the economic (Bourdieu 1991: 170). It is cultural capital, as Ngugi argues in *Decolonising the Mind*, that enables the ruling class to rule the mental universe of the dominated—the most important area of domination. Controlling people's minds, the powerful determine how people see themselves and their relationship to the world. 'Economic and political control can never be complete or effective without mental control. To control a people's culture is to control their tools of self-definition in relationship to others' (Ngugi 1986).

The relationship between cultural capital and the maintenance of power cannot be understood without understanding the politics of education. Despite some democratic changes in recent years, the education system, by and large, remains the stronghold of the social elite. It is the elite who function as intellectual interpreters of the past and present. Knowingly or unknowingly, they reproduce culture and education in a way that safeguards their caste-class interests and normalizes the structures of hierarchy. For example, caste elites (as we saw in previous chapters) generally present caste as a division of labour and a uniquely indigenous way of resolving socio-ethnic differences. In their eyes, caste is not a system of discrimination but a way of life.

Contesting the claims of disinterested nature of cultural production, as Bourdieu shows, the school and university reproduce hierarchy in society and remain the main centres of the propagation of the elite culture. The elite institutions build up the cultural and intellectual competence of the privileged, who invest their talents to reproduce and perpetuate caste-class distinctions. Above all, the educational centres themselves create power hierarchies in the struggle for cultural capital. Any discipline, in this respect, becomes like an enclosed space with its own set of ascriptive norms and hierarchies. Such academic politics are made invisible by communicating ideas and researches in a specialist language that serve the dual function of warding off the non-specialists and concealing the hierarchical power politics of its practitioners (Bourdieu 1977; 1988).

Without decoding this knowledge-power nexus, it is impossible to grasp the elite's superficial support for democracy and justice and expose their hegemonic design. But the public remains in the dark about the real social facts and phenomenon like hegemony. The common people have yet to grasp the underlying ideas about nationality, race, caste, class, and gender. Exceptions apart, their minds remain enslaved to the dominant constructions of the ruling class as they remain submerged in the established power relationships. Ideas and images of the social world and one's place in it—implanted in the people's minds since their childhood—take years to eradicate, if they ever can be.

It is not easy to embrace democratic values when those values are routinely contradicted in our everyday life. Awakening from the slumber of centuries is not easy. Opening one's long-closed eyes is especially painful in the beginning. Not surprisingly, many people want to avoid the self-struggle that is absolutely necessary for a new social life. This problem is aggravated by the ruling class which never fails to spot the potential revolutionaries among the oppressed, who are promptly given ticket to success—prizes, prestige, applause—and taught the lucrative value of being traitors to their own suffering communities. Similarly, due to elitist manipulation and their own lack of critical consciousness, the oppressed sometimes become the instruments of oppression of other oppressed. That explains the notorious boast of American railway financer Jay Gould, 'I can hire half the working class to shoot the other half.'

It is indeed a cruel irony of history that the oppressed have been known to taunt, torment and torture other oppressed. The victims fight, injure, and are cruel to one another because the oppressors do not just oppress them but also see to it that the people harass and fight one another. But the issue remains (yet to be overcome): one may be oppressed, and still vile in one's interaction with the other oppressed.

Oppression dehumanizes and divides the oppressed, delegating physical violence on which it rests to the oppressed themselves. When institutionalized oppression acquires an aura of normalcy, it induces the victims to regulate themselves. There is a tendency among the common people—actively promoted by vested interests—to imitate the norms, values, and behavioural patterns of those who have a higher status or are more powerful. The internalization of dominant norms and values is the most corrosive injury inflicted on the victims who at terrible cost to their own humanity embrace the value of their oppressors. Hemmed in on all sides by the dominant values, the oppressed are forced to validate hierarchy, tolerate discrimination, and thus, limit the possibilities of their emancipation. Generations of subservience to the higher ups induce passivity, credulity and docility in the oppressed.

The oppressed are so demoralized that some of them even come to respect their oppressors. The fear of freedom is drilled so deep in them that they learn to internalize their sufferings; they learn to remain silent, and even give away their right to speak to the higher-ups. It is an old saying that ten people who speak make more noise than ten thousand who do not open their mouths. In the democratic era too, the people remain prone to hero worship false leaders who speak the rhetoric of change while actually they safeguard the status quo. This allows the wily and the vocal to keep the multitude in the dark about things that matter. The powerful offer themselves—in a spirit of sacrifice (!)— to think, see, talk and act on the people's behalf. Like this shameless publicity for a modern politician:

You don't need to think, he thinks for you!
You don't need to see, he sees for you!
You don't need to talk, he talks for you!
You don't need to act, he acts for you!
(Publicity for a Brazilian politician, in Freire 2005: 51)

But people can, and will, think and liberate themselves and others, and this is what we turn to in the following pages.

RETHINKING AND DEMOCRATISING EDUCATION

The ruling class pays lip service to justice and inclusiveness, but refuses to reorganize society and education on a democratic line. The education system is still oriented to domesticate the student and prepare her to fulfil a function in the established hierarchy of society and production system. First in school, and later in college, the design is to mould the individual into a clog in the social machine—in a hierarchy of jobs and roles. The basic idea is to imprison youth in thousands of prefabricated pigeon-holes in which social rank is measured by the quantity of education and the money made. The purpose of elite-led education is not to disturb the established power relationships in society.

In India, the education system, on the whole, conceals the reality of mass deprivation and discrimination under the fanciful theories of diversity and pluralism, which in fact validate the brahmanic argument that different castes, ethnicities, and genders have different essences, different inclinations, and that traditional India has been wonderfully sensitive to their need of differential existences! Such arguments not only amount to eliding the historical oppressions perpetrated against toiling castes and women, especially their historical exclusion from education, but also obliquely suggesting that culture and education are not meant for everyone. In other words, by hiding social contradictions and oppression, caste elites camouflage discriminations with cultural differences, thus negating the basic spirit of democracy that calls for demolition of all discriminations.

The viability of a democracy depends on equality of conditions, since in its essence it is, more than a form of governance, a way of life that has to be built brick-by-brick by breaking old habits and re-educating minds. As emancipation of the oppressed is a basic promise of democracy, it must constitute an integral part of educational excellence. By encouraging critical thinking and equipping citizens for appropriate choice in their life, democratic education must begin with questioning the social role of education, the structures of school systems and the university as well as the content and value of received knowledge and culture. In other words, an alternative envisioning of education demands dismantling the elitist fiefdoms of knowledge-construction and structuring a public discourse that helps forge a vibrant civil society.

Committed to equality and dignity for everyone, democratic education aims at levelling, but as Benjamin Barber (1992) makes clear, this is levelling up, not levelling down. Democratic politics and education bring about an improvement for the whole society, without reducing everyone to the same identity, or stifling the special talents of anyone. In a democracy, a fair and equal treatment of other people is one of the preconditions for one's own flourishing. Such conditions prepare a level playing field where one does not have to trample over others for one's creativity and success. The promise of democracy is to generate equal opportunities for everyone, especially by enabling the hitherto disadvantaged people to realize their potential. Democratic education stands for the idea that no caste, class, race, or sex has a monopoly on brilliance, beauty, or power; and that there is room for everyone to excel. The common good means that it is good for everyone. For this, education has to be freed from entrenched interests; it must pave the way for the hitherto oppressed groups to liberate themselves and remake their lives.

Democratic education in the Indian context means an education that leads towards emancipation of the demoralized majority. The emerging dalit-subaltern studies, women's studies, minorities' studies and research on other subjugated segments of society will contribute to such democratization. These studies will complement each other, and find ways to engage and integrate all oppressed groups as the voices of togetherness for an exploitation-free world. New education should be based on the idea that the only community is the one that embraces all humanity. Phule visualized it as *ekamay loka*; people who have emerged as a new society transcending caste, class, gender, and other exploitation. Such a world cannot be constructed without building bridges of solidarity among all the oppressed, converging and merging their emancipatory aspirations into the new education. Although its core curriculum and its basic objectives will have to be widely discussed and debated before reaching at a broad consensus, there is little doubt that the new education has to be directed towards undermining the status quo, disrupting the power structure of everyday life, and challenging the claim of the dominant group to represent and dominate all others.

In other words, the realm of ideas, education, and communication should form a crucial site for emancipatory struggle—from slums to universities. Exploring possibilities for change, democratic education has to open up fresh debates about the age-old yet unresolved problems facing humanity. It has to expose the structure and the mindset that foster sexist, casteist, homophobic, and other oppressive ideas and practices. It has to critique the institutions, attitudes and relationships that weave the web of injustice and exclusion. For this, the new education will have to challenge the intellectual strongholds and resorts of the ruling classes—*Todane hi honge math or garh sab*, as the Hindi poet Gajanan Madhav Muktibodh put it in the 1960s. This means that we go to the roots of problems, so that we can grasp and discard canons and constructs that oppress and suppress, and replace them with a liberating vision and will for reconstruction. Above all, new education will require a new language and a new sensibility. The master's tools, in Audre Lorde's words, will never bring down the master's house.

Among other things, the new education will have, necessarily, to contend with the principal contradiction in Indian history and culture, that is, the long-drawn dialectical opposition between *shastra* (the brahmanic intellectual tradition and its modernization in contemporary knowledge-construction) and *loka* (society at large). In a famous poem, Kabir gives voice to this divide between *shastra* and *loka*, when he says that his criteria for assessing reality is *aakhin ki dekhi* (his own first-hand experience and observation) while the brahman takes recourse to *kaagad ki lekhi* (fictitious and false writings) to pull wool over people's eyes:

How can our minds—yours and mine—meet!
I say what I have seen.
You say what you have read.
I want to disentangle the complexity of truth.
And you keep it under wraps to
Further complicate the matter! (For the original in Hindi, see Dwivedi 1999: 247)

This dialectical opposition between elitist knowledge and oppressed humanity continues in new forms to this day, irrespective of changes on the surface. The elitist grammar and language have changed dramatically, but not the mindset that reproduces exclusion. On the whole, academia and intellectual constructions remain under elitist control, the mainstream of intellectual currents in India remains brahmanic. This is the context and the raison d'être for reconstructing knowledge and education. Let us now discuss some of the important issues related to this challenge.

New Stratum of Intellectuals, Identity and Representation

Educational transformation requires people, especially the oppressed, to think for themselves. The notion that an intellectual activity is the abstract cogitation of a few professional intellectuals has to be changed, and instead seen as a concrete social activity in which, implicitly, all people are engaged. It must first be shown, we may recall with Gramsci, that all men and women are intellectuals, as all people have thinking faculties. And though all do not have the social functions of intellectuals, everyone is capable of taking an active part in the creation of history and developing their conception of the world (Gramsci 1996: 5–23). Recall Buddha's maxim *atta dipo bhava, atta saran* (be your own lamps, be your own refuge). The new intellectuals would be the thinking and organizing element among the commonality, whom Gramsci calls organic intellectuals. He distinguishes between a traditional intelligentsia which sees itself—wrongly—as a class apart, and the thinking groups which every class produces from its own ranks. Such organic intellectuals do not simply describe social life in accordance with the established rules, but rather articulate the feelings and experiences which the masses could not express for themselves. Stressing the need to create a new people's culture for a democratic education, Gramsci asserts that the common people, like privileged groups, are capable of developing from within their own ranks their own philosophers: 'It is essential to destroy the widespread prejudice that philosophy is a strange and difficult thing just because it is the specific intellectual activity of a particular category of specialists or of professional and systematic philosophers' (ibid.: 323).

However, unlike traditional professional intellectuals, literary, philosophical, and scientific, it is not sufficient for organic intellectuals to have just expertise and specialized knowledge. They must also be willing to work with people, learn from their experiences, and participate in the struggle for the formation of a liberating cultural paradigm. To be *directive* as well as *specialized*, the new intellectuals must be able to elaborate their specialized knowledge into social and political knowledge. 'The mode of being of the new intellectual can no longer consist in eloquence, which is an exterior and momentary mover of feelings and passions, but in active participation in practical life, as constructor, organizer, "permanent persuader"'(ibid.: 10). It will be the job of the organic intellectual to know things deeply and profoundly, to know more than the traditional intellectuals with a superior conception of humanity and history. They will empower people by opening their minds rather than inducing dependency.

Thus the role of new thinkers is not just to observe and articulate or formulate long-term necessities, but to perceive initiatives, to stimulate minds, to coordinate social action, and above all, to assist in raising public consciousness. It is less a matter of leadership than of being an integral part of a movement to evolve new patterns of life through a new pedagogy: a pedagogy of revolution and a pedagogical revolution.

The new intellectuals and the common people must be fused in a way that develops the democratic character of new education and intellectual activity. Intellectuals of the masses and public-spirited scholars of academia and elsewhere must be recognized and integrated into the process. Together, they must help evolve a public debate and public reason in which all individuals can participate as free and equal individuals. Anyone, irrespective of social background, who wants to be a part of the ongoing liberation struggle can help in this enterprise, though the bulwark of cultural and academic initiatives for transformation must come from the sufferers of the system themselves. Those joining the liberation struggle will have to prove their revolutionary integrity, as Bertolt Brecht points out in his poem 'The Interrogation of the Good':

Step forward: we hear
That you are a good man.
You cannot be bought, but the lightning
Which strikes the house, also
Cannot be bought.
You hold to what you said.
But what did you say?
You are honest, you say your opinion.
Which opinion?
You are brave.
Against whom?
You are wise.
For whom?
You do not consider your personal advantages,
Whose advantages do you consider then?
You are a good friend.
Are you also a good friend of the good people? (Brecht, tr. Zizek, in idem, 2001: 150–1)

The oppressed are tired of being represented by others. Men at the helm of a feminist struggle, or brahman-bourgeois leading a democratic struggle no longer enthuse the struggling women and the dalit-bahujan. The advocacy of self-representation, however, is not to be reduced as a proposal for a narrow-minded identity politics, or indulgence in essentialism. If ever one has to take recourse to essentialism, it has to be strategic (under specific circumstances) and committed to a radical politics. Strategic fight provides a break here and there, it may uplift some groups or bring some palliative reforms, but it makes no systemic difference; it does not change the system. A strategy, however brilliant, cannot be a substitute for ideology.

The question of identity is important, and the challenge before the oppressed is not to be defined or confined by their inherited humiliating identity, but to forge a new emancipatory one. In fact, a shudra has not only to cast off her degrading shudra identity, but ultimately also persuade or force the brahman to give up her oppressive brahman identity. Shudra or brahman identity has to be rejected because as long as there is a brahman, there will be a shudra, and vice versa—a fact many *progressive* brahman men and women do not understand. If our focus is to shift from brahman to brahmanism (as many caste elites insist and rightly so), this necessitates that the brahman gives up his brahman identity. This is not easy, but we have to make a move in that direction.

True, a social or cultural identity cannot have meaning without reference to the past, to tradition, to origins, and to 'who we were.' Yet the emancipatory struggle should not be centred on just 'who are we?' and 'how did we become what we are today?' It must undergird transformational visions of the present and future. History has never been an unalterable given, the nature of which is agreed upon by all. All cultural identities are 'imagined' or 'invented' rather than simply discovered from the past. Roy Wagner (1975) sees all cultures to be invented but he naively sees such inventions as unconscious and spontaneous. Hobsbawm and Ranger (1983) suggest that the invention of culture and tradition is always a deliberate, conscious, and politically motivated act. As cultures and traditions are human products, they are not eternal; they change all the time. Drawing on this perspective, two scholars have put it forthrightly,

> Though they seem to invoke an origin in a historical past with which they continue to correspond, actually identities are about questions of using the resources of history, language and culture in the process of becoming rather than being: not 'who we are' or 'where we came from', so much as what we might become, how we have been represented and how that bears on how we might represent ourselves. (Stuart Hall and Paul du Gay, quoted in Bauman 2008: 101)

History is a flexible source for justifying change and also defending the status quo. 'History may be servitude, history may be freedom.' As the common people have been either 'hidden from history' or grossly misrepresented, there is a need for reconstruction of people's experience as 'a source of inspiration and understanding.' If a consciousness of the triumphant experiences in the past is justified for the oppressive groups, the need of 'lifting the veil', or a realistic representation of the past, is many times more justified for exploited castes and communities. As a feminist historian puts it, women and other oppressed classes

> cannot afford to lack a consciousness of a collective identity, one which necessarily involves a shared awareness of the past. Without this, a group [is] . . . vulnerable to the impositions of dubious stereotypes, as well as limiting prejudices about what is right and proper for it to do or not to do. (Johansson 1976: 427)

The lesson that the past teaches is seldom precise and often contradictory, but a fair knowledge of the duality of past is the key to understanding the present.

Besides comforting the afflicted and afflicting the comfortable, identity-based radicalism expresses aspirations of the oppressed for self-representation. But more desirable is the construction of a new emancipatory identity and politics based on a new education, encompassing powerful symbols and instrumental orientations for change. It has to be thoughtfully developed as an antidote to internalized mindsets of domination and submission. It has to clearly recognize that the foundation on which tyranny is built is the unified, interrelated matrices of caste, class, and patriarchy. Justice for all will come with a reconstruction of knowledge, and casting off of deeply ingrained mindsets of hierarchy and ascription.

Core Issues and Orientation

Educational transformation is an academic enterprise, animated by an emancipatory vision. Critiquing structures of dominance and intellectual status quo, it holds up a mirror to the whole of society so that the oppressed can see their enslavement and the oppressor their privileges and complicity in institutionalized injustice. It goes beyond the usual anthropological studies of customs and life styles of the marginalized communities, and instead undertakes a critical review of the entire spectrum of society.

> Studying 'up' as well as 'down' would lead us to ask many 'common sense' questions in reverse. Instead of asking why some people are poor, we should ask why other people are so affluent. How on earth would a social scientist explain the hoarding patterns of the American rich and middle class? How can we explain the fantastic resistance to change among those whose options 'appear to be many'? (Nader 1972)

Thus, studying the ruling class and unmasking the false normalization of established order must form an integral part of emancipatory education. The entire gamut of politics and pedagogy must come under its purview. Broadly speaking, research and writing must undermine existing hegemonies and produce what a social scientist calls 'a culturally suspicious, trouble-making readership.' Education has, necessarily, to be a transgressive and anti-establishment practice, oriented to call all canons and constructs of culture into question. Even as it contests the status-quoist classroom politics and the subterranean dominant ideologies that underlie its texts, it must create the synergy for a collective will to reconstruct knowledge—and the human world.

Emancipatory education has to navigate the academic jungle and expose the high priests for their pretended impartiality and actual collusion with the institutional and professional structures of hegemony that leave no scope for any meaningful engagement with the larger society, especially the suffering communities. The fiction of academic neutrality or scholarly apoliticism must be probed and exposed for what they actually are. Any cultural product, whether art, literature, academic writing or theorization needs to be seen in its historical setting. Any text has to seen as socially produced, as a product of a particular cultural milieu, and not as an inspiration. As Polish poet Wisława Szymborska underlines in her poem, 'Children of Our Age':

Whether you like it or not,
your genes have a political past,
your skin, a political cast,
your eyes, a political slant. . . .
Apolitical poems are also political,
and above us shines a moon
no longer purely lunar.
To be or not to be, that is the question.
And though it troubles the digestion
it's a question, as always, of politics. . . .
Meanwhile, people perished,
animals died,
houses burned,
and the fields ran wild
just as in times immemorial
and less political.

To pretend to be apolitical—neutral—is to be partisan, and taking a status quo-ist position. Thomas Mann argues in his 'Culture and Politics' (1939) that being apolitical amounts to being anti-democratic. Chinua Achebe, known for calling a dog a dog, dismisses the so-called *neutral* literature as 'deodorized dog shit'. Indeed, no serious writer can escape from societal politics and power structures that shape human life and worldviews—she or he has to take sides either with the establishment or those opposed to that. As Ngugi argues, 'Every writer is a writer in politics. The only question is what and whose politics.'

Today, there is a crisis of intellectual confidence for cultural transformation, and the dalit-bahujan studies, adivasi studies, women's studies, and other studies of marginalized communities must strive to reconstruct education as well as produce a committed, capable intelligentsia, especially, though not necessarily, from amongst the dalit-subaltern, women and other oppressed groups. As Freire argues,

> The pedagogy of the oppressed [is] a pedagogy which must be forged with, not for, the oppressed (be they individuals or peoples) in the incessant struggle to regain their humanity. This pedagogy makes oppression and its causes objects of reflection by the oppressed, and from that reflection will come their necessary engagement in the struggle for their liberation. And in the struggle this pedagogy will be made and unmade. (Freire 1996: 30)

Such pedagogy cannot be conceived for the oppressed but with them and by them, on the basis on their own reading of the world. The new teaching can only be a dialogue, not giving knowledge from 'outside'. The oppressed cannot be treated as the object of teaching; they are the subject. By illuminating the subjectivities ignored in the traditional teaching, radical pedagogy mingles with radical politics. For Freire, who struggled to resolve the problem of adult illiteracy in Brazil, teaching reading is inseparable from reading the world and becoming aware of one's position in it, and then discovering in one's needs the way to the effort—individual and collective—that will lead to liberation from oppression. Contrary to the education that pretends to be neutral but functions as an instrument which is used to facilitate the integration of people into the logic of an existing system (and bring about conformity) the new education becomes the practice of freedom. In Freire's pedagogy, the very first words read also interpret the social reality that they symbolize. The learners do not just learn facts, but ask questions. Authentic education is learning to see the world with new eyes, to deal critically with an oppressive reality and discover how to participate in the transformation of the world. This way of learning changes not only one's attitude towards the world, but also one's attitude towards oneself. The learner comes to realize that the world around us is not an unchangeable given, and the learner herself a thing, with no option but to fall in line with other things in the world. Central to the philosophy of emancipatory pedagogy is the idea of 'learning to perceive social, political, and economic contradictions, and to take action against the oppressive elements of reality' (Freire 1996).

The new education is to assist the suffering people, submerged in the reality of an unequal and unjust society, to emerge from this situation by becoming aware of the causes of their subjugation and of the possibility of changing this reality to make it respond to human needs.

The worst consequence of social hierarchy is the lower orders' internalization of oppressive norms and values of the higher orders. The elites know that their greatest asset in manipulating society and maintaining their dominance is the mind of the oppressed. Liberation begins with the desire of the oppressed to be free, but at the outset, since they have no other model, to be free means to be an oppressor. Instances of the working class adopting middle-class values, lowered castes imitating brahmanic norms, or women working hard to be like men are scattered around us. A crucial task of the new education, therefore, is to make the oppressed aware that the life of the oppressor is unacceptable. Those seeking their freedom and humanity must not copy the oppressor and covet, like the latter, acquisition of wealth and power as the goal of life. They must endeavour to break the sinister cycles of humiliation of one person or one class of people by another. Radical breaks with the oppressive order must constitute a fundamental part of the new pedagogy and politics.

The oppressor is not the one who can lead a liberating movement; it is only the oppressed who have to wage this struggle. Thus, the education of the oppressed, animated by authentic ethical concern for everyone (unlike the false generosity of the dominant class) has to be the education for a new humanity. Changing the structures, methods, and content of existing education will thus become an integral part of a cultural movement which will delineate contradictions in society and strive to overcome the social causes of alienation and dehumanization.

Above all, the new education must aim for ending the divisive structures of education which perpetuate all other conflicts, especially the question of manual and intellectual work which separates the class from the mass. The sharp division between manual and mental work has for long been the fulcrum of social hierarchy. Historically, intellectual work was the province of the ruling groups, which also decided how labour was put to use. Manual work was given to the 'lesser' humans who were denied good life and education and systematically turned into slaves or lower orders. The ruling class, thus, doubled up as the intellectual class and kept the working people uneducated, divided, and demoralized. The sharp separation of physical and cerebral work in a particular mode continues still. All awards, rewards, and prestige are cornered by the people who invent things, manage machines, and above all, supervise and manipulate people. This is especially so in the technology-driven era of economic globalization when the essential productive force is no longer labour-intensive land and machines, but knowledge, technology, and financial wizardry in the service of the capitalist who exploits and directs them to maximize profits.

The primacy accorded to the manipulation of people can be easily seen in the hierarchy of a multinational company (MNC). On an average, its chief executive officer (CEO) gets 500 times, or more, salary than the person at the gate—and in between there are hundreds of salary hierarchies in which employees are placed. And the billionaire owner has many times more income or profit than his highest paid CEO. However, the gatekeeper gets more than a skilled worker who works for a lowly firm. And then there are unskilled labour outside the gate of the lowly firm who get even less. And then there is an army of unemployed, unlettered and unskilled people in countries like India, for whom any wage is a good wage. A person who spends Rs. 29 a day in urban area and Rs. 22 a day in rural area is not poor in the eyes of the Indian government whose ministers and bureaucrats may spend Rs. 50,000 on lunch. Capitalism brutally discriminates between different kinds of manual labour and intellectual skills. In market society, money becomes the arbiter with the best and the worst. Ideas, innovations, and creativity are judged on the basis of the monetary values of their expected commercial exploitation.

Grasping the corrosive nature of capitalism is necessary not simply because it is materially exploitative, but because its system of impersonal market forces compel individuals to treat one another as potential competitors or as means to an end. The issue is not simply a mechanized and monetized society over which humanity has lost control, but the inner dullness and ethical disintegration that it fosters. At stake is not class concerns and revolution, but the survival of humanity.

In short, to resolve the dualism between intellectual and manual work, alongside the conflict between the profit-over-people mechanism and the progressive possibilities of individual and social development requires a radical overhaul of the educational system. The goal is not simply educational reform, but a cultural revolution. The full implications of changing the structures of education only become clear in this context.

Renewal will not come from embracing the latest technology of communication and teaching but from a change in structures, methods, and content of education. The purpose of education is to form individuals able not only to keep society functioning but also to renew social life and activity in a better direction. Its aim is to form complete humans—responsible beings in a specific sector of production, capable of reflection on the ends of the whole society, important participants in the new course of civilization. Imagination and ingredients for such transformation cannot be imparted to society from the top or the outside but must emanate from specific cultural conditions of countries. This cannot be done without going to the roots of problems which Marx considered the hallmark of a genuine radicalism, calling for 'a merciless criticism of everything existing, merciless in two senses: this criticism must not be afraid of its own conclusions and must not shrink from a collision with the established powers' ([1843c] 1978).

Critiquing everything existing must go hand in hand with self-criticism and self-struggle (as we discussed at length in Chapter 1). The initiative to humanize the world must begin with humanizing ourselves. Without the ethical core of love and compassion, all pedagogy and politics are bound to end in bitterness and bigotry. Freire visualises revolution as 'an act of love' because of its creative and liberating nature:

> . . . The revolution is made by people to achieve their humanization. What, indeed, is the deeper motive that moves individuals to become revolutionaries, but the dehumanization of people? The distortion imposed on the word love by the capitalist world cannot . . . prevent the revolutionaries from affirming their love of life. (Freire 1996: 70)

Without connecting with other people on the basis of imaginative sympathy and understanding, there is little hope of challenging and changing the system. This dialogic spirit and willingness to cooperate with others will provide the ground for a collective struggle for liberation. The need for such reciprocity and generosity cannot be overstressed:

> Survival in fact is about the connections between things; in Eliot's phrase, reality cannot be deprived of the 'other echoes [that] inhabit the garden.' It is more rewarding—and more difficult—to think concretely and sympathetically, contrapuntally, about others than only about 'us'. But this also means not trying to rule others, not trying to classify them or put them in hierarchies, above all, not constantly reiterating how 'our' culture is number one (or not number one for that matter). (Said 1993: 408)

Indulgence in self-serving politics is self-defeating—and against the foundational principle of educational revolution. Self-confinement or separation from other suffering communities also gives a chance to the establishment to set one marginalized group against another. It opens the way for dividing the oppressed into various categories of ethnic or religious minorities, keeping them in their ghettos. Any meaningful struggle has to be reciprocal to and supportive of struggles of other suffering communities. Dalits and adivasis, workers and artisans, poor Indians and poor Pakistanis must stand for each other's rights. The oppressed everywhere must be united—and transformed—into a force to overcome oppressive forces. 'Life in common', as Hardt and Negri (2004: xv, 228) say, is the bond that binds all the productive people in the multitude: 'The multitude is neither an identity, nor uniform (like the masses), the internal differences of the multitude must discover the common that allows them to communicate and act together. The common we share, is in fact, not so much discovered as produced.' They rightly argue that 'becoming common presents the possibility of not only the equality of various forms of labour but also their free exchange and communication. Producing in common presents the possibility of the production of the common.'

A Holistic, Critical and Constructive Approach

Emancipatory education must enunciate its rationale in social and intellectual terms. Its basic justification, like any education, is that it enhances our social understanding and possibility for a better world. However, to replace the existing body and framework of education requires the creation of an alternative and definitive body of literature in both social sciences and humanities. Such works should establish the focus and rationale of the new education as well as its alternative theories, paradigms, research methods and strategies. Interrogating the status quo, it must come up with relevant data, categories, and concepts that can provide intellectual resources for an alternative vision and paradigm. In theory and presentation, it has to adhere to core democratic values and thematics that express its concerns and priorities, and help develop a critical perspective on major problems. What should be the core characteristics of such a body of literature?

Emancipatory education must adopt a holistic approach that enables us to see the whole and the parts at the same time. We can better grasp it with the parable of the elephant and the blind men that Buddha narrated to highlight the futility of viewing reality in fragmented bits, and missing the core. Holistic vision enables us to avoid the trap into which the blind people fell. By adopting an integrated perspective, we are freed from mistaking the trees for the wood. In the Indian context, adopting a holistic approach means a comprehensive investigation into a longstanding hierarchical society where millions of people continue to be oppressed. Such an approach is based on the premise that structures of caste, class, gender as well as several other cultural-regional and political factors are interrelated and interactive. All these structures and substructures have their own components and roles to play but are not independent of each other. There are symbiotic interconnections and overlaps between factors, which are social (caste, family, ethnic identities), economic (class, material aspects and social relations of production), cultural (religion, art, literature, mass media, film and television), and gender-based (patriarchy, equation between sexes, politics of sexuality and reproduction). All these factors are always in flux as they constantly interact and mould each other, and thus keep changing their colours and contours. The failure to view them in their totality limits our intellectual perception and hinders our political action for change.

It is important, therefore, not to put all emphasis on just one factor, be it social (caste) or economic (class) or gender (inequality between men and women), that can deny or undermine the role of other factors, which mutually reinforce the status quo. For example, the full force of caste discrimination cannot be understood if its study is divorced from its economic (class) and religio-cultural and gender moorings. Similarly, women in India face the brutality of rape, dowry deaths, domestic violence in everyday life and gang rapes and killings during riots not just because they are women, but because they are dalit women, adivasi women, Muslim women, women who are poor and of a particular caste, tribe or ethnicity. As Noam Chomsky argues,

> It makes sense to seek out and identify structures of authority, hierarchy, and domination in every aspect of life, and to challenge them; unless a justification for them can be given, they are illegitimate. And should be dismantled, to increase the scope of human freedom. That includes political power, ownership and management, relations among men and women, parents and children, our control over the fate of future generations . . . Naturally this means a challenge to the huge institutions of coercion and control; the state, the unaccountable private tyrannies that control most of the domestic and international economy, and so on . . . the burden of proof has to be placed on authority, and that it should be dismantled if that burden cannot be met. (Chomsky 2004)

Only a holistic understanding can unite the communities who have been pushed to the margins, and forge them together in a collective struggle based on collective aspirations. One of the main reasons behind divisions and fragmentations among oppressed communities is the intellectual failure to develop an alternative inclusive vision. The new education must take up this challenge and strive to create an intellectual ferment for such a vision.

A holistic approach also implies a critical approach—an objective, incisive approach to evaluate and orient the reality. It means subverting stereotypes, easy simplifications and rigid preconceptions. It means eschewing dogmatic formulations, not shunning nuance and ambiguity, and developing the capacity to grasp complexity and contradictions so that we can better meet the challenge. It is desirable to transcend narrations of victimhood, and instead dig beneath the surface and superficiality to bring out the political behind the personal. Similarly, it is vital to grasp that dominant intellectual constructs and clichés trickle into people's consciousness, tower over cultural commonsense, and paralyse intellectual and moral resistance to injustices. There must be special efforts to understand and overcome the widespread acceptance and internalization of oppressive values of gender, caste, and class. The greatest weapon in the oppressors' armoury, as Fanon said, is the mind of the oppressed. Emancipating the mind from layers and layers of oppressive constructs is not easy: it requires painstaking and prolonged effort. But this is a revolutionary challenge and must be engaged with. Criticality also means recognizing human imperfections, including our own, and developing a healthy disdain for strident moral judgement and stereotypical certitudes.

Recent years have witnessed the publication of many outstanding works from the perspective of the oppressed, and we must learn from them. The subversive potential of subaltern and gender subjectivity—amply evident in the pan-Indian emergence of dalit literature and women's writings—is obvious enough, but it is important to politicize the personal, and vice versa. Through adopting a sociological language, one's lived experiences can be narrated to ask passionate and probing questions, sparking a debate and dialogue with a wider audience. For example, Kancha Ilaiah's *Why I Am Not a Hindu* can be cited as a subversive text. So also Sharan Limbale's *Akkarmashi* (The Outcaste); Omprakash Valmiki's *Joothan: A Dalit Life*; Bama's *Karukku*; Vasant Moon's *Growing Up Untouchable in India*; Baby Halder's *A Life Less Ordinary*; Baby Kamble's *The Prisons We Broke*; Manikuntala Sen's *In Search of Freedom*, and many other dalit-subaltern and feminist autobiographical works.

The emergent subjectivity of dalit-subaltern and women's literatures may help us better understand the social psychology of collective behaviour. As Georges Lefebvre, the historian who first used the term 'history from below', has argued, 'Social history cannot be limited to describing the external aspects of antagonistic classes. It must also come to understand the mental outlook of each class' (cited by Kaye 1995: xi). Why intellectual and social participation of individuals from the privileged castes in anti-caste movements have not always produced desired results could be gauged from a perceptive comment by Rabindranath Tagore wherein he speaks of the schizophrenic disjunction between the principle and practice of traditional elites in India.

> For a long time past we have been in the habit, in our life and endeavour, of setting apart one place for our emotions and another for our practices. Our intellect has all the time remained dormant, because we have not dared to allow it scope. That is why, when we have to rouse ourselves to action, it is our emotion which has to be requisitioned, and our intellect has to be kept from interfering by the hypnotism of some magical formula—that is to say we hasten to create a situation absolutely inimical to the free play of our intellect. (Tagore, cited in Biswas 2001: 146)

Emancipatory education should delve into the social pathology of caste and patriarchal culture, and try to bring out not only what Ambedkar termed the 'lawless laws' of the Hindu tradition but also their subtle and seductive reinvention in the contemporary times. There is a need to revisit and bring out the ambiguities and contradictions of that soul-stirring phrase 'freedom struggle' including the roles of national heroes such as Gandhi and Nehru, on the caste question and their quintessentially brahmanic vision of Indian society that was primarily responsible for their failure to make common cause with anti-caste intellectuals like Ambedkar and Periyar (Aloysius 1997; Mani 2005).

Holistic and critical approach should culminate in a reconstructive approach. It can go beyond the traditional academic parameter of explanation, evaluation and criticism to an orientation towards transformation. Reconstruction entails not only developing a new way of looking at humanity and society, but also to find ways to link new knowledge-construction and epistemology to social practice. This requires, among other things, reconstructing history in the image and interests of the common people. Thus, we must seek to demonstrate how the historically specific struggles of dalits and adivasis, working men and women, peasants and artisans have been crucial to whatever positive changes or social mobility took place in Indian society. It is vital to grasp that the struggles against caste and brahmanism under multiple socio-political banners right from the shramanic-Buddhist resistance to the explosion of popular protests in the radical streams of the medieval Bhakti movement to the more recent anti-caste campaigns of Jotirao Phule, Iyothee Thass, Narayana Guru, Ambedkar and Periyar were inspired by the vision of an equalitarian society (Mani 2005). It is up to the new generation of radicals to make creative use of these cultural resources to lay the foundation of a new politics of transformation.

Today, the dalit-bahujan movement is in ideological and ethical disarray, and by and large unable to grasp and face the challenges of a fast changing world. Behind the smoke-screen of 'political radicalism' in recent years symbolized by the rise of some dalit-bahujan politicians in regional and national power politics, there is the disturbing sign of their capitulation and compromise for personal gain. On the whole, the dalit-bahujan politics is being driven by personal ambition, rather than by larger social and political ideas. Retrieval of the legacy of anti-caste movements from the corrupt power politicians has become a huge challenge for all Phule-Ambedkarites and promoters of emancipatory education.

Diverse struggles against injustice since the time of Buddha have to be reinterpreted in the contemporary language to present a viable alternative to the brahmanic envisioning of Indian society. This requires avoiding the tendency to highlight just one movement or culture hero, and ignore the rest, or worse, pit one emancipatory movement and its leaders against another, according to a narrow allegiance to one's own caste, creed, ethnicity, or region. Moreover, invoking the names of great individuals and examples from the past cannot be a substitute for engaging with the present and its formidably complex challenges. The new education must have a forward-looking approach. It must raise public consciousness against all forms of human hierarchy and promote self-conscious practices that undermine and ultimately overcome dominant ideology and praxis.

Lastly but immensely important, practitioners and promoters of emancipatory education must establish in discourse and practice their commitment to transformational change. We cannot afford the pomposity of feigned and fictitious neutrality of established academia. All academic work, like any cultural endeavour, takes place in a socio-cultural context, which either reinforces or undermines the status quo. When even the researches or inventions of natural sciences—as the neo-Gandhian scholars in India imitating the postmodernist anti-Enlightenment framework have been parroting for the past many years, in order to defend their pre-modern caste and brahmanism (Dharampal 1983; Nandy 1983)—are not isolated from the politico-economic imperative of the societies in which they emanate, is it possible for the theories and postulations of social sciences to be pure? The brahmanic fad of the 'pure' and 'detached' should not unnecessarily detain the practitioners of the new education. Instead, its practitioners should openly declare their intentions and unambiguously align with the oppressed and their struggle for liberation.

In the Indian context, scholars such as Gail Omvedt, G. Aloysius, Kancha Ilaiah, Uma Chakravarti, Meera Nanda, Christophe Jaffrelot, to name just a prominent few, have done notable work in recent years, which can be used, enriched, and taken forward to give a solid intellectual foundation to the new education. These authors and their works that challenge the basic tenets of brahmanic canons and constructs must be critically appreciated and carried forward by the practitioners of the emancipatory education. Such works can serve as models to produce quality reading material for emancipatory education. Attempts should also be made to render important works into many languages. Knowledge, after all, belongs to the whole of society. To produce an alternative body of knowledge and then give it back to the people, who need it the most in their liberation struggle, must be the cherished aim of emancipatory education.

The Necessity of Hope: The Revolution-in-Action

Transformative education and struggle cannot take off without hope. In the struggle that is life, there is no greater weapon than an unwavering sense of hope. The belief that tomorrow will be better than the present enthuses us to imagine alternative realities with the confidence that we can achieve them. Since a positive outlook enhances the odds of survival, and makes better things possible, hope abides in all of us. We even see our misfortune as a blessing in disguise. Resurrection and revolution, individual and collective, hinge on hope.

George Orwell says, 'The mental connection between pessimism and a reactionary outlook is obvious enough.' Revolutionaries such as Phule and Ambedkar wanted everyone to like the dreams of the future better than the history of the past. Towering above them, Buddha and Jesus, two paradigmatic figures of humanity, set the examples that the dream of a better life, of a noble and fair world, would never perish from the earth.

In other words, what matters even more than our experience and knowledge of the world is the meaning we give to them. It is what we think that determines how we act. It was to stress this point that Buddha said, 'You become what you think.'

Our aspirations are our possibilities. Diminishing aspiration amounts to diminishing life. As Marcel Proust once observed, 'If a little dreaming is dangerous, the cure for it is not to dream less but to dream more, to dream all the time.' And according to Oscar Wilde, 'A map of the world that did not show Utopia would not be worth consulting.'

For mould-breaking creativity, we need vision and imagination and courage. We need youthful thinkers (not necessarily in appearance but in ideas) with ambitious spirits. We need men, women and children—with dreams and attitudes—who can say, 'I will think and act as if what I do makes a difference.'

We need Prometheus and Spartacus who can dare the lords of heaven and earth to ignite the fire of human freedom and dignity.

We need Savitri and Jotirao Phule, and Marx and Ambedkar who can choose to do what is noble and liberating rather than what is traditional and expedient.

We need Pandita Ramabai and Helen Keller for whom life is a daring adventure or it is nothing.

We need Harriet Tubman, 'the Moses of her people', who threatened to shoot the very African-American slaves she had freed; as fearing an unknown freedom, they wanted to go back to captivity.

We need Sojourner Truth, the black revolutionary, baring her breasts to the white sisters at a women's convention (in 1851) and asking, 'Ain't I a woman?' We need people like her who can speak truth to the power, and whose flaming words can become the symbol of indomitable spirit of humanity: 'I have been forty years a slave and forty years free and would be here forty years more to have equal rights for all.' If Sojourner Truth, forty years a slave, can dream of changing the world at the age of 80, how can we despair of humanity?

When people do not have hope, they give up struggle. When there is no positive vision of life, people perish. Negative expectations shape outcomes in a negative way. Positive expectations propel us to surmount the greatest of odds. Courage is contagious, and so is hope. Elie Wiesel is right in insisting, 'Hope is like peace. It is not a gift from God. It is a gift only we can give one another.'

As an impassioned advocate of democracy and public education, Benjamin Barber (1993), put it: 'When we wish it and will it, what we wish and will has happened. Our successes are willed; our failures seem to happen when will is absent. There are, of course, those who benefit from the bankruptcy of public education and the failure of democracy. But their blame is no greater than our own: in a world where doing nothing has such dire consequences, complacency has become a greater sin than malevolence.'

Our first and foremost task is to unleash opportunities for hope. Keeping hopes alive in the face of oppressive circumstances and taking the road less travelled make all the difference. Hope means hoping when everything seems hopeless. Like the poignant self-encouragement of a lonely young struggler in a far away country represented in a touchingly awkward poem, 'An Epilogue', by John Masefield:

I have seen flowers come in stony places;
And kind things done by men with ugly faces;
And the gold cup won by the worst horse at the races;
So I trust, too.

Hope has the power to transform reality. Alone, however, it does not amount to much—and just to hope, without the commitment and struggle, is to hope in vain. But without hope, the struggle will be weak and wobbly: 'Without a minimum of hope, we cannot so much as start the struggle. But without the struggle, hope . . . loses its bearings, and turns into hopelessness' (Freire 2004: 3).

Real hope is doing something—*with* and *for* the hopeless. Walter Benjamin believed that 'it is only for the sake of the hopeless that hope is given to us'. Only such a hope can nurture—and lead to—the change that we want to see.

Hope, like all beautiful things in life, has conventionally been the preserve of the privileged. For most of human history, only a few have been used to hope that the future would be better and brighter. But if things are to change for the better, people must dream. If the world is to be reimagined and changed, we must dream that things will change; that we shall overcome; that whatever the difficulties, we shall integrate and liberate ourselves and others.

All liberation depends on an enhanced consciousness. No aspiration turns into reality without being positive, open and enthusiastic. No liberating breakthrough can be achieved without believing, like Sartre, that 'life begins on the other side of despair' and that 'people are powerless only when they admit they are'.

Yes, it is easy to be discouraged by life as it is; it is easy to be subsumed by the lies, deceit, and injustice that surround us. The world is unjust and life unfair for a large number of people. It is easy to be discouraged by powerful forces that do not allow the disprivileged children to blossom. But if suffering people decide to change the course of their life, and if the wider community lends them love and support in their struggle, things will change. If the seemingly powerless people persist in their creative struggle, things will change.

APPENDIX

Resources for Transformation

I have attempted to make a list of books for the general reader. The education system produces a populace able to read but unable to distinguish what is worth reading. Even the politically engaged among us do not read much and what we do does not often help us better grasp the world and ourselves. It has been said that 'the trouble with radicals is that they only read radical literature, and the trouble with conservatives is that they don't read anything'. This crisis has taken a dangerous turn with consumerist marketing of books, the glimpse of which we see in the glut of self-help literature along with pulp, porn, and other profit-driven books or magazines that greet us everywhere. It was this situation that impelled me to work this reading list. The books selected here are admittedly in the English language, with a few translations.

Challenging and illuminating, many of the listed books blend the personal with the political, and the local with the universal. Some of them are acknowledged masterpieces. But as Virginia Woolf underlines in *A Room of One's Own*, 'Masterpieces are not single and solitary births; they are the outcome of many years of thinking in common, of thinking by the body of the people, so that the experience of the mass is behind the single voice.' Many books in our suggested reading qualify this criterion—and thus should be part of our mental horizon.

Many of the selected books jolt us out of our stupor of fond belief, half truth, and conventional ideas. Sometimes with wit and imagination, sometimes with sheer empiricism and force of logic, the authors of these books strip away disguises and fossilized mindsets of caste, class, and other oppressive categories. Some of them have the power and passion to cultivate hope and awaken the dead. They stretch our thinking and challenge us to reconsider many 'settled' attitudes and ideas. The diversity of issues and plurality of approaches notwithstanding, these works are bound together in a broader sense by a common quest for human liberation.

Since the list of books is not small, it is categorized and divided into various sections. There are, for example, dozens of books related to women's issues, and so they have conveniently been put under 'Patriarchy and Gender'. In reality, we cannot understand them in isolation from the books covered under 'Caste, Race and Class' and other sections. Each section is related to others as the books represented here converge on a common point of justice for everyone and everywhere. In multiple ways and contexts, they bring out a major truth that the human world can be much better—even for the oppressor—without oppression.

Some of the chosen books are recognized as classics; some others deserve to be considered so; while the rest are important for grappling with vital issues that still await better works by better minds. The list of readings, though by no means comprehensive, takes into account the need of both social and individual reconstruction. Hence, I have included some books concerning our inner and emotional lives. The authors included here do not necessarily agree in emphasis or even in substance or viewpoints with each other, neither do all of them align with the perspective I have presented in my book. Divergent, open-ended, even contradictory viewpoints, I hope, would encourage readers to arrive at their own conclusions. Many titles announce the subject and author's intentions straight away. However, a brief introductory note is given, which may be of help to the reader, especially the young. Some classics are listed without publishing information as they are easily available in a number of editions or translations. The same applies for the works that figure in the bibliography but are included here to underline their importance.

GENERAL / UNCATEGORISED

ABERCROMBI, NICHOLAS, STEPHEN HILL AND BRYAN S. TURNER. *The Dominant Ideology Thesis* (London: Allen and Unwin, 1980). Discusses in depth whether a set of beliefs constitutes the dominant ideology in a particular society, or social formation involves a host of complex theoretical and empirical issues. Provides a clear-eyed analysis of theories on the role of ideology in supporting social inequalities as well as in bringing transformational change.

ACHEBE, CHINUA. *Hopes and Impediments* (New York: Random House, 1988). These essays take us beyond *Things Fall Apart* (1958), Achebe's celebrated novel which explores the effects, overwhelmingly corrosive, of British colonialism on Nigeria. This anthology includes his famous essay 'Racism in Conrad's *Heart of Darkness*', and reveals the impediments that stand in the way of transparent dialogue between blacks and whites. Advocating cultural decolonization, Achebe stresses the social and ethical dimensions of art and literature, and argues why it is necessary to discard prejudiced perceptions and see truth in its diversity. In 'Colonialist Criticism', he writes, 'Whatever faults the black man may have or whatever crimes he committed (and they were, and are, legion) he did not bring racism into the world. And no matter how emancipated a man may wish to appear or how anxious to please by his largeness of heart, he cannot make history simply go away. ... For colonialism itself was built also on an ideology (although its adherents may no longer realize it) which, despite many setbacks, survives into our own day.'

ADLER, MORTIMER J. *Six Great Ideas* (New York: Collier Books, 1981). Dispelling the notion that philosophy is the fiefdom of the specialist, this work strives to make serious thinking a part of everyone's life. Gives a lucid analysis of truth, goodness, and beauty (the ideas we judge by), and liberty, equality, and justice (the ideas we act on). Makes clear some fundamentals that can help us better cope with the political, social and moral issues that confront us everyday.

ALTHUSSER, LOUIS. 'Ideology and Ideological State Apparatuses', in idem, *Lenin and Philosophy and Other Essays*. Transcending the dogmas of economic determinism and humanism that view social change reflecting a pre-given and essentially fixed human nature, Althusser argues that it is ideology, largely determined by *Ideological State Apparatuses* (ISA) such as the legal and educational system, the media, religious institutions, that structures our consciousness. The crux of his argument is that the ISA have some degree of flexibility and freedom of their own but on the whole they are oppressive because the ideology that they generate moulds people into compliant subjects who conform to the norms of existing class relations but fancy themselves as free agents. The dominant ideology sucks in the individual in such a way that the world cannot be seen in any other way, and thus the dominant class is able to reproduce its class domination.

AMIN, SAMIR. *The World We Wish to See: Revolutionary Objectives in the Twenty-first Century* (Delhi: Aakar Books, 2009). A manifesto for revolutionary action to overcome capitalism's new offensive through globalism. Takes a realistic note of new problems and critical changes in the global capitalism, but rejects both the neoliberal notion of 'no alternative' and the left's abandonment of revolution. Amin recognizes the failures of past revolutions but reaffirms the necessity for revolution and socialism, arguing that revolutions 'make it possible for creative utopian ideas to win over minds and, eventually, achieve the supreme ambition of modernity, which is to make human beings the active subjects of their own history'. The social movements that he visualizes to serve as the agent of a new revolution are to be defined by three features: social progress, by which he means the elimination of exploitation and oppression; democratic methods and forms of organization; and respect for diversity and national autonomy.

ANDERSON, PERRY. *The Indian Ideology* (Gurgaon: Three Essays, 2012). Officially, India is a Socialist, Secular, Democratic Republic. The establishment and its intellectuals take this 'Idea of India'—producing a 'stable political democracy, a harmonious territorial unity, and a steadfast religious impartiality'—as the unquestionable truth, writing off the massive injustice and violence as aberrations in an otherwise marvellous Republic. Anderson's book challenges this official view, which is pervasive in India's mainstream intellectual life. Even those who are critical of inequalities of Indian society, he contends, remain imprisoned in the romantic myths of freedom struggle, the roles of its top leaders such as Gandhi and Nehru, and the glory of the world's biggest democracy. He shows that the ills and flaws of India are not few and episodic, the result of the recent misconduct of its rulers, but rather pervasive and deep-seated, structurally, culturally, and politically. Revisiting the events of over a century, especially the national movement which culminated in the transfer of power from British rule to Congress in a divided subcontinent, in the light of how the majority of Indians fare in the Republic today, he unravels many suppressed realities of the past and present, and urges the Indian intellectuals to engage with them in a meaningful manner.

BENJAMIN, WALTER. *Illuminations*. Benjamin's brilliance and uncanny insight can be especially seen in two of his most renowned essays that are included here, 'The Work of Art in the Age of Mechanical Reproduction' and 'Theses on the Philosophy of History'.

BERGER, JOHN. *Ways of Seeing*. In this illuminating text on art criticism, Berger makes us grasp the delicate relation between what (and how) we see and what (and how) we know. He argues that the real meaning of many images has been obscured by academics, changed by photographic reproduction, and distorted by monetary value. In Western art the nude objectified women, and this tradition has been continued by photography. Making the point that art often celebrates the power of money, Berger cites the example of oil painting which has, because of its realism, a strong link to ownership and the buying power of money. The best part of the book comes in the closing chapter which establishes the link between ownership and art by critically looking at modern consumer society and advertising photography. Two riveting passages from this work are cited in Chapter 3 of our book.

BERGER, PETER AND THOMAS LUCKMANN. *The Social Construction of Reality*. This classic tract of social constructionism presents an analysis of 'everything that passes for knowledge' in society. This study—and development of a theory—of institutions, legitimization and socialization shows that they are neither a given nor encoded in our DNA. Social order is not part of the *nature of things*.

BOAL, AUGUSTO. *The Theatre of the Oppressed* (New York: Theatre Communications Group, 1979). An alternative vision of theatre. Argues that theatre can be a vehicle for transformation but will have first to challenge and transgress the Aristotelian–Machiavellian theatre where only the feelings and pain of the powerful matter, whereas the suffering and oppression of ordinary people are kept in the background, obscured or hidden. Boal's thesis is that capitalism oppresses everyone, and its theatre, film, and television which glorify greed and base instincts, work as a tool to promote capitalism. Thus are debased the individual and society.

BOHM, DAVID. *On Dialogue*. This classic makes us grasp that dialogue is not merely an exchange or discussion, but an effort to create a situation where we suspend our opinions and judgements in order to be able to listen to each other. As it 'enables inquiry into, and understanding of, the sorts of processes that fragment and interfere with real communication between individuals, nations and even different parts of the same organization', it can be a way of exploring—and overcoming—the roots of the many crises that diminish and jeopardize humanity. But such conversation is hardly taking place: 'Shared meaning is really the cement that holds society together, and you could say that the present society has very poor quality cement.' Hence, an increasing inability to live together in a world full of stunning technological advances. Bohm stresses that what we need is a painful and difficult dialogue, in which 'each person is participating, partaking of the whole meaning of the group, and also taking part in it'.

BOURDIEU, PIERRE. *Distinction: A Social Critique of the Judgement of Taste*, tr. Richard Nice (Cambridge, MA: Harvard University Press, 1984). In this cultural critique (which can be compared to Veblen's 1899 classic *Theory of the Leisure Class*), Bourdieu illuminates the world of pretensions, showing that our taste is acquired in a class-divided society, and hence no judgement of taste is innocent. He bases this thesis on a vast ethnographical study of the France of 1960s and 1970s and a superb analysis of the middle class mind. Like Veblen, he demonstrates that various aesthetic choices, contrasting attitudes of classes and masses towards art and beauty, are all choices made in opposition to those made by other classes. This creates a symbolic system grounded in power relationships, in which distinctions of taste become the basis for social judgement. This understanding is the basis of Bourdieu's conception of cultural capital which refers to the distinctive forms of knowledge and ability that students acquire—at home, at school, and in the relations between the two. This capital—literary, artistic, or musical qualifications—is to be regarded like an asset just like economic capital such as money or a house, inherited and transmitted from one generation to the next. 'And, just as there are mechanisms for converting one form of economic capital (property) into another (money), so there are mechanisms for converting cultural capital into economic capital, and back again.'

BRONOWSKI, JACOB. *The Ascent of Man* (1973). A scientist with a flair for communication traces the development of science in its social setting and context, offering an illuminating perspective not just on science but on civilization itself.

CARSON, RACHEL. *Silent Spring* (Houghton Mifflin Harcourt, [1962] 2002). Her love of nature combined with her exceptional literary and scientific passions enabled Carson to produce this classic that challenged blind faith in technological progress and set the stage for the global environmental movement. Derision and threats of lawsuits (from the corporate lobby and pesticide industry) failed to stop her from researching and writing on the dangers of new chemical pesticides. The book's most poignant chapter, 'A Fable for Tomorrow', depicts a nameless American town where all life—from birds and fish to apple blossoms and human children—has been silenced by the insidious effects of DDT. She said a little before she died in 1964, 'Man is a part of nature, and his war against nature is inevitably a war against himself.'

CESAIRE, AIME. *Discourse on Colonialism*, tr. Joan Pinkham (New York: Monthly Review Press, [1955] 2000). This classic text of anti-colonialism brings forth with passion and poetry—Cesaire was an extraordinary poet—the inherent racism and injustice that dominated the colonial discourse. Showing how colonialism dehumanizes the colonized and the colonizer, Cesaire makes the point, dripping with sarcasm, that a society which creates and justifies colonialism is a sick civilization—implicit in the imperial brutality—and 'calls for its Hitler, . . . its punishment'. Arguing thus that Nazism was the result of accumulation of the decades of imperial thought, he reminds us that 'the relationship between consciousness and reality are extremely complex. . . . It is equally necessary to decolonize our minds, our inner life, at the same time that we decolonize society'.

CHE GUEVARA. *Che Guevara Reader: Writings on Politics and Revolution*, ed. David Deutschmann (Ocean Press, 2003). A signature anthology of an ignited and restless mind. Especially notable for blending political radicalism with love and empathy.

DUNHAM, BARROWS. *Man Against Myth* (Delhi: National Book Trust, [1946] 2007). With sparkling common sense, this work demolishes many entrenched myths—'the rich are fit and the poor unfit'; 'there are superior and inferior races'; 'you cannot be [both] free and safe', and so on. Shows how the maintenance of such pervasive and interconnected myths has benefited the privileged and legitimized inequality.

EAGLETON, TERRY. *Ideology: An Introduction* (London: Verso, 2007). A cogent book on a confused subject. Eagleton analyzes different definitions of ideology before he interprets its complex history from Enlightenment to postmodernism. A Marxist critic and commentator, he has written extensively on the place and role of religion in today's world. Rejecting simple-minded atheist denunciation of religion, he takes into account its ethical–political dimension, but condemns the regressive role of organized religion, thus ruffling feathers on both sides of the God debate. Worth reading are his *Reason, Faith, and Revolution: Reflections on the God Debate* (2011); *Meaning of Life* (2008); and *Terry Eagleton Presents Jesus Christ: The Gospels* (2007), all marked by his distinctive wit, verve and erudition.

ETZIONI, AMITAI. *The Moral Dimension: Toward a New Economics* (New York: Free Press, 1988). Moral sentiments that make up a core part of who we are, and how we think, feel, and act also apply to economics. Etzioni argues here that no human decision-making can be fully grasped if we ignore the moral sensibilities that inevitably inform all social choices, including monetary and commercial decisions.

FANON, FRANZ. *The Wretched of the Earth.* Written in a heroic burst of energy by a dying man, this work shows Fanon at the height of his subversive thinking. It covers themes such as the idea of emancipatory violence (the necessity of violence by colonized people against the colonizers); the role of the poor as the main force of revolution; the betrayal of commoners by a native middle class that merely replaces and imitates the old colonial power; and the emergence of a new national culture after the struggle. Fanon calls for nothing less than the creation of a new human. Related to this is his another classic, *Black Skin, White Masks* which examines the psychological origins and effects of racism. Delving into his own feelings of alienation as a black man, he shows how the identity problem—black skin—is created by the dominant group's exploitative stereotypes which are eventually internalized by the repressed.

FARMER, PAUL. *Pathologies of Power: Health, Human Rights and New War on the Poor* (University of California Press, 2003). This book is an impassioned plea to think about health care as a fundamental human right. It challenges conventional thinking within human rights circles and exposes the relationship between political and economic injustice, on one hand, and the suffering and illness of the powerless, on the other. Farmer uses harrowing stories and eyewitness accounts from the prisons of Russia and the beleaguered villages of Haiti to link the lived experiences of individual victims with a broader structural violence. These brutal examples are linked to Farmer's guarded optimism that new medical and social technologies will develop in tandem with a more informed sense of social justice. Otherwise, he concludes, we will be guilty of managing social inequality rather than addressing structural violence.

FOUCAULT, MICHEL. *The History of Sexuality*, Vol. I. Why was there an explosion of discussion about sex in the West since the seventeenth century? Foucault unravels the centuries-old rise of a complex deployment of sex, 'for getting us to believe in the sovereignty of its law when in fact we are moved by the power mechanisms of sexuality'. We are reminded of religious or traditional injunctions to make us detest the body, 'but let us ponder all the ruses that were employed for centuries to make us love sex, to make the knowledge of it desirable and everything said about it precious'. If sexual prudery does not make sense, liberation through sex is similarly nonsensical, since sex is subordinate to sexuality and not vice-versa. By saying yes to sex, one does not say no to power.

GALEANO, EDUARDO. *Memory of Fire* (the trilogy contains *Genesis, Faces and Masks*, and *Century of the Wind*). From its first English-language publication in the 1980s, this riveting history of the Western colonization of the Americas is considered a classic of political engagement, original research, and a new way to write and understand history. In vivid prose and beautifully resurrected anecdotes, vignettes, stories and poetry, Galeano covers the large swathe from pre-Colombian creation myths and the first European voyages of discovery and conquest, to the Age of Reason and the beauty and beastliness of the twentieth century. Its running theme and indictment: rapacious greed snuffing out a world of human knowledge and experience—the powerful inflicting atrocities and genocides, and making mincemeat of the defenceless.

Galeano writes from the point of view of the most ordinary people—the powerless, the dispossessed, the voiceless—in the most extraordinary manner. His blend of story-telling and cultural critique finds devastating expression in his new book *Mirrors* (2009), which retells the history of the world in a series of vignettes. What I want to say is perfectly stated in the book's blurb: 'In *Mirrors*, Galeano smashes the narrative of conventional history and arranges the shards into a new pattern, to reveal the past in radically altered form. From the Garden of Eden to 21st-century cityscapes, we glimpse fragments in the lives of those who have been overlooked by traditional histories: the artists, the servants, the gods and the visionaries, the black slaves who built the White House, and the women who were bartered for dynastic ends.'

GEORGE, SUSAN. *How the Other Half Dies: The Real Reasons for World Hunger* (London: Penguin, 1991). Not overpopulation or bad weather or changing climate but the food control by the overfed—the multinational agribusiness corporations, Western governments, and development organizations in cahoots with local elites and governments everywhere—cause mass hunger in the age of plenty. What is required, George suggests, to feed the world is not population control or the Green Revolution but social change towards justice. With that, the poor could resolve most of their problems themselves. The interested can also read her trenchant critique of the World Bank, *A Fate Worse Than Debt* (1988).

GOULD, STEPHEN JAY. *The Mismeasure of Man* (New York: Norton, 1983). Gould, along with Richard Leontin, is known for challenging the way 'the doctrine of DNA' (according to which the genes hold culture on a leash) has been used to 'justify inequalities within and between societies and to claim that those inequalities can never be challenged'. *The Mismeasure of Man* is a historical study—and exposé—of scientific racism and sexism, tracing it through monogeny and polygeny, phrenology, recapitulation, and hereditarian IQ theory. Illustrating the logical inconsistencies of the pseudo-scientific theories and the prejudicially motivated misuse of data in each case, Gould lays bare the fatal flaws of biological determinism—the proposition that society follows nature, and social stratifications (hierarchies of advantage and disadvantage) follow the dictates of biology. He shows that the enterprise of setting a biological value upon human groups is irrelevant, intellectually unsound and highly injurious. *Social rank does not reflect one's innate worth and stratification does not reflect biology.* The more interested can read Leontin's *The Doctrine of DNA: The Biology as Ideology* (1991), and his earlier work (with Steven Rose and Leon J. Kamin), *Not in Our Genes: Biology, Ideology and Human Nature* (1984), which exposes the nefarious politics of DNA research and evolutionary biology.

GRAMSCI, ANTONIO. *The Prison Notebooks*. Gramsci is an outstanding Marxist thinker, and this book shows us his creative originality. Rejecting the tendency to see all cultural and ideological conceptions as direct derivatives of economic facts, he sees politics as 'an autonomous activity' within the context and limits set by historical development. Societies are more than structures of economic domination and political power, and they have a certain cohesion even when riven by class struggle. This led Gramsci to think and theorize a new kind of socialist politics to transform human life, to create a socialist society, and this is his major contribution. His concept of *hegemony* through which the ruling class establishes its 'intellectual and moral leadership' and imposes a general direction upon social life that maintains the status quo was not completely unknown before him. What is new in Gramsci is the observation that hegemony is not automatic but achieved through political action and organization. His writings make us grasp how economic–corporative organization becomes political hegemony, and 'why even the most militant trade unionism remains a subaltern part of capitalist society'. Thus the difference between dominant/hegemonic and subaltern classes is fundamental, and the challenge of socialist revolution is to make a hitherto subaltern class capable of hegemony. The theorization that revolution is the struggle for hegemony, which must be waged before the transition of power, as well as during and after it, calls for both popular mobilization and self-transformation. Gramsci applied his mind to this task in his theory of politics, history, philosophy, education, the modern state, and above all, the role of intellectuals.

HARDT, MICHAEL AND ANTONIO NEGRI. *Empire* (Cambridge, MA: Harvard University Press, 2000). This book, hailed in some progressive circles as the communist manifesto for the twenty-first century, presents the concept of non-territorial Empire of victorious global capitalism, and the 'multitude' around the world ranged against it, fighting for a full-blown global democracy. *Empire* needs to be read with the writer duo's related work *Multitude: War and Democracy in the Age of Empire* (2005).

HERMAN, EDWARD AND NOAM CHOMSKY. *Manufacturing Consent: The Political Economy of the Mass Media* (1988). A classic leftist look at the ways public opinions and choices are moulded by a monopolistic media which work at the behest of dominant political and economical interests in society.

HIGLEY, STEPHEN RICHARD. *Privilege, Power, and the Place: The Geography of the American Upper Class* (Lanham, MD: Rowman and Littlefield, 1995). Geographer Higley argues here that people in the US have sorted themselves residentially by class and status. Geographic proximity, he shows, is an essential pillar of upper class identity and solidarity. The life changes and lifestyles are deeply moulded by the geography of one's social class.

HOBSBAWM, ERIC. *How to Change the World: Marx and Marxism* (London: Little, Brown, 2011.) Few intellectuals attempted to change the world as Marx did. However, the socialism to which he dedicated his life, has for the last thirty years or so seen a stunning reversal at the hands of capitalism. Though capitalism appears stronger than ever, its corrosive greed and contradictions point otherwise. If it is not replaced by socialism but some sort of barbarism, fascism, or ecological disaster (Marx had ominously hinted at one place in the *Communist Manifesto* that capitalism might end in the 'common ruin of the contending classes'), it will indeed be a catastrophe. This collection of essays by an iconic Marxist historian makes us aware of such a dire possibility, and the need to learn from the past and do our best for a socialist world. The essays give an overview of Marxism and covers such wide-ranging topics as pre-Marxian socialism, Marx on pre-capitalist formations, Gramsci, Marx and labour, and two absorbing chapters on the *Communist*

Manifesto and Engels's *The Condition of the Working Class in England*. Hobsbawm is the author of classics such as *The Age of Revolution* and *The Age of Extremes*, and ranks among those rare authors whose concepts and language have become part of everyday conversation and the way we have come to understand the modern world.

JAMESON, FREDRIC. *Postmodernism: Or, the Cultural Logic of Late Capitalism* (1992). A brilliant attack on postmodernism and a defence of Marxism. An important and illuminating book in the realm of contemporary ideas.

JASPERS, KARL. *Socrates, Buddha, Confucius, Jesus: The Paradigmatic Individuals*, ed. Hannah Arendt, tr. Ralph Manheim (New York: Harcourt Brace Jovanovich, 1962). These extracts from Jaspers' history of philosophy present his brilliant reading of what he calls 'the paradigmatic individual'. Fascinating insights into the four fabulous lives that changed the course of intellectual–moral landscape of humanity.

JOHNSON, ALLAN G. *The Forest and the Trees: Sociology as Life, Practice, Promise* (Philadelphia: Temple University Press, 1970). Johnson uses the example of the forest and the trees as a metaphor to bring home the point that we are always participating in something larger than ourselves. Sociology is the art and science of understanding both the forest and the trees and how they are related to each other. He argues that individualistic perspectives that dominates current thinking about social life blunt the sociological imagination, making us see only individuals, not the social structures and institutions that shape diverse group experiences.

KRANTZ, FREDERICK, ed. *History from Below: Studies in Popular Protest and Popular Ideologies in Honour of George Rude* (Montreal: Concordia University, 1985). In this volume, Eric Hobsbawm, Christopher Hill and other pioneers of the people's history examine approaches to the people's movements in the context of specific periods and events. Frederick

Krantz presents a vivid account of the life, career and contribution of George Rude.

LACLAU, ERNESTO AND CHANTAL MOUFFE. *Hegemony and Socialist Strategy: Towards a Radical Democratic Politics* (London: Verso, 1985). This book generates a new set of ideas that rejects the dogma of economic determinism and primacy of class but retains the socialist and ethical passion for justice, freedom, and the need for human solidarity. A necessary read for understanding what has come to be known as *post-Marxism.*

LAMONT, MICHELE, AND MARCEL FOURNIER. *Cultivating Differences: Symbolic Boundaries and the Making of Inequality* (Chicago: University of Chicago Press, 1992). Helps us better understand the social construction of inclusion or exclusion. Though symbolic boundaries are distinct from 'social boundaries' that are objectified forms of social differences (manifested in unequal access to social resources and opportunities), this work shows how the two—the mental boundaries and physical boundaries—are deeply interconnected. It covers four topic areas—the institutionalization of cultural norms; the exclusionary effects of high culture; the role of ethnicity and gender in shaping symbolic boundaries; and, the role of democracy in creating inclusion or exclusion.

LASSWELL, HAROLD. *Politics: Who Gets What, When, How* (1936). Takes a practical and historical approach to politics, viewing the elite as the primary holders of power. The title—and its elucidation in the book—now serves as the standard definition of politics. Lasswell is also known for a similar theorization of communications: *Who (says) What (to) Whom (in) What Channel (with) What Effect.*

LEVI, PRIMO. *If This Is a Man: Remembering Auschwitz* (New York: Summit Books, 1985). First published in 1947 in Italian, this renowned account of the Holocaust is also a superb study of humanity. Levi introduces the book with a poem which has become famous and which explains the title and the theme of the book—humanity in the midst of inhumanity. As Philip Roth says, Levi was in touch with the 'minutest workings of the most enduring human events and the most contemptible. . . . [This work carries not only] his memory of the unbearable, but also . . . his delight in what made the world exquisite to him'.

LUCAS, JOHN, ed. *Writing and Radicalism* (New York: Longman, 1996). Chronicles the diversity and development of radical Western writing in literature, history and politics over four centuries. The contributors engage with both well-known as well as neglected documents and source materials, and reveal the variety of intellectual responses to events of political upheaval and social change. These begin with the Commonwealth period, then the French Revolution, Chartism, the Suffragette Movement, important interwar issues as the General Strike and the Spanish Civil War and conclude with women's movements in recent times. The study addresses crucial themes such as urbanization, the development of class consciousness, the subversive potential of popular culture, and extends the parameters of the current debate about the role in and significance of radical writing to political movements.

LUKACS, GEORG. *History and Class Consciousness*, tr. Rodney Livingstone (Delhi: Rupa, [1923] 1993). In these controversial essays, Lukacs elaborates on ideology, false consciousness, reification, and class consciousness. Explores the hold of capitalist ideas on people's consciousness and how it can be broken. Notable for insight into theories of alienation, these essays deepen the Marxist critique of capitalism that commodification has the effect of giving relations between people the character of things, thereby 'reifying' them.

LYKES, M.B. et al., eds. *Myths about the Powerless: Contesting Social Inequalities* (Philadelphia: Temple University Press, 1996). Contributors of this collection unmask the underlying assumptions such as victim-blaming that sustain social inequality. They challenge the neo-conservative logic that dominates public debate and legislative agendas, and point out the primary things that must be addressed to dismantle institutionalized discrimination.

MAO ZEDONG. *Four Essays on Philosophy* (Beijing: Foreign Languages Press, 1968). Mao's writings run to many volumes, but these four essays—'On Practice' (1937); 'On Contradiction' (1937); 'On the Correct Handling of Contradictions Among the People' (1957); 'Where Do Correct Ideas Come From?' (1963)—neatly sum up his philosophical thought. 'On Contradiction' is emblematic of his attack on dogmatism by which he meant a tendency to apply airy-fairy Marxist theory without any regard to socio-political reality. Questioning the theory that base always determines superstructure, he argued that reversal of the role of aspects is possible in any contradiction. 'When the superstructure (politics, culture, etc.,) obstructs the development of the economic base, political and cultural changes become principal and decisive.' The brilliance of Mao was to put such understanding in the fight against the bourgeois-feudal forces 'triumphant [for centuries] at the cost of the misery of the multitude'. His weaknesses and excesses were many, but his greatest 'crime' was to galvanize the commoners to bring revolution to an old, authoritarian, and terribly complex country. Coming from a peasant family, he worked with peasants and workers throughout China, indoctrinating them in socialism. The man of the Long March, the Great Leap Forward and the Cultural Revolution could not be a hero to an elite whose reactionary threats forced him to rally the young with slogans like 'Politics in Command', 'Bomb the Headquarters', and 'Destroy the Old, Establish the New'. Perhaps he was a synthesizer, too, who could think 'women hold up half the sky' and 'let a hundred flowers blossom and a hundred schools of thought contend'.

MANNHEIM, KARL. *Ideology and Utopia: An Introduction to the Sociology of Knowledge*, tr. Luis Wirth and Edward Shils

(New York: Harvest Books, 1936). Different social groups in the course of the struggle for power create different forms of knowledge. Showing that 'ideologies' and 'utopias' emerge from such struggle, Mannheim argues that ideologies reflect the interests of the ruling class and generally obscure realities in order to stabilize society. Utopias, on the other hand, represent processes of thoughts or imaginations, such as symbols, fantasies, dreams, ideas, and the like of the oppressed groups which do not actually exist but which the people yearn to bring into existence. Bearing the brunt of a cruel and unjust world, the oppressed make themselves a moral paradise of sweet dreams and visions. Thus, though utopianism does not receive its inputs from the direct force of social reality, it is not an escapist flight from the horrors of everyday life but a necessity for mass action and transformation. If it is also lost 'man would lose his will to shape history and his ability to understand it'.

MARCUSE, HERBERT. *One-Dimensional Man: Studies in the Ideology of Advanced Industrial Society* (1964). In this powerful critique of modern capitalism, Marcuse sees the nexus of capital and technology as constituting new forms of social control and domination that reduce individuals—a One-Dimensional Man formed from a One-Dimensional Society that frames a One-Dimensional Thought. 'The capabilities (intellectual and material) of contemporary society are immeasurably greater than before—which means that the scope of society's domination over the individual is immeasurably greater than ever before.' Some aspects of this 1960s treatise have of course become dated, but its basic point remains relevant. 'The totalitarian dimensions of the one-dimensional society render the traditional ways and means of protest ineffective—perhaps even dangerous because they preserve the illusion of popular sovereignty. This illusion contains some truth: "the people", previously the ferment of social change have "moved up" to become the ferment of social cohesion. Here rather than in the redistribution of wealth and equalisation of classes is the new stratification of advanced industrial society.'

MARX, KARL AND FRIEDRICH ENGELS. *The Communist Manifesto* (1848). One of the most radical tracts ever written to understand the world, and also a call to arms to change it. From its opening ('A spectre is haunting Europe—the spectre of communism') to the closing remark ('The proletarians have nothing to lose but their chains. They have a world to win. Working men of all countries, unite!'), it has a 'dark, laconic eloquence', its 'compelling power as literature', and its political rhetoric which has 'an almost biblical force', as Eric Hobsbawm puts it. Though it appeared under the joint authorship of Marx and Engels, the latter conceded (in his Preface to the English edition of 1888) that its fundamental proposition—'the whole history of mankind has been a history of class struggle'—belongs to Marx.

This tract outlines this dialectical history and describes the achievements of the bourgeoisie before launching a broadside against the latter: '[M]odern bourgeois society, which has conjured up such gigantic means of production and of exchange, is like the sorcerer, who is no longer able to control the powers of the underworld he has called up ... Bourgeois relations have become too narrow to encompass the wealth created by them.' These words capture with stunning accuracy an image of contemporary globalized capitalism. Of course, Marx hoped that the disastrous development would lead to 'a revolutionary reconstitution of society at large' with a proletariat victory, but he did not exclude the alternative: capitalism may be replaced not with socialism but with fascism or barbarism. In a significant and often overlooked phrase, he writes ominously, that capitalism might end 'in the common ruin of the contending classes'. Some aspects of Marxism have of course become out-of-date, and there are things (such as the possibility of technology-led disaster or social democracy wiping out revolutionary fervour) which Marx could not visualise. But the critique of capitalism and the need to replace it with a system and 'an association in which the free development of each is the condition of the free development of all' remains relevant and inspiring. Marx's writings (especially *Economic and Philosophical Manuscripts of 1844, The German Ideology,* and above all, *Das Kapital*) provide a powerful framework for the analysis of history, economy and society. As a philosophy and praxis, Marxism may not be the panacea for the present crisis but as long as capitalism endures, Marxist literature deserves to be critically read and debated.

MATSON, FLOYD AND ASHLEY MONTAGU, eds. *The Human Dialogue: Perspectives on Communication* (New York: The Free Press, 1967). 'The field of communication is today more than ever', the editors stress in their introduction, 'a battlefield contested by two opposing conceptual forces—those of monologue and dialogue.' The monological approach views communication as essentially the transmission and reception of symbolic stimuli—messages or commands. In contrast, the dialogical approach regards communication as the quest for understanding others and the basis for self-discovery. The selections here from the work of many eminent thinkers on the subject not only examine the challenges in communication, but also show the way for the real dialogue.

MIDGLEY, MARY. *The Myths We Live By*. Myths are everywhere but can myth coexist and flourish with science? Underlining that myths are not simply fiction but a network of powerful symbols for understanding the world, Midgley argues that far from being the opposite of science, myth is a central part of it. Debunking scientific and non-scientific pretensions alike, she takes examples from evolutionary psychology, consciousness, the study of nature, environment, and animals, and points out the absolutist degeneration of science into a pseudo-religion. But science is not religion, and this book reminds us to take our emotional and imaginative life seriously.

MILIBAND, RALPH. *Divided Societies: Class Struggle in Contemporary Capitalism* (Oxford: Oxford University Press, 1989). Under capitalism, 'developed' as well as 'developing' societies are more unequal and divided than ever. Miliband raises this question and explains how capitalism limits democracy and the meaning of citizenship. See also his *Marxism and Politics* (1977) and *Socialism for a Sceptical Age* (1995).

MILLS, C. WRIGHT. *The Power Elite* (1956). Mills challenges the dominant academic view that society remains stable through shared norms and values, arguing that such functionalist ideology supports the status quo and serves the vested interests. A sharp analysis of the US system of power, this work exposes the reality of domination by an elite presiding over business, politics, and the military. It shows that their power is derived from their institutional location rather than their individual talents. 'For power is not of a man. Wealth does not centre in the person of the wealthy. Celebrity is not inherent in any personality. To be celebrated, to be wealthy, to have power requires access to major institutions, for the institutional positions men occupy determine in large part their chances to have and to hold those valued experiences.' Mills developed these insights and argued for a humanist social science connecting the personal, social, and historical dimensions in our lives in his classic work *Sociological Imagination* (1959). See also *Power, Politics and People: The Collected Essays of C. Wright Mills*, ed. Irving Louis Horowitz (1963).

MOORE, BARRINGTON. *Injustice: The Social Bases of Obedience and Revolt* (London: Macmillan, 1978). Explores responses to injustices in a stratified society—ranging from acquiescence to resistance—from a perspective which is not the captive of economic determinism. 'Without strong moral feelings and indignation, human beings will not act against the social order. In this sense moral convictions become an equally necessary element for changing the social order, along with alterations in the economic structure.'

MORE, THOMAS. *The Best State of a Commonwealth and the New Island of Utopia* (1516). *Utopia* (Greek for nowhere), added more than an adjective (utopian) to the English language. A typical work of Renaissance humanism, it embodies a vision of a new world—uniting reason with emotion, universalism with concern for the particular and its diversities—quite different from what actually came after the advent of a more imperialistic and violent Europe. Signifying a challenge to the evils of contemporary English society, it is a document of social protest, or a blueprint of (as some have termed it) Christian communism. It lashes out at dynastic warfare, the abuse of power, the cult of predatory acquisitiveness, the greed of the wealthy, the poverty of the toiling classes, the cruelties of the criminal law, and other evils of the time. The fable of the ideal island where people lived in peace, equality, collective ownership and useful labour was a call to build an alternative society with strong ethical values. A man who preferred death to give in to demands made upon him by the king of England (and the subject of Robert Bolt's famous play *A Man for All Seasons*), More was committed to a moral revolution, not to a mere change in the form of government or a shift of power from one group to another. The only true revolution, he believed, was moral, and hence any political change will be of limited value unless the new regime produces good humans.

NANDA, MEERA. *Prophets Facing Backward: Postmodernism, Science, and Hindu Nationalism* (Delhi: Permanent Black, 2004). Underpinning the importance of science and rationality in creating the possibility of universal measures of judgement for truth, justice and progress, this book argues that at the heart of the hyper-nationalism of the Hindu right lies 'a postmodernist assumption: that each society has its own norms of reasonableness, logic, rules of evidence, and conception of truth'. A trenchant critique of this assumption, it exposes the intellectual and cultural sources of the rise of reactionary forms of modernism in India—the coming together of cutting-edge technologies, including nuclear weapons, with the aggressive right-wing promotion of obscurantism in the guise of 'Vedic sciences'. Advocating a critical sensibility and authentic Indian modernity committed to social change, this book explores the importance of Ambedkar's project of combing a socially engaged Buddhism with the rationalist pragmatism of John Dewey, which presents a progressive alternative to the half-baked ideas of Gandhi, Nehru and Tagore.

O'HEAR, ANTHONY. *Beyond Evolution: Human Nature and the Limits of Evolutionary Explanation* (Oxford: Oxford University Press, 1997). This work shows that our ability to think-reflect-consider differentiates our world from the natural world: many of our ideals and goals cannot be justified in terms of survival-promotion or reproduction advantage. In fact, our self-consciousness allows us to go beyond not only our biological but also cultural inheritance. 'We are prisoners neither of our genes nor of the ideas we encounter as we each make our personal and individual way through life.'

PAINE, THOMAS. *The Rights of Man* (1791). This classic on democracy (and a defence of the French Revolution) invented a language of politics that ignited millions of minds for people's rights, national independence, revolutionary war, and people-centred development. As a pioneer of the democratic revolution, Paine wanted politics to enter the realm of economics, and took the lead in demanding state-funded public education, employment for casual worker, child and maternity benefits, old age pensions, etc.

PARENTI, MICHAEL. *Inventing Reality: The Politics of News Media* (New York: St. Martin's, [1986] 1993). This work helps us better grasp what we read and see daily. Shows how the media stay within the prevailing ideological orthodoxy that serves the interests of the few while appearing to serve the many. Arguing that journalists' careers depend mainly on their ability to equate dominant views with 'objectivity', it unravels example after example of news bias and identifies the means by which the media misrepresent reality. Parenti is a public intellectual, and has written on a wide range of subjects. His notable works include *Power and the Powerless* (1978), *History as Mystery* (1999), and *Democracy for the Few* ([1974] 2007).

PARKIN, FRANK. *Class, Inequality and Political Order* (London: McGibbon and Kee, 1971). A powerful analysis of dominant ideologies and counter ideologies, their social roles, and their relationships to social class.

PIVEN, FRANCES FOX AND RICHARD CLOWARD. *Poor People's Movements: Why They Succeed, How They Fail* (New York: Vintage, 1979). Focussing on theory as well as strategy, this disturbing yet inspiring study of four movements from below challenges us to think differently about resistance by the oppressed. Useful for both scholars and participant-makers of such movements.

POSTMAN, NEIL. *Amusing Ourselves to Death: Public Discourse in the Age of Show Business* (1985). An indictment of the media hysteria and television onslaught, and how they are shaping our lives in a negative way, obstructing public discourse and public affairs. 'Who is prepared to take arms against a sea of amusements? To whom do we complain, and when, and in what tone of voice, when serious discourse dissolves into giggles? What is the antidote to a culture's being drained by laughter?' Unravelling the danger of media-induced trivialization of issues facing society, Postman suggests that 'before we hand over politics, education, religion and journalism to the show-business demands of the television age, we must recognize the ways in which the media shape our lives and the ways we can, in turn, shape them to serve our highest goals'.

RIFKIN, JEREMY. *The Age of Access: The New Culture of Hypercapitalism Where All of Life Is Paid-For Experience* (New York: Tarcher/Putnam, 2000). In the new global economy, 'experience industries' such as travel and entertainment will increasingly make the industrial production and the exchange of property (that currently dominate the market economy) secondary. Up for sales will be human experience itself and all cultural activities will be gradually commodified. The danger, this work implies, lies in concentration of services being provided globally by fewer and fewer players who will focus on the lowest common denominator in order to expand consumption. Rifkin is suggesting—and warning—that this 'hypercapitalism' will bring in a fundamental debasement of culture and our relationships with our homes, our communities and our world.

RIIS, JACOB A. *How the Other Half Lives: Studies Among the Tenements of New York City* (New York: Penguin, 1997). A pioneering classic of photojournalism, first published in 1890, Riis' moving words are matched by his telling photographs that bring alive the horrendous living conditions of the poor of the city. A document that reminds us of the terrible miseries of millions still imprisoned in slums across the world.

ROY, ARUNDHATI. *The Algebra of Infinite Justice* (Delhi: Penguin, 2002). If Roy's novel *The God of Small Things* (1997) is an effective poetic protest against caste, class, and oppressive power relationships between men, women and children, her political essays, collected in this anthology, carry this forward in a daring and moving language. These essays generate anger and revulsion against nuclear weapons ('The End of Imagination'), the destructive politics of development ('The Greater Common Good'), the state and its institutions, a showy democracy and corporate globalization that together play havoc against the weak and the defenceless.

RUSSELL, BERTRAND. *Sceptical Essays* (London: Routledge, [1928] 2004). One of the founders of modern analytical philosophy, Russell was a public intellectual who wrote on a wide range of social, political and moral issues, disproving that profound things cannot be discussed in public and in a language that can be grasped by everyone. Wit and lucidity that contains subtlety and profundity, this signature Russell book begins with these words: 'These propositions may seem mild, yet, if accepted, they would absolutely revolutionize human life.' He holds forth here on key philosophical issues that affect our quotidian life—freedom, happiness, emotions, ethics, and beliefs, and advocates a spread of rational scepticism for good life. Brimming with common sense, open-mindedness and unpleasant truths, his other popular works such as *Principles of Social Reconstruction, What I Believe, Why I Am Not a Christian, Education and the Social Order, Marriage and Morals*—all of them still in circulation—played a positive role in the revolution in social attitudes that separated the twentieth century from the Victorian age.

RYAN, WILLIAM. *Blaming the Victim* (1971). 'Justifying inequality by finding defects in the victims of inequality' is built on the premise of the Just World hypothesis which ignores the social environment and structure as underlying causes for social problems. Though the phenomenon of seeing the world as a just place where people ultimately get what they deserve is well known in human psychology and history, Ryan's was the first book to establish it as an ideology employed to justify racism and social injustice against the blacks in the US. It demonstrates that social problems are a function of the social arrangements of society, and that such problems are both predictable and preventable. It blasts elitist myths such as poor children perform poorly in school because they are 'culturally deprived'; Afro-Americans are handicapped by a family structure that is typically unstable and matriarchal; poor people suffer from bad health because of ignorance and lack of interest in proper health care. It identifies these truisms as part of the system of denial that even the best-intentioned elites have constructed around the unpalatable realities of race and class. Still relevant for its diagnosis of the psychic underpinnings of social injustice.

SAID, EDWARD. *Orientalism: Western Conceptions of the Orient* (London: Penguin, 1978). In this brilliant polemic of intellectual history, Said explores Western attitudes towards the East, especially the Arab and Islamic world—as subject, as representation, as institution. Though he fails to take into account the collusion between the Western power and the native elites for mutual benefit on which colonialism was based, at least in the case of India, he succeeds in underlining the nexus between false knowledge, power, and oppression. In a related work, *Culture and Imperialism* (1993), he traces the relationship between the Western culture and imperialism that mutually reflected and reinforced each other. Rereading many classics of the Western canon, he makes the point that the justification for colonization was deeply embedded in the cultural imagination of the West, so much so that most of its leading intellectuals and writers were complicit in its imperialism. In another important work *Representations of the Intellectual* (1994), Said sees the intellectual not as the specialized servant of special interests but as a rebel whose role it is 'to speak the truth to power' even at the risk of ostracism or imprisonment. Excellent selections from his major works can be found in *The Edward Said Reader*, edited by Moustafa Bayoumi and Andrew Robin (2000).

SANDEL, MICHAEL. *What Money Can't Buy: The Moral Limits of Markets* (London: Allen Lane, 2012). Sandel wrote a chapter on 'Markets and Morals' in his very popular book *Justice* (2009) in which he raised two key questions: 'How free are the choices we make in the free market? And are there certain virtues and higher goods that markets do not honour and money cannot buy?' He addresses these questions extensively and in a lively manner in this book which aims at breaking the spell of market thinking that has 'drained public discourse of moral and civil energy, and contributed to the technocratic, managerial politics that afflicts many societies today'. He makes the point that with market triumphalism, what we have today is not just a market economy but a market society: we have 'a way of life in which market values seep into every aspect of human endeavour . . . [and] social relations are [being] made over in the image of the market'. Citing several examples that show the alarming role and reach of markets in social and personal realms, he argues that these and related questions touch on contested visions of the good society and the good life. He stresses the need for a reasoned public debate on these questions—questions that are moral and political, not merely economic.

SCHUMACHER, E.F. *Small Is Beautiful: A Study of Economics as if People Mattered* (London: Vintage, [1973] 1993). In this offbeat study of world economics, Schumacher presents a case against the capitalist pursuit of profit and 'progress', which promotes giant organizations and increased specialization, and says they inevitably lead to economic inefficiency, environmental pollution, and inhuman working conditions. He proposes a system of Intermediate Technology based on smaller working units, communal ownership, and regional workplaces utilizing local labour and resources.

SCOTT, JAMES C. *Domination and the Arts of Resistance: Hidden Transcripts* (New Haven and London: Yale University Press, 1990). Brings the subtle and often hidden layers of confrontations between the powerful and the powerless. Uses examples from literature, history and politics of cultures around the world, and makes us think afresh on subordination, hegemony, resistance, folk culture, and the ideas behind revolt. See also Scott's earlier and related work, *Weapons of the Weak: Everyday Forms of Peasant Resistance* (1985).

SHIRER, WILLIAM. *The Rise and Fall of the Third Reich.* A major narrative history of Hitler's reign, its publication in 1960 helped put Hitler and the Holocaust in the public domain. Some academics do not find the book scholarly enough, but most agree with Theodore H. White who called it 'a monumental work, a grisly and thrilling story'.

SHRIVASTAVA, ASEEM AND ASHISH KOTHARI. *Churning the Earth: The Making of Global India* (Delhi: Penguin, 2012). Rich with statistics and stories, it maps the political economy of both the socio-economic consequences and ecological impact of India's 'economic rise'. Showing that the predatory nature of 'growth' is destroying ordinary Indians and their environment, it makes a profound case for 'a radical ecological democracy based on the principles of environmental sustainability, social equity and livelihood security'.

SINGER, PETER. *Animal Liberation* (New York: Avon Books, [1975] 1990). Brings to light the tyranny of humans over animals, and shows why the ethical principle of the equal consideration of interests on which human equality rests requires us to extend this to animals too. Linking discrimination based on race and sex with oppression of animals, the author makes the point that animal liberation is human liberation too. Singer has written on some of the most important issues facing humanity. His essay 'Affluence and Morality' raises the question whether it is morally defensible for affluent people to spend money on luxuries while the poor are starving. Also notable are his works on moral philosophy *Practical Ethics* (1979), and *How are We to Live: Ethics in an Age of Self-interest* (1995).

STIGLITZ, JOSEPH. *The Price of Inequality* (London: Allen Lane, 1912). When the impact of inequality is terrible (higher violence and crime, and physical and mental illness) and well-known, why is it growing, what are its causes, and who are responsible for it? Stiglitz shows that markets are neither free nor fair as politics shapes economics, and vice-versa, that advantage the richest over the rest, leading to concentration of money and power in the hands of the few rather than engendering competition. Also shows that moving money from the middle and bottom to the top, far from stimulating entrepreneurship, actually produces slower growth, lower GDP and, above all, social instability. Analysing the current crisis, he suggests democratic ways to arrest the dangerous drift.

THOREAU, HENRY DAVID. *Civil Disobedience and Other Essays*. The author of *Walden, or, Life in the Woods* (1854) was not the fabled eccentric who went into the woods to live monastically; he was interested in critiquing society rather than in persuading people to shun society and live in a shack in the wild. These essays show his strong opposition to slavery, and his eagerness to make people think for themselves (instead of carrying the dead wood of the past). His 'Civil Disobedience' (1849) exalts the law of conscience over civil law, and his abolitionist essays 'Slavery in Massachusetts' and 'A Plea for Captain John Brown' attack the government support for slavery. 'Life without Principles' presents his philosophy of self-reliance, simplicity and deliberateness in everyday life, and 'Walking' celebrates the joy of walking and pleads for conservation of the world's wild places.

VEBLEN, THORSTEIN. *The Theory of the Leisure Class* (1899). This classic work presents a fascinating social critique of an indulgence-driven culture that wallows in abundance, waste, and conspicuous consumption. It sees conspicuous leisure, pleasure and extravagance as the application of money—to display a higher social status. 'In order to gain and to hold the esteem of men it is not sufficient merely to possess wealth or power. The wealth or power must be put in evidence, for esteem is rewarded only on evidence.' Seeing envy and hunger for esteem as the primary psychological spurs to economic success, Veblen detested the domination of business interests over the common interests, and was among the first academics to condemn conspicuous consumerism as fundamentally wasteful and disastrous for the commoners. He argued that modern economic life was driven by the vestiges of the traditional social stratification (as the division of labour was still according to one's inherited status group) rather than by larger social and economic utility.

WEINER, MYRON. *The Child and the State in India: Child Labour and Education Policy in Comparative Perspective* (Princeton: Princeton University Press, 1991). Weiner shows that 'those who are educated have power over those who are not', and in India, the educated (who run and manipulate the state) have kept the poor deliberately uneducated fearing the subversive power of mass schooling. In the land of caste, 'Educators and officials do not regard education as an equalizer, as an instrument for developing shared attitudes and social characteristics, but rather as a way of differentiating one class from another.' More than two decades after the author wrote these words, India has the largest number of non-school-going working children in the world. This book explains why the government has not removed children from the labour force and made it mandatory that they attend school, as have the governments of all developed and many developing countries. This comparative study first looks at why and when other states have intervened to protect children against parents and employers. By examining Europe of the nineteenth century, the United States, Japan, and a number of developing countries, Weiner rejects the argument that children were removed from the labour force only when the incomes of the poor rose and employers needed a more skilled labour force. Regarding India, he shows that its policies emanate from a discriminatory culture, rather than from economic conditions. Identifying the values that elsewhere led educators, social activists, religious leaders, trade unionists, and bureaucrats to make education compulsory and to end child labour, he explains that similar groups in India fear mass education because of its potential to subvert the social order.

WESTEIN, ALAN. *Privacy and Freedom.* This 1967 book assumes relevance as privacy is threatened more than ever before—not so much by the Orwellian Big Brother, but the ever-expanding big business with technology-generated abilities to collect, store, and distribute details about people's private lives. Facts by themselves mean little, but the ability to tie immense number of facts together—data files on the computer—is the name of the power game.

WILKINSON, RICHARD AND KATE PICKETT. *The Spirit Level: Why More Equal Societies Almost Always Do Better* (2009). Comprehensive data and evidence gathered here leave no scope for ambiguity that the root cause of social ills is inequality, not poverty. Unless policymakers address that and break the practice of seeing each problem in isolation such attempts are doomed to disappoint. The authors show how differences in status and wealth, and super rewards to stimulate the innovation on which growth depends, are proving disastrous everywhere. 'We have got close to the end of what economic growth can do for us.' The way out of the morass, they argue, is evenly distributed wealth and incomes through harsh taxes on the rich, and small differences in pay.

WILLIAMS, RAYMOND. *Keywords: A Vocabulary of Culture and Society* (New York: Oxford University Press, 1983). A renowned cultural critic introduces the histories of 155 words that have acquired cultural and social significance, showing how these words we use to understand the world take on new meanings and how these changes reflect the political dynamics and values of society.

WRIGHT, RONALD. *Stolen Continents: 500 Years of Conquest and Resistance in the Americas*. A tragic yet incendiary account of the brutality, destruction and genocide leading to the creation of settler states that, unlike those in Asia and Africa, could never be decolonized. Focuses on the interaction between colonizers and colonized, and about the myths settlers created and the native narratives they caused.

ZELDIN, THEODORE. *An Intimate History of Humanity* (New York: HarperCollins, 1994). This unusual history with an intimacy of tone reveals the past and present of human world that often remains (though all pervasive in our lives) hidden from our eyes. Exploring how feelings and personal relationships have changed through the ages, Zeldin attempts here to illumine what humans have in common, rather than what divides them. In the process, he explains what has thwarted people in their efforts to deepen humanity, to learn the art of living, and to cope with anger and cruelty. Sometimes by hierarchizing morality and sometimes by adopting a cynical amorality, 'compassion has been the most frustrated of emotions, more so than sex. ... All sorts of philosophies and prejudices have been like chastity belts, keeping it firmly under control'. Stressing that choices made in the past are not necessarily irreversible, Zeldin points out the options that remain untried, and the meetings between individuals, cultures and religions that have not yet taken place.

ZINN, HOWARD. *On History* (New York: Seven Stories Press, 2011). A collection of shorter writings of a self-taught working class intellectual, who fought for justice and peace, with his belief that we cannot be neutral on a moving train—that history has no bystanders, only participants. His writings enrich us with a true picture of race, class, and injustice in American society. This book takes us into his intellectual workshop and opens the window into his radical perspectives. He narrates his experiences in the civil rights and anti-war movements which taught him that change happens not because what people-in-power decide, but when people's movements force the powers to be to act responsibly and justly. Included here are his important essays such as 'The Uses of Scholarship' and 'Empire or Humanity? What the Classroom Didn't Teach Me About the American Empire.' The more interested should read *The Zinn Reader* and his masterpiece *A People's History of the United States.*

Class, Caste and Race

Aloysius, G. *Nationalism Without a Nation in India* (1997). A searing critique of modern Indian history, nationalist historiography, and top national leaders such as Gandhi and Nehru. Analyzing the anti-caste movements during the colonial period within the framework of nationalism as a congruence of power and culture, it explores the reasons why nationalism in India failed to accommodate the forces fighting against caste and brahmanism. It comes to the conclusion that 'internal cleavages within the Indian society, rather than the obvious external contradiction between Indian people and the British, were responsible for the outcome of the national movement and failure of the nation to emerge'. See also Aloysious' *Religion as Emancipatory Identity: A Buddhist Movement among the Tamils under Colonialism* (1998), and *The Brahminical Inscribed in Body Politic* (2010).

Ambedkar, B.R. *Annihilation of Caste* (1936). This famous essay is emblematic of Ambedkar's ideological and political struggle against caste. It lays bare the flawed assumption of 'Hindu society', the odious reality of brahmanic scriptures, the senseless law of caste and karma, and thus builds up a devastating critique of Hinduism, a subject that he engages with in several of his writings. His numerous works on caste, untouchability, identity, religion, economics, nationalism, constitutionalism and law—now easily available—will get you close to a restless and ignited mind with an alternative vision of society based on social democracy in terms of economic, political and cultural empowerment of the oppressed. Like Phule, Ambedkar was a rare system-builder in modern India. And, in all likelihood, a greater visionary than Gandhi and Nehru, a recognition that a society (still) in grip of caste and its consequences refuses to give him for obvious reasons. With the slogan of 'educate-agitate-organize', the liberation movement that he led from the 1920s until his death in 1956 in the teeth of vicious *savarna* opposition, united and inspired millions of caste-oppressed for self-respect, education, political representation, a new cultural identity and conversion to Buddhism and other casteless religions. His writings and speeches are now available in twenty-plus volumes, under the title *Dr. Babasaheb Ambedkar: Writings and Speeches*. A selection of his key writings in a single volume can be found in *Essential Writings of B. R. Ambedkar*, edited by Valerian Rodrigues (2002).

ANNER, JOHN, ed. *Beyond Identity Politics: Emerging Social Justice Movements in Communities of Colour* (Boston: South End Press, 1999). Articles collected here take a critical look at the emerging struggles within and surrounding communities of colour, and discuss complex issues ranging from building ethnic and class solidarity to fighting immigrant rights.

BASU, TAPAN, ed. *Translating Caste: Stories, Essays, Criticism* (Delhi: Katha, 2002). This anthology contains representative texts on the theme of caste, spanning disciplines, genres and perspectives. Uma Chakravarti's 'Through Another Lens: Men, Women, and Caste' presents an illuminating overview of caste—a necessary read for anyone interested in understanding caste and its consequences.

BERREMAN, GERALD. *Caste and Other Inequities: Essays on Inequality* (Meerut: Folklore Institute, 1979). Caste is not organic solidarity but 'institutionalised discrimination' (against the lowered castes). These scholarly essays shatter the myth, popular in academia in India and abroad, that there was consensual acceptance of the caste system among the various castes in Indian society.

BROWN, DEE. *Bury My Heart at Wounded Knee: An Indian History of the American West* (London: Vintage Books, 1991). First published in 1970 to eloquent acclaim and disclaim, this work unravels the story of systematic destruction—authenticated by council records, autobiographies, firsthand descriptions—of the native Indian culture by the US government during the second half of the nineteenth century.

DAHIWALE, S.M., ed. *Understanding Indian Society: The Non-Brahmanic Perspective* (Delhi: Rawat, 2005). Sociologists and activists come together in this collection of essays to unsettle the settled, and present a new perspective on older—conventional and brahmanical—historiographical interpretations of Indian society.

DANGLE, ARJUN, ed. *Poisoned Bread: Translations from Modern Marathi Dalit Literature* (Bombay: Orient Longman, 1992). Abused, humiliated, kept away from knowledge and the truth of their own dehumanized lives for centuries, dalits have started a remarkable fight-back in modern India, not just politically but also culturally and intellectually. This trailblazing anthology is an example of this rebellion. A range of dalit activist-writers—inspired by the Ambedkarite liberation movement—strip themselves bare in these writings, exposing the Indian apartheid in a way that jolts us out of the illusion of living in a civilized society. These raw, powerful, deeply moving writings—poems, stories, autobiographies and essays—are nothing short than a manifesto of revolt against caste and cultural oppression.

DELAGO, RICHARD, ed. *Critical Race Theory: The Cutting Edge* (Philadelphia: Temple University press, 1995). Critical race theory is a critical examination of society and culture, and intersection of race, law, and power. This anthology brings together some of the best writings on the subject.

DHARMA THEERTHA. *No Freedom With Caste*, ed. G. Aloysius (Delhi: Media House, 2004.) First published in 1941 under the title *History of Hindu Imperialism*, this work is a critical survey of caste and its consequences. One of the first and finest of such attempts, it exposes brahmanism and its nefarious role in keeping the masses ignorant and divided for exploitation. 'The claim of a superior [Hindu] culture is an utterly false imposture and a clever manoeuvre, with the help of ancient books and theories intended to conceal the hideousness of Hindu life and the brutality of its caste masters.' The author also shows how the oppressive tradition modernized itself during the colonial period under the mask of nationalism, perpetuating the culture of caste and discrimination. Leaders like Gandhi and Nehru, notwithstanding their democratic rhetoric, carried forward this brahmanic politics that only helped strengthen the traditionally dominant forces within the Indian society.

DOUGLASS, FREDERICK. *Narrative of the Life of Frederick Douglass, An American Slave*, ed. Houston A. Baber, Jr. (New York: Penguin, [1845] 1986). The stirring story of Douglass' self-education against the dreadful captivity of slavery and of his escape to freedom and fame. His narrative reveals how an unfettered mind reacts to a system that keeps him and his entire community in slavery. 'The more I read, the more I was led to abhor and detest my enslavers.' After publication of an early version of his story, Douglass fled to Great Britain to evade arrest. He returned after two years, and became famous throughout the country for his continued writings and work for the abolition of slavery. When the Civil War began, there was no plans to free the slaves, but Douglass 'managed to get Lincoln's ear and helped convince the president that it would further the war effort to free them'.

DU BOIS, W.E.B. *The Souls of Black Folk* (New York: Signet Classic, [1903] 1995). This collection of 14 essays combines the academic language of sociology with the lyrical beauty of spirituality. This is a manifesto for a new culture: an anguished cry for erasing the colour line and judging people by their souls, not by their skins. Written by one of the greatest Afro-American thinkers of the twentieth century, it has inspired many—and not just in the US—to learn from the past, question the status quo, and fight for a just society.

DYSON, MICHAEL ERIC. *Reflecting Black: African-American Cultural Criticism* (Minneapolis: University of Minnesota, 1993). A quest for criticism that would celebrate the positive aspects of black culture without ignoring its weaknesses.

The essays and reviews of this anthology plead to reject essentialism while recognizing the interweaving of cultural and political experience in African-American culture.

FRADY, MARSHALL. *Martin Luther King, Jr.: A Life* (New York: Penguin: 2002). An intimate portrait of a political and religious hero whose complicated life and leadership is often reduced to hagiography.

FRANKLIN, JOHN HOPE AND ALFRED A. MOSS JR. *From Slavery to Freedom: A History of African Americans* (New York: Alfred A. Knopf, 2000). This definitive history of African Americans, first published in 1947 and since then continuously updated, bridges the gap between black history and American history, documenting how blacks and whites coexisted and how widely their experiences differed. Franklin's challenge, as he put it, was 'to weave into the fabric of American history enough of the presence of blacks so that the story of the United States could be told adequately and fairly'. Records the experiences of blacks from the time they left Africa to their struggle for equality at the end of the previous century. Describes the rise of slavery, the interaction of European and African cultures in the New World, and the emergence of a distinct culture among slaves and free blacks. It examines the period after slavery, including the struggle for citizenship and equality; educational efforts; literary and cultural changes; problems in housing, health, juvenile matters, and poverty; the expansion of the black middle class; and the persistence of discrimination in the administration of justice.

FRANCO, FERNANDO, et al. *Journeys to Freedom: Dalit Narratives* (Kolkata: Samya, 2004). Offers interviews with dozens of dalits of Gujarat, a state where the militancy of right-wing Hindu politics has kept the traditionally subjugated communities particularly demoralized. Despite these obstacles, dalits have found their voice and have undertaken difficult journeys to liberty and dignity.

GEETHA, V. AND S.V. RAJADURAI. *Towards a Non-Brahmin Millennium: From Iyothee Thass to Periyar* (Kolkata: Samya, 1998). An outstanding work on south India's Non-brahman movement from its beginning at the end of the nineteenth century to Periyar's Self-Respect movement of the 1920s and 1930s. Meticulously researched and elegantly written, it brings alive a remarkable social movement in all its glories and limitations. The authors also include the issues concerning women and how the movement handled them.

GENOVESE, EUGENE. *Roll, Jordan, Roll: The World the Slaves Made* (New York: Vintage, 1972). A history of slavery of the US south. A reassessment of the master-slave relationship in American history.

GURU, GOPAL, ed. *Humiliation: Claims and Context* (Delhi: Oxford University Press, 2009). Essays in this collection examine the meanings, contexts, forms, and languages of humiliation, and also interrogate the structures that both underlie and renew various forms of humiliation—racial humiliation in the context of colonialism; caste-based humiliation through the practice of untouchability; multiple forms of gender humiliation, etc.

HALEY, ALEX. *Roots* (1976). This riveting story traces an Afro-American family back through seven generations. As Haley says, '*Roots* is not just a saga of my family. It is the symbolic saga of a people.'

ILAIAH, KANCHA. *Why I am Not a Hindu* (1996). A sociological autobiography and a hard-hitting critique of caste and Hinduism. Ilaiah, a leading intellectual of dalit-bahujan movement in India, emphasizes the difference in cultural, religious and material life between the exploitative 'upper-caste' Hindus and the productive masses who are now classified as dalits and OBCs. His other important work is *God as Political Philosopher: Buddha's Challenge to Brahminism* (2000) which presents an alternative reading of ancient Indian history. Also notable are his 'Dalitism and

Brahmanism: The Epistemological Conflict in History', in Ghanshyam Shah (ed.), *Dalit Identity and Politics* (2001), and an anthology of journalistic writings *Buffalo Nationalism: A Critique of Spiritual Fascism* (2004) in which he holds forth from a distinct dalit-bahujan perspective on issues such as caste, communalism, religion, politics, globalization, and education. His *Turning the Pot, Tilling the Land: Dignity of Labour in Our Times* (2007) is a tribute to contributions of toiling communities in the evolution of civilization and science in India. His latest work, *Post-Hindu India: A Discourse on Dalit-Bahujan Socio-Spiritual and Scientific Revolution* (2009), tries to synthesize all his earlier works, concerns and struggles for a socio-cultural revolution in India.

JONDHALE, SURENDRA AND JOHANNES BELTZ, eds. *Reconstructing the World: B. R. Ambedkar and Buddhism in India* (Delhi: Oxford University Press, 2004). This collection of essays analyzes Ambedkar's thoughts, his sociology of religion, and his construction of a 'new' Buddhism. Having considered the multi-faceted dimension to the Ambedkarite Buddhism, the scholars conclude that his worldview was one that transcended the dalit issue, and in fact attempted to provide a blueprint for the egalitarian reconstruction of society.

JOSHI, BARBARA. *Untouchable! Voices of the Dalit Liberation Movement* (Delhi: Select Book Service Syndicate, 1986). A documentation of dalit expression that anticipated the rise of dalit literature and politics of the 1990s. As Joshi says in her incisive introduction, 'They would have to find their own ways of financing and amplifying independent voices. They have found some. They would find others. This book is an attempt to bring some of those independent and courageous untouchable voices to a wider audience.'

JUERGENSMEYER, MARK. *Religious Rebels in the Punjab: The Ad Dharma Challenge to Caste* (Delhi: Navayana, [1982] 2009). A groundbreaking study of religious and political activism of dalits in the north India. Based on extensive field research, interviews and archival resources, this work shows why and how their wider movement for social change was also a religious movement. This historical study has relevance to the continuing struggles of dalit-subalterns for justice and dignity.

KING, MARTIN LUTHER, JR. *I Have a Dream: Writings and Speeches that Changed the World* (New York: HarperCollins, 1992). All of King's important speeches, essays, and books are included here. A superb anthology.

KUMAR, RAJ. *Dalit Personal Narratives: Reading Caste, Nation and Identity* (Delhi: Orient BlackSwan, 2009). A comprehensive, multidisciplinary, and in this sense pioneering study of dalit autobiographies. It examines examples of traditional autobiographical practices in the West as well as India, and shows how dalit personal narrative as a genre is 'comparatively new and completely different' from the existing autobiographical traditions in India and abroad.

MALCOLM X, written with Alex Haley. *The Autobiography of Malcolm X* (New York: Ballantine Books, [1964] 1992.) Story of an extraordinary activist whose militancy of attitude and thoughts challenged both blacks and whites. A classic of the Afro-American struggle for justice.

MANI, BRAJ RANJAN. *Debrahmanising History* (2005). Arguing that the axis of inequality in India is caste rooted in the ideology and politics of brahmanism (defined here as a historical-ideological weapon of multidimensional dominance), this work not only corners the dominance, but also generates thoughts for a new emancipatory politics. It brings alive a tradition of counter-culture, resurrecting many known and unknown champions of peoples' causes, from Buddha to Ambedkar. Many old and new myths about India, caste and Hinduism lie shattered in this book which stresses that 'caste consciousness and the brahmanical mindset persist' in modern garb, in defiance of democratic ideals, causing India to remain one of the most unequal and unjust societies.

MOHANTY, MANORANJAN, ed. *Class, Caste, Gender* (Delhi: Sage, 2004). Essays of this collection, written by some of India's leading thinkers on the subject, analyze basic conceptual issues and place them in the context of India's current social situation and political developments.

MONTAGU, ASHLEY. *Man's Most Dangerous Myth: The Fallacy of Race* (Walnut Creek, CA: AttaMira, [1942] 1997). The idea that race is a racist idea was by and large unknown when this classic work made the argument that race is a social construction, and not constitutive of significant biological differences between peoples. Montagu's radical hypothesis—accepted knowledge today—was ahead of its time in 1942, when Nazism ruled the roost, and the African-Americans were forced to sit at the back of the bus. This abridged and updated edition is a valuable read for a better understanding of the multi-ethnic society and culture we live in.

NARASU, LAKSHMI P. *A Study of Caste* (1922). Drawing from rational-humanist ideology, Narasu shows that humans are fundamentally alike, and nothing can be more dehumanizing than the arbitrary division of castes. Seeing caste as the mainstay of Hinduism and the necessity of a cultural struggle for a casteless society, he was among the pioneers in modern India to rediscover Buddhism in an egalitarian light. His 1907 book *The Essence of Buddhism* is still a favourite of many Buddhist enthusiasts. Ambedkar declared it 'the best book on Buddhism that has appeared so far', and reissued it in 1948 with an introduction of his own in which he hailed Narasu for his splendid fight against caste inhumanity, Hindu orthodoxy, and European authoritarianism 'all under the inspiring banner of the teachings of the great Buddha'.

NATRAJAN, BALMURALI AND PAUL GREENOUGH, eds. *Against Stigma: Studies in Caste, Race and Justice Since Durban* (Delhi: Orient BlackSwan, 2009). Essays in this anthology offer cutting-edge perspective on two of the most odious and divisive concepts in the history of humanity, enriching our understanding of human rights, race relations, caste studies, and the politics of socio-cultural exclusion.

OBAMA, BARACK. *Dreams from My Father: A Story of Race and Inheritance* (New York: Three Rivers Press, 2004). This memoir of the famous son of a black African father and a white American mother takes us to the difficult terrain of identity, class, and race. Perceptive and moving.

OMVEDT, GAIL. *Dalits and the Democratic Revolution* (1994). Omvedt bases her analysis on a new historical materialism that takes into account the complex realities of caste, class and gender. Engaging with Phule-Ambedkar's ideology and struggle for a democratic society, she shows how through the rightist concoction of seamless national unity against colonialism on the one hand and the leftist class vision (that subsumes all realities of caste and discrimination) on the other, the dalit movement has been distorted and marginalized in the historiography of both the nationalist and Marxist varieties. Omvedt has authored several books related to this subject. In *Ambedkar: Towards an Enlightened India* (2004), she compares the Ambedkarite struggle against exploitative social structures with the Gandhian movement for freedom, arguing that the former fought for 'a broader liberation from exploitation and oppression'. Her writings expose the elitist tendency to equate Indian tradition with Hinduism and Hinduism with brahmanism, stressing that even the progressive-secular minds remain imprisoned within this mindset. She carries forward this debate in *Seeking Begumpura: The Social Vision of Anti-caste Intellectuals* (2008).

PERIYAR, E. V. RAMASAMY. *Collected Works of Periyar E.V.R.*, compiled by K. Veeramani (Chennai: The Periyar Self-Respect Institute, 2000). This translation (from the original Tamil) and editing leave much to be desired, but there is no good anthology of Periyar's writings in English—a revealing fact in itself. Periyar did not have the education and English like

Ambedkar to operate on a pan-India level, yet he was, along with the latter, one of the two key anti-caste intellectuals of the previous century grappling with all the conflicting ideological and political issues of the time. Carrying a distinct Tamil sensibility, his critique of caste, patriarchy, Hinduism, nationalism, and a host of related issues, was forged during his long and spectacular Dravidian and Self-Respect movement, and remains one of the most original and penetrating in modern India, a glimpse of which can be seen in this anthology.

PHULE, JOTIRAO. *Slavery* ([1873] 2002). This is Phule's best-known work, and has recently been rendered into a graphic book, *A Gardener in the Wasteland: Jotiba Phule's Fight for Liberty* (Navayana, 2011). Written originally in Marathi in the form of a dialogue between Phule and a friend of his, *Slavery* is a hard-hitting satirical account of brahmanism and its caste ideology. The 'Preface', in Phule's own English, shows that he could, when necessary, write powerfully in this language too. It is notable that he never uses the term Hindu or Hinduism; he refers to brahman and brahmanism instead. Attacks on caste and brahmanism, though not unknown before, reach a turning point with Phule. He sees slavery in the very structure of caste, and conceptualizes it in a way that shifts attention from social mobility within the caste hierarchy to a rejection of the system itself. What makes him a revolutionary is his ability to see the interconnections between caste, class, and gender, and his radical politics to smash this oppressive matrix through a socio-cultural action based on solidarity—through a critical education—of all the oppressed. As he wanted to fight all forms of injustice and monopoly of power, he was passionate about building a cultural foundation for such a transformation. After a century of elitist trivialization, Phule, along with Ambedkar, is now being read and recognized as a pioneering figure of social justice in modern India.

RAVIKUMAR AND R. AZHAGARASAN, eds. *The Oxford India Anthology of Tamil Dalit Writing* (Delhi: Oxford University Press, 2012). Traces the rise and evolution of dalit writing from the late nineteenth century to the present in Tamil Nadu. Introduction provides the historical and socio-cultural contexts of the writings collected here.

RODRIGUES, VALERIAN. *Dalit-Bahujan Discourse* (Delhi: Critical Quest, 2008). A sensitive and insightful interpretation of dalit-bahujan thoughts in modern India centred around social, cultural and economic emancipation of the oppressed majority 'as compared to other currents of social and political thought in India or even elsewhere.'

SATYANARAYANA, K. AND SUSIE THARU, eds. *No Alphabet in Sight: New Dalit Writing From South India.* Dossier 1: Tamil and Malayalam (Delhi: Penguin, 2011). The editors call this volume a dossier to emphasize the range of documents—fiction, poetry, cultural critique, social analysis, and political speech—collected and translated from the south Indian languages. A long Introduction puts these accounts, experiences and perspectives in the socio-political context. Underpinning the emergence of 'national debate on caste' and 'the rediscovery of Ambedkar as a national figure' in the wake of the 1990 reservation debate, it shows the significance of the dalit-subaltern writings, noting that caste remains a 'contemporary form of power' as it works in renewed forms in modern contexts and institutions. It is not just a problem the lower castes suffer from, but entwined with the entire socio-economic and educational infrastructure that enables caste elites to successfully negotiate modern society and institutions, keeping the lower castes, especially dalits, in their place. The diverse writings collected here vindicate the editors' claims. They straddle a range of issues and bring alive the discrimination, pain, and humiliation that dalits still have to face in everyday life. Shows not only how caste is being reproduced in education, culture, law, the arts and the media, but also the Ambedkarite resolve of dalit youth to fight and crush this scourge.

SEABROOK, JEREMY. *No-Nonsense Guide to Class, Caste and Hierarchies* (Oxford: New Internationalist, 2002). Gives a realistic picture of how class and caste still affect people's lives in the globalized world. The hierarchies, in fact, show no sign of disappearance since those at the top would have too much to lose. It also identifies the rich, the celebrities and others who obscure the ugly social reality and play a significant role in reconciling the poor to their wretched condition.

SINGH, KUMAR SURESH. *Birsa Munda and His Movement 1872-1901: A Study of a Millenarian Movement in Chotanagpur* (Kolkata: Seagull, 2002). An account of the best-known millenarian movement in tribal India, and the legendary hero who led the movement from the front.

STOWE, HARRIET BEECHER. *Uncle Tom's Cabin* (1852). Stowe wrote this novel to highlight the cruelty of slavery in the USA, giving it a human name and face, so that people could relate, empathize, and fight on the behalf of the enslaved blacks. This 'highest moral art', as Tolstoy described it, not only created popular revulsion against slavery but also galvanized many against it. This work, some believe, swelled the ranks of abolitionists, and set the stage for the Civil War. Lincoln called Stowe 'the little lady who made this big war'.

THOMPSON, E.P. *The Making of the English Working Class* (London: Vintage, 1966). Social conscience and impeccable research that one sees in this work is an example of how people's social history should be written. As Thompson writes in the Preface: 'I am seeking to rescue the poor stockinger, the Luddite cropper, the "obsolete" hand-loom weaver, the "utopian" artisan, and even the deluded follower of Joanna Southcott from the enormous condescension of posterity.' He brings out the life-experience and struggles of these people, who were not just the victims of history: 'The working class made itself as much as it was made.' He uses the term 'working class' rather than 'classes' to emphasize the growth of a working-class consciousness: 'In the years between 1780 and 1832 most English working people came to feel an identity of interests as between themselves, and as against other men whose interests are different from (and usually opposed to) theirs.' This consciousness is at the core of this book, manifested in the values of collectivism, mutuality, and a common aspiration for radical change. Thompson was a Marxist and this book was his way of steering the Left towards democratic socialism as opposed to the Stalinist totalitarianism.

WEST, CORNEL. *Race Matters* (Boston: Beacon Press, [1994) 2001). In this collection of essays, West analyzes social issues through a humanistic and moral lens, and re-energizes the debate on race by including issues of class, gender, and citizenship. Going beyond the established language of political debate, his criticism questions moral authority, encourages self-criticism, and confronts the reader with *what is to be done?*

ZELLIOT, ELEANOR. *From Untouchable to Dalit: Essays on Ambedkar Movement* (Delhi: Manohar, 1992 [1998]). The title suggests the idea that the untouchables of India had themselves chosen a new identity, that of dalit—oppressed—to indicate their resentment against their traditional oppression. The essays collected here get us close to the continuing innovation, diversity and vitality of the Amebedkar movement.

ZELLIOT, ELEANOR, AND ROHINI MOKASHI-PUNEKAR, eds. *Untouchable Saints: An Indian Phenomenon* (Delhi: Manohar, 2005). In the land of caste, even saints can be damned and despised as untouchables! A collection of illuminating essays on the phenomenon of religious voices from the lowest order of society—Nandanar and Tiruppan Alvar in the south, Chokhmela and his family in the Marathi territory, and Ravidas in the north.

PATRIARCHY AND GENDER

AGNES, FLAVIA. *My Story, Our Story: Building Broken Lives* (Bombay: Forum Against Oppression of Women, [1984] 1988). A moving autobiography of an activist and advocate of women's rights. An important work for understanding sexuality and subordination in Indian society. See also her *Law and Gender Inequality: The Politics of Women's Rights in India* (1999).

ANDERSEN, MARGARET L. AND DANA HYSOCK WITHAM. *Thinking about Women: Sociological Perspectives on Sex and Gender* (New York: Pearson, 2010). A superb text on the sociology of gender. This updated edition offers a comprehensive review of feminist scholarship in the social sciences.

ANDERSEN, MARGARET L. AND PATRICIA HILL COLLINS, eds. *Race, Class, and Gender: An Anthology*, 8th edn. (Belmont CA: Wadsworth, 2012). This excellent anthology provides a multidimensional perspective on a number of social issues. Includes many interdisciplinary readings, and each section is brilliantly introduced by the editors.

ANDERSON, BONNIE S., AND JUDITH P. ZINSSER. *A History of Their Own: Women in Europe from Prehistory to the Present*, two volumes (New York: Oxford University Press [1990] 1999). Brings women's history into focus. Restoring many forgotten or unwritten facts or events to historical record, it discovers models of female action and achievements.

ASHTON-JONES, EVELYN, GARY OLSON AND MERRY G. PERRY, eds. *The Gender Reader*, 2nd edn. (New York: Longman, [1991] 1999). The selections provide a comprehensive overview of the sociology of gender roles.

BACA ZINNE, MAXINE, PIERRETTE HONDAGNEU-SOTELO AND MICHAEL A MESSNER. *Gender Through the Prism of Difference*, 4th edn. (New York: Oxford University Press, 2010). This work examines gender by focussing on how social inequalities and identities impact gender. Selections here, many of them based on latest research, cover contemporary topics.

BELENKY, MARY FIELD, et al. *Women's Ways of Knowing: The Development of Self, Voice, and Mind* (New York: Basic Books, 1986). An outstanding book on women, knowledge, and identity. Based on in-depth interviews of 135 women, it demystifies the troubled world of women who feel silenced in their families and in schools, notwithstanding the progress of the women's movement. Compels us to think in better ways about what constitutes knowledge and therefore the aim of education for both women and men.

BENOKRAITIS, NIJOLE V. *Subtle Sexism: Current Practice and Prospects for Change* (Thousand Oaks, CA: Sage, 1997). Documents a range of discriminations that many women experience on a daily basis. Examines sexism as a social control, and also offers ways to overcome this menace.

BLEIER, RUTH. *Science and Gender* (New York: Oxford University Press, 1984). One of the very first and important books on the subject.

BORDO, SUSAN. *The Flight to Objectivity: Essays on Cartesianism and Culture* (Albany: State University of New York Press, 1987). This book tells us how the masculinization of thought—with stress on objectivity and emotional detachment, qualities traditionally associated with masculinity, as essential aspects of knowledge—began with the very foundation of civilization. Feminine qualities such as subjectivity and emotional involvement were considered hindrances in the advancement of knowledge. The epistemic 'masculinization' reached a watershed at the beginning of modernity with Descartes' scientific attempt to interpret the world. But women's life and experiences—marked by menstruation, childbirth, nursing, and caring for others—are *embodied* experiences that cannot be abstracted into clear-cut Cartesian dualism of mind and body. Bordo thus brings home the point that 'Cartesian modernity is inherently linked to the repression of nature and women.' The result is that objectivity rather than meaning became the main philosophical concern.

BRITTAN, ARTHUR AND MARY MAYNARD. *Sexism, Racism, and Oppression* (Oxford: Basil Blackwell, 1984). The oppressed are 'those who are coerced by others. Their freedom of action is limited by the superior power of those who are in a position to ensure their compliance'. Making this point, the authors stress the need to eliminate both sexism and racism to overcome oppression.

BROWNMILLER, SUSAN. *Femininity* (New York: Fawcett Columbine, 1985). A lucid exposition of powerful nuances involved in the construction of femininity—body, hair, clothes, voice, skin, movement, emotion, ambition.

CHAFETZ, JANET SALTZMAN. *Masculine, Feminine or Human? An Overview of the Sociology of the Gender Roles* (Illinois: F.E. Peacock, 1978.) A little dated, but this work is still important for making us see how boys and girls are conditioned from childhood to polarized gender attitude and behaviour.

CHAKRAVARTI, UMA. *Gendering Caste: Through a Feminist Lens* (Calcutta: Stree, 2003). Most academic feminists in India come from privileged castes and for them caste simply does not matter; some of them such as Madhu Kishwar even dare to celebrate caste. Chakravarti is the rare feminist scholar who sees crucial linkages between caste and gender, and has worked brilliantly and extensively on brahmanic patriarchy in Indian society, and this work is an excellent example of this. Her other notable works include *Social Dimensions of Early Buddhism* (1987); *Rewriting History: The Life and Times of Pandita Ramabai* (1998); and *Everyday Lives, Everyday Histories: Beyond the Kings and Brahmanas of Ancient India* (2006).

CHOW, REY. *Woman and Chinese Modernity* (Minneapolis: University of Minnesota Press, 1991). As the entry point of modernity in eastern societies is linked to the history of Western imperialism, this work focuses on 'the politics of reading between East and West'.

COLLINS, PATRICIA HILL. *Black Feminist Thought: Knowledge, Consciousness, and the Politics of Empowerment* (New York: Routledge, [1990] 2000). Explores the work and ideas of black women and their pursuit of knowledge and empowerment against the odds of white hegemonic power structures and knowledge systems. Black feminist epistemology, the author argues, must question any system that does not take into account the collective experience of race, gender, and class oppression.

CONNELL, R.W. *Gender and Power: Society, the Person and Sexual Politics* (Cambridge: Polity Press, [1987] 1997). An excellent book for understanding gender as both an object and category of analysis. Integrates the social analysis of sex and gender with the larger social and political theorization, with the aim of challenging and changing the traditional paradigms.

CROW, BARBARA, ed. *Radical Feminism: A Documentary Reader* (New York: New York University Press, 2000). Radical feminism of the 1960s and 1970s continues to be a controversial subject—it has both supporters and detractors. Resurrecting the original voice—essays, pamphlets, manifestoes, etc.—of radical feminists, this panoramic collection permits them to speak for themselves.

CROWLEY, HELEN AND SUSAN HIMMELWEET, eds. *Knowing Women: Feminism and Knowledge* (United Kingdom: Polity Press, 1992). Exploring developments in feminist ideology, this work engages the reader in the debates concerning women's status as both objects and subjects of knowledge.

DAVIS, ANGELA. *Women, Race and Class* (Delhi: Navayana, [1981] 2011). An outstanding book on the subject in the context of women's movement in the US.

DE BEAUVOIR, SIMONE. *The Second Sex* (1949). This classic of feminist literature argues that all through history, woman has been denied the rights and opportunities to rise to her full potential. Social custom—created by man—relegated woman to a secondary, dependent, inferior position. 'One is not born, but rather becomes a woman.' Though most women mistakenly look for salvation in love and marriage, this is not essentially 'feminine' nature. This manifesto of a 'complete economic and social equality' between sexes—which some radical feminists find problematic for giving alibi to emulation of masculine values and ideals—inspired women the world over for gender equality.

EPSTEIN, CYNTHIA FUCHS. *Deceptive Distinctions: Sex, Gender, and the Social Order* (New Haven, CT: Yale University Press). Presents a lucid synthesis of feminist scholarship, and shows how distinctions between the sexes are maintained by the established social order and its ideology.

ESTES, CLARISSA PINKOLA. *Women Who Run With the Wolves: Myths and Stories of the Wild Woman Archetype* (New York: Ballantine Books, 1995). Celebrates pristine feminine nature filled with good instincts, creativity, and wisdom. Through stories and commentaries, it attempts to free the 'looted, driven back, and ever-built' female nature and psyche. A protest against 'society's attempt to civilize us into rigid roles [that] has muffled the deep, life-giving messages of our own souls'.

FIRESTONE, SHULAMITH. *The Dialectic of Sex: The Case for Feminist Revolution* (New York: Bantam, 1971). Argues that sex, more than class or race, has been the matrix of domination and social stratification. This fundamental division cannot be overcome without ushering in a feminist revolution, which will be more challenging than the socialist revolution because this involves 'a larger problem, with an oppression that goes back beyond recorded history to the animal kingdom itself'.

FRANKENBERG, RUTH. *The Social Construction of Whiteness: White Women, Race Matters* (Minneapolis: University of Minnesota Press, 1993). This work takes on the white feminists who see the source of all evil in gender. 'Race shapes white women's lives. In the same way that both men's and women's lives are shaped by their gender...white people and people of colour live racially structured lives. ...[A]ny system of differentiation shapes those on whom it bestows privilege as well as those it oppresses.'

FRIEDAN, BETTY. *The Feminine Mystique* (New York: Norton, 1963). This work heralded a new wave of feminist consciousness with a message that even affluent, middle class women lead a frustrated, restricted lives—'the problem that has no name'. 'We can no longer ignore that voice within women that says: I want something more than my husband and my children and my home.'

FRYE, MARILYN. *The Politics of Reality: Essays in Feminist Theory* (1983). A brilliant exposition of the structural perspective that lies at the heart of gender oppression. Oppression, unlike cases of individual suffering in society, is systemic—structured into the fabric of social institutions. Gender is the product of cultural and economic structures which create and enforce rigid patterns of sex-marking and sex-announcing behaviour which mould the human species as dominators or subordinates. As Frye put it, they construct two classes of people, the masculine and the feminine, where another constellation of forces might have constructed three or five categories, and not necessarily hierarchically related. Individual acts and practices which reinforce those structures are sexist. Resistance to sexism, thus, is that which undermines those structures by social and political action and by projects of reconstruction and revision of ourselves.

GEETHA, V. *Gender* (Calcutta: Stree, 2002). One of the best Indian books on the subject. Clear, sharp, and purpose-driven.

GILBERT, PAM, AND SANDRA TAYLOR. *Fashioning the Feminine: Girls, Popular Culture and Schooling* (Sydney: Allen & Unwin, 1991). A critique of the roles played by popular culture and education in the construction of teenage female identity, it explores the possibilities for changing that identity from a feminist viewpoint.

GOODMAN, ELIZABETH, ed. *Literature and Gender* (London: Routledge & London Open University, 1996). An anthology of literary texts (in all three major genres—poetry, fiction, drama) which demonstrate the relevance of gender to the study of literature.

GREER, GERMAINE. *The Female Eunuch.* This 1970 work challenges the 'sense of [female] inferiority and natural dependence', and explores why women themselves accept degrading and debilitating stereotypes into their living reality. Greer debunks the myth of love and marriage as the ultimate female destiny, and says that being 'an object of male fantasy' actually desexualizes women, and that 'cooking, clothes, beauty and housekeeping' become compulsive, anxiety-producing activities.

HANSEN, KAREN, AND ILENE J. PHILIPSON, eds. *Women, Class, and the Feminist Imagination: A Socialist-Feminist Reader* (Philadelphia: Temple University Press, 1990). This collection of stimulating essays shows the contribution of American socialist-feminists of the 1960s and 1970s in expanding feminist debates and progress in critical areas.

HOLLAND, DOROTHY, AND MARGARET EISENHART. *Educated in Romance: Women, Achievement, and College Culture* (Chicago: University of Chicago Press, 1990). Brings into focus the pervasive 'culture of romance' on campus which encourages young women to prioritize romantic love above other forms of life and learning. The case studies presented here show how young women often sell themselves short academically in order to enter into stereotyped relationships where their attractiveness to men counts the most.

HOOKS, BELL. *Feminist Theory: From Margin to Centre* (Boston: South End Press, 1984). Challenges the academic status quo and claims that theory should be objective and detached from activism. Arguing that much of the academic theories reflect dominant, white, patriarchal structures, Hooks challenges the notion of the centre as powerful and the margin as powerless. Instead, she sees the margin as a potential power base since globally more people occupy the margins than the centre. She attacks the feminism fashioned by white women which ignores social inequalities and the fact that women themselves are divided by sexist attitudes, racism, and class privilege. By insisting on the common oppression of women, the white women in the movement, she argues, have not allowed the most victimized women to speak out for themselves. 'Every problem raised by white feminists has a disproportionately heavy input on blacks.' Since feminism is a struggle to end gender oppression, it is necessarily a struggle to eradicate the ideology of domination as well as a commitment to reorganizing society so that the self-development of people can take precedence over imperialism, economic expansion, and material greed. Hooks' other notable works include *Teaching to Transgress: Education as the Practice of Freedom* (1994), and (written with Cornel West) *Breaking Bread: Insurgent Black Intellectual Life* (1991).

JACOBS, HARRIET. *Incidents in the Life of a Slave Girl* (New York: Oxford University Press, [1861] 1988). One of the first slave narratives written by a woman, this heart-wrenching account of Jacobs' suffering, and her search for her own voice, prefigure the rise of Afro-American women writers in the coming decades.

JAGGAR, ALISON AND SUSAN R. BORDO, eds. *Gender/Body/Knowledge: Feminist Reconstructions of Being and Knowing* (New Brunswick, N. J.: Rutgers University Press, 1989). A superb anthology of feminist analyses of epistemological and metaphysical issues.

JAGGAR, ALISON, ed. *Living with Contradictions: Controversies in Feminist Social Ethics* (Boulder: Westview Press, 1994). An important collection of articles on sexism and related issues in connection with a wide range of moral issues.

JOHN, MARY E., ed. *Women's Studies in India: A Reader* (Delhi: Penguin, 2008). Maps out the rise of a new and constantly expanding field of study in India. This anthology shows 'not just how vast the field has become, but also how contested it continues to be'.

JONES, JACQUELINE. *Labour of Love, Labour of Sorrow: Black Women, Work, and the Family from Slavery to the Present* (NewYork: Basic Books, 1985). Despite being crushed under the weight of racial humiliation and sexual discrimination, black women have shouldered the responsibility as bread winners and guardians of family and community stability. This historical study lends voice to the epic, yet unrecorded, struggle of black women from the depths of slavery to the ongoing fight for civil rights.

JUNG, ANEES. *Breaking the Silence: Voices of Women from Around the World* (Delhi: Viking /Unesco, 1997). Presents a powerful, often moving, account of the emergent new woman in patriarchal societies with a personality and a voice of her own. Amplifying women's cries for freedom and equality everywhere, the author seems to suggest that it is the woman herself who has to wage her freedom struggle—individually and collectively with her sisters.

KELLY, JOAN. *Women, History and Theory: The Essays of Joan Kelly* (Chicago: University of Chicago Press, 1984). This important anthology has Kelly's famous essay 'Did Women Have a Renaissance?' First published in 1977, it challenged the conventional view of the cultural movement, arguing that women's power and agency actually declined during the Renaissance period of the 1350s to 1530s. It was primarily an artistic and literary movement, and the art works and literature produced during the time to celebrate life also emphasized the gendered division of labour—keeping women confined to household duties and child-care. As 'the relations of sexes were restructured to one of female dependency and male domination', the women did not have a Renaissance.

KLEIN, ETHEL. *Gender Politics: From Consciousness to Mass Politics* (Cambridge, MA: Harvard University Press, 1984). This work explains the phenomenon of the 1960s and 1970s which witnessed the rise of a spectacular women's movement. Klein begins her probe by asking two questions: what are the common concerns that mobilize women, and how these concerns shape political activism. The necessary ingredients of a movement—grievances, leaders, organization, and resources—were already there before the 1960s; what was missing was, she says, a constituency to support women's demands. In that period, group consciousness among women grew, and so did popular support, and the two factors coalesced in the rise of activism and a full-blown women's movement.

KUMAR, RADHA. *The History of Doing: An Illustrated Account of Movements for Women's Rights and Feminism in India* (Delhi: Kali for Women, 1993). Recaptures the debate around women's issues during the reform and national movement, its subsequent disappearance from the agenda of public debate until the women themselves came forward with demands of equality and justice in the 1960s and 1970s.

LALITHA DHARA, ed. *Phules and Women's Question* (Mumbai: Dr Ambedkar College of Commerce and Economics, 2011). A useful anthology of articles on women-related work and writings of Savitribai and Jotirao Phule, underlining relevance of their thoughts for women's liberation.

LERNER, GERDA. *The Creation of Patriarchy* (New York: Oxford University Press, 1986). A classic work on the subordination of women and the institution of masculine power in Western civilization—one of the first to link historical understanding with theoretical arguments. Lerner's account demonstrates that male dominance over women was not 'natural' or biological; it was created at a specific time in history out of many complex processes. Using history, literature, artistic, and archaeological evidences, she traces the development of the ideas and institutions, symbols and metaphors, which were incorporated in the construction of patriarchy and female powerlessness. The argument that Lerner makes in this work is powerful: as patriarchy as a system of organizing society was established historically, it can and must be ended by a historical process. Also see her related work *The Creation of Feminist Consciousness* (1993).

LORBER, JUDITH. *Paradoxes of Gender* (New Haven, CT: Yale University Press, 1994). Gender is so pervasive in our society that we assume it is bred into our genes. 'And everyone "does gender" without thinking about it. . . . Much of what we take for granted about gender and its causes and effects either does not hold up or can be explained differently.'

LORDE, AUDRE. *Sister Outsider* (California: Crossing Press, 1984). A multifaceted author and poet engages here with age, race, class, and sex.

MACKINNON, CATHARINE A. *Feminism Unmodified: Discourse on Life and Law* (Cambridge, MA: Harvard University Press, 1987). This collection of speeches and write-ups includes MacKinnon's influential essay 'Sexual Harassment and Sexual Politics'. Her writings interpret the structure of government as the reflection of persistent patterns of male domination.

MENON, NIVEDITA. *Recovering Subversion: Feminist Politics Beyond the Law* (Delhi: Permanent Black, 2004). This work attempts to show that the Indian state and the law have often been more a hindrance than a help to ethical and emancipatory impulses of feminist politics.

MESSNER, MICHAEL. *The Politics of Masculinities* (Thousand Oaks: Sage, 1997). Using personal accounts, Messner unravels three key considerations in the study of masculinity. First, the institutionalized nature of male privilege that gives men as a group power over women as a group. Then, he shows that the limiting definition of masculinity damages—hardens—men in many ways. Finally, he takes up inequalities and differences among men that give white, heterosexual men more power than others in the American culture. In his earlier work, *Power at Play: Sports and the Problem of Masculinity* (1992), Messner shows how the narrow masculinity that men learn in sports connects—and plays havoc—with other forms of social dominance. Class and racial-ethnic differences affect the construction of masculine identities by boys and men within the world of organized sports.

MILES, ROSALIND. *The Women's History of the World* (London: Harper Collins, 1988). Offers a gendered reappraisal of history—retrieving her story that has been subsumed in his story, history. Celebrates millions of unknown women who contributed to the making of civilization, authenticating it with tales of individual women who shaped history.

MILLER, CASEY AND KATE SWIFT. *Words and Women* (Indiana: iUniverse, [1976] 2001). An intense and extensive look at the impact language has had on the perception and identity of women. Laying bare the pervasive sexism of language and speech, the authors talk of a 'semantic polarization' in which people use masculine words to convey good meanings and feminine words to convey bad and obscene meanings. Similarly, our speech can be casteist and racist. How can we speak to each other, about each other, with dignity and accuracy is still a vital question, a contested territory, and so is the relevance of such works.

MILLET, KATE. *Sexual Politics* (1970). Analyzes patriarchy as a political institution. Arguing that politics is all about 'power-structured relationships', Millet stresses that the one between the sexes is a 'relationship of dominance and subordinance'. Women are idolized and patronized at the same time. Separating sex from politics will not be possible without a liberating vision and a long-drawn struggle based on it.

MORAGA, CHERRIE AND GLORIA ANZALDUA, eds. *This Bridge Called My Back: Radical Writings by Women of Colour* (New York: Kitchen Table Press, [1981] 1983). An impressive array of women of colour from diverse backgrounds come together in this anthology to challenge the forces that put all women and feminism in one category. Raising the issues related to race and class, they laid the foundation of what is called 'third wave feminism'. *This Bridge* offers 'a rich and diverse account of the experience and analyses of women of colour, with its collective ethos, its politics of rage and regeneration, and its mix of poetry, critique, fiction, testimony, it challenges the boundaries of feminist and academic discourse'.

MURTHY, LAXMI AND RAJASHRI DASGUPTA, eds. *Our Pictures, Our Words: A Visual Journey Through the Women's Movement* (Delhi: Zubaan, 2011). This beautiful book brings alive the complex and multilayered campaigns for women's rights spread over the last three decades through posters and other visual representation—photographs, drawings, stickers, wall writing, reports, brochures, pamphlets—with matching words.

OGELSBY, C. A., ed. *Women and Sport: From Myth to Reality* (Philadelphia: Lea and Febiger, 1978). Offers a feminist perspective to reassess women's role, rights, experiences, and future in sport in light of socio-historical and legislative concerns.

OKIN, SUSAN MOLLER. *Justice, Gender, and the Family* (New York: Basic Books, 1989). Challenges Rawls' theory of justice and the possibility of a gender-free rationality. As Okin says, there is a 'blindness to the sexism of the tradition in which Rawls is a participant. ...A feminist reader finds it difficult not to keep asking, *Does this theory apply to women?*'

No fair theory of justice, she argues, can fail to include an analysis of justice within the family, since family is still the primary shaper of personality, as well as of basic attitudes of self-respect, gender, race or caste. Yet, almost all theories of justice tend to ignore the status of all family members, while the findings of feminism point to how 'deeply and pervasively' gendered-structured our society is. 'They have largely bypassed the fact that the society to which their theories are supposed to pertain is heavily and deeply affected by gender, and faces difficult issues of justice stemming from its gendered past and present assumptions.'

ORTNER, SHERRY AND HARRIET WHITEHEAD, eds. *Sexual Meanings: The Cultural Construction of Gender and Sexuality* (Cambridge: Cambridge University Press, [1981] 2000). A collection of articles about the way in which gender and sexuality are conceptualized in various cultures, the volume also attempts to understand the consequences of such conceptions in social, political and cultural contexts.

PIPHER, MARY. *Reviving Ophelia: Saving the Selves of Adolescent Girls* (New York: Ballantine Books, 1995). Despite the advances of feminism, girls continue to be grossly sexualized and those who are not 'attractive' scorned. So much so that the girls themselves become promoters of nasty sexual stereotypes. This book lays bare the everyday reality of female teenagers in a 'look-obsessed, media-saturated, girl-poisoning culture' that teaches them 'don't worry about feeling good or being good, worry about looking good'. It pleads to change the toxic and intoxicating world of sexism and violence that surround young girls and restore their self-esteem and creative spirit.

POLLACK, WILLIAM. *Real Boys: Rescuing Our Sons from the Myths of Boyhood* (1999). Shows that many of man's self-destructive ways are nurtured on the persistent image of the strong, dispassionate, action-oriented male that damages the boys who 'lose their voice, a whole half of their emotional selves' at a very young age. 'Their vulnerable, sad feelings and sense of need are suppressed or shamed out of them' by their parents, peers and glorification of violence in entertainment industry.

RAO, ANUPAMA, ed. *Gender and Caste* (Delhi: Kali for Women, 2003). An important collection of articles on caste and gender, especially issues related to dalit women.

REGE, SHARMILA. *Writing Caste/Writing Gender: Reading Dalit Women's Testimonios* (Delhi: Zubaan, 2006). An important theoretical articulation of the multiple oppression experienced by dalit women through the study of autobiographies of dalit women from Maharashtra.

ROWBOTHAM, SHEILA. *Feminism and Social Action* (New York: Routledge, 1992). A classic work on women, politics, and activism.

ROY, KUMKUM. *The Politics of Gender and the Gender of Politics: Explorations in Early Indian History* (Delhi: Oxford University Press, 2010). Essays collected here present a gendered analysis and underscore the importance of such studies in the reconstruction of India's past.

SANGARI, KUMKUM AND SUDESH VAID, eds. *Recasting women: Essays in Colonial India* (Delhi: Kali for Women, 1989). Incisive essays of this anthology enable us to better understand the historical processes which constituted patriarchy in colonial India, reflected both in the policies of the colonial state and the national politics of 'reform' movements. Especially noteworthy are Uma Chakravati's 'Whatever Happened to the Vedic Dasi?: Orientalism, Nationalism, and a Script for the Past' , and Lata Mani's 'Contentious Traditions: The Debate on *Sati* in Colonial India'.

SCHWARTZ, PEPPER AND VIRGINIA RUTTER. *The Gender of Sexuality: Exploring Sexual Possibilities* (Rowman & Littlefield, 1998). The relationship of gender to sexuality is often underestimated. The social influences on sexual desire, this book demonstrates, are huge, almost decisive. Sexuality, sexual orientation, and sexual identity are not simply a matter of biology—attraction to and desire for a male or female. With examples culled from all over, the authors point to the social context of masculinity and femininity and the significance of social processes in determining sexual desire.

SCOTT, JOAN W. 'Gender', in *Coming to Terms: Feminism, Theory, Politics*, ed. Elizabeth Weed (New York: Routledge, 1989). Brilliantly explains gender as a construct and category of analysis. Also see her *Gender and the Politics of History* (1988).

SMITH, DOROTHY. *The Everyday World as Problematic: A Feminist Sociology* (Toronto: University of Toronto Press, 1987). Contesting the traditional—androcentric—sociological study, Smith argues that the very nature of such study reinforces the exclusion of women from major institutions of culture which are dominated by the men of privileged class. Such study keeps reproducing the dominant ideas in politics, economics, education, law, and medicine. Rejecting this dominant ideology, which objectifies women in academic research and devalues them within society, this book shows the way to develop a feminist discourse and epistemology based on women's experience.

THARU, SUSIE AND K. LALITA, eds. *Women Writing in India*, Volume I: 600 BC to the Early Twentieth Century; Volume II: The Twentieth Century (Delhi: Oxford University Press, 1991 and 1993). The first such anthology to emerge from India. Introduction dissects the institutionalized denial of language and voice to women; despite these huge barriers, the writings gathered here show, Indian women from various social groups have, over the centuries, been successful (to varying degree) in recording their experiences and dissent.

WERTHEIM, MARGARET. *Pythagoras' Trousers: God, Physics and the Gender Wars* (London: Fourth Estate, 1997). An important book on science and gender.

WOOD, JULIA T. *Gendered Lives: Communication, Gender, and Culture*, 10th edn. (Boston: Wadsworth, 2013). One of the best textbooks on the subject, this is also a rewarding read for general readers.

WOOLF, VIRGINIA. *A Room of One's Own*, ed. Morag Shiach (Oxford: Oxford University Press, [1929] 1992). Today's radicals don't think much of Woolf as a feminist, but she still makes for captivating reading, and is read by people who would never read most feminist writing. Despite her elitism, she brings forth the issue of women's emancipation and entrenched patriarchal opposition to it in these essays. 'The history of men's opposition to women's emancipation is more interesting perhaps than the story of that emancipation itself. An amusing book might be made of it.' She adds that men hate women but very few women have any clue about it. What makes this work remarkable is her powerful argument that women's talents have so far been largely frustrated and wasted. She contemplates many gifted women from the past and their predictable pathetic fate. Hauntingly vivid is her invention of Judith, Shakespeare's sister, as gifted as her brother. She, too, came to London with stars in her eyes but was denied any opportunity to show her talents. Humiliated and broken, she kills herself one winter's night and lies buried in some part of the city. But 'she lives in you and me, and in many other women who are not here tonight, for they are washing up the dishes and putting the children to bed', Woolf says in this essay, which was first delivered as a lecture at Cambridge.

WOLLSTONECRAFT, MARY. *A Vindication of the Rights of Woman*. In this trailblazing 1792 work, a pioneer of women's rights sets the tone of an idea whose time had yet to come. Prior to this she had penned a pamphlet 'A Vindication of the Rights of Men' (1790) in support of the French Revolution. As a champion of liberty, equality, and fraternity, she links women's subordination to the social and political structure of the society. She argues that the existing property rights, laws, and class distinctions are mechanism of control that deny women their freedom and demean their lives.

KNOWLEDGE, EDUCATION, PEDAGOGY

ALINSKY, SAUL. *Rules for Radicals: A Pragmatic Primer for Realistic Radicals* (New York: Random House, 1971). Describes theory and methods of grassroots organising, drawing upon the author's own experiences. Alinsky says, '*The Prince* was written by Machiavelli for the Haves on how to hold power. *Rules for Radicals* is written for the Have-Nots on how to take it away.'

ANDRESKI, STANISLAV. *Social Sciences as Sorcery* (Manchester: Penguin, 1974). Demonstrates with compelling illustrations that the dominant tendency in modern academia is to obscure reality, obfuscate issues, and conceal discrimination under the pretext of non-partisan scholarship. Elite social scientists—behind the smokescreen of scholasticism, oriented towards amassing recondite facts, obscure original sources, and endless bibliographies complete with jargon, euphemism, ellipsis, and ponderous prose—are writing about less and less, making even 'the simplest truth appear unfathomably obscure'. In this exposé of the mumbo-jumbo—'a torrent of meaningless verbiage and useless technicalities'—that riddles the literature of social sciences, Andreski reveals that deliberate obscurity and disguised propaganda have become the order of the day in much of academic writing. 'The bent towards sterility and deception in the study of human affairs stems from cultural, political and economic trends of our time...evasion and deception are as a rule much more profitable than telling the truth.' This book is important because the fraud and the rot that Andreski saw in the social sciences in his time have deepened with the time.

APPLE, MICHAEL W. *Education and Power* (London: Routledge, 1982). In this and his other works such as *The Politics of Official Knowledge* (1993), Apple explains issues of class, gender, power, and hegemony from a fresh Marxist perspective. Presenting a critique of cultural and economic reproduction in education, he delineates how the school process, curriculum form, the transmission of knowledge, and teaching in general are linked to the reproduction of existing structures and ideologies of the dominant social order. Also see his edited work with L. Weis, *Ideology and Practice in Education* (1983).

BOURDIEU, PIERRE AND JEAN-CLAUDE PASSERON. *Reproduction in Education, Society and Culture* (California: Sage, 1977). The most extensive theoretical work on the educational reproduction. It shows how the reproduction of a culture through education plays a crucial role in reproduction of the whole social system. Bourdieu and Passeron argue that education carries an essential arbitrary cultural scheme, which is actually, though not in appearance, based on power. Drawing on the Marxist tradition, they make the point that schooling produces certain deep-seated ways of understanding and perceiving—they call this process 'habitus'—that allow the dominant class to maintain its status without resorting to physical violence or coercion. Passed from one generation to the next, the 'habitus' keeps different social and cultural groups separate from each other, allows subordinate groups to be reproduced, and gives legitimacy to the symbols of the dominant culture. In other words, in the established education, 'symbolic violence' substitutes for physical violence. This work gives impressive empirical evidence to support its analysis, but many of its compelling arguments are based on commonsense observations.

BROOK, JAMES AND IAIN A. BOAL. *Resisting the Virtual Life: The Culture and Politics of Information* (San Francisco: City Lights, 1995). A range of critical voices on the technology-driven communications—known variously as information age, information superhighway, cyberspace, virtuality and the proliferating variants. This work exposes the rhetoric of liberation attached to the information industry, as the write-ups here connect technologies with the abstract, virtual existence, showing how they are engendering estrangement, not affection.

CARNOY, M. *Education as Cultural Imperialism* (New York: David McKay, 1974). Presents an analysis of education as a tool of domination.

DEWEY, JOHN. *Democracy and Education* (1916). Here, a champion of progressive education makes an enduring statement of the social role of schooling in a democratic society. A key feature of the book is teaching for the development of intelligence and creative thinking. Though Dewey displays a naive faith in science as a repository of both rational and moral inspiration to reconstruct society as well as the tendency to underplay power divisions within society, his pragmatic vision of uniting pedagogical theory and practice for desirable social change remains important.

DIXON, BOB. *Catching Them Young: Sex, Race and Class in Children's Fiction*, Vol. I, and *Catching Them Young: Political Ideas in Children's Fiction*, Vol. II (London: Pluto Press, 1977). The first major study of ideology as a concern of children's literature criticism. Dixon extensively examines 'the ideas, attitudes, and opinions which authors convey to children through novels and stories' and the ways in which this is done.

FERRO, MARK. *The Use and Abuse of History, Or How the Past is Taught* (London: Routledge, 1984). In advancing understanding of the past, history has to question the traditional conception of a 'universal history' which involves separating the myth from reality. Recognizing and deflating myths as well as explaining their origins and significance constitute a vital part of the function of history. Ferro has demonstrated this in his study of the way history is taught around the world.

Foucault, Michel. 1980. *Power/Knowledge* (New York: Vintage, 1980). Foucault's main ideas are presented here in an accessible language.

FREIRE, PAULO. *Pedagogy of the Oppressed* (1970). Freire sees education in the wider context, linking it with history, politics, and class as well as the concept of culture and power. His conviction that illiteracy and poverty are directly related to oppressive social structures and power relationships led him to design his educational programmes to transform these structures by empowering people to engage in social analysis, political activism, and reading the world in order to change it. Since education involves social relations and political choices, central to his theory is the idea that education is a political act. For him, the whole point of education is about the ability to read the world. As all educational policies and practices have social implications, one cannot be neutral in any educational project. Every educator has a choice, either to go along with reproduction of exclusion or injustice in society, or be a part of challenging and changing the oppressive conditions. Those seeking change have necessarily to discard the traditional school system which promotes dominant knowledge and naturalizes the oppressive relationships. Freire presented an instance from his own educational groundwork in his native Brazil. His philosophy and praxis combines social radicalism, personal humbleness and commitment with intellectual coherence consistent with an ethical outlook. In his other work, especially in *Education for Critical Consciousness*, he proposes the use of cultural capital of the oppressed to promote forms of consciousness that will lead people to social action for change.

GIROUX, HENRY. *Theory and Resistance in Education: A Pedagogy for the Opposition* (Boston: Bergin and Garvey, 1983). This work views theoretical struggle and the construction of a new language—'language of possibility'—as a crucial aspect of counter-hegemonic mobilisation within the academy. Drawing on Freireian critical literacy, Giroux says,

'What is at stake here is the goal of giving working-class students and adults the tools they need to reclaim their own lives, histories, and voices.'

GREENE, MAXINE. *Landscapes of Learning* (New York: Teachers College Press, 1978). The volume consists of essays explicating concepts such as praxis, aesthetics, justice, mythification of education and technology, all of which are animated by Greene's profound belief in the potential of each individual for which she emphasizes the need to be 'wide-awake', alive to ourselves and others, alive to our landscapes, both internal and external. 'To be in touch with our landscapes is to be conscious of our evolving experiences, to be aware of the ways in which we encounter our world.'

HABERMAS, JURGEN. *Knowledge and Human Interests* (Boston: Beacon Press, 1968). Attempts to reconcile an interpretivist view with positivist methods of science by developing a critical theory of communication.

KARABEL, J. AND A. H. HALSEY. *Power and Ideology in Education* (New York: Oxford University Press, 1977). Readings collected here represent some of the major positions in the sociology of education and provides a variety of ways to view the relationship between education and power.

KOZOL, JONATHAN. *Savage Inequalities: Children in America's School* (New York: HarperPerennial, 1991). Examining the extremes of affluence and deprivation in cities and suburbs, this work indicts the American school system for scorning the poor children. In his other book, *Amazing Grace: The Lives of Children and the Conscience of a Nation* (1995), the poor children speak movingly about how they are wounded by poverty and racial isolation. But such callousness and cruelty, Kozol found to his amazement, have not hardened their hearts—a rare grace to which the society must respond.

KUMAR, KRISHNA. *Prejudice and Pride: School Histories of the Freedom Struggle in India and Pakistan* (Delhi: Penguin,

2001). This comparative and critical study of history textbooks of India and Pakistan reveals that they keep children away from real history and instead (mis)lead them into self-serving perspectives of two master narratives. An indictment of 'official knowledge' as well as pedagogic poverty, this work tries to set the records straight on both sides, and makes a strong plea for constructing education, especially history, differently.

LILLA, MARK. *The Reckless Mind: Intellectuals in Politics* (New York: New York Review of Books, 2001). An indictment of some of the most exalted philosophers, this work serves as a reminder of the intellectual's temptation to succumb to the allure of an idea, and how passion can blind even the best of minds to its tyrannical potential.

LYND, ROBERT. *Knowledge for What? The Place of Social Science in American Culture* (Princeton: Princeton University Press, 1939). Dated but still relevant as the social and ethical issues involved in knowledge-construction and the pressure put by vested interests as trustees or donors to university research and education—brilliantly raised in this volume—have increased with the neoliberal privatization of education.

MACKIE, ROBERT, ed. *Literacy and Revolution: The Pedagogy of Paulo Freire* (New York: Continuum, 1981). An excellent volume on the work of a revolutionary educationist. Contains commentary on Freire's work, a bibliography of books and write-ups by and about Freire, interviews with him, and readings that provide a context for his work.

MACLAREN, PETER. *Life in Schools: An Introduction to Critical Pedagogy in the Foundations of Education* (New York: Longman, 1994). Combines theory and practice to critically introduce political, social and economic issues underlying classroom practices and the social world of modern schools. Stresses the need for transcending all forms of education that limit the project of human liberation, and provides insight and hope for emancipatory education.

NEEDLEMAN, JACOB. *The Heart of Philosophy* (New York: Knopf, 1982). Teaching philosophy through dialogue to high school students and their parents, Needleman impresses us with his offbeat ideas about education, society, and the need for philosophy.

NGUGI, WA THIONG'O. *Decolonizing the Mind* (London: James Currey, 1986). An impassioned book on the politics of language and culture by a brilliant African intellectual. Ngugi contends here that language is much more than a means of communication, it carries the soul of a society, and, by adopting foreign languages, Africans are committing a 'linguicide', which in effect, has killed off their memories as a people and as a culture. Setting an example, he changed his name from James Ngugi to Wa Thiong'o Ngugi, and stopped writing in English after the publication of *Decolonizing the Mind.*

NUSSBAUM, MARTHA C. *Cultivating Humanity: A Classical Defence of Reform in Liberal Education* (Cambridge, MA: Harvard University Press, 1997). Making a plea for an inclusive humanity, Nussbaum suggests that education should make a practical difference in our life. She regrets that few professional intellectuals use their intellect and theories to improve the human condition by fighting for equality, justice and freedom. Decrying exclusions of many people and their lives from the domain of knowledge, she pleads for an academy 'in which the world will be seen to have many different types of citizen and in which we can all learn to function as citizens of that entire world'.

PACKARD, VANCE. *The Hidden Persuaders* (1957). Reveals for the first time how everyone's mind, feelings, and thinking are constantly bombarded by technologized mass communication and advertising. Exposing the psychological tricks advertisers use to sell anything from soap to idea, Packard argues that we have become victims of such communication, rather than communication being a means by which we find ourselves in our relation with fellow beings in a community of mutual criticism and helpfulness.

PERSELL, CAROLINE HODGES. *Education and Inequality: A Theoretical and Empirical Synthesis* (New York: Free Press, 1977). Probing the relationship of education to social stratification, Persell shows that a structure of dominance and supportive ideology influence educational structures, the expectations and behaviour of teachers, and ultimately both cognitive and uncognitive outcomes of schooling.

SHOR, IRA AND PAULO FREIRE. *A Pedagogy for Liberation: Dialogues on Transforming Education* (New York: Bergin and Garvey, 1987). In this engaging and lively exchange, two renowned educationists discuss the problems of education system in relation to those of the larger society. Arguing for the need to transform the classroom, they show the effectiveness of dialogue in action as a practical means by which teachers and students can become active participants in the learning process. Also see Shor's *Critical Teaching and Everyday Life* (1987).

SLAUGHTER, SHEILA AND GARY RHOADES. *Academic Capitalism and the New Economy: Markets, State, and Higher Education* (Johns Hopkins University Press, 2009). Analyzes the new corporate regime in higher education and research, and how they have been tamed and turned into an instrument of power and control both within the US and across the world. Shows that with gradual decline of state support, personal cost of education has risen sharply, and inequalities—of race, region, and class—are widening.

WALKER, STEPHEN AND LEN BARTON, eds. *Gender, Class, and Education* (London: Falmer Press, 1983). This collection of essays offers an in-depth study of the intersection of gender and class in schooling and cultural locations.

WILLIS, PAUL. *Learning to Labour: How Working Class Kids Get Working Class Jobs* (New York: Columbia University

Press, 1977). This is an ethnographic study set in England. 'The difficult thing to explain about how working-class kids get working-class jobs is why they let themselves.' The way Willis puts this question suggests that the working-class children have some choice in determining their fate. His analysis rejects Bourdieu's theory of cultural reproduction, and he seems to indulge in a bit of system-justification argument, but such works must be debated and discussed by the people who see a revolutionary role of education.

SELF-STRUGGLE AND INNER TRANSFORMATION

ANGELOU, MAYA. *And Still I Rise* (1978). 'All my work is meant to say, "you may encounter defeats but you must not be defeated".' This irrepressible spirit pervades this verse anthology as well as Angelou's several autobiographical works, of which *I Know Why the Caged Bird Sings* (1969) is most renowned.

AUGUSTINE. *Confessions*. This fifth century classic by a restless, self-made Christian (who said, 'a Christian is made, not born') blazed the trail of a new literary genre that came to be known as autobiography. Augustine still sounds contemporary in this honest, brooding, introspective blend of philosophy and journal writing.

BUBER, MARTIN. *I and Thou* (1923). In this classic on communication, Buber contrasts the two ways in which we approach existence—the I-Thou relationship, and the I-It. The difference between the two is not the nature of the object to which one relates. Not every relation between persons is the I-Thou one, nor is every relation with nature or animal an I-It. The difference lies in the nature of relationship. I-Thou is a relationship of mutuality and openness—it may be between human and human, or between a human and a dog or a work of art—and through all of these with God, the 'eternal Thou'. In contrast, I-It is the subject-object relationship in which other people or things are an instrument that is known and used without consideration of their subjectivity. Thus dialogue depends on mutuality which implies 'experiencing the other side' of the relationship. Buber stresses that 'all real living is meeting'. Here, he introduces these ideas (in dense and difficult prose) that most of his later works develop in a more accessible language. It may be a good idea, therefore, to read his *Between Man and Man* and *Pointing the Way*, alongside this work.

CARTER, STEPHEN L. *Integrity* (New York: HarperCollins, 1996). When everyone accepts integrity as a virtue, why is it diminishing in our personal and public life? Why do people care more about winning than about playing by the rules? This book makes us grasp the difficulties involved in trying to teach or legislate integrity. Without the assumption of personal integrity, humanity will be trapped in a cultural and political morass.

DE SAINT-EXUPERY, ANTOINE. *The Little Prince*. The enduring popularity among children as well as adults of this 1943 French classic reflects a profound human desire for intimate relationships. The meaning behind the deceptively simple story is that we can know and enjoy only that which we can make our own through love and a shared experience of understanding and appreciation. As the fox in the story says to the Little Prince, 'It is only with the heart that one can see rightly; what is essential is invisible to the eye.'

DUBOS, RENE. *So Human an Animal* (New York: Charles Scribner's Sons, 1968). A biologist well versed in philosophy and literature shows that science is indispensable but not omnicompetent. Sounds a warning—losing our humaneness to the mechanized surroundings as we live in a confusion of concrete and steel, trapped 'in the midst of noise, dirt, ugliness, and absurdity'—and offers an insight into how the trend towards dehumanization can be reversed.

FRANKL, VIKTOR E. *Man's Search for Meaning: An Introduction to Logotherapy* (New York: Pocket Books, [1946] 1963). This harrowing account of the author's life in a concentration camp is especially remarkable for conversion of those experiences into a form of philosophic therapy. 'When we are no longer able to change a situation, we are challenged to change ourselves.'

FRANK, ANNE. *The Diary of a Young Girl.* A personal document of World War II, this unusual classic of war literature has moved millions, showing the human face to the barbarity of Holocaust. What did this young Jewish girl do to arouse Hitler's wrath? Written in the secret den where Anne hid with her family for more than two years before her life was snuffed out, the diary captures the budding personality of a bright and complex teenager who is curious about life, religion, and sex; caustic about her parents; and above all, ill at ease with herself for her perceived flaws and contradictory nature. Her acute awareness of her vanity and quickness to fight makes her realize the value of dignity, generosity, and a sense of purpose. A year before her death in the Bergen-Belsen camp, she writes, 'I want to be useful or give pleasure to people around me who yet don't really know me. I want to go on living even after my death!'The diary represents the human spirit in the face of terrible odds, but it is also a literary triumph that symbolizes the power of the book. Making this point, Roger Rosenblatt says, 'In a way, the Holocaust began with one book [*Mein Kampf*] and ended with another. Yet it was Anne's that finally prevailed—a beneficent and complicated work outlasting a simple and evil one.'

FROMM, ERICH. *The Art of Loving* (1956). A pithy and poignant classic, not a self-help book—don't get misled by its title. Its chapter on the disintegration of love is a superb humanistic analysis of modern society. Set against the consumerism that leads to a commodification of love, Fromm diagnoses the pathology, the 'wrong' loves that confound individuals and make it hard for them to achieve a true loving experience. 'Love is possible only if two persons communicate with each other from the centre of their existence. . . . Love, experienced thus, is a constant challenge; it is not a resting place, but a moving, growing, working together.'

GOFFMAN, ERVING. *The Presentation of Self in Everyday Life* (New York: Anchor Doubleday, 1959). This everyday sociology tells us that we come into the world as individuals, acquire character, and become persons wearing masks, many masks. The word person, in its first meaning, is a mask. Everyone, everywhere, more or less purposefully plays a role. All of us, Goffman says, try to put forward a certain impression of self in order to get something from others! Our behaviour may not be so cynical, but he seems right that we try to manage the impression that others have of us.

HALDER, BABY. *A Life Less Ordinary*, tr. Urvashi Butalia (Delhi: Zubaan & Penguin, 2006). Heart-wrenching story of a Bengali domestic help who survives poverty, hardship, and violence to write this stunning autobiography of courage, integrity, and grace.

HANH, THICH NHAT. *Living Buddha, Living Christ* (New York: Riverhead, 1995). If Buddha and Jesus were to meet today, what would each think of the other's precept and practice? In this illuminating book, a Buddhist sage brings together the two great meditative and compassionate traditions, showing the connection between personal evolution, inner peace, and peace on earth.

HARDOT, PIERRE. *The Inner Citadel: The Meditations of Marcus Aurelius*, tr. Michael Chase (Cambridge MA: Harvard University Press, 1998.) A profound mediation on Marcus' meditation. The interested can also read Hardot's *Philosophy as a Way of Life* (1995), which combines scholarly brilliance with spiritual depth and a superb philosophical taste.

HOCHSCHILD, ARLIE RUSSELL. *The Managed Heart: The Commercialization of Human Feeling* (Berkeley: University of California Press, [1983] 2003). Emotion is one of the unique qualities that make us human. In our private and social life, all of us try to manage our feelings to the best of our abilities. But what happens when emotion becomes a commodity; when feelings are bought and sold in the market for 'emotional labour'; when private capacities for empathy and warmth are put to corporate uses? Using primarily the experiences of air attendants, sociologist Hochschild raises these disturbing questions, and points to the danger of control and commercialization of feelings in service interactions, especially in an atmosphere of sexism, socio-economic inequalities, and the rationalization of the workplace in the corporate pursuits of profit-maximization. The interested can also see Hochschild's related work *The Outsourced Self: Intimate Life in Market Times* (2012).

HOWE, REUEL L. *The Miracle of Dialogue* (Winston Press, 1975). Howe says that dialogue is at the heart of human life. 'Every man is a potential adversary, even those whom we love. Only through dialogue are we saved from this enmity toward one another. Dialogue is to love, what blood is to the body. When the flow of blood stops, the body dies. When dialogue stops, love dies and resentment and hate are born. But dialogue can restore a dead relationship ... [though it] is not easy and comfortable to achieve, a fact which may explain why it occurs so rarely.'

KELLER, HELEN. *The Story of My Life* (1903). The relationship of the deaf-dumb-blind Keller and her teacher, Anne Sullivan, makes this slim book an epic of hope and inspiration. How riveting is the description of the transformation that came over the young Keller when she discovered (with the help of her teacher) that words were related to things! This made her grasp that language had the power to liberate people like her. Her schooling and then college education: 'I fall, I stand still . . . I trudge on, I gain a little . . . I get more eager and climb higher and begin to see the widening horizon. Every struggle is a victory.' Thus was born a visionary who personified her noble words, 'Although the world is full of suffering, it is also full of the overcoming of it.' As a grateful disabled admirer put it, Keller was our first star as she 'altered people's perception of the disabled and remapped the boundaries of sight and sense'. But there were other dimensions to her life and struggle. She was a fierce advocate of justice, a fighter for racial and gender equality: 'My work for the blind has never occupied a centre in my personality. My sympathies are with all who struggle for justice.' Those who know her only as the Miracle Worker, will be surprised to know that in her eyes Lenin, Edison, and Chaplin were the most important people of the twentieth century.

MacIntyre, Alasdair. *After Virtue* (Indiana: University of Notre Dame Press, 1981). An exposition that virtues are necessary for society and human development, and excellence and community flourish together.

Merton, Thomas. *New Seeds of Contemplation* (New York: New Directions, 1961). A classic on the contemplative life, interspersed with insights from literature, philosophy, psychology, and Catholic theology.

Pearson, Carol S. *The Hero Within: Six Archetypes We Live By* (New York: Harper and Row, 1989). Combines literature, anthropology and psychology to define six heroic archetypes—Innocent, Orphan, Wanderer, Warrior, Martyr, Magician—to subsume a rich complex patterns of human relationships. Insightful and self-revelatory, these archetypes say a lot about us and our life-journeys.

Peck, M. Scott. *The Road Less Travelled: A New Psychology of Love, Traditional Values and Spiritual Growth* (New York: Touchstone, [1978] 2003). A rewarding book for those who seek self-transformation. Peck's take on discipline, love, and grace are not simple though. He suggests salvation in love, which he defines as 'the will to extend one's self for the purpose of nurturing one' own or another's spiritual growth'.

Raymo, Chet. *Sceptics and True Believers: The Exhilarating Connection Between Science and Religion* (New York:

Walker, 1998). In this book, a scientist with a soul sets out to heal the gratuitous rifts between science and spirituality, knowledge and morality—and succeeds in this difficult task with his brilliance, insight and refreshing humility. Raymo recognizes the beauty of mystery, aesthetics and imagination, but warns against the attractions of religious dogmatism and romantic assault on science by the likes of Bryan Appleyard and Vaclav Havel. A rewarding read for anyone drawn to reflect on life's meaning and purpose.

ROGERS, CARL R. *On Becoming a Person* (1961). A classic on the human potential for growth and creativity. Rogers' recipe for release of personal potential shifts the areas of power and control. Contesting the hierarchical concepts on which society operates, he makes the point that influence is gained as power is shared, and control is more constructive when it is self-control. The process of a good and productive life involves the stretching and growing more and more of one's potentialities. 'It involves the courage to be. It means launching oneself fully into the stream of life.'

RUSSELL, BERTRAND. *The Conquest of Happiness* (London: Routledge, [1930] 2006). Conveys a simple truth, inspired by common sense and confirmed by Russell's own experience and observation that happiness comes with an active outward engagement with life, work and relationships and is lost by self-obsession, anxieties and passivity. As the world has become even more self-obsessed than in the days of Russell's, this work retains its verve and weight.

SAUL, JOHN RALSTON. *On Equilibrium: The Six Qualities of the New Humanism* ([2001] 2004). Lucid and brilliantly argued, this work shows that the consciousness of our humaneness—through judicious application of common sense, ethics, imagination, intuition, memory, and reason—can be enhanced and employed to achieve personal growth as well as to foster an ethical and just society.

SCHUMACHER, E. F. *A Guide for the Perplexed* (1977). Its title notwithstanding, it is concerned not just with the perplexed but with all society, aiming at the full actualization of human potential. Philosophical and practical at once, it presents a compelling defence of the civilizational values of Buddhist-Christian humanism against the scientific pretensions of recent centuries.

SENNET, RICHARD and JONATHAN COBB. *Corrosion of Character: The Hidden Injuries of Class* (New York: Random House, 1973). Following Veblen, Sennet and Cobb argue in this classic work that the rich indulge in conspicuous consumption to show off their wealth; the working-class people, even when able to afford basic necessities of life, are unable to show their social worth to others because they have no wealth to display. Though estranged from the work they do, working-class parents work extra hours and sacrifice in several other ways for their children's education and future so that the next generation will not have a life like theirs. Their lives are not a 'model' but a 'warning' to their children. If the children do not succeed in fulfilling the parents' wishes, they are a failure in their parents' and their own eyes; if they do succeed and rise above their family's status, the parents may become an embarrassment to their children. The everyday experience of class thus goes well beyond economic stability or instability. People are caught in a vicious circle of resentment, hostility and shame. Presenting a powerful sociological critique of everyday life, the authors show that hierarchies of class keep everyone in a game of one-upmanship in which no one is the ultimate victor; true humanism can be achieved only by egalitarianism and rediscovering diverse concepts of human dignity.

SHAKESPEARE, WILLIAM. *Hamlet* (1603). This classic Shakespearean play brings out the truth that breaking of a moral law inevitably leads to all-round disaster. A play of intrigue, ambiguity and suspended action, it is thematically rich and varied: the pervasiveness of betrayal (wife of husband, brother of brother, parent of child, friend of friend); the opposing demands made on Hamlet that he avenge his father's murder and that he adhere to the Christian ethic against killing; the nature of kingship and the need to rule oneself before ruling others, besides several others. Hamlet's fabled indecisiveness and tragedy are related to difficult choices—of belief, of action, of love, of justice, of conscience—that he is presented with throughout the play.

SLATER, PHILLIP. *The Pursuit of Loneliness* (Boston: Beacon Press, 1970). An acute assessment of the relationship between self-chosen reliance on technology and quality of life. Disturbing but moving, this forty-year old book is still a pleasure to read and reflect upon.

STEINEM, GLORIA. *Revolution from Within: A Book of Self-Esteem* (Boston: Little, Brown, 1992). This memoir of a feminist icon makes the point, powerfully and tenderly, citing personal examples, that overcoming a lack of self-esteem and respecting the self are vital for empowering the powerless—be they women, men, children, or even nations.

WALKER, ALICE. *Anything We Love Can Be Saved: A Writer's Activism* (1997). The author of *The Colour Purple* and *In Search of Our Mothers' Gardens* writes intimately about her life as an activist, and her fundamental belief that the world is savable, only if we act and love. Hers was an activism rooted in the love of nature and a delight in human beings. In this spiritual autobiography, Walker explores many important public and private issues: family and identity, feminism and friends, religion and the spirit, writing and language, politics and change.

WEST, CORNEL. *Keeping Faith* (1993). Eclectic and personal, this collection of essays by a leading Afro-American intellectual critiques the traditions of Western philosophy and modernity, exposing the structures of power and oppression as they operate within American society. Opens a debate about a new way of thinking about human dignity and difference.

Bibliography

Acemoglu, Daron and James Robinson. 2012. *Why Nations Fail: The Origins of Power, Prosperity and Poverty*. London: Profile Books.

Alam, Javeed. 2012. *Who Wants Democracy?* Delhi: Orient Black Swan.

Ali, Daud, ed. 2002. *Invoking the Past: The Uses of History in South Asia*. Delhi: Oxford University Press.

Aloysius, G. 1997. *Nationalism without a Nation in India*. Delhi: Oxford University Press.

———. 1998. *Religion as Emancipatory Identity: A Buddhist Movement among the Tamils under Colonialism*. Delhi: New Age International.

———. 2000. 'Caste in and above History', in S.L. Sharma and T.K. Oommen, eds., *Nation and National Identity in South Asia*, pp. 151–73. Delhi: Orient Longman.

———. 2010. *The Brahminical Inscribed in Body-politic*. Delhi: Critical Quest.

Althusser, Louis. 1971. 'Ideology and Ideological State Apparatuses', in idem, *Lenin and Philosophy and Other Essays*, pp. 121–73. London: New Left Books.

Ambedkar, B.R. 1987–2003. *Dr Babasaheb Ambedkar: Writings and Speeches* (*BAWS*), vols. 1-17, ed. Vasant Moon et al. Bombay: The Education Department, Govt. of Maharashtra. *Annihilation of Caste* (1936), vol. 1; *The Revolution and Counter-Revolution in Ancient India*, unfinished work (1956), vol. 3; *Who were the Shudras?* (1946) and *The Untouchables* (1948), vol. 7; *What Congress and Gandhi Have Done to the Untouchables* (1945), vol. 9; *The Buddha and His Dhamma* (1957), vol. 11.

Ambedkar, B.R. 2002. *The Essential Writings of B.R. Ambedkar*, ed. Valerian Rodrigues. Delhi: Oxford University Press.

Anderson, Benedict. 1983. *Imagined Communities*. London: Verso.

Anderson, Margaret L. 2003. *Thinking About Women: Sociological Perspectives on Sex and Gender*, 6th edn. New York: Pearson.

Anderson, Perry. 2012a. *The Indian Ideology*. Gurgaon: Three Essays Collective.

———. 2012b. 'Respect Gandhi If You Will, Don't Sentimentalize Him', *Outlook*, see www.outlookindia.com/article.aspx?282832

Anderson, Walter Truett, ed. 1996. *The Fontana Postmodernism Reader*. London: Harper Collins.

Angar Ee, HaBir. 1994. *Pali is the Mother of Sanskrit*. Nagpur: Tarachand Chavhan.

Aristotle. [350 BCE] 1992. *The Politics*, ed. Trevor J. Saunders, tr. T.A. Sinclair. London: Penguin.

———. 1984. *The Complete Works of Aristotle*, ed. Jonathan Barnes. Princeton: Princeton University Press.

Atwood, Margaret. 1992. 'The Female Body', in idem, *Good Bones*. Toronto: Couch House Press.

Bacon, Francis. 1974. *The Advancement of Learning* [1605] *and New Atlantis* [1626], ed. Arthur Johnston. Oxford: Oxford University Press.

———. [1623] 2012. *Novum Organum*. Charleston SC: Forgotten Books.

Bacon, Roger. [1267] 1928. *The Opus Majus of Roger Bacon*, ed. Robert Belle Burke. Kessinger Publishing.

Bagehot, Walter. [1872] 2007. *Physics and Politics*. New York: Cosimo.

Bailkey, Nels M., ed. 1987. *Readings in Ancient History*. Massachusetts: D.C. Heath and Co.

Ball, Terence and Richard Dagger. 2004. *Political Ideologies and the Democratic Ideal*, 5th edn. New York: Pearson Longman.

Balzac, Honore de. [1835] 1951. *Old Goriot*, tr. Marion Ayton Crawford. London: Penguin.

Bapat, P.V., ed. [1956] 1997. *2500 Years of Buddhism*. Delhi: Publications Division, Govt. of India.

Barber, Benjamin. 1992. *An Aristocracy of Everyone: The Politics of Education and the Future of America*. New York: Oxford University Press.

Barber, Benjamin. 1993. 'America Skips School', *Harper's Magazine*, November issue.

Barnes, Jonathan. 2006. *Aristotle: A Very Short Introduction*. Delhi: Oxford University Press.

Barnes, Julian. [1989] 2009. *A History of the World in $10^{1/2}$ Chapters*. London: Vintage.

Basham, A.L., ed. 1985. *A Cultural History of India*. Delhi: Oxford University Press.

Bassham, Gregory, et al., eds. 2002. *Critical Thinking*, 2nd edn. Boston: McGraw Hill.

Bauman, Chad M. 2008. *Christian Identity and Dalit Religion in Hindu India, 1868–1947*. Cambridge: Eerdmans Publishing Co.

Baxi, Upendra. 2000. 'Emancipation as Justice: Legacy and Vision of Dr. Ambedkar', in K.C. Yadav, ed., *From Periphery to Centre Stage: Ambedkar, Ambedkarism and Dalit Future*, pp. 49–74. Delhi: Manohar.

———. 2012. *The Future of Human Rights*. Delhi: Oxford University Press.

Bayly, Susan. 2000. *Caste, Society and Politics in India: From the Eighteenth Century to the Modern Age*. Cambridge: Cambridge University Press.

Bazaz, Premnath. 2002. 'The Role of the Bhagavad Gita in Indian History', *The Radical Humanist*, August issue.

Benedict, Ruth. 1962. *Race: Science and Politics*. Revised edn. Viking Press.

Benjamin, Walter. 1969. *Illuminations*, ed. Hannah Arendt. New York: Harcourt Brace.

———. 1996. *Selected Writings 1913–26*, vol. I. Cambridge, MA: Belknap Press.

Berger, John. 1981. *Ways of Seeing*. London: BBC/Penguin.

Berger, Peter and Thomas Luckmann. 1966. *The Social Construction of Reality: A Treatise in the Sociology of Knowledge*. New York: Doubleday.

Berlin, Isaiah. 2003. *The Crooked Timber of Humanity: Chapters in the History of Ideas*. London: Pimlico.

Bernstein, Carl. 1992. 'The Idiot Culture', *The New Republic*, 8 June.

Berreman, Gerald D. 1991. 'The Brahmanical View of Caste', in Dipankar Gupta, ed., *Social Stratification*, pp. 84–92. Delhi: Oxford University Press.

Beteille, Andre. 1997. 'Caste in Contemporary India', in C.J. Fuller, ed., *Caste Today*, pp. 150–79. Delhi: Oxford University Press.

Bhaskar, Roy. 2002. *From Science to Emancipation: Alienation and the Actuality of Enlightenment*. Delhi: Sage.

Bible, King James Version. [1611] n.d. Colorado: International Bible Society.

Biswas, Oneil. 2001. *Dalits after Partition*. Delhi: Blumoon Books.

Biswas, Swapan K. 1998. *Gods, False Gods and the Untouchables*. Delhi: Orion.

Bloch, Marc. 1953. *The Historian's Craft*, tr. Peter Putnam. New York: Vintage Books.

Bodley, John H. 1999. *Victims of Progress*, 4th edn. California: Mayfield Publishing.

Bohm, David. 2004. *On Dialogue*. London and New York: Routledge.

Bougle, C. 1991. 'The Essence and Reality of the Caste System', in Dipankar Gupta, ed., *Social Stratification*, pp. 64–73. Delhi: Oxford University Press.

Bourdieu, Pierre and Jean-Claude Passeron. 1977. *Reproduction in Education, Society and Culture*, tr. Richard Nice. California: Sage.

Bourdieu, Pierre. 1988. *Homo Academicus*, tr. Peter Collier. Cambridge: Polity.

———. 1991. *Language and Symbolic Power*, ed. John B. Thompson. Cambridge: Polity.

———. 1998. *On Television and Journalism*. London: Pluto Press.

Brecht, Bertolt. [1935] 1959. 'Questions from a Worker Who Reads' as 'A Worker Reads History' in *Selected Poems*, tr. H.R. Hays. New York: Grove Press.

———. [1944] 1996. *The Caucasian Chalk Circle*, ed. Ray Speakman. London: Heinemann.

Bronowski, Jacob and Bruce Mazlish. 1963. *The Western Intellectual Tradition*. Harmondsworth: Penguin.

Bronowski, Jacob. 1973. *The Ascent of Man*. Boston: Little Brown.

Brown, Donald E. 1988. *Hierarchy, History and Human Nature: The Social Origins of Historical Consciousness*. Tucson: University of Arizona Press.

Buber, Martin. [1923] 2000. *I and Thou*, tr. Ronald Gregor Smith. New York: Simon & Schuster.

Cahn, Steven M. 1970. *The Philosophical Foundations of Education*. New York: Harper & Row.

Calhoun, Craig. 1997. *Nationalism*. Minneapolis: University of Minnesota Press.

Caputo, John D. 2001. *On Religion*. London and New York: Routledge.

Carrithers, Michael. 1992. *Why Humans Have Cultures*. Oxford: Oxford University Press.

Carroll, Harry, et al., eds. 1969. *The Development of Civilisation: A Documentary History of Politics, Society, and Thought*, vols. I & II. Illinois: Scott, Foresman & Co.

Cassirer, Ernst. 1954. *The Question of Jean-Jacques Rousseau*. New York: Columbia University Press.

Cesaire, Aime. [1955] 2000. *Discourse on Colonialism*, tr. Joan Pinkham. New York: Monthly Review Press.

Chakravarti, Uma. [1987] 1996. *The Social Dimensions of Early Buddhism*. Delhi: Munshiram Manoharlal.

———. 1998. *Rewriting History: The Life and Times of Pandita Ramabai*. Delhi: Kali for Women.

Chalam, K.S. 2007. *Caste-based Reservations and Human Development of India*. Delhi: Sage.

Chatterjee, Debi. 2010. *Ideas and Movements Against Caste in India*. Delhi: Abhijeet Publications.

Chhibber, Pradeep and Rahul Verma. 2013a. 'A Platform of, by and for the Connected', *The Indian Express*, Delhi, 14 January.

Chhibber, Pradeep and Rahul Verma. 2013b. 'No Denying the Family', *The Indian Express*, Delhi, 24 January.

Chibber, Vivek. 2006. *Locked in Place: State-building and Late Industrialization in India*. Princeton University Press, 2006.

Chisti, Seema. 2009. 'The Chosen Ones', *The Indian Express*, Delhi, 28 September.

Chomsky, Noam. 1996. *Powers and Prospects*. Delhi: Madhyam Books.

———. 2004. *Language and Politics*, ed. Carlos Otero. Oakland, CA: A.K. Press.

Churchill, Winston. 1943. Speech at Harvard University, 6 September.

Clement, Catherine. 1983. *The Lives and Legends of Jacques Lacan*. New York: Columbia University Press.

Conrad, Joseph. 1988. *Heart of Darkness*, ed. Robert Kimbrough. New York: Norton.

Coomaraswamy, Ananda K. [1909] 1981. *Essays in National Idealism*. Delhi: Munshiram Manoharlal.

———. 1943. *Hinduism and Buddhism*. New York: Philosophical Library.

Corry, Stephen. 1976. *Towards Indian Self-Determination in Columbia*. Survival Document no. 2.

Crichton, Michael. 2006. 'Why Politicised Science Is Dangerous', in idem, *State of Fear*. Delhi: Harper Collins.

Dangle, Arjun, ed. 1992. *Poisoned Bread: Modern Marathi Dalit Literature*. Bombay: Orient Longman.

Darwin, Charles. 1962. *The Voyage of the Beagle*. New York: Doubleday Anchor Books.

———. [1859] 2003. *The Origin of Species*. New York: Signet Classics.

Davies, Robertson. 1977. 'The Conscience of the Writer', in idem, *One Half of Robertson Davies*. London: Macmillan.

Dawkins, Richard. [1976] 2006. *The Selfish Gene*. Oxford: Oxford University Press.

De Beauvoir, Simone. [1949] 1953. *The Second Sex*, tr. H.M. Parshley. London: Jonathan Cape.

Delany, Sheila, ed. 1971. *Counter-Tradition: The Literature of Dissent and Alternatives*. New York: Basic Books.

Deleury, Guy. 2005. *India: The Rebel Continent*, tr. Florence D'Souza. Delhi: Macmillan.

Denby, David. 1996. *Great Books*. New York: Simon & Schuster.

Derrida, Jacques. 2004. *Specters of Marx*, tr. Peggy Kamuf. London: Routledge.

Desai, Meghnad. 2010. 'The Raging Battle', *The Sunday Express*, 23 May.

Descartes, Rene. 1968. *Discourse on Method* [1637] *and the Meditations* [1641], tr. F.E. Sutcliffe. London: Penguin.

Deshpande, Ashwini. 2011. *The Grammar of Caste: Economic Discrimination in Contemporary India*. Delhi: Oxford University Press.

Deshpande, Satish. 2004. *Contemporary India: A Sociological View*. Delhi: Penguin.

Dharampal. 1983. *The Beautiful Tree: Indigenous Indian Education in the Eighteenth Century*. Delhi: Biblia Impex.

Dharma Theertha. [1941] 1992. *History of Hindu Imperialism*. Madras: Dalit Educational Literature Centre.

Dickens, Charles. 1998. *Great Expectations*. London: Wordsworth classics.

Dickens, Peter. 2002. *Social Darwinism*. Delhi: Viva Books.

Dirks, Nicholas. 2002. *Castes of Mind: Colonialism and the Making of Modern India*. Delhi: Permanent Black.

Doniger, Wendy and Brian Smith, eds. 1991. *The Laws of Manu*. Delhi: Penguin.

Dostoevsky, Fyodor. [1880] 1982. *The Brothers Karamazov*, tr. David Magarshack. London: Penguin.

Dreze, Jean and Amartya Sen. 2011. 'Putting Growth In Its Place,' *Outlook*, 14 November.

Dumont, Louis. [1970] 1998. *Homo Hierarchicus: The Caste System and Its Implications*, revised English edn. Delhi: Oxford University Press.

Durkheim, Emile. [1912] 2001. *The Elementary Forms of Religious Life*, tr. Carol Cosman. Oxford: Oxford University Press.

Dwivedi, Hazari Prasad. [1940] 1999. *Kabir*, in Hindi. Delhi: Rajkamal.

Easwaran, Eknath, tr. 1986. *The Dhammapada*. London: Routledge & Kegan Paul.

Einstein, Albert. 1981. *Albert Einstein the Human Side*, eds., Helen Dukas and Banesh Hoffman. New Jersey: Princeton University Press.

Emerson, Ralph Waldo. 1912. 'Fable', in *Yale Book of American Verse*, ed. Thomas R. Lounsbury. New Haven: Yale University Press.

Engels, Friedrich. 1978. 'The Origin of Family, Private Property, and State' [1884]; and 'Speech at the Graveside of Karl Marx' [1883], in *The Marx-Engels Reader*, ed. Robert C. Tucker. New York: Norton.

Enzensberger, Hans. 'Karl Heinrich Marx.' See www.tumblr.com/karl_heinrich_marx

Euripides. [Fifth century BCE] 1954. *The Bacchae and Other Plays*. Harmondsworth: Penguin.

Fallows, James. 1996. *Breaking the News: How the Media Undermine American Democracy*. New York: Pantheon Press.

Fanon, Frantz. [1963] 2005. *The Wretched of the Earth*, tr. Richard Philcox. New York: Grove Press.

———. [1952] 2008. *Black Skin, White Masks*, tr. Richard Philcox. New York: Grove Press.

Fernandez-Armesto, Felipe. 1995. *Millennium: A History of the Last Thousand Years*. New York: Scribner.

Fiori, G. 1970. *Antonio Gramsci: Life of a Revolutionary*. London: New Left Books.

Foucault, Michel. 1980. *Power/Knowledge: Selected Interviews and Other Writings 1972–77*, ed. Colin Gordon. New York: Vintage.

———. [1976] 1990. *The History of Sexuality*, vol. I, tr. R. Hurley. London: Penguin.

———. 1991. *The Foucault Reader*, ed. Paul Rabinow. London: Penguin.

Freire, Paulo. [1970] 1996. *Pedagogy of the Oppressed*, tr. Myra Bergman Ramos. London: Penguin.

———. 2004. *Pedagogy of Hope*. London: Continuum.

———. 2005. *Education For Critical Consciousness*. London: Continuum.

French, Patrick. 1998. *Liberty Or Death: India's Journey to Independence and Division*. London: Flamingo.

———. 2010. *India: A Portrait*. Delhi: Penguin.

Freud, Sigmund. [1930] 2002. *Civilisation and Its Discontents*, tr. David McLintock. London: Penguin.

Friedman, Thomas. 2005. *The World is Flat: A Brief History of the Twenty-First Century*. New York: Farrar, Straus and Giroux.

Frye, Marilyn. 1983. *The Politics of Reality: Essays in Feminist Theory*. New York: Crossing Press.

Frykenberg, Robert Eric. 2001. 'The Emergence of Modern Hinduism', in G.-D. Sontheimer and Hermann Kulke, eds., *Hinduism Reconsidered*, pp. 82–107. Delhi: Manohar.

Fukuyama, Francis. 1992. *The End of History and the Last Man*. New York: Free Press.

Funkenstein, Amos. 1992. 'History, Counter-history and Narrative', in S. Friedlander, ed., *Probing the Limits of Representation: Nazism and the 'Final Solution'*. Cambridge, MA: Harvard University Press.

Galbraith, J.K. 1999. 'How to Get the Poor Off Our Conscience', in G.L. Hatch, ed., *Arguing in Communities*, 2nd edn., pp. 376–80. California: Mayfield Publishing.

Galeano, Eduardo. 2010. *The Memory of Fire: Genesis*, rpt. London: Basic Books.

Gandhi, M.K. 1925. *Young India*, 17 September.

———. 1935. 'If I Had Power to Legislate.' *Harijan*, 5 May.

———. 1967. 'My Jail Experiences XI.' *Young India*, 11 September 1924, in *The Collected Works of Mahatma Gandhi*, vol. XXV. Delhi: The Publication Division, Govt. of India.

———. 1970. *My Theory of Trusteeship*. Bombay: Bharatiya Vidya Bhavan.

———. 1993. *The Penguin Gandhi Reader*, ed. Rudrangshu Mukherjee, includes *Hind Swaraj* (1909) and *Varna Vyavastha* (1934). Delhi: Penguin.

Geetha, V. and S.V. Rajadurai. 1998. *Towards a Non-Brahmin Millennium: From Iyothee Thass to Periyar*. Calcutta: Samya.

Gellner, Ernest. 1983. *Nations and Nationalism*. Oxford: Basil Blackwell.

Ghurye, G S. 2000. *Caste and Race in India*, 5th edn. Bombay: Popular Prakashan.

Gill, Rosalind. 2009. 'Supersexualize Me!: Advertising and the Midriffs', in Feona Attwood, ed., *Mainstreaming Sex: The Sexualization of Western Culture*, pp. 93–109. London: I.B. Tauris.

Glendinning, Simon. 2011. *Derrida*. London: Oxford University Press.

Goldman, Emma. 1996. 'The Social Importance of the Modern School' [1917], in *Red Emma Speaks: Selected Writings and Speeches*, ed. Alix Kates Shulman, 3rd edn. New York: Humanity Books.

Gopalakrishnan, Amulya. 2011. 'Schooled in Elitism', *The Indian Express*, Delhi, 19 September.

Gramsci, Antonio. [1971] 1996. *Selections from the Prison Notebooks*, tr. Quintin Hoare and Geoffrey N. Smith. Chennai: Orient Longman.

———. 1975. *Letters from Prison*, tr. Lynne Lawner. London: Jonathan Cape.

Gray, John. 1998. *False Dawn: The Delusions of Global Capitalism*. New York: The New Press.

Greene, Robert. 2004. *The 48 Laws of Power*. Delhi: Viva Books.

Greer, Germaine. 1970. *The Female Eunuch*. London: MacGibbon & Kee.

Guha, Ranajit. [1983] 1999. *Elementary Aspects of Peasant Insurgency in Colonial India*. Delhi: Oxford University Press.

———. 1997. *Dominance without Hegemony: History and Power in Colonial India*. Cambridge: Cambridge University Press.

Guignon, Charles. 2004. *On Being Authentic*. London and New York: Routledge.

Gupta, Shekhar. 2011. 'The Caste of Corruption', *The Indian Express*, Delhi, 24 December.

Gupte, Amol. 2009. 'No Favours to Anybody', *The Week*, 18 January.

Guru, Gopal. 2010. 'How Egalitarian are the Social Sciences in India?' in Achin Vanaik and Rajeev Bhargava, eds., *Understanding Contemporary India: Critical Perspectives*. Delhi: Orient Black Swan.

Gyan Prakash. 2010. 'We Pine to Shine', *The Times of India*, The Crest Edition, First Anniversary Special, 9 October.

Habermas, Jurgen. 1968. *Knowledge and Human Interests*. Boston: Beacon Press.

Hakim, Catherine. 2011. *Honey Money: The Power of Erotic Capital*. London: Allen Lane.

Hall, Stuart and Paul de Gay. 2008. Quoted in Chad M. Bauman, *Christian Identity and Dalit Religion in Hindu India, 1868–1947*. Cambridge: Wm. B. Eerdmans Publishing Co., 2008.

Hamilton, Clive. 2009. *The Freedom Paradox*. Noida: Allen-Unwin with Viva.

Hamilton, Sue. 2006. *Indian Philosophy: A Very Short Introduction*. Delhi: Oxford University Press.

Hande, Harish. 2011. 'How Many IITians have done Research for a Good Cooking Stove? Where is the Contribution of the IITs to the Real India?' *The Indian Express*, Delhi, 20 September.

Hanh, Thich Nhat. 1995. *Living Buddha, Living Christ*. New York: Riverhead.

Hanisch, Carol. [1970] 2000. 'The Personal is Political', in Barbara A. Crow, ed., *Radical Feminism: A Documentary Reader*. New York: New York University Press.

Hardt, Michael and Antonio Negri. 2004. *Multitude: War and Democracy in the Age of Empire*. New York: Penguin.

Hargreaves, Ian. 2005. *Journalism: A Very Short Introduction*. Oxford: Oxford University Press.

Harrington, James. 1992. *The Commonwealth of Oceana* [1656] *and A System of Politics*, ed. J.G.A. Pocock. Cambridge: Cambridge University Press.

Harriss-White, Barbara. 2004. *India Working: Essays on Society and Economy*. Delhi: Cambridge University Press.

Harriss, John. 2006. *Power Matters: Essays on Institutions, Politics and Society in India*. Delhi: Oxford University Press.

Harvey, C. et al. eds. 1970. *Industrialisation and Culture*. London: Macmillan.

Hawkins, Mike. 1997. *Social Darwinism in European and American Thought 1860–1945*. Cambridge: Cambridge University Press.

Hegel, G.W.F. [1807] 1977. *Phenomenology of Spirit*, tr. A.V. Miller. Oxford: Oxford University Press.

Herman, Arthur. 1997. *The Idea of Decline in Western History*. New York: The Free Press.

Herman, Edward and Noam Chomsky. 1988. *Manufacturing Consent: The Political Economy of the Mass Media*. New York: Pantheon.

Herman, Edward and Robert McChesney. 1998. *The Global Media: The New Missionaries of Corporate Capitalism*. Delhi: Madhyam Books.

Hertz, Noreena. 2002. *The Silent Takeover*. London: Arrow.

Hess, Linda and Sukhdev Singh. 1986. *The Bijak of Kabir*. Delhi: Motilal Banarsidass.

Hirschman, Albert. 1977. *The Passions and the Interests: Political Arguments for Capitalism Before its Triumph*. Princeton: Princeton University Press.

Hite, Shere. 1976. *The Hite Report on Female Sexuality*. New York: Dell.

Hobbes, Thomas. [1651] 2008. *Leviathan*, ed. J.C.A. Gaskin. Oxford: Oxford University Press.

Hobsbawm, Eric and Terence Ranger, eds. 1983. *The Invention of Tradition*. Cambridge: Cambridge University Press.

Hofstadter, Richard. 1944. *Social Darwinism in American Thought*. Boston: Beacon Press.

Holder, John H., tr. 2006. *Early Buddhist Discourses*. Indianapolis: Hackett, 2006.

Holloway, Carla F.C. 1995. *Codes of Conduct: Race, Ethics, and the Colour of Our Character*. New Jersey: Rutgers University Press.

Hoover, Kenneth and Todd Donovan. 1995. *The Elements of Social Scientific Thinking*, 6th edn. New York: St. Martin's Press.

Hope, Samuel. 2001. 'Introduction', in *Justice For All*, ed. Jake B. Schrum. Georgetown, Texas: Southwestern University.

Horkheimer, Max and Theodor Adorno. [1947] 1972. *Dialectic of Enlightenment*. New York: Herder and Herder.

Hume, David. 1953. 'Of the Origin of Government', in Charles Hendel, ed., *Political Essays*. New York: Liberal Arts Press.

———. [1740] 1978. *A Treatise of Human Nature*, ed. L.A. Selby-Bigge. Oxford: Clarendon Press.

Huxley, Aldous. 1998. *The Brave New World*. Harper Perennial.

Ilaiah, Kancha. 1996. *Why I Am Not a Hindu*. Calcutta: Samya.

———. 2000. *God as Political Philosopher: Buddha's Challenge to Brahminism*. Calcutta: Samya.

Inden, Roland. 1990. *Imagining India*. London: Basil Blackwell.

Jaffrelot, Christophe. 1999. *The Hindu Nationalist Movement and Indian Politics*. Delhi: Penguin.

———. 2004. *Dr Ambedkar and Untouchability: Analysing and Fighting Caste*. Delhi: Permanent Black.

Jaini, Padmanabh, ed. 2001. *Collected Papers on Buddhist Studies*. Delhi: Motilal Banarsidass.

Jaiswal, Suvira. 2000. *Caste: Origin, Function and Dimensions of Change*. Delhi: Manohar.

Jameson, Fredric. 1992. *Postmodernism: Or, the Cultural Logic of Late Capitalism*. London: Verso.

Johansson, Sheila R. 1976. 'Herstory as History: A New Field or Another Fad?' in Berenice A. Carroll, ed., *Liberating Women's History*. Illinois: Illinois University Press.

Joshi, Lal Muni. 2007. *Brahmanism, Buddhism, and Hinduism*. Delhi: Critical Quest.

Kailasapathy, K. 1987. 'The Writings of the Tamil Siddhas', in K. Schomer and W.H. McLeod, eds., *The Sants: Studies in a Devotional Tradition of India*, pp. 385–411. Delhi: Motilal Banarsidass.

Kalupahana, David J. 1976. *Buddhist Philosophy: A Historical Analysis*. Hawaii: University Press of Hawaii.

Kandasamy, Meena. 2011. 'All You Who Make Love to Mannequins', *Outlook*, 26 December.

Kaufmann, Walter. 1974. *Nietzsche: Philosopher, Psychologist, Antichrist*, 4th edn. Princeton: Princeton University Press.

Kautilya. 1997. *The Arthashastra*, tr. R.P. Kangle. Delhi: Motilal Banarisidass.

Kaye, Harvey. 1995. 'Foreword' to George Rude's *Ideology and*

Popular Protest. Chapel Hill: The University of North Carolina Press.

Kearney, Richard. 2002. *On Stories*. London and New York: Routledge.

Keer, Dhananjay. [1954] 1971. *Dr. Ambedkar: Life and Mission*. Bombay: Popular Prakashan.

Keer, Dhananjay. [1964] 2000. *Mahatma Jotirao Phule: Father of Indian Social Revolution*. Bombay: Popular Prakashan.

Keith, A.B. 1948. *A History of Sanskrit Literature*. Oxford: Oxford University Press.

Keller, Helen. 1911. Letter published in *Manchester Advertiser*. 3 March.

———. 1927. *My Religion*. New York: Swedenborg Foundation.

Kilbourne, Jean. 1999. *Deadly Persuasion: Why Women and Girls Must Fight the Addictive Power of Advertising*. New York: The Free Press.

Killingley, Dermot. 1993. *Rammohun Roy in Hindu and Christian Tradition: The Teape Lectures 1990*. Newcastle: Grevatt & Grevatt.

King, Martin Luther, Jr. 1992. *I Have a Dream: Writings and Speeches that Changed the World*, ed. James M. Washington. New York: Harper Collins.

Kingsnorth, Paul. 2003. *One No, Many Yeses: A Journey to the Heart of the Global Resistance Movement*. London: Free Press.

Kochhar, Rajesh. 2000. *The Vedic People: Their History and Geography*. Delhi: Orient Longman.

Kopf, David. 1969. *British Orientalism and the Bengal Renaissance: The Dynamics of Indian Modernization 1793-1835*. Berkeley: University of California Press.

Kosambi, D.D. [1965] 1992. *The Culture and Civilisation of Ancient India in Historical Outline*. Delhi: Vikas.

———. [1962] 2000. *Myth and Reality*. Mumbai: Popular Prakashan.

Kropotkin, Peter. [1902] 2008. *Mutual Aid: A Factor of Evolution*. Forgotten Books.

Kunhappa, Murkot. 1988. *Sree Narayana Guru*. Delhi: National Book Trust.

Langer, William L. 1992. 'The Diplomacy of Imperialism, 1890-1902', in Brian Tierney et al., eds., *Great Issues in Western Civilisation*, 2nd edn., pp. 553–9. New York: McGraw-Hill.

Lappe, Frances Moore. 1971. *Diet for a Small Planet*. New York: Ballantine Books.

———. 2008. 'A Shortage of Democracy, not Food', *The Progressive*, July issue.

Lasn, Kalle. 2000. *Culture Jam*. New York: Quill /Harper Collins.

Lasswell, Harold. 1936. *Politics: Who Gets What, When, How*. New York: McGraw-Hill.

Le Guin, Ursula K. 1975. *The Dispossessed*. New York: Avon Books.

———. 1992. 'Bryn Mawr Commencement Address', in Toby Fulwiler and Arthur Biddle, eds., *A Community of Voices*, pp. 397–408. New York: Macmillan.

Levi, A.W. 1974. *Philosophy and Social Expression*. Chicago: University of Chicago Press.

Levi, Primo. 1993. *Survival in Auschwitz*. New York: Simon & Schuster.

Lingat, Robert. [1967] 1998. *The Classical Law of India*, tr. J.D.M. Derrett. Delhi: Oxford University Press.

Lipset, Seymour Martin. 1959. 'Some Social Requisites of Democracy: Economic Development and Political Legitimacy', *American Political Science Review* 53, pp. 69–105.

Locke, John. [1690] 1995. *An Essay Concerning Human Understanding*. New York: Prometheus Books.

Maalouf, Amin. 2011. *Disordered World: Setting a New Course for the Twenty-First Century*. London: Bloomsbury.

MacGuire, Randall and Robert Paynter. 1991. *The Archaeology of Inequality*. Oxford: Blackwell.

Machiavelli, Niccolo. [1513] 2003. *The Prince*. London: Penguin.

Mandela, Nelson. 2005. Public Address in London, during the G7 Finance Ministers' Meet, 3 February.

Mani, Braj Ranjan. 2005. *Debrahmanising History: Dominance and Resistance in Indian Society*. Delhi: Manohar.

———. 2007. *Resurgent Buddhism: Ambedkar's Predecessors in Modern India*. Delhi: Critical Quest.

Mani, Braj Ranjan and Pamela Sardar, eds. 2008a. *A Forgotten Liberator: Life and Struggle of Savitribai Phule*. Delhi: Mountain Peak.

Mani, Braj Ranjan. 2008b. 'Neo-brahmanism, Human Rights and Social Democracy', www.voicesforfreedom.org/index.php?... neobrahmanism.

Mann, Thomas. 1939. *Culture and Politics*. USA: Survey Graphic.

———. 2002. *The Cambridge Companion to Thomas Mann*, ed. Ritchie Robertson. Cambridge. Cambridge University Press.

Marcuse, Herbert. 1956. *Eros and Civilisation: A Philosophical Inquiry into Freud*. London: Routledge.

———. 1964. *One-Dimensional Man: Studies in the Ideology of Advanced Industrial Society* (Boston: Beacon Press).

Marger, Martin N. 2005. *Social Inequality: Patterns and Processes*. New York: McGraw-Hill.

Marmot, Michael. 2004. *Status Syndrome*. London: Bloomsbury.

Marshall, P.J., ed. 1970. *The British Discovery of Hinduism in the Eighteenth Century*. Cambridge: Cambridge University Press.

Marx, Karl. [1845] 1970. *The German Ideology*. New York: International Publishers.

———. 1975. 'Reflections of a Young Man on the Choice of a Profession' [1837], in Marx and Engels' *Collected Works*, vol. 1. Moscow: Progress Publishers.

———. 1978. *The Marx-Engels Reader*, ed. Robert C. Tucker, 2nd edn. Includes 'Contribution to the Critique of Hegel's Philosophy of Right' (1843a), 'On the Jewish Question' (1843b), 'Letter to Arnold Ruge' (1843c), 'Economic and Philosophic Manuscripts' (1844), 'The German Ideology' (1845a), 'Theses on Feuerbach' (1845b), 'The Communist Manifesto' (1848), '18th Brumaire of Louis Bonaparte' (1852). New York and London: Norton.

Maslow, Abraham H. 1970. 'Peak Experiences in Education and Art', *The Humanist*, September-October issue.

Masson, Jeffrey and Susan McCarthy. 1995. *When Elephants Weep: The Emotional Lives of Animals*. New York: Delta Book.

May, Rollo. 1966. 'Antidotes for the New Puritanism', *The Saturday Review*, 26 March.

McMahon, Darrin. 2006. *The Pursuit of Happiness: A History from the Greeks to the Present*. London: Penguin.

Mead, G.H. 1934. *Mind, Self and Society: From the Standpoint of a Social Behaviourist*. Chicago: The University of Chicago Press.

Mead, Margaret. [1928] 2001. *Coming of Age in Samoa*. London: Harper Collins.

———. 1951. 'Our Awareness Controls Human Destiny', in *This I Believe* talk series.

Mehta, Pratap Bhanu. 2011. 'Questions Lit Up', *The Indian Express*, Delhi, 26 October.

———. 2012a. 'Sin of Littleness', *The Indian Express*, Delhi, 29 May.

———. 2012b. 'Breaking the Silence: Why We Don't Talk About Inequality', *The Caravan*, October issue.

Menand, Louis. 2009. *The Marketplace of Ideas: Reform and Resistance in the American University*. New York: Norton.

Mencher, Joan. 1991. 'The Caste System Upside Down', in Dipankar Gupta, ed., *Social Stratification*, pp. 93–109. Delhi: Oxford University Press.

Menon, Dilip. 2006. *The Blindness of Insight: Essays on Caste in Modern India*. Delhi: Navayana.

Midgley, Mary. 2011. *The Myths We Live By*. London and New York: Routledge.

Miles, Rosalind. 1988. *The Women's History of the World*. London: Harper Collins.

Mill, John Stuart. 2006. *On Liberty and The Subjection of Women*, ed. Alan Ryan. London: Penguin.

Miller, Casey and Kate Swift. 2001. *Words and Women*, updated edn. Indiana: iUniverse.

Miller, James. 1993. *The Passion of Michel Foucault*. London: Harper Collins.

Millet, Catherine. 2002. *The Sexual Life of Catherine M*. London: Serpent's Tail.

Mills, C. Wright. 1956. *The Power Elite*. New York: Oxford University Press.

———. [1959] 2000. *The Sociological Imagination*. London: Oxford University Press.

Mitra, Ashok. 1995. *Caste and Class in Indian Society*. Calcutta: The Asiatic Society.

———. 2010. 'Snakepit', *The Telegraph*, Calcutta, 7 May.

Mooney, Linda A. et al. 2002. *Understanding Social Problems*, 3rd edn. Belmont, CA: Wadsworth.

More, Thomas. [1516] 2009. *The Best State of a Commonwealth and the New Island of Utopia*. London: Penguin.

Morrison, Toni. [1993] 2009. *The Nobel Lecture in Literature, 1993*. New York: Knopf Doubleday.

Moya, Paula et al. 2001. *Reclaiming Identity: Realist Theory and the Predicament of Postmodernism*. Hyderabad: Orient Longman.

Mulgan, Geoff. 2006. *Good and Bad Power: The Ideals and Betrayals of Government*. London: Allen Lane.

Muktibodh, G.M. 2008. *Pratitidhi Kavitayen*. Delhi: Rajkamal Prakashan.

Nader, Laura. 1972. 'Up the Anthropologist—Perspectives Gained in Studying Up', in Dell Hymes, ed., *Reinventing Anthropology*, pp. 284–311. New York: Pantheon Books.

Nandy, Ashis. 1980. *At the Edge of Psychology: Essays in Politics and Culture*. Delhi: Oxford University Press.

———. 1983. *The Intimate Enemy: Loss and Recovery of Self Under Colonialism*. Delhi: Oxford University Press.

Narasu, P. Lakshmi. [1922] 2003. *A Study of Caste*. Delhi: Blumoon Books.

Narasu, Lakshmi. [1907] 2004. *The Essence of Buddhism*. Delhi: Winsome Books.

Narke, Hari, ed. 1993. *Mahatma Phule: Sahitya Aur Vichar*, in Hindi. Bombay: Govt. of Maharashtra.

Nash, Knowlton. 1998. *Trivial Pursuit: How Showbiz Values are Corrupting the News*. Toronto: McClelland & Stewart.

Nehru, Jawaharlal. 1960. Address to the National Institute of Science of India. *Proceedings of the National Institute of Science of India*, vol. 27.

———. [1946] 1996. *The Discovery of India*. Delhi: Nehru Memorial Fund/Oxford University Press.

———. [1936] 1999. *An Autobiography*. Delhi: Nehru Memorial Fund/Oxford University Press.

Ngugi, Wa Thiong' O. 1986. *Decolonising the Mind: The Politics of Language in African Literature*. London: James Curry.

Nietzsche, Friedrich. [1880s] 1968a. *Will to Power*. New York: Random House.

———. [1895] 1968b. *The Anti-Christ*, tr. R.J. Hollingdale. Harmondsworth: Penguin.

———. [1883–5] 1974. *Thus Spoke Zarathustra*, tr. R.J. Hollingdale. Harmondsworth: Penguin.

Nirala, Suryakant Tripathi. 2003. 'Gahan Hai Yeh Andhakara', in *Prasad, Nirala, Pant, Mahadev Ki Shreshtha Kavitaen*, ed. Vachaspati Pathak, rpt. Allahabad: Lok Bharati Prakashan.

North, Robert C. 1976. *The World That Could Be*. New York: Norton.

Oakeshott, Michael. 1966. *Experience and its Modes*. Cambridge: Cambridge University Press.

O'Hanlon, Rosalind. 1985. *Caste, Conflict and Ideology: Mahatma Jotirao Phule and Low Caste Protest in Nineteenth-Century Western India*. Cambridge: Cambridge University Press.

Olivelle, Patrick. 2005. *Manu's Code of Law*. Delhi: Oxford University Press.

Omvedt, Gail. 1994. *Dalits and the Democratic Revolution: Dr Ambedkar and the Dalit Movement in Colonial India*. Delhi: Sage.

———. 2003. *Buddhism in India: Challenging Brahmanism and Caste*. Delhi: Sage.

———. 2011. *Understanding Caste: From Buddha to Ambedkar and Beyond*. Delhi: Orient Black Swan.

O' Neill, Onora. 2002. *A Question of Trust: The BBC Reith Lectures 2002*. Cambridge: Cambridge University Press.

Oommen, T.K. 2013. 'Analyzing India's Social Transformation: The Missing Subaltern Perspective', the Ambedkar Memorial Lecture on 5 February at NISWASS, Bhubaneswar.

Orwell, George. [1946] 1981. *A Collection of Essays*. San Diego and London: Harcourt.

———. [1949] 2000. *1984*. London: Penguin.

Outlook. 2012. 'Story of An Op Lost', 16 July.

Packard, Vance. [1957] 2007. *The Hidden Persuaders*. New York: I.G. Publishing.

Paglia, Camille. 1994. *Vamps and Tramps: New Essays*. New York: Vintage.

Paine, Thomas. [1791] 1984. *Rights of Man*. New York: Penguin.

———. [1794] 2004. *The Age of Reason*. New York: Dover Publications.

Pamuk, Orhan. 2007. 'My Father's Suitcase', the Nobel Lecture, in idem, *Other Colours*, tr. Maureen Freely. London: Faber and Faber.

Pandian, M.S.S. 2007. *Brahmin & Non-Brahmin: Genealogies of the Tamil Political Present*. Delhi: Permanent Black.

Panini, M.N. 1996. 'The Political Economy of Caste', in M.N. Srinivas, ed., *Caste: Its Twentieth Century Avatar*. Delhi: Viking Penguin.

Parekh, Bhiku. 1989. *Gandhi's Political Philosophy: A Critical Examination*. Indiana: University of Notre Dame.

———. 2001. *Gandhi: A Very Short Introduction*. London: Oxford University Press.

Paul, Daniel. 2000. *We Were Not the Savages: A Mi'kmaq Perspective on the Collision between European and Native American Civilizations*. Winnipeg: Fernwood.

Paz, Octavio. 1992. *The Collected Poems*, 1957–87, ed. and tr. Eliot Weinberger. Delhi: Rupa and Co.

Perkins, John. 2006. *Confessions of An Economic Hit Man: The Shocking Inside Story of How America REALLY Took Over the World*. London: Ebury Press.

Phule, Jotirao. 1991. *Collected Works of Mahatma Jotirao Phule*, vols. I & II, tr. P.G. Patil. Bombay: Educational Department, Govt. of Maharashtra.

———. 2002. *Selected Writings*, ed., G.P. Deshpande, with *Slavery* [1873] and *Cultivator's Whipcord*. Delhi: Left Word.

Pilger, John. 1998. *Hidden Agendas*. London: Vintage.

Plato. [c. 380 BCE] 1957. *The Republic of Plato*, ed. A.D. Lindsay. New York: EP Dutton.

———. 1997. *Plato: Complete Works*, ed. John Cooper. Indiana: Hackett.

Polanyi, Karl. 1957. *The Great Transformation*. Boston: Beacon Press.

Popper, Karl. [1945] 2010. *The Open Society and Its Enemies, Vol. One: The Spell of Plato*, Indian rpt. Noida: Routledge.

Postman, Neil. 1985. *Amusing Ourselves to Death: Public Discourse in the Age of Show Business*. New York: Penguin.

Pound, Ezra. 1952. *Collected Shorter Poems*, London: Faber and Faber.

Proudhon, Pierre Joseph. [1840] 1970. *What is Property? An Inquiry into the Principle of Right and of Government*, tr. Benjamin Tucker. New York: Dover.

Queen, Christopher S., and Sallie B. King, eds. 1996. *Engaged Buddhism: Buddhist Liberation Movements in Asia*. Albany: State University of New York Press.

Radhakrishnan, S. 1962. *Indian Philosophy*, vol. 1. London: George Allen and Unwin.

———. [1956] 1997. 'Foreword' to P.V. Bapat, ed., *2,500 Years of Buddhism*. Delhi: Publications Division, Govt. of India.

Ratner-Rosenhagen, Jennifer. 2012. *American Nietzsche: A History of an Icon and his Ideas*. Chicago: University of Chicago Press.

Reich, Wilhelm. 1969. *The Sexual Revolution: Toward a Self-Governing Character Structure*, 4th edn. New York: Farrar, Straus & Giroux.

Report of an Expert Group to Planning Commission. 2008. 'Development Challenges in Extremist Affected Areas.' New Delhi: Govt. of India.

Rhode, Deborah. 2011.*The Beauty Bias: The Injustice of Appearance in Life and Law*. New York: Oxford University Press.

Rhode, Eric. 1976. *A History of the Cinema from Its Origin to 1970*. London: Allen Lane.

Rhys Davids, T.W. [1902] 1981. *Buddhist India*. Delhi: Motilal Banarsidass.

Rosenblatt, Roger. 1999. 'The Diarist Anne Frank', *Time*, 14 June.

Rosselson, Leon. 1981. *For the Good of the Nation*. London: Journeyman Press.

Rousseau. 1987. *Jean-Jacques Rousseau: The Basic Political Writings*, includes 'Discourse on the Origin of Inequality' [1754], tr. Donald A Cress. Indianapolis: Hackett.

———. [1762] 1998. *The Social Contract*, tr. H J Tozer. London: Wordsworth.

Rothman, William. 1997. *Documentary Film Classics*. Cambridge: Cambridge University Press.

Rowse, Arthur. 2002. *Drive-by Journalism: The Assault on Your Need to Know*. Monroe, Maine: Common Courage Press.

Roy, Arundhati. 2004. *An Ordinary Person's Guide to Empire*. Massachusetts: South End Press.

———. 2010. 'Indian TV in Grip of a Small, Incestuous Clique', *The Times of India, The Crest Edition*, 8 November.

Russell, Bertrand. 1988. *Education and the Social Order*. London: Routledge.

Ryan, William. [1971] 1976. *Blaming the Victim*. London: Vintage.

Said, Edward. 1978. *Orientalism: Western Conceptions of the Orient*. London: Penguin.

———. 1983. 'Opponents, Audiences, Constituencies and Community', in W.J.T. Mitchell, ed., *The Politics of Interpretation*. Chicago: University of Chicago Press.

———. 1993. *Culture and Imperialism*. London: Vintage.

———. 1994. *The Politics of Dispossession*. New York: Vintage.

Sainath, P. 1996. *Everybody Loves a Good Drought*. Delhi: Penguin.

Sainath, P. 2010. 'Media has Lost its Sense of Priorities', *The Hindu*, Delhi, 1 July.

Sanghvi, Vir. 2009. 'No Room for Outsiders in Indian Politics', *Hindustan Times*, Delhi, 27 September.

Sankrityayan, Rahul et al. 1990. *Buddhism: The Marxist Approach*. Delhi: People's Publishing House.

Sardesai, S.G. 1994. *Progress and Conservatism in Ancient India*. Delhi: People's Publishing House.

Sarkar, N.K. 1978. *Social Structure and Development Strategy in Asia*. Delhi: People's Publishing House.

Sarkar, Sumit. 1983. *Modern India 1885–1947*. Delhi: Macmillan.

Sarkar, Sumit. 1997. *Writing Social History*. Delhi: Oxford University Press.

Saul, John Ralston. 2004. *On Equilibrium: The Six Qualities of the New Humanism*. Delhi: Penguin.

Savarkar, V.D. [1923] 1999. *Hindutva—Who is a Hindu?* 7th edn. Mumbai: Savarkar Rashtriya Smarak.

Scharffstein, Ben-Ami. 1995. *Amoral Politics: The Persistent Truth of Machiavellism*. New York: State University of New York Press.

Schopenhauer, Arthur. 1995. *On the Basis of Morality*. Indianapolis: Hackett.

Schouten, J.P. 1995. *Revolution of the Mystics: On the Social Aspects of Virashaivism*. Delhi: Motilal Banarsidass.

Schumacher, E.F. 1977. *A Guide for the Perplexed*. New York: Harper and Row.

Scruton, Roger. 2011. *Beauty: A Very Short Introduction*. London: Oxford University Press.

Sen, Amartya. 2005a. *The Argumentative Indian: Writings on Indian History, Culture and Identity*. London: Penguin.

———. 2005b. 'Foreword' to K.M. Sen's *Hinduism*, pp. vii-xxiii. Delhi: Penguin.

———. 2009. *The Idea of Justice*. London: Penguin.

Sen, Amiya P. 1993. *Hindu Revivalism in Bengal 1872–1905*. Delhi: Oxford University Press.

Sen, K.M. [1961] 2005. *Hinduism*. Delhi: Penguin.

Senge, Peter M. 2004. Preface to Bohm's *On Dialogue*. London and New York: Routledge.

Sharma, R.S. 1983. *Perspective in Social and Economic History of Early India*. Delhi: Munshiram Manoharlal.

———. [1958] 1990. *Shudras in Ancient India*. Delhi: Motilal Banarsidass.

Shirer, William. [1961] 1991. *The Rise and Fall of the Third Reich*. London: Mandrin.

Shrivastava, Aseem, and Ashish Kothari. 2012. *Churning the Earth: The Making of Global India*. Delhi: Penguin.

Sidhanta, N.K. 1929. *The Heroic Age of India*. London: Kegan Paul.

Singh, Malvika. 2010. 'No Time to Look Behind', *The Telegraph*, Kolkata, 11 May.

Sloan, Bill. 2001. *I Watched a Wild Hog Eat My Baby! A Colourful History of Tabloids and their Impact*. New York: Prometheus.

Smith, Adam. [1759] 1984. *The Theory of Moral Sentiments*, eds. D.D. Raphael and A.I. Macfie. Indianapolis: Liberty Fund.

Smith, Adam. [1776] 2005. *An Inquiry into the Nature and Causes of the Wealth of Nations*, electronics classics series. Pennsylvania: Pennsylvania State University.

Smith, Brian K. 2012. *Veda and Varna*. Delhi: Critical Quest.

Smith, Linda T. 1999. *Decolonising Methodologies: Research and Indigenous Peoples*. London and New York: Zed Books.

Soccio, Douglas J. 2001. *Archetypes of Wisdom: An Introduction to Philosophy*. Belmont, CA: Wadsworth.

Sorokin, Pitirim A. 1957. 'Integralism Is My Philosophy', in Whit Burnett, ed., *This Is My Philosophy*, pp. 180–89. New York: Harper & Brothers.

Soros, George. 1998. *The Crisis of Global Capitalism: Open Society Endangered*. New York: Public Affairs.

Srinivas, M.N. [1962] 1985. *Caste in Modern India*. Bombay: Media Promoters.

Ste Croix, G.E.M. de. [1981] 1997. *The Class Struggle in the Ancient Greek World: From the Archaic Age to the Arab Conquests*. London: Gerald Duckworth.

Steinem, Gloria. 1978. 'If Men Could Menstruate', *Ms*. VII, October issue.

———. 1992. *Revolution From Within*. Boston and Toronto: Little Brown.

Stiglitz, Joseph. 2012. *The Price of Inequality*. London: Allen Lane.

Stone, I.F. 1988. *The Trial of Socrates*. Toronto: Little Brown.

Strindberg, August. 1983. *The Ghost Sonata* [1907], in *Five Plays*. Los Angeles: University of California Press.

Stubbs, Marcia and Sylvan Barnet. 1996. *The Little Brown Reader*, 7th edn. New York: Harper Collins.

Stumpf, Samuel Enoch. 1993. *Socrates to Sartre*, 5th edn. New York: McGraw Hill.

Surve, Narayan. 2011. *Narayan Surve Yancha Samagra Kavita*, in Marathi. Mumbai: Popular Prakashan.

Symborska, Wislawa. 'Children of Our Age'. See www.poemhunter.com/wislawa-symborska

Szasz, Thomas. 1974. *The Second Sin*. London: Routledge and Kegan Paul.

Taylor, Charles. 1992. *Multiculturalism and The Politics of Education*. Princeton: Princeton University Press.

Thapar, Romila. [1961] 1999. *Ashoka and the Decline of the Mauryas*. Delhi: Oxford University Press.

———. 2001. 'Syndicated Hinduism', in G.-D. Sontheimer and H. Kulke, eds., *Hinduism Reconsidered*. Delhi: Manohar.

The Economist. 2008. 'Why We Are, As We Are', 18 December.

———. 2009. 'How to Feed the World', 19 November.

———. 2011. 'The Rich and the Rest: A Special Report on Global Elite', 22 January.

———. 2012. 'True Progressivism', 13 October.

The Hindu. 2011. 'Poverty is a Human Rights Violation', Delhi, 26 October.

———. 2012. 'Battling Bias', Delhi, 6 July.

The Indian Express. 2010. 'Paid News Could Mark Death of Journalism', Delhi, 23 July.

———. 2012. 'Top Naxals are Two 15-yr-old Toppers', Delhi, 2 July.

The Times of India. 2011. 'Black is Bountiful', Delhi, 21 September.

———. 2012. 'Growth Pangs', Delhi, 3 June.

The Week. 2009. 'Get Lost, Goodness', 22 March.

Theekkuni, Pavithran. 2012. 'A Poet Feeds on Hunger, Literally', *The Hindu*, Delhi, 23 July.

Thorat, Sukhdeo and Katherine Newman, eds. 2010. *Blocked by Caste: Economic Discrimination in Modern India*. Delhi: Oxford University Press.

Thoreau, Henry David. 1993. *Civil Disobedience and Other Essays*. New York: Dover Publications.

Thucydides. [431 BCE] 1954. *History of the Peloponnesian War*, tr. Rex Warner. Baltimore: Penguin.

Tidrick, Kathryn. 2006. *Gandhi: A Political and Spiritual Life*. London: I B Tauris.

Tierney, Brian, et al., eds. 1992. *Great Issues in Western Civilization*. New York: McGraw-Hill.

Tocqueville, Alexis de. [1840] 1988. *Democracy in America*, vol. 2, ed. J P Mayer. New York: Harper-Perennial.

Tolstoy, Leo. 1987. 'On Patriotism' [1894], in idem, *Writings on Civil Disobedience and Non-Violence*. Philadelphia: New Society Publishers.

Trouillot, Michel-Rolph. 1995. *Silencing the Past: Power and the Production of History*. Boston: Beacon Press.

Truth, Sojourner. 1851. 'Ain't I A Woman?', speech delivered at Women's Rights Convention, Akron, Ohio.

———. 1867. Address to the first annual meeting of the American Equal Rights Association, New York City, 9 May.

Turner, Bryan S. 1983. *Religion and Social Theory*. London: Heinemann.

Valla, Lorenzo. [1431] 1977. *On Pleasure: De Voluptate (Of the True and the False Good)*, ed. M. Lorch, tr. A. Kent Hiett and M. Lorch. New York: Albaris Books Inc.

Vajpeyi, Kailash, ed. 2000. *An Anthology of Modern Hindi Poetry*. Delhi: Rupa.

Varadarajan, Siddharth. 2010. 'This War Can't Be Won by Mines and Bullets', *The Hindu*, Delhi, 20 May.

Varma, V.P. 1974. *Studies in Hindu Political Thought and its Metaphysical Foundations*, revised edn. Delhi: Motilal Banarsidass.

———. 1956. 'The Origins of Buddhism', *The Journal of the Bihar Research Society*, Buddha Jayanti spl. issue, vol. 2.

Varshney, Ashutosh. 2012. 'India's Moment of Truth', *The Indian Express*, 11 June.

Veblen, Thorstein. [1899] 2005. *The Theory of the Leisure Class*. Delhi: Aakar Books.

Verardi, Giovanni. 2011. *Hardships and Downfall of Buddhism in India*. Delhi: Manohar.

Vishwanathan, Gauri. 2001. *Outside the Fold: Conversion, Modernity, and Belief*. Delhi: Oxford University Press.

Vora, Neera, ed. 1999. *Gandhiji's Dialogue with Christianity*. Delhi: Swaraj Peeth Trust.

Wagner, Roy. 1975. *The Invention of Culture*. New Jersey: Prentice-Hall.

Walker, Alice. 1997. *Anything We Love Can Be Saved: A Writer's Activism*. New York: Random House.

Walker, Benjamin. 1983. *Hindu World*, vols. I and II. Delhi: Munshiram Manoharlal.

Wall, Daniel. 2001. 'Perspective of a White Male by Daniel Wall', in Jake B. Schrum, ed., *Justice For All*. Georgetown, Texas: Southwestern University.

Watson, Peter. 2000. *A Terrible Beauty: The People and Ideas That Shaped the Modern World*. London: Phoenix.

Webster, John C.B. 2000. *Religion and Dalit Liberation: An Examination of Perspectives*. Delhi: Manohar.

West, Cornel. 1993. *Keeping Faith*. London: Routledge.

Wheen, Francis. 2008. *Marx's Das Kapital*. Bhopal: Manjul Publications.

Wiesel, Elie. 1960. *Night*, tr. Stella Rodway. New York: Batman Books.

Wilde, Oscar. [1891] 1905. *The Soul of Man Under Socialism*. Portland, Maine: Thomas B. Mosher.

Wilkinson, Richard and Kate Pickett. 2009. *The Spirit Level: Why More Equal Societies Almost Always Do Better*. London, Penguin.

Williams, Paul. 1989. *Mahayana Buddhism: Doctrinal Foundations*. London: Routledge.

Williams, Raymond. 1977. *Selections from Marxism and Literature*. Oxford: Oxford University Press.

Winstanley, Gerrard. [1651] 2006. *Winstanley: The Law of Freedom and Other Writings*, ed. Christopher Hill. Cambridge: Cambridge University Press.

Woodward, F.L. and E.M. Hare. 1932–6. *Anguttara Nikaya*, translated as *The Book of Gradual Sayings*, 5 vols. London: Pali Text Society.

Wright, Ronald. 2005. *Stolen Continents: 500 Years of Conquest and Resistance in the Americas*. Boston: Mariner Books.

Zelliot, Eleanor. 1979. 'The Indian Rediscovery of Buddhism', in A.K. Narain et al., eds., *Studies in Pali and Buddhism*, pp. 389–406. Delhi: B.R. Publishing.

———. 1996. *From Untouchable to Dalit: Essays on the Ambedkar Movement*. Delhi: Manohar.

Zinn, Howard with David Barsamian. 2006. *Original Zinn: Conversations on History and Politics*. New York: Harper Collins.

Zizek, Slavoj. 2001. *On Belief*. London and New York: Routledge.

Index